RECLAIMING HUMAN RIGHTS IN A CHANGING WORLD ORDER

*Providing new perspectives and
knowledge on an increasingly complex,
uncertain, and interconnected world.*

The Chatham House Insights Series
Series Editor: Caroline Soper

The Insights series provides new perspectives on and knowledge about an increasingly complex, uncertain, and interconnected world. Concise, lively, and authoritative, these books explore, through different modes of interpretation, a wide range of country, regional, and international developments, all within a global context. Focusing on topical issues in key policy areas, such as health, security, economics, law, and the environment, volumes in the series will be written accessibly by leading experts—both academic and practitioner—to anticipate trends and illuminate new ideas and thinking. Insights books will be of great interest to all those seeking to develop a deeper understanding of the policy challenges and choices facing decision makers, including academics, practitioners, and general readers.

Published or forthcoming titles:

David Lubin, *Dance of the Trillions: Developing Countries and Global Finance* (2018)

Keir Giles, *Moscow Rules: What Drives Russia to Confront the West* (2019)

Nigel Gould-Davies, *Tectonic Politics: Global Political
Risk in an Age of Transformation* (2019)

Jamie Gaskarth, *Secrets and Spies: UK Intelligence
Accountability after Iraq and Snowden* (2020)

Sten Rynning, Olivier Schmitt, and Amelie Theussen (eds.), *War Time:
Temporality and the Decline of Western Military Power* (2021)

Kerstin Bree Carlson, *The Justice Laboratory: International Law in Africa* (2022)

Christopher Sabatini (ed.), *Reclaiming Human Rights in a Changing World Order* (2022)

Chatham House, the Royal Institute of International Affairs, is a world-leading policy institute based in London. Its mission is to help governments and societies build a sustainably secure, prosperous, and just world.

Chatham House does not express opinions of its own. The opinions expressed in this publication are the responsibility of the author(s).

RECLAIMING HUMAN RIGHTS IN A CHANGING WORLD ORDER

CHRISTOPHER SABATINI

EDITOR

BROOKINGS INSTITUTION PRESS
Washington, D.C.

CHATHAM HOUSE
The Royal Institute of International Affairs
London

Copyright © 2023
THE BROOKINGS INSTITUTION
1775 Massachusetts Avenue, N.W.
Washington, D.C. 20036
www.brookings.edu

The Brookings Institution is a private nonprofit organization devoted to research,
education, and publication on important issues of domestic and foreign policy. Its
principal purpose is to bring the highest quality independent research and analysis
to bear on current and emerging policy problems. Interpretations or conclusions in
Brookings publications should be understood to be solely those of the authors.

Library of Congress Cataloging-in-Publication Data has been applied for.

ISBN 978-0-8157-3975-3 (pbk)
ISBN 978-0-8157-3976-0 (ebook)

9 8 7 6 5 4 3 2 1

Typeset in Adobe Garamond

Composition by Westchester Publishing Services

Contents

Foreword

As I prepare to leave Chatham House, after fifteen years as director, my thoughts—sparked also by recent events—inevitably turn to the changes to the international system in the past decade and a half. One of the main changes has been to the liberal values that have underpinned international and regional human rights regimes, which is the central theme of this book.

Beyond its timeliness, what sets this book apart is its comprehensiveness. The chapters that follow trace many of the multiple factors undermining rights regimes, globally and domestically. Nationalism, renewed claims of national sovereignty over international collective commitments, and new technologies that grant unaccountable power to states are not exclusively the domain of illiberal states. Increasingly, democratic governments, including the original architects of the liberal system have become enablers in the dissipation of the international, regional, and national protections of human rights.

As a policy think-tank, Chatham House combines rigorous academic analysis with practical recommendations. This book's chapters build on both the theoretical and day-to-day causes of weakening human rights commitments and practice to produce original policy recommendations to policymakers, activists, and academics for future action and research. The recommendations highlight the multidimensionality of the challenges and the responsibilities of stakeholders to rise to them. This book seeks to provide actionable proposals. They include the reframing of competition among global powers; reforming of the multilateral system; and adapting public debates to the threats of populist nationalism and the rise of new constituencies. Some of these are amenable to progressive human rights, some fundamentally oppose even to the funding, organization and the recruitment of human rights–focused international bodies. Many of those recommendations are in the conclusion—developed through Chatham House consultations with academic, policymaking, and activist networks—but they also conclude each chapter.

We need look no further than the recent developments in Europe to understand both the relevance and human urgency of this book. As we go to print, thousands of innocent lives are being lost in Ukraine. The invasion and its human consequences provide a clear example of what happens when a leader believes he (or she) is unconstrained by any political checks and balances, independent media, or civil society, and the state narrative is validated by official and social media state propaganda and disinformation.

But if Vladimir Putin's actions demonstrate the costs of unaccountable leadership, the international reaction has exposed the willingness of a growing international bloc to countenance the violation of international norms—or at least to not stand up in their defense. Forty-five countries abstained in the UN General Assembly vote to condemn Russia's action, including major democracies like India and South Africa. And only thirty-nine countries have imposed sanctions on Russia to signal their opposition to its actions.

This reflects, to a large extent, the sense of Western double standards about human rights that the Ukraine invasion raises in many parts of the world. Where were U.S. and European concerns about human rights when Basher al-Assad was massacring his own citizens, including with the use of chemical weapons? And are these same governments sufficiently concerned about the disastrous impacts that their sanctions on Russia, as well as Putin's war, are having on global food and other commodity prices and, therefore, on the human rights of hundreds of millions of the world's poorest people? For these reasons, one of the central aims of this book is to build on the views and analyses of scholars and activists from the Global South.

Ukraine is a microcosm of the central theme of this book. Liberal democracies and the world's main multilateral institutions are now on the defensive. Their leaders have believed—consistently—that the purpose of international order is to provide a secure, external framework for the protection of their citizens' individual human rights and, at the same time, to create an environment in which these rights could and would be extended to others around the world.

What lies at the core of the definition of human rights in a liberal democracy is the right and the ability for individuals to lead a life of liberty and opportunity, without abuse by the powerful or dominance by the majority. It is the job of government to provide the institutional framework and policies to deliver these human rights for their citizens. In doing so, they must balance absolute human rights with the responsibility that individuals carry for the welfare of others in human society—in other words, the pursuit of one individual's or group's human rights should not undermine the rights of others. These tenets are defined and underlined in the UN's Universal Declaration of Human Rights.

As this book reveals and explains, the tide has now turned for three reasons. First, the rise of China under the Communist Party of China (CPC) has offered an alternative path to politicians around the world. The CPC believes that it has the lead responsibility for delivering individual economic rights, which trump citizens' individual and collective political rights. As the guarantor of state sovereignty and security, the CPC believes it is and should be domestically unchallengeable. The CPC is offering a model that others may try to emulate. And it is incentivising others to prioritize central political and economic control by offering large amounts of foreign aid and investment to governments around the developing world. Unfortunately, corrupt politicians like Robert Mugabe in Zimbabwe and Najib Razak in Malaysia used Chinese financing to help entrench their political power while undermining human rights in the process.

Second, technological advances in digital communications have, so far, facilitated these efforts to centralize political control, with China again both leading the way and facilitating others, from Central Asia to sub-Saharan Africa and the Gulf States. The fact is, whether autocratic leaders fail or succeed in delivering economic progress to their citizens is not the point; their priority is always the same: not to relinquish power.

Third, since the mid 2000s, the upholders of the UN Declaration have become increasingly ambivalent about supporting the principles they had previously championed. The two main reasons are simple: first, the failed interventions in Afghanistan, Iraq, and Libya have deeply embedded strategic caution among Western policy communities over pursuing or tying foreign policy goals to ill-defined or far-reaching liberal ideals; and second, the failed Arab uprisings in Egypt, Bahrain, and, eventually, Syria. We also saw Barack Obama shy away from and Donald Trump openly deriding international democratic activism.

At the same time, Western governments have had to contend with the deep unhappiness of their own populations in the wake of unchecked globalization, the financial crisis and the austerity that followed, and now the disruption of the COVID-19 pandemic. Managing the political fallout from these trends and events has meant a concentrated period of trying to put their own houses in order, coinciding with the rise of parties offering some of the same simplistic populist answers as their autocratic counterparts.

Russia's invasion of Ukraine has reunited the liberal democracies in defense of their political systems, as well as of their sovereignty. But, with the leaderships in Moscow and Beijing convinced of the interconnection between strong central political control and the future of their own sovereignty, multilateral institutions have become battlegrounds between two antithetical approaches to human rights, one prioritizing the state and the other the individual. But this long overdue reform of international and regional human rights norms and institutions is not a fight that Western states of the developed North should confront or address alone.

The deepening divide between these two systems is eroding the operation of multilateral institutions, not only the political ones, such as the UN's Security Council and Human Rights Council, but also the economic ones, such as the World Trade Organization (WTO). The sense in democratic capitals is that autocracies are using trade and investment to embed autocracy, rather than use economic development as the stepping stone to greater political openness.

Unfortunately, so far in response, officials in Europe and the United States have focused on narrower issues. Key among them has been the economy. One of the principal forums that has brought together these like-minded countries has been the informal Group of Seven (G7). As an economic grouping, however, its members (Canada, France, Germany, Italy, Japan, the United Kingdom, and the United States) are more invested in facilitating favored treatment for production and investment in each other's markets and those of Western-allied Pacific allies, such as Japan, South Korea, and Taiwan—what Federal Reserve Chair Janet Yellen has termed, "friend-shoring"—and of constructing closed supply chains to guarantee access to critical technologies at a time of growing geo-economic competition, than they are in strengthening global rules.

As necessary as these defensive steps might be, ultimately, as a select grouping of developed economies, the G7 cannot be the proper forum for addressing the growing challenges for human rights defense and demands to upgrade its frameworks. Many of those demands have come from the Global South. Their absence in a select group of potential reformist states indicates the lack of effective forums for addressing the issues discussed in this book.

The best that can be hoped for in this context is that liberal democracies do not give up on external engagement with countries whose systems of governance remain in flux. This means sustaining diplomatic and economic relations even with autocratic governments, so long as they are not exporting autocracy or actively seeking to undermine other democracies. It will also mean democracies cultivating constructive relations with their more autocratic partners, but within clear boundaries that do not empower leaderships that abuse human rights. Hopefully, this will buy time for liberal democracies to become, once again, role models for inclusive economic development that others might want to emulate. It will also afford time to reengage the Global South in the inclusive reforms required to strengthen and improve international human rights, away from the efforts by China and Russia to bend or break them to their autocratic interests.

As I conclude my tenure at Chatham House and assess the state of international affairs today, I can't help wondering if, with more foresight, the process of strengthening human rights conventions by making their new design more inclusive should have started ten or even twenty years ago. But I am confident that this timely book will reenergize the discussion on international human rights, and how to shore up the system of liberal values that underpins them, for years to come.

Sir Robin Niblett, KCMG,
Director and Chief Executive Officer,
Chatham House (2006–2022)

Acknowledgments

Any book project, particularly an edited volume of this scope and ambition, has a cast of characters to thank. First and foremost is the Ford Foundation for their belief in and support for the project, and particularly Otto Saki for his advice and patience throughout the process. That patience became particularly important when the COVID-19 pandemic shut down travel and in-person work just as we were beginning to pull the project together. We had planned a series of author workshops in 2020 and 2021, but these obviously became impossible during the lockdown. Instead, like much of the world, we got by on Zoom, first for the discussions with our reviewers and later for two workshops we conducted—one with young leaders associated with Chatham House (in part through our Common Future Conversation project and the South African Institute of International Affairs), and another with activists.

From the beginning Caroline Soper, editor of the Chatham House/Brookings Institution Press *Insights* book series, helped shepherd the project along, keeping us all on track, coordinating between reviewers, copyeditors, and the Brookings Institution, and generally being a tough—but fair—taskmaster. Kerstin Bree Carlson (Roskilde University) and Bronwyn Leebow (University of California, Riverside) provided valuable perceptivity and thorough comments on all the chapters, of course all via Zoom. (It was Kerstin who urged me to move the discussion of the young leaders to the front of the book, saying "You're burying the lead!" She was right.) I am also grateful to the anonymous reviewer who provided both constructively critical comments and encouragement for the book and its conclusions. Whoever you are, thank you.

At Chatham House there are a number of people to thank. Rose Abdollahzadeh first suggested the book be part of the *Insights* series and introduced me to Caroline and to Amanda Moss, who helped ease the process and kept it moving forward. Renata Dwan recommended two of the authors for the chapters and chaired the early workshop with the authors. Anar Bata and Courtney Rice were closely involved with this project at various stages of the two-year process; but one of their most important contributions was keeping in order all the different drafts of chapters we had floating around. And last but not least, Margaret May was an excellent and dogged copyeditor, catching grammatical errors, questionable word choices, and incomplete references large and small.

William Finan, Director of the Brookings Institution Press, our *Insights* publishing partner, was a welcoming and encouraging editor. Our thanks to him and his publishing team at Brookings.

The participants in the two invaluable workshops mentioned above deserve special acknowledgment. The young leaders, brought together by Martina Carlucci, Nairomi Eriksson, and Ben Horton of Chatham House, and Steve Gruzd of the South African Institute of International Affairs, were an impressive group of students and young professionals who willingly gave their time to share their views on human rights. They included Hafsa Ali, Michel Alimasi, Tessa Dooms, Giuseppe Grieco, Mohamed Hachem, Leyla Helvaci, Amira Ismail, Gift Jedida, Salome Nzuki, Samantha Potter, Oliver Taylor, Sanne Thijssen, Mondher Tounsi, Araminta Watson, and Sophie Zinser. Since this book is intended to provide practical recommendations, the second workshop was conducted as we were wrapping up our drafts. Ana Lankes, Anar Bata, and Courtney Rice convened a diverse group of human rights activists from around the world: Peace Oliver Amuge, Nicholas Bequelin, Edmund Foley, Rez Gardi, Kumaravdivel Guruparan, Mateo Jarquín, Omer Kanat, Leanne Macmillan, Rahima Mahmut, Jacqueline Rowe, Changrok Soh, José Miguel Vivanco, Marta Welander, and Sarah Whitson. Their spirited, passionate comments and reflections on their experiences helped us think through our analyses and better hone our recommendations to policymakers, academics, and activists to bolster and improve international human rights today. More than anything, they reminded us of the human impact of our project.

Many of the authors—myself included—asked friends and colleagues to review early drafts of chapters. For their time and thoughtful comments, we would particularly like to thank Nicholas Bequelin, Daniel Cerqueira, Carl Conetta, Ariel Dultizky, Kate Jones, Emily Kent, Ana Lankes, and Harriet Moynihan.

Finally, my thanks more generally to Chatham House for its support of this project. It has been an honor to pull together this book under its auspices.

Christopher Sabatini

Acronyms and Abbreviations

ACERWC	African Committee of Experts on the Rights and Welfare of the Child
ACHPR	African Commission on Human and Peoples' Rights
ACHR	American Convention on Human Rights (American Convention)
ACLED	Armed Conflict Location & Event Data Project
ACtHPR	African Court on Human and Peoples' Rights
AI	artificial intelligence
AICHR	ASEAN Intergovernmental Commission on Human Rights
AIIB	Asian Infrastructure Investment Bank
APEC	Asia-Pacific Economic Cooperation
ASEAN	Association of South-East Asian Nations
AUC	African Union Commission
AWS	autonomous weapon systems
BRI	Belt and Road Initiative (China)
BRICS	Brazil, Russia, India, China, South Africa
CAT	Committee against Torture (UN)
CCP	Chinese Communist Party

CERD	International Convention on the Elimination of All Forms of Racial Discrimination
CHR	Commission on Human Rights (UN)
CIS	Commonwealth of Independent States
CODESRIA	Council for the Development of Social Science Research in Africa
CoE	Council of Europe
CSCE	Conference on Security and Co-operation in Europe
CSO	civil society organization
CSTO	Collective Security Treaty Organization
DLT	decentralized ledger technologies (blockchain)
DNS	domain name system
EAEU	Eurasian Economic Union
ECHR	European Convention on Human Rights
ECNL	European Center for Not-for-Profit Law
ECOSOC	Economic and Social Council
ECtHR	European Court of Human Rights
ETIM	East Turkestan Islamic Movement
FDI	foreign direct investment
GIEI	Grupo Interdisciplinario de Expertos Independientes
GONGO	government-organized nongovernmental organization
HDIM	Human Dimension Implementation Meeting (OSCE)
HRC	Human Rights Council
HRIs	human rights organizations
IACHR	Inter-American Commission on Human Rights
IACtHR	Inter-American Court of Human Rights
IASHR	Inter-American System of Human Rights
ICC	International Criminal Court
ICCPR	International Covenant on Civil and Political Rights
ICESCR	International Covenant on Economic, Social, and Cultural Rights
ICISS	International Commission on Intervention and State Sovereignty
ICJ	International Court of Justice
ICNL	International Center for Not-for-Profit Law
ICRC	International Committee of the Red Cross
ICTSD	International Centre for Trade and Sustainable Development
ICTY	International Criminal Tribunal for the Former Yugoslavia

IDEA	International Institute for Democracy and Electoral Assistance
IEEE	Institute of Electrical and Electronics Engineers
IETF	Internet Engineering Task Force
IGE	Institute for Global Engagement
IIIM	International, Impartial, and Independent Mechanism
IJOP	Integrated Joint-Operations Platform
IoT	Internet of Things
IP	internet protocol
IRFA	International Religious Freedom Act (1998)
ISO	International Organization for Standardization
ISP	internet service provider
ITU	International Telecommunications Union
LGBT(I)	Lesbian, Gay, Bisexual, Transgender (Intersex)
MFN	most favored nation
NGO	nongovernmental organization
OAS	Organization of American States
ODIHR	Office for Democratic Initiatives and Human Rights
OHCHR	Office of the High Commissioner for Human Rights
OIC	Organisation of Islamic Cooperation
OSCE	Organisation for Security and Co-operation in Europe
P5	Permanent Five UN Security Council members
PRC	People's Republic of China; Permanent Representatives Committee (AU)
QCCM	Quadrilateral Cooperation and Coordination Mechanism
R2P	Responsibility to Protect
RIPE NCC	Regional Internet Registry for Europe Network Coordination Centre
SADC	Southern Africa Development Community
SARS	Severe Acute Respiratory Syndrome
SCO	Shanghai Cooperation Organization
SDGs	Sustainable Development Goals (UN)
SDO	standards developing organization
TBT	technical barriers to trade (WTO)
UAE	United Arab Emirates
UDHR	Universal Declaration of Human Rights
UN	United Nations Human Rights Council
UNASUR	Union of South American Nations
UNCCW	UN Convention on Conventional Weapons

UNGGE	Group of Governmental Experts (on Lethal Autonomous Weapon Systems)
UNSC	United Nations Security Council
W3C	World Wide Web Consortium
WCF	World Congress of Families
WHO	World Health Organization
WTIO	World Trade Organization
WTSA	World Telecommunication Standardization Assembly

Introduction

CHRISTOPHER SABATINI

In preparing for this book, Chatham House convened an extended, informal discussion among young scholars and activists from Africa, Asia, Europe, the Middle East, and the United Kingdom with the aim of better understanding the views of a diverse generation of youth with regard to human rights.

Given growing concerns about economic insecurity and the divisive, hateful rhetoric of demagogues and xenophobes, I expected to hear shades of skepticism about the seemingly antiquated notions of political and civil liberties. Instead, rather than concentrating on the potential irrelevance of the international human rights system, or how human rights have failed to meet the promises of seventy-five years ago (though the discussion did touch on those too), the young participants emphasized their faith in human rights and their potential. There was some debate regarding the indivisibility of human rights and whether some should be prioritized over others, but by and large, participants not only praised the philosophical centrality of human rights today but also emphasized how they have shaped their own lives. As one woman from Africa said, they are the generation that "grew up in human rights."

If the discussion challenged my pessimistic assumptions about the opinions of at least an internationally engaged segment of youth, it also reinforced my belief in the importance of preserving and reforming today's international system of human rights. In January 2020, I published an op-ed in the *Washington Post,* titled "Why Is the U.S. Joining Venezuela and Nicaragua in Discrediting a System to Protect Human Rights?"[1] My argument was that the administration of Donald J. Trump was undermining international bodies intended to monitor and defend the rights that the United States claimed to champion. Of course, the administration's hypocrisy wasn't news to those who had watched the forty-fifth president embrace politicians such as Russia's leader Vladimir Putin, President Recep Tayyip Erodoğan of Turkey, or Hungary's prime minister Viktor Orbán. What was ironic was that in the United States' own neighborhood, the White House was undermining independent human rights bodies in implicit alliance with two members of what the administration's national security adviser John Bolton called the "troika of tyranny"—Venezuela and Nicaragua, along with Cuba.[2] I had moved to Britain a few months earlier, just as my adoptive country was engaging in the vitriolic and complicated process of extricating itself from the European Union. Both countries were in different ways pulling back from international commitments and restraints on their power that formed part of the broader network of the postwar liberal institutional order. But something deeper, more systemic, it seemed, was afoot. At the same time that these two countries were questioning, even challenging, elements of the post–World War II liberal international order, nondemocratic regimes in China, Russia, and Latin America were actively seeking to recast global human rights norms and multilateral bodies.

The changing and complicated positions in the United States' foreign commitments to human rights transcend parties. Just half a year into President Joe Biden's administration, his government followed through with a plan to pull U.S. troops out of Afghanistan. As the Taliban quickly retook the country and the U.S.-backed elected government collapsed—leaving behind thousands of Afghans who had worked with the United States and Western nongovernmental organizations (NGOs) to promote human rights—President Biden struck an almost Trumpian, realpolitik tone. The United States' mission, despite promises of restoring democracy and rolling back the Taliban's mistreatment of women, was not to defend human rights. As the Democratic president said, "We [the United States] had no vital national interest in Afghanistan other than to prevent an attack on America's homeland and our friends."[3] For those Afghans who had placed their faith and lives on the promise of a democratic new era in Afghanistan, and for the rest of the world, which had spent blood and treasure on the liberal promise of an Afghanistan that protected women's rights to education and the rule of law, the rapid withdrawal and the United States' dismissive shrug over the reversal of over twenty years of work could only seem a betrayal. But more than this abandonment of the lofty rhetoric of the values of the expanded mission, the United States' glibness over the consequences of its actions sent a powerful signal to current and future allies in other countries that its commitment at one moment to the advancement of principles of human rights and liberalism could quickly evaporate in the face of defeat and domestic popular and political opinion.

Globally the threats to the international rights regime today are multiple and complex. The bare power calculations of states' national security, economic, and diplomatic interests still present the primary challenge to compliance with human rights norms. But threats to the international rights framework are emerging from three new directions: increased geopolitical competition with new powers whose views of state sovereignty are at odds with human rights obligations, the rise of xenophobic and populist domestic movements, and the spread of surveillance technologies. In addition, for billions of citizens living in poverty or conflict zones, the notion of an international legal regime to which they can appeal for the protection of their rights remains a distant fiction. More than simply challenging individual norms and institutions, these factors are undermining the fragile, imperfect consensus that developed around human rights since 1945.

This book examines these emerging challenges to the international human rights regime and offers recommendations for activists, policymakers, and academics to better understand and address them. It emerged from discussions with the Ford Foundation on how scholars, youth, policymakers, and activists could weigh in on the partisan, often gloomy, global discussion around human rights. As the project unfolded over the course of two years, we held a series of virtual workshops with authors and informal meetings with human rights experts and activists to share ideas, explore and develop cross-chapter themes, and reality-check our analyses and conclusions.

To be sure, there are other threats than those described above. The impact of climate change on human rights is a major one. Another is the rapid growth of global inequality, accelerated by the COVID-19 pandemic and the economic crises that accompanied it. Even before the pandemic, poverty, inequality, and deprivation were undermining not just the guarantees of economic and social rights described in the following chapters but also the substance and perceived legitimacy of political and civil rights protections. Arguably, as citizens feel their economic insecurity more acutely in the postpandemic recovery, autocrats and demagogues will seek to exploit economic insecurity to consolidate personal power. Partisan attempts to parlay popular fears over the economy will lead to worsening treatment of refugees and asylum seekers and the declining power of multilateral and regional organizations to enforce international commitments for their protection and humane treatment.

Of course, we could not address all these issues in a single volume. Our goal was more modest: to focus on the structural, political, and technical challenges or threats to international and regional human rights regimes. However, many of the other issues listed above are addressed indirectly. Climate change, for example, has an impact on many of the themes addressed here. Extreme weather is already a factor in increased migration and domestic and international conflict. The rise of populism and the breakdown of regional human rights bodies' enforcement of protections for migrants and refugees have fueled the deterioration in attitudes toward them, and in their treatment. And although economic and social rights are not addressed here as a discrete topic, many of the authors in this book explain how economic, social, and political inequality have both increased the pressures for the realization of the broad guarantees of human rights and weakened the appeal of the West and indeed much of the Global North's traditional focus on civil and political rights.

Structure of the Book

The chapters are grouped into four related clusters: the rise—or return of—global great power competition and the efforts of global autocracies and to remake the global order; the persistence of populist and transnational religious groups that are shaping international human rights policies and institutions; the emergence of new technologies, which has placed greater authority in the hands of states, corporations, and individuals; and the struggles of regional human rights systems to adapt to these challenges.

After my historical and contextual overview in chapter 1, the first section explores the effect of geopolitical competition on human rights. Chapter 2, by Rosemary Foot, examines the dynamics and implications of rising U.S.–China antagonism, both within China and globally. In chapter 3 Nandini Ramanujam and Vishakha Wijenayake look at Russia's role in shaping the international rights system and how the international failure to address economic and social rights has aided President Vladimir Putin's efforts to undermine political and civil rights domestically and abroad. Alexander Cooley discusses in chapter 4 how China and Russia have sought to create new institutions of global governance that promote their self-interested views of illiberalism and national sovereignty at the expense of human rights in an attempt to remake the global order to their own advantage. When we initially sketched out the outlines of this book project, the term COVID-19 did not exist, but in chapter 5 Rana Moustafa explains how rising geopolitical competition weakened the global response to the pandemic and how multilateral institutions have failed in guaranteeing human rights protections during domestic responses.

The second thematic section deals with the impact of domestic politics on international human rights policies. The influence of domestic politics on the foreign policies of states is, of course, nothing new.[4] But the sorts of national populist movements described by Roger Eatwell and Matthew Goodwin, often stoked by economic insecurity, are targeting commitments and policies to defend human rights, not just domestically but internationally.[5] In chapter 6, Gerald Neuman builds on his previous work on this topic[6] to examine these pressures and explore how the reassertion of national sovereign claims might be balanced against international norms. Within and outside those populist movements, evangelical churches and leaders in Brazil, the Philippines, Uganda, the United States, and elsewhere are asserting themselves in foreign policy and human rights matters. Chapter 7, by Melani McAlister, examines the tension between the narrower interpretation of rights advanced by evangelical movements and the progressive rights agenda of many human rights NGOs and multilateral organizations.

Section III examines the threats of new technologies to human rights, and the gaps and weaknesses in responses by existing institutions. Emily Taylor, Kate Jones, and Carolina Caeiro consider in chapter 8 how attempts by the Chinese government to alter internet protocols will likely impinge on rights to privacy; freedom of expression and opinion; freedom of thought, religion, and belief; and due process. In chapter 9, Thompson Chengeta highlights the racially discriminatory effects of autonomous weapons systems and artificial intelligence and the lack of accountability regarding their use.

The last thematic grouping, section IV, focuses on regional human rights systems in Europe; Latin America; and Africa; and political upheaval, geopolitics, and human rights in the Middle East and North Africa. In chapter 10, Urfan Khaliq analyzes the European system of human rights, which was once considered an exemplary model (wrongly, he believes), and how domestic and intraregional tensions have weakened its effectiveness. Chapter 11, by Santiago Canton and Angelita Baeyens, argues that unless governments in the Americas dramatically reform the inter-American system of human rights, sometimes described as the "crown jewel" of the Western hemisphere's multilateral system, the Organization of American States, will become obsolete. In the case of the African human rights system, Solomon Dersso argues in chapter 12 that the continent is not immune to contemporary pressures facing the global human rights regime, including populism, nationalism, bigotry, the assertion of national sovereignty, and intensifying rivalry among global actors. In each of these cases, reimagining the function and duties of these systems and their bureaucracies will be essential if they are to remain relevant to the mission of defending human rights and lives. While the Middle East and North Africa do not have a regional human rights system similar to those in Europe, Latin America, and Africa, there too citizens and governments have become caught up in the rising demands for accountable government, geopolitics, and decreasing U.S. commitment to advancing human rights globally, as Aslı Bâli details in chapter 13.

The book concludes with a series of recommendations for policymakers and activists alike. These build on a separate, virtual discussion Chatham House held between the authors and international and frontline human rights activists from Africa, Asia, Latin America, and the United States. Those discussions and earlier discussions of draft chapters produced a set of practical and personal perspectives that we include in our recommendations here. Some of those recommendations call for the drafting and updating of treaties and covenants to address new challenges. Others focus on changing or expanding the mandate of existing multilateral bodies or outlining new agendas for activism and future scholarship.

This book seeks to provide concrete, practical policy recommendations in response to these modern challenges and to the gaps in policy, advocacy, and scholarship. If, indeed, the international consensus over human rights and the legitimacy and functions of international institutions to defend human rights are fraying or fragile, to what extent can they be recovered? More optimistically, can the present moment represent an opportunity to hear the voice of the Global South more clearly and to expand its role in redefining human rights domestically and internationally? What can activists, policymakers, and citizens do to shore up and protect the human rights system in which so many of us—as the young participant in the Chatham House roundtable reminded us—have grown up? And for those who are aware of the promises of political, civil, economic, and social rights but have yet to benefit, or who are watching them become increasingly distant—as in Brazil, China, Myanmar, the Philippines, Russia, Saudi Arabia, Venezuela, and Zimbabwe—what can be done to realize or recover them?

We hope the analyses and recommendations presented here match the urgency of human rights challenges in a difficult, fluid, multipolar world, and point a way forward to renew the commitment to these rights. We believe that in sketching out some of the broader geopolitical and domestic threats to the international human rights regime, we can, in a limited way, start to deepen future discussion and research on this topic.

Notes

1. Christopher Sabatini, "Why Is the U.S. Joining Venezuela and Nicaragua in Discrediting a System to Protect Human Rights?," *Washington Post,* January 17, 2020, www.washingtonpost.com/opinions/2020/01/17/why-is-us-joining-venezuela -nicaragua-discrediting-system-protect-human-rights/.

2. Julian Borger, "Bolton Praises Bolsonaro While Declaring 'Troika of Tyranny' in Latin America," *The Guardian,* November 1, 2018, https://www.theguardian.com /us-news/2018/nov/01/trump-admin-bolsonaro-praise-john-bolton-troika-tyranny -latin-america.

3. "Remarks by President Biden on the End of the War in Afghanistan," August 31, 2021, https://www.whitehouse.gov/briefing-room/speeches-remarks/2021/08/31/remarks -by-president-biden-on-the-end-of-the-war-in-afghanistan/.

4. Robert Putnam, "Diplomacy and Domestic Politics: The Logic of Two-Level Games," *International Organization* 42, 3 (Summer 1988), pp. 427–60, www.jstor.org /stable/2706785?seq=1.

5. Roger Eatwell and Matthew Goodwin, *National Populism: The Revolt against Liberal Democracy* (London: Penguin Books, 2018).

6. Gerald Neumann (ed.), *Human Rights in a Time of Populism: Challenges and Responses* (Cambridge University Press, 2020).

PART I
Geopolitics

ONE

Human Rights

From Evolution to Devolution?

CHRISTOPHER SABATINI

The modern international human rights system that emerged from World War II as well as the creation of the United Nations (UN) survived the Cold War and anarchic international society of state competition to evolve, adapt, and expand. Over the course of its seventy-five–year history, what was originally a set of ideals based on the dignity of human beings, their fundamental rights, and the obligations of states to protect them grew imperfectly into a set of international norms, treaties, and international and regional institutions. This international normative, institutional infrastructure helped spark the formation of a community of local and transnational activists, and this in turn, together with the post–World War II human rights architecture, has helped consolidate and realize the promotion and defense of human rights promised in the early articulation of these ideals.

The process was never linear and certainly never balanced. Great-power politics, the Cold War, national interests, humanitarian crises, socioeconomic inequality, and lack of state capacity challenged the high-minded notion that human rights would be applied to all states equally or that all people would enjoy access to them. And for decades, from governments across the ideological spectrum, rhetoric and policy in defense of human rights have been instrumentalized for political agendas and national interests. Yet despite this, particularly after the 1970s, the moral, legal, and political principles and obligations of human rights took root and grew.

The formation and expansion of the international and regional human rights systems coincided with the broader emergence and consolidation of international law in the postwar era on issues of trade, norms for the conduct of war, refugees, and the environment. But arguably, human rights treaties and practice were the most intrusive in terms of national sovereignty. These historic and subversive ideals placing the power of human dignity above state rights informed international and domestic discourse, captured the imagination of citizens and activists, shaped popular demands on governments and policymakers, and, in many countries, formed the basis of domestic law and principles of jurisprudence. Human rights and the treaties and customary laws that embodied and reflected them—together with a global human rights movement—helped curb state abuse and in some cases contributed to the downfall of autocratic governments in Africa, Asia, Eastern Europe, and Latin America.

The Early Years and the Cold War

There are long-standing debates about the genesis of the idea of human dignity and rights and the accountability or responsibility of rulers and states to defend them. For some the philosophical foundations extend to ancient Greece, Roman law, the Enlightenment, or the debates and activism in Europe to end slavery.[1] For others the basis of social contract theory that a ruler's legitimacy rests on the consent of the governed arises from English liberal philosophers of the seventeenth and eighteenth centuries. Whatever the roots of human rights, such discussion does have a bearing on their universality. As the argument goes, human rights—especially civil and political rights—are a Western concept and have little relevance to other societies and their experiences. But the formation of this concept in the West, especially as it defines and defends the dignity of individuals and their liberties, does not preclude its applicability to the human condition elsewhere—much as philosophical insights into the human condition arising in non-Western societies and traditions have universal applicability.[2] Others have pointed out that concepts of human dignity that are the core of human rights exist in Islam and Hinduism,[3] and lawyers and scholars representing different cultures and religions contributed to the drafting of the Universal Declaration of Human Rights (UDHR).[4] Indeed, norms and promises of political and civil rights—especially when interpreted collectively as the right of self-determination—served as moral and political leverage against colonial powers for independence leaders and movements in Africa and Asia.[5]

It was the United Nations in 1945 that launched the concept of universal human rights in international law, though narrower treaties had introduced the limited notion of rights before this. In its preamble, the UN Charter declares: "We the people of the United Nations . . . reaffirm faith in fundamental human rights, in the dignity and worth of the human person, in the equal rights of men and women," and goes on to commit the UN to "promoting and encouraging respect for human rights and for fundamental freedoms for all without distinction as to race, sex, language or religion."[6] While the language did not extend as far as some representatives gathered in San Francisco wanted (including those from Latin America), the charter listed the promotion of human rights as one of the mandates of the new multilateral body and called for the creation of a commission by the Economic and Social Council (ECOSOC) to monitor and oversee this new international commitment.

The Universal Declaration of Human Rights, formulated soon after, was adopted as a resolution by the UN General Assembly in 1948. By setting out the notion that human rights were universal and thus, to quote John Simmons, "rights possessed by all human beings (at all times and in all places, simply by virtue of their humanity)," the charter and the UDHR extended those rights to all peoples.[7] By inscribing the concept of equal rights and, in the case of the declaration, defining these rights as universal, through language and status, both these instruments committed members to protect them domestically.

However, while the UDHR was originally conceived as a broad proclamation that would include political, civil, economic, and social rights, its preparation and ratification into a legally binding treaty became caught in the ideological and geopolitical tensions between the United States and the Soviet Union. The set of economic and social rights was not entirely foreign to the United States: President Franklin Roosevelt's 1941 State of the Union address, in which he laid out the "Four Freedoms," spoke of freedom of speech and expression, freedom of worship, *freedom from want,* and freedom from fear (emphasis mine).[8] Nevertheless, after 1948 the Soviet Union and a large bloc of developing countries shied away from the largely liberal West's greater emphasis on political and civic rights, focusing instead on the economic and social components of the treaty. In 1966, with the support of the Soviet bloc and developing countries, the UN approved two separate sets of rights: the International Covenant on Economic, Social, and Cultural Rights and the International Covenant on Civil and Political Rights. These instruments set the rights originally outlined in the Universal Declaration on a legally binding footing and placed the responsibility for implementation firmly on states; by 2021 more than 160 states were parties to each. But the reluctance of the United States and many of the Western democracies to accord the same importance to economic and social rights as to the political and civil rights that defined their political systems gave the former a seeming secondary status, despite repeated UN declarations and summits that reinforced the indivisibility and interdependence of political/civil and economic and social rights. A raft of other treaties were adopted around this process, more of them in the mold of political and civil rights, including the International Convention on the Elimination of All Forms of Racial Discrimination (1965), the Convention on the Elimination of All Forms of Discrimination Against Women (1981), the Convention Against Torture and Other Cruel, Inhumane or Degrading Treatment or Punishment (1987), and the Convention on the Rights of the Child (1990).

These international treaties and agreements gave birth to a set of bodies intended to monitor (and in the case of some regional human rights bodies, to adjudicate) these obligations. In 1946 the UN created the UN Commission on Human Rights (later re-formed as the UN Human Rights Council [UNHRC] in 2006), establishing an institutional body and procedural means to promote protection of these rights. Both are political bodies with state members, not legal arbiters of rights compliance. As such they have both strengths and weaknesses in monitoring and criticizing human rights practices in countries. As political entities they have had the capacity to wield significant political pressure to change state behavior in certain cases. In other cases, they have been at the mercy of powerful states, regional blocs, and alliances, and this has led to a distorted focus on certain issues and anomalous failures to censure egregious behavior. Nevertheless, even within those limitations, innovations such as the creation of special rapporteurs to investigate and report on specific countries and themes, and the Universal Periodic Reviews in which countries—and nongovernmental organizations (NGOs)—review and comment on human rights practices of UN member countries, have given the UNHRC an importance beyond its original conception. Through these processes, states periodically report on their compliance and attend oral hearings. In the 1990s, the role of the UN High Commissioner for Human Rights was added. The Office of the Commissioner for Human Rights is charged with assisting governments to meet their human rights obligations, but perhaps inevitably it has become a focal point for local human rights groups and has helped draw attention to cases of human rights abuse, recently, for instance, in Syria and Venezuela.

At the same time, regional multilateral bodies were developing their own normative infrastructure for human rights. In Europe, the European Convention on Human Rights was adopted in 1950 to safeguard civil and political rights, and the European Court of Human Rights followed in 1959. The Lisbon Treaty, which entered into effect at the end of 2009, made the Charter on Fundamental Rights a binding element of European Union (EU) law. In the Americas, the Inter-American Convention on Human Rights of 1969 drew from the charter of the Organization of American States that declared the regional body's commitment to human rights. When the Inter-American Convention entered into force in 1979, it reorganized and strengthened the Inter-American Commission on Human Rights and created the Inter-American Court of Human Rights based in San José, Costa Rica. In Africa human rights treaties and bodies came later: the African Charter on Human and Peoples' Rights was originally drafted under the Organization of African States (later the African Union) in 1981 and passed into effect in 1986. The Charter led to the creation of the African Commission on Human and People's Rights and the African Court on Human and People's Rights, in 1987 and 1998, respectively. To date, there have been no similar regional human rights–based treaties or bodies in the Middle East or Asia. In 2009 members of the Association of Southeast Asian Nations (ASEAN) established an Intergovernmental Commission on Human Rights, but the body has only weakly defined powers, mostly relying on states' self-monitoring and reporting. In some countries international human rights principles and norms also became a key part of domestic law and jurisprudence. In Argentina, Mexico, and South Africa, for example, such norms have either become officially part of constitutional or local law or can be drawn on by local courts and judges.

Post–Cold War Human Rights

The decade after the end of the Cold War could arguably be called the high-water mark of international human rights, despite the lack of a global consensus. There was a broader and more active acceptance that states and multilateral bodies had a legitimate right to speak out and monitor human rights. With this came the expansion of human rights activism to include democratic rights such as the right to free and fair elections, demonstrated by the wide acceptance of international election monitoring at the time. During this period states also took steps to protect populations through international criminal law. In 1993 the UN Security Council (UNSC) created the International Criminal

Tribunal for the Former Yugoslavia (ICTY) to investigate and try cases of genocide, war crimes, and crimes against humanity committed during the civil war in the former Yugoslavia. The following year, the UNSC created a similar court, the International Criminal Tribunal for Rwanda (ICTR), to investigate the horrific bloodletting that had occurred in that country. In 1998, states signed the Treaty of Rome that would form the basis for a permanent court with jurisdiction over genocide, war crimes, and crimes against humanity, "when committed as part of a widespread or systematic attack directed against any civilian population."[9] Two years later the International Criminal Court (ICC) was established in Geneva. In 2018, the crime of aggression was added to the ICC's mandate. A total of 125 countries submitted to its jurisdiction, though the Philippines and Burundi later withdrew.

Since its creation the ICC has been controversial. Under the administration of President George W. Bush, the United States refused to place itself under the Court's authority and sought to prevent it from prosecuting U.S. citizens.[10] The Bush administration's hard-nosed opposition to the Court (even using the threat of cutting international assistance to extort agreement from poorer countries not to prosecute U.S. officials) demonstrated that at least one major global state would not consistently submit to its jurisdiction. There were also complaints about the slow pace of investigations and prosecution under the ICC's first prosecutor, Argentinian jurist Luis Moreno Ocampo.[11] Its efforts to prosecute leaders and groups involved in conflict, such as the president of Sudan, Omar Hassan Ahmed al-Bashir, in 2009 and 2010, raised the concern that by aggressively giving notice that current combatants or heads of state would face prosecution and likely prison, the ICC was reducing the potential for negotiations or for leaders to step aside peacefully. Critics also worried that the ICC was focusing its attention too much on Africa, creating—or, for some, reinforcing—the impression that the global criminal court was an instrument of international and human rights law that applied only to the weak.[12] South Africa and The Gambia almost withdrew over this apparent Africa-centric focus. Overall, in twenty years the ICC has achieved only ten convictions.[13] Nevertheless, by its creation and through its public role, it has built a sense among activists, international jurists, and citizens that impunity for egregious, systematic crimes against humanity will no longer be the norm, even if the avenue for justice is imperfect and many of its indictments may remain—for now—public recognition of their crimes.

A further step toward the international enforcement of human rights was taken in 2001 with a report from the International Commission on Intervention and State Sovereignty in what became known known as the Responsibility to Protect or R2P. The goal was to prevent a recurrence of the sort of horrors witnessed in Rwanda in the early 1990s. It was an admission of the international community's collective guilt and its sense of responsibility for failing to intervene early to stop the genocide. At the 2005 high-level UN World Summit, member states declared their preparedness to take military or other collective action, if authorized by the UNSC, to help protect populations from genocide, war crimes, ethnic cleansing, and crimes against humanity. But R2P's star has waned since 2011, when the UNSC, having authorized the use of force to protect Libyan civilians under attack by forces loyal to Muammar Qaddafi, changed course midway through the mission, to overthrow the Qaddafi regime. The shift from protection to regime change, the loss of civilian life during the operation, and the chaos that followed reinforced the fears that R2P was a cover for the agenda of great powers and when used bluntly could itself become a threat to human rights and civilians.[14]

Civil Society: Breathing Life into Human Rights Norms

None of the push to realize the goals of the UN and liberal ideals or to expand human rights norms and jurisprudence would have been possible without the emergence and consolidation of transnational human rights and grassroots organizations and networks. Their growth picked up in the 1970s in the wake of a series of coups d'état in countries such as Greece (1967), Czechoslovakia (1968, brought about by Soviet intervention), Chile (1973), and Argentina (1976), and the repression that followed in all these cases—often exposed by local activists and the media. As Samuel Moyn has argued, the independence movements of former colonies in Asia and Africa gave historical momentum and definition to the idea of self-determination and individual rights and to the modern-day human rights system. That momentum found its formal recognition as a central theme on the world stage and as a policy of state among the great powers with the election of President Jimmy Carter (1977–1981), who positioned human rights as a core element in U.S. foreign policy.

The number of international and domestic nongovernmental human rights groups rose dramatically in the period. The first was Amnesty International, founded in 1961 in London in response to an article, "The Forgotten Prisoners," published on May 28 in *The Observer*. By profiling and personalizing the individuals held in detention, the U.K.-based organization focused international attention on the existence and plight of political prisoners, bringing the expression "prisoner of conscience" into popular currency—the term referring not just to the injustice but also to the victims' higher moral calling. A year after Amnesty International won the Nobel Prize in 1977, Helsinki Watch was formed. Initially created to monitor human rights in the Soviet Union and Eastern bloc countries that were signatories to the 1970 Helsinki Accords, the organization, renamed Human Rights Watch in the 1980s, expanded its scope to the United States and Latin America and later globally. These pioneering nongovernmental organizations did more than just open a new field of human rights research and advocacy; they and the hundreds if not thousands that followed, and their networks, helped embed human rights in public consciousness and international relations.[15] International human rights groups served as training grounds for new activists and built bridges between homegrown local church groups, community organizations, social movements, trade unions, foundations, and the like across borders and to international organizations and other governments. According to Margaret Keck and Kathryn Sikkink, between 1983 and 1990 alone, the number of human rights NGOs across the world doubled.[16]

The change was not just in numbers, networks, and public discussion. This new transnational movement created a sense of community that brought new ideas, information, and testimonials to international attention and, by relaying information to sympathetic governments and appropriate officials in multilateral organizations, pressed for action to address human rights abuses. The network embodied the newfound concept of sovereignty expressed in the original human rights declarations, moving away from the concept of a state's sovereign right to govern in its own manner within its borders, to one where it was now accountable to the independent voices within its own population and to the criticism of other states and multilateral bodies. This was much the intention of the original body of the UN and other international and regional human rights treaties and conventions, but by citing examples that cataloged and humanized the abuses, providing access to independent objective information, and fostering the alliances and advocacy of a transnational community of committed citizens, civil society helped realize those norms—if not always in enforcement, then at least in domestic and international debates and in perceptions of accountability. Actions facilitated by local activists and international forensic scientists established the culpability of the military junta for disappearances in Argentina; dissidents such as Andrei Sakharov and Elena Bonner in the Soviet Union and Václav Havel in then Czechoslovakia gained international attention and, in some cases, release from prison thanks to the international attention brought to their cases by this global web of conscientious activism.

In later years, this spirit and these civil networks expanded and adapted to other aspects of the extension of human rights, particularly as autocratic governments from southern Europe, Latin America, the Eastern bloc, Asia, and Africa during the late 1970s to the 1990s gave way to elected governments—in no small part because of the awareness and pressure brought by transnational civil society. Later, Indigenous; women's; environmental; and lesbian, gay, bisexual, and transgender (LGBT) rights drew their inspiration from the rights explicit or implicit in the original texts of the treaties from the 1940s and subsequent ones that advocated for their expansion, applying many of the same tactics and often working with some of the same founding human rights organizations. Civil society's by this time well-worn process is well-explained by Bob Clifford: "First, politicized groups frame long felt grievances as normative claims. Second, they place these rights on the international agenda by convincing gatekeepers in major rights organizations to accept them . . . third, states and international bodies, often under pressures from gatekeepers and aggrieved groups, accept new norms. Finally, national institutions implement the norms."[17] This process has become so standard that today it almost seems organic and natural, to the extent that it has been imitated by nondemocratic states (such as Russia and China) in their efforts to roll back human rights and undermine criticism.

The recognition, pursuit, and protection of human rights norms internationally, whether through state foreign policy or through multilateral institutions, was never uniform or consistent. The on-the-ground successes in curbing the human rights abuses of governments, such as those mentioned above, occurred primarily in smaller, weaker countries and were at times (as in U.S. policy toward Cuba) driven more by domestic politics.[18] These were states that were more susceptible to leverage through suspension of trade privileges or the curtailment of bilateral or multilateral economic or military assistance. Such tools have been notably less successful in the case of China, which, given its large internal economy, lacks the exposure to outside economic pressures—in no small part because it often enjoys the support of international businesses deeply invested in and reaping profits from the large Chinese market and its global trade. These norms and processes have also proved weak in protecting the rights of individuals and communities in a growing number of situations of state collapse, such as in Libya, Syria, or Venezuela.

The global fissures over human rights that existed at their birth in international treaties in the 1940s and that would assume greater prominence in the 2000s were already evident in 1993. At that year's World Conference on Human Rights in Vienna, the United States hoped for a clear post–Cold War reaffirmation of the global commitment to human rights. Those hopes hit a snag in a bloc of countries including China, Iran, Pakistan, Singapore, and

Syria, which argued that human rights, as a Western fabrication, did not apply to other societies—in particular, their countries. The conference's final Vienna Declaration and Programme of Action repeated states' commitment to the international bill of rights (as the UDHR, the International Covenant on Civil and Political Rights—plus two additional protocols—and the International Covenant on Economic, Social and Cultural Rights became known collectively), but with the caveat that "the significance of national and regional particularities and various historical, cultural, and religious backgrounds must be borne in mind."[19] While the declaration reiterated the universality of human rights and created the UN High Commissioner for Human Rights, in the following thirty years the rift between the developed North and China, Iran, and other countries widened, especially as domestic politics shifted and global great-power competition returned.

Debates and Doubts

To retrace these founding moments and celebrate them is not to project a narrative of their evolution as teleological or even as perfect public good.[20] Even in the "good times," the realities of power politics, global economic inequality, ideological prejudices and alliances, and the inherent lack of autonomy of multilateral organizations remained. The successes were selective, at best; despite the lofty rhetoric, they rarely triumphed over realpolitik; autocratic states that abused human rights were left largely free of vocal government criticism if they possessed resources or economic power (Saudi Arabia and China) or were critical to regional peace (Egypt), or if the cost of the potential turmoil from possible regime collapse was deemed too high (Algeria, Iraq before 2003, or Uganda). And in the worst cases, human rights were used as a cover for intervention and the bald extension of a state power (in part, Iraq in 2003, especially after the invading forces failed to find the promised weapons of mass destruction). There were also often the unintended consequences of even the best intentions (such as in Libya in 2011) or of struggling to find a balance between accountability for abuses and reconciliation (as Colombian president Juan Manuel Santos argued in defense of his 2016 Colombian Peace Agreement).

As human rights norms, institutions, and jurisprudence have developed, a number of criticisms have been directed at the heart of the UDHR and the broader human rights movement. For scholars such as Makau Mutua and Samuel Moyn, the distinction between civil and political liberties and economic and social rights, and the emphasis on the former, led to distortion that disadvantaged the rights most relevant to the needs of many citizens in the Global

South.[21] Moyn recently extended this argument to make the powerful case that by failing to address extreme inequality and socioeconomic needs, the current human rights movement has lost the "imaginative near-monopoly as a framework for reform."[22] By focusing on political and civil rights, Moyn argues, the rights agenda has ignored—even implicitly legitimated—inequality. Without a broader attention to an agenda of social rights now with the rise of populism, he asserts, the achievements of human rights can be "easily reversed."[23]

At the same time, there are concerns over the "justiciability" of economic and social rights. Economic and social rights, for instance, to housing, health care, and education, are related more to state capacity that many countries in the developing world lack, and are not directly enforceable—a fact acknowledged in the covenant but that nevertheless hampers their implementation through traditional justice systems and international bodies. Unlike violations of civil and political rights, there is not an immediate, identifiable perpetrator; poverty, inequality, and lack of access to public goods are linked to a complex web of factors rather than the result of intentional abuse by state or nonstate actors. For some this leads to the argument that for practical reasons, economic and social rights are best considered aspirational rights or public policy goals rather than absolute rights. Amartya Sen and Martha Nussbaum go further. They argue that civil and political rights are essential to the condition of human dignity that is core to the philosophical and practical conditions and process of development.[24] In this view and others like it, it is therefore impossible to imagine and promote economic and social development, and the rights associated with it, without civil and political rights, and hence the four aspects cannot be separated. Nevertheless, popular discontent and global concern over endemic poverty, and with it the political and social exclusion that threatens human dignity, have led to a growing movement, especially within the Global South, of a "right to development." In 1986 the UN General Assembly adopted the Declaration on the Right to Development. declaring this to be an "inalienable right" "subject to the relevant provisions of both International Covenants on Human Rights."[25]

Another criticism relates to what Michael Ignatieff has called "rights inflation."[26] He and others argue there has been an increasing tendency to imbue any desirable public good—development, progressive economic policy, environmental protection, constraints on the abuses of transnational corporations (and recently even anticorruption measures, as Santiago Canton and Angelita Baevens discuss in chapter 11)—with the moral authority, urgency, and legal doctrine of human rights law.[27] As the argument goes, this risks expanding the theoretical basis of human rights and so diluting their effectiveness, as well as endowing human rights with a quasi-religious quality, capable of remedying all perceived evils, rather than remaining on firm legal ground. As an example of this trend, Hurst Hannum calculates that in 1990 the special procedures and expert investigations of the UN Human Rights Commission (later Council) included a narrow set of issues primarily linked to physical security, civil rights, and socioeconomic rights, whereas by 2017 the Council had forty-four special procedures and experts on topics ranging from the disposal of hazardous material; foreign debt; and a clean, healthy environment; to transnational corporations. Very few of these later topics had specific links to treaties or obligations, and some—such as on debt and transnational corporations—targeted nonstate actors.[28]

There is an additional point implied in many of these criticisms: that the human rights agenda had a false teleology, deriving from a tendency to imagine the philosophical and practical evolution of human rights as an expression of the natural historical order that will continue to progress as such. A criticism of this view formed part of Moyn's revisionist history of the human rights movement—though his claims of the shallowness of rights consciousness and political and social commitment to them have been challenged.[29] This sense of human rights determinism has led to a naivete about the security and progress of human rights relative to pressing socioeconomic needs, and a dangerously impractical view about how the world *should* work.[30]

None of this is to deny the very real (though admittedly fragile) progress and impact that the focus on human rights has had on world affairs, the evolution of domestic rule of law, and the protection of lives and freedoms. Popular beliefs and expectations have changed: according to Pew Global surveys, in 2020 a median of 64 percent of citizens in thirty-four countries supported the view that individuals should have the right to express themselves. The same surveys revealed that 74 percent of citizens believed women should have the same rights as men, and 68 percent supported freedom of religion.[31] These gains in civil and political rights are seen, for example, in the declining use of the death penalty and torture, the proliferation of independent media, and the expansion of women's rights in the past seventy-five years. Improvements in poverty levels, literacy, children's school enrollment, and health care increased attention to the rights of Indigenous and minority cultures and traditions; the formulation of and advances toward the UN development goals are also evidence of the progress of economic, cultural, and social rights—despite their seeming lower priority in international discussions and advocacy.

Seventy-five years of human rights have transformed our belief in human dignity and the obligations of states and societies, and have inspired generations of citizens and activists. The jailed protesters in Hong Kong, those killed on the streets defending democracy in Myanmar, demonstrators demanding fair elections in Belarus, harassed LGBT activists in Russia, or dissidents in North Korea or Cuba are all struggling for more than a philosophical concept or a vestige of Western culture. These lives, their stories, and the values that inspired them will not be easily extinguished, whatever happens to the normative and institutional infrastructure of human rights internationally and domestically, or in the debates among academics.

But Then There's Today

Despite the successes and enduring popular commitment to human rights, the infrastructure of rules, processes, and institutions, and efforts to apply liberal norms in world affairs and domestic law and policy have eroded in recent years. Thirty years on from the World Conference on Human Rights in Vienna, the consensus around human rights has frayed.

The same debates continue—about the notion that rights are universal or mediated by local cultures, whether calling out violations amounts to foreign interference in sovereign affairs, and what to do about spoiler states—but rights abusers have become more outspoken and are finding unlikely partners. As they resist the legitimacy of international norms and the authority of multilateral organizations, NGOs, and other states to weigh in on human rights concerns, this new generation of autocrats is finding allies; China and Russia, which have in some cases provided financial support and diplomatic backing, are cheering on such autocrats and human rights abusers by asserting the rights of national sovereignty and noninterference. And at times even some of the states that created and defend the modern human rights system have given autocrats diplomatic and ideological cover, as with former U.S. president Donald Trump's embrace of populist regimes from Brazil to eastern Europe and professed admiration for Vladimir Putin in Russia. The former president of the Philippines, Rodrigo Duterte, saying he "doesn't care about human rights" and encouraged his supporters to kill drug addicts.[32] Russia and Poland have both asserted their sovereign prerogatives over the jurisdiction of the European Court of Human Rights.[33] Hungary's prime minister, Viktor Orbán, has lambasted human rights as a product of "liberal imperialism."[34] In Nicaragua, despite the protests of much of the developed world and sanctions imposed by the United States and the European Union, President Daniel Ortega violently repressed peaceful protesters, closed down independent media, and jailed or held under house arrest all of the main opposition leaders in the run-up to the

2021 presidential elections. Myanmar's military junta was invited to an ASEAN conference only weeks after overthrowing a democratically elected government in a military coup, and after years of conducting genocide against the Rohingya people in Rakhine State. China's genocide of the Uyghurs has met little international resistance. Even beyond the formal and rhetorical alliances among these human rights–abusing regimes, their individual and collective ability to avoid international accountability is also having an intangible, cumulative demonstration effect on other aspiring autocrats.

Human rights protections have even diminished within Western democracies. The rise of far-right parties across Europe has diluted these countries' international commitments to protest the rights of asylum seekers. Syrian refugees in Denmark are being sent to Damascus because it has been deemed "safe" by the country's immigration offices;[35] its Parliament also passed a law to establish internment camps outside Europe, possibly in Rwanda, to process asylum applications. The United Kingdom in 2022 attempted to implement a similar policy. These efforts resemble Australia's notoriously cruel policy, restarted in 2013, of harboring asylum seekers in offshore detention centers in Papua New Guinea and the island of Nauru.[36] The European Union has signed agreements with Libya and Turkey to keep migrants from reaching its borders, despite evidence that such policies fuel rights abuses in both countries.[37] In the United States, judicial challenges delayed the Biden administration's plans to dismantle his predecessor's widely criticized policy of forcing asylum seekers attempting to cross the U.S.-Mexico border to remain in Mexico while their applications were being processed.

These domestic strains, and even attacks against human rights, have spilled over into foreign policy and the efficacy and legitimacy—if not the survival—of regional and international human rights bodies. Recent years have not been a smooth ride for the European system of human rights, whether through the Council of Europe or through the EU and its commitment to human rights norms and the democratic health of its members. In one example, an EU resolution criticizing China's human rights record at the UN was blocked by Greece, allegedly because of the influence of Chinese investments in that member state.[38] The EU has also struggled to uphold its own commitments to the rule of law in Hungary and Poland. Brexit has created not only concerns about the United Kingdom's commitment to the liberal order it helped found but also deeper tensions over its commitment to the European human rights system. In one example, after a series of judgments by the European Court of Human Rights against U.K. law limiting the right of felons to vote, the then prime minister David Cameron condemned the Court's right to weigh in on domestic laws, criticizing it for not taking into account the "democratic decisions by a national parliament" and threatening that failure to do so would discredit rights.[39] It was an argument that could have been made by a number of populist governments in eastern member states against the European human rights system.

In the United States similar sentiments rejecting human rights institutions and international norms have grown, reinforced by a deepening nationalist/populist strain in domestic politics. While U.S. claims of exceptionalism have always meant that these currents run deeper, in recent years the United States has sought to openly undermine human rights institutions and norms. During the "war on terror," the administration of President George W. Bush rejected international outcry over its systematic use of torture and the jailing of alleged terrorists without due process in Guantánamo.[40] While Barack Obama pledged to reverse the policies, the prisons there remain open, and the rejection of international human rights was resurrected with even greater hostility under Donald Trump's America First agenda. The Trump administration withdrew the United States from the UN Human Rights Council (a decision later reversed by President Joe Biden), and its use of human rights as a blunt weapon to punish China for economic issues unrelated to human rights seemed a cynical (though not original) conflation of U.S. principles and economic interests. At the same time, President Trump's enthusiastic personal embrace of human rights–abusing governments in Brazil, Hungary, the Philippines, Poland, and Russia scrambled what many believed was a consensus among liberal democracies to maintain political distance, at the very least, from such governments as they dismantled the rule of law and attacked political and civil rights.

Under the Trump administration, the United States also cut funding to multilateral and regional human rights organizations and temporarily placed sanctions on jurists in the ICC, including chief prosecutor Fatou Bensouda for investigating U.S. troops in Afghanistan for war crimes (another policy decision reversed by President Biden).[41] Domestically too, various concerns were raised over the Trump administration's treatment of migrants and domestic protesters. When the Inter-American Commission on Human Rights attempted to hold hearings on U.S. policies toward migrants, the administration either refused to accept the Commission's authority or refused to attend.[42] This cycle of rejection and limited compliance appears unlikely to abate given the political temperature in the United States today, despite Biden's attempt to recover lost ground.

Within this divergence and discord among the historical post–World War II defenders of human rights have come not-so-subtle efforts by countries such as China and Russia—often in collaboration with current governments in Hungary, Nicaragua, the Philippines, Poland, Turkey, and Venezuela (among others)—to reset the human rights consensus internationally in their own favor. China's compelling example of its authoritarian-led development successes has served it well as an example of the long-standing sentiment among many governments and citizens in the Global South that economic and social rights were downplayed or even ignored in favor of political and civil rights. Speaking often in the rhetoric of noninterference and solidarity within the Global South, Beijing's nondemocratic development success, nonideological approach to building alliances, and offers of economic assistance and trade have become powerful alternatives to the once unipolar vision of an irreversible liberal tide and new world order.

At the same time, China has sought to fill the diplomatic and financial vacuum left by the United States and offer alternatives within and alongside existing multilateral institutions. In a move strikingly similar to the Trump administration's liberal use of targeted personal sanctions over alleged corruption and human rights cases, China imposed its own sanctions on European officials and academics in retaliation for EU sanctions for the treatment of Uyghurs. The move turned against the West one of its own trusted tools to combat alleged perpetrators of human rights abuses. It is a weapon that many economically weaker states in the Global South have lacked.

Recent developments have added other challenges. Technological advances are placing unprecedented and potentially unaccountable power in the hands of liberal democracies and autocracies alike. The potential for abuse exists for any government, especially since in many cases these new technologies and their uses have outstripped the institutional scope and capacity of international human rights bodies and NGOs. Global tensions, nationalist populism, and gaps in multilateral preparedness have also provided unique opportunities for competition among states and a breakdown in cooperation, not just over the response to the COVID-19 pandemic but also over humanitarian crises and global inequality. The legacy of the pandemic and its aftermath is an even more economically insecure and unequal world from the one that already existed in early 2020. This will require even greater attention to the economic and social guarantees of the international human rights agenda while still protecting and expanding political and civil rights.

These challenges differ sharply from those that the global and regional human rights regime faced, and under which it evolved, seventy-five years ago. The question today is not whether those norms and institutions are fit for purpose for those novel pressures—they are not—but whether and how they can be reformed to meet them. The new forces should also perhaps prompt a reevaluation of the original goals of the human rights system, as Moyn has powerfully argued, challenging the human rights community to place greater emphasis on distributive justice.[43] This is a responsibility not just of the institutions themselves, but of the states that make them up and give them the force of moral, political, and economic power, and of the human rights NGOs and community that gave them life. When the human rights system inaugurated in 1945 with the adoption of the Universal Declaration of Human Rights reaches its hundredth anniversary, will we still celebrate its successes and capacity for change and survival? We can hope; fortunately, we are beginning to learn what the challenges are.

Notes

1. See Rowan Cruft, Matthew Liao, and Massimo Renzo, *Philosophical Foundations of Human Rights* (Oxford University Press, 2015).

2. Jack Donnelly, "Human Rights and Human Dignity: An Analytic Critique of Non-Western Conceptions," *American Political Science Review* 76, 2 (June 1982), pp. 433–49.

3. Boaventura de Sousa Santos, "Human Rights as an Emancipatory Script?," in *Another Knowledge Is Possible: Beyond Northern Epistemologies*, edited by Boaventura de Sousa Santos (London: Verso, 2008).

4. Ahmed Shaheed and Rose Parris Richter, "Are Human Rights a 'Western' Concept?," IPI Global Observatory, October 17, 2018, https://theglobalobservatory.org/2018/10/are-human-rights-a-western-concept/.

5. Steven Jensen, *The Making of International Human Rights: The 1960s, Decolonization, and the Reconstruction of Global Values* (Cambridge University Press, 2016).

6. United Nations Charter, Preamble, www.un.org/en/about-us/un-charter/full-text.

7. A. John Simmons, "Human Rights and World Citizenship: The Universality of Human Rights in Kant and Locke," in *Justification and Legitimacy: Essays on Rights and Obligations,* edited by A. John Simmons (Cambridge University Press, 2001), p. 185.

8. Cass R. Sunstein, *The Second Bill of Rights: FDR's Unfinished Revolution and Why We Need It More Than Ever* (New York: Basic Books, 2004).

9. Rome Statute of the International Criminal Court, Article 7, www.icc-cpi.int/resource-library/Documents/RS-Eng.pdf.

10. Jean Galbraith, "The Bush Administration's Response to the International Criminal Court," Penn Law Legal Scholar Repository (University of Pennsylvania Carey Law School, 2003), https://scholarship.law.upenn.edu/cgi/viewcontent.cgi?article=2450&context=faculty_scholarship.

11. David Kaye, "Who's Afraid of the International Criminal Court?," *Foreign Affairs*, May/June (Council on Foreign Relations, 2011), www.foreignaffairs.com /articles/2011-04-18/whos-afraid-international-criminal-court.

12. Mary Kimani, "Pursuit of Justice or Western Plot?," *Africa Renewal, UN,* October 2009, www.un.org/africarenewal/magazine/october-2009/pursuit-justice-or -western-plot.

13. See International Criminal Court, "'Facts and Figures," https://www.icc-cpi .int/about.

14. Calum Inverarity and James Kearney, "Recalibrate the Responsibility to Protect," Chatham House Expert Comment, June 12, 2019, www.chathamhouse.org /2019/06/recalibrate-responsibility-protect; Cristina Stefan, "On Non-Western Norm Shapers: Brazil and the Responsibility While Protecting," *European Journal of International Security* 2, 1 (February 2017), pp. 88–110, https://doi.org/10.1017/eis.2016.18.

15. See Aryeh Neier, *The International Human Rights Movement: A History* (Princeton University Press, 2021).

16. Margaret Keck and Kathryn Sikkink, *Activists beyond Borders* (Cornell University Press, 1998), p. 90.

17. Bob Clifford, "Introduction: Fighting for New Rights," in *The International Struggle for New Human Rights*, edited by Bob Clifford (University of Pennsylvania Press, 2009), p. 4.

18. Tony Evans, *US Hegemony and the Project of Universal Human Rights* (New York: St. Martin's Press, 1996).

19. Office of the United Nations High Commissioner for Human Rights, "Vienna Declaration and Programme of Action," 1993, www.ohchr.org/en/professionalinterest /pages/vienna.aspx.

20. Samuel Moyn, *The Last Utopia: Human Rights in History* (Cambridge, Mass.: Belknap Press, 2010).

21. Makau Mutua, *Human Rights: A Political and Cultural Critique* (University of Pennsylvania Press, 2008), and Moyn, *The Last Utopia.*

22. Samuel Moyn, "Human Rights Have Lost Their Monopoly as a Framework for Reform," *OpenGlobalRights*, May 19, 2021, www.openglobalrights.org/human -rights-have-lost-their-monopoly-as-a-framework-for-reform/?lang=English.

23. Ibid.

24. Martha Nussbaum, *Creating Capabilities: The Human Development Approach* (Harvard University Press, 2011); Amartya Sen, *Resources, Values and Development* (Cambridge University Press, 1984), ch. 13, "Rights and Capabilities"; Amartya Sen, *Development as Freedom* (New York: Anchor, 1999); and Amartya Sen, "Democracy as a Universal Value," *Journal of Democracy* 10, 3 (July 1999).

25. United Nations, Office of the High Commissioner for Human Rights, "Declaration on the Right to Development," https://www.ohchr.org/en/professionalinterest /pages/righttodevelopment.aspx.

26. Michael Ignatieff, "Human Rights as Idolatry," in *Human Rights as Politics and Idolatry*, edited by Amy Gutman (Princeton University Press, 2003).

27. Eric Posner, *The Twilight of International Human Rights Law* (Oxford University Press, 2014).

28. Hurst Hannum, "Reinvigorating Human Rights for the Twenty-First Century," in *Human Rights and 21st Century Challenges: Poverty, Conflict, and the Environment,* edited by Dapo Akande et al. (Oxford University Press, 2020), p. 37.

29. See Sarita Cargas, "Questioning Samuel Moyn's Revisionist History of Human Rights," *Human Rights Quarterly* 38, 2 (2016), pp. 411–26.

30. For an overview of the academic debates and responses, see Stephen Hopgood, Jack Snyder, and Leslie Vinjamuri, *Human Rights Past, Present and Future* (Cambridge University Press, 2017).

31. Richard Wike and Shannon Schumacher, "Attitudes toward Democratic Rights and Institutions," Pew Research Center, February 7, 2020, www.pewresearch.org/global/2020/02/27/attitudes-toward-democratic-rights-and-institutions/.

32. Jodesz Gavilan, "Groups Slam Duterte Gov't Rights Summit as 'Desperate Charade,'" *Rappler,* December 9, 2020, www.rappler.com/nation/groups-statements-duterte-government-human-rights-summit-attempt-vs-accountability-violations, and "One Year On, Duterte Remains a Human Rights Nightmare," Amnesty International, July 3, 2017, www.amnesty.org/en/latest/news/2017/07/one-year-on-duterte-remains-a-human-rights-nightmare/.

33. "Russia Overrules the European Court of Human Rights," *EurActiv,* July 14, 2015, www.euractiv.com/section/europe-s-east/news/russia-overrules-the-european-court-of-human-rights/.

34. "Civil Organisations Will Have to Disclose Foreign Funds," Reuters, June 19, 2020, www.reuters.com/article/eu-hungary-ngo-orban-idINKBN23Q1JF.

35. Regin Winther Poulsen, "How the Danish Left Adopted a Far-Right Immigration Policy," *Foreign Policy,* July 12, 2021, https://foreignpolicy.com/2021/07/12/denmark-refugees-frederiksen-danish-left-adopted-a-far-right-immigration-policy/.

36. Elaine Pearson, "Seven Years of Suffering for Australia's Asylum Seekers, Refugees," Human Rights Watch, July 16, 2020, www.hrw.org/news/2020/07/16/seven-years-suffering-australias-asylum-seekers-refugees.

37. No Escape from Hell," Human Rights Watch, January 21, 2019, www.hrw.org/report/2019/01/21/no-escape-hell/eu-policies-contribute-abuse-migrants-libya.

38. Helena Smith, "Greece Blocks European Union's Criticism at UN of China's Human Rights Record," *The Guardian,* June 18, 2017, www.theguardian.com/world/2017/jun/18/greece-eu-criticism-un-china-human-rights-record. The point is also made in chapter 4 by Alexander Cooley.

39. "Concept of Human Rights Being Distorted, Warns Cameron," *BBC News,* January 25, 2012, www.bbc.com/news/uk-politics-16708845.

40. Philippe Sands, *Torture Team: Rumsfeld's Memo and the Betrayal of America's Values* (London: Palgrave Macmillan, 2008).

41. "International Criminal Court Officials Sanctioned by US," *BBC News,* September 2, 2020, www.bbc.co.uk/news/world-us-canada-54003527.

42. Christopher Sabatini, "Why Is the U.S. Joining Venezuela and Nicaragua in Discrediting a System to Protect Human Rights?," *Washington Post*, January 17, 2020, www.washingtonpost.com/opinions/2020/01/17/why-is-us-joining-venezuela -nicaragua-discrediting-system-protect-human-rights/.

43. Moyn, "Human Rights Have Lost Their Monopoly as a Framework for Reform."

TWO

Positioning Human Rights in China-U.S. Relations

ROSEMARY FOOT

Human rights issues have always added a layer of complexity to the China--U.S. relationship since the normalization of ties in the late 1970s. Today that complexity has been magnified for three main reasons. First, geopolitical rivalry between the two states has deepened as a result of China's emergence as a peer competitor; second, in both countries a rise in illiberal practices has damaged the standing of human rights; and, third, there has been a turn on both sides toward arguments emphasizing that the two protagonists are engaged in a clash of values. The ambitions of the current Chinese leadership include a greater willingness to promote its own beliefs about how rights can best be protected, to confront the notion of the universality and indivisibility of human rights, and to close down any perceived challenge to the rule of the Chinese Communist Party (CCP), including on human rights grounds, in both the domestic and the international spheres. On the U.S. side, the Trump administration shifted from outright dismissal of the value of human rights diplomacy to an unconvincing attempt to present it as a core cause of the breakdown in Sino-American relations. The final stages of the Trump presidency, as well as the start of the Biden administration, came to cast the struggle against a resurgent People's Republic of China (PRC) as one that pits a democratic against an autocratic way of life, the outcome of which will shape the nature of global order in the decades to come.

This chapter traces the evolution of human rights matters in this bilateral relationship, noting the wider impact of these developments on the progress of the international human rights regime. It focuses first on the forms of leverage on which both the Chinese and U.S. governments have been able to draw when positioning this issue in their relationship. Changing policy priorities have affected not only the extent to which they have focused on rights in their bilateral relations, but also how these two states have operated within such multilateral bodies as the United Nation's Human Rights Council (UNHRC) and its forerunner, the UN Commission on Human Rights (UNCHR).

This chapter then illustrates two matters that have negatively affected the current vitality of the rights regime. It notes the disruptive nature of the Trump administration's own attitude toward human rights and how it addressed that issue in relation to China. It next considers the consequences of the coincidence of these disruptive policies with a more ambitious and politically influential Chinese leadership seemingly determined to advance its own beliefs about human rights.

Finally, the chapter argues that the coupling of China's ideational power with its material assets has generated some support for its policy stance on human rights within UN bodies including the HRC. Beijing has also established additional, non-UN–related human rights bodies, such as the South-South Forum on Human Rights, to underscore the support it receives from some other governments and to afford it additional opportunities to elaborate its perspectives. These developments have added to the difficulties that the Biden administration faces as it attempts to recover U.S. standing in this area, to address the wider repercussions posed by an authoritarian state, as well as to work with China on shared-fate issues. In consequence, the revitalization of the international human rights regime, to which the Biden administration wishes to add its weight, is in peril, and the notion of the universality and indivisibility of rights is significantly challenged.

U.S. Trade-Offs and China's Levers

From the time of the Sino-American rapprochement, U.S. administrations have been expected, or have had as an objective, to include a human rights dimension in their policy toward China.[1] This has never been an easy task, not least because China, as a major power in global politics, has drawn on its resources to constrain U.S. policy choices, underlining their contingent nature on this issue.

China's strategic leverage has been manifested in earlier times in relation to the former Soviet Union, and more consistently as a potentially veto-wielding permanent member of the UN Security Council. Later, U.S. calculations and China's behavior began to be affected by the latter's growing attractiveness as a trading, aid, and investment partner. With China's economy continuing to advance after the 2008–2009 global financial crisis and its offer of global public goods—including the inauguration in 2013 of the Belt and Road Initiative and the establishment in 2016 of the Asian Infrastructure Investment Bank— Beijing determined it would become more active in defining its approach to human rights. In particular, it sought various ways to promote economic development as a priority right and to reduce forms of accountability for human rights violations. Successes in these policy areas demonstrated that other states were willing to follow China's lead.[2]

Beijing's ability to use these two major levers was plain from the start of the Sino-American rapprochement. President Jimmy Carter, for example, chose to give priority to the rights record of the former Soviet Union, to highlight that both Beijing and Washington viewed Moscow as their major strategic enemy, and to argue that Beijing under paramount leader Deng Xiaoping had turned a significant political corner, leaving behind the mass violations of rights associated with the Maoist era.[3]

Inevitably, however, the regime's bloody crackdown on demonstrators in Tian'anmen Square in 1989 signified a major turning point in Sino-American relations, sharply highlighting the need to hold China to account for its human rights violations. The U.S. Congress took a particularly firm position, and the administration itself quickly determined that it would suspend all sales of weapons and ban diplomatic exchanges between military leaders. It later announced it would curtail all meetings with the Chinese government above the level of assistant secretary. U.S. representatives at the World Bank and Asian Development Bank were instructed to postpone consideration of new loans to Beijing, and some 45,000 Chinese students and senior scholars in the United States had their visas extended.

Nevertheless, Beijing also benefited from having its crackdown on demonstrators occur during the presidency of George H. W. Bush, who argued forcefully on strategic and economic grounds that it was necessary to maintain some contact with China. Relatively swiftly, various U.S. bans on diplomatic exchanges were set aside, not least because as a permanent member of the UN Security Council, and with veto power, China had bargaining clout. This was used to good effect as Washington sought Beijing's support of, or abstention on, a U.S.-backed Security Council resolution authorizing the use of force to eject Saddam Hussein's armed forces from Kuwait. Over the course of this Gulf crisis, China voted for all ten UN resolutions that imposed political, military, and economic sanctions on Iraq and, crucially, abstained on Resolution 678, which legitimated the use of force against Iraqi troops. That abstention was enough to persuade President Bush to receive the Chinese foreign minister in Washington.[4]

Strategic developments aided China again during the George W. Bush presidency, highlighting once again the conditional nature of U.S. attention to Beijing's human rights record. Certainly, the promotion of religious freedom was a prominent part of the administration's policy: Bush met the Tibetan spiritual leader, the Dalai Lama; spoke out on China's harsh treatment of Falun Gong practitioners; and condemned a repressive wave in Xinjiang in October 2001. However, China enjoyed positive repercussions from its support for the United States after the terrorist attacks on U.S. soil in September 2001. Beijing had voted for UN resolutions condemning the attacks and hosted an Asia-Pacific Economic Cooperation conference in Shanghai in October 2001 that facilitated the negotiation of a supportive statement. More importantly still, China interceded with its close ally Pakistan to persuade it to provide access to U.S. armed forces in their fight against al Qaeda and its Taliban supporters in Afghanistan.

China's rewards included the U.S. decision in August 2002 to designate the so-called East Turkestan Islamic Movement (ETIM) as a terrorist organization, though few specialists on Xinjiang have ever regarded this grouping as a significant presence in that province. The designation has been used by China, to this day, to justify its claims that the terrorist threat explains its policy of "re-education" with respect to Muslim Uyghurs residing in Xinjiang. Bush also attended the 2008 Olympic Games in Beijing even though these had acquired the meme of the "Genocide Olympics" as a result of China's close relationship with the rights-abusing government in Sudan.[5]

President Barack Obama came into power promising to position human rights "not as a secondary interest" but as a "top priority that must be translated into concrete actions, and supported by all of the diplomatic, economic and strategic tools at [the U.S. government's] disposal."[6] However, a determination to emphasize the cooperative and not solely the more adversarial areas of the relationship with Beijing led Washington to draw attention regularly to issues where their relationship could be viewed as complementary: for example, conflict resolution in Afghanistan, counterterrorism, climate change, and the nonproliferation of nuclear weapons.[7]

Thus, over three decades or more, strategic interventions regularly resulted in a struggle for human rights issues to become a consistent, high-level, priority in U.S. policy toward China. Beijing took its opportunities where it could to protect itself from external criticism and advance its own policy positions (as in the case of the ETIM designation), as well as to highlight that U.S. inconsistencies in this policy area cast doubt on the universality of the rights regime and exposed its politicization. China also started to mimic the State Department's annual report on human rights practices around the world, producing its own record of U.S. human rights violations, especially highlighting racism and gun violence in American society.

As China's economic strength grew, U.S. policy toward that country underscored yet further how the powerful could protect themselves from human rights criticisms, while less well-endowed states attracted negative attention. In the 1990s, for example, the United States attempted to make China's Most Favored Nation (MFN) trading status conditional on domestic improvements in human rights protection. However, the U.S. business lobby publicly urged President Bill Clinton to renew MFN unconditionally: some eight hundred representatives of large and small businesses, trade associations, and farming and consumer groups wrote to the president, insisting that U.S. jobs and profits were at stake in the steadily expanding China market. Within a year of the introduction of his linkage policy, the president capitulated.[8]

President Obama similarly found economic issues interfering in efforts to give prominence to human rights questions, particularly as a result of the urgent need to deal jointly with the global financial crisis. The U.S. secretary of state, Hillary Clinton, controversially implied that "serious exchanges on global issues" with Beijing, including the workings of the international economy, would lead to a sacrifice of attention to human rights.[9] China's significant holdings of U.S. treasury bonds led her to remark privately to Australian prime minister, Kevin Rudd, in March 2009: "How do you deal toughly with your banker?"[10]

China's Trade-Offs and U.S. Levers

However, leverage has not only worked in one direction. Since the start of China's Reform and Opening policy in late 1978, Beijing has desired American goods and investment, as well as access to the U.S. market. It has also sought to cultivate an image as a "responsible great power," and one that has complied with dominant global norms.[11]

This concern with image provided the United States and its mainly European partners with leverage in international bodies such as the UN Commission on Human Rights (CHR). To some degree "naming and shaming" worked with Beijing. At the CHR, Washington drafted or cosponsored resolutions critical of rights protections inside China nearly every year after 1990 until

2005, some dealing explicitly with the situation in Tibet, others referencing instances of abuse elsewhere in China. In all but one year (1995), China successfully organized a "no-action" motion that prevented further progress on these draft resolutions. But the success of those no-action motions required the use of China's political and economic capital and strong lobbying tactics.

Moreover, despite the inability to pass these condemnatory resolutions, China's resort to such a tactic served to keep the issue of its human rights record on the international agenda and helped to draw Beijing into the rights regime. To defuse criticism, Beijing decided to invite the UN's Special Rapporteur on Religious Intolerance, as well as the UN's Working Group on Arbitrary Detention, to visit. In 1995 China also produced a new White Paper on Human Rights that described its citizens' increased abilities to claim their rights as guaranteed by law.[12]

Image mattered in bilateral ties too, with the Clinton administration making use of scheduled summits with President Jiang Zemin to encourage concessions from China. In October 1997, on the eve of Jiang's visit to Washington, he announced Beijing's signature of the International Covenant on Economic, Social, and Cultural Rights (ICESCR, ratified in March 2001) and voiced a commitment to the indivisibility of rights. The Sino-American communiqué, while acknowledging "major differences," also referred positively to the standing of the Universal Declaration of Human Rights.

It additionally pledged both to exchange legal experts and legal materials, and to start legal training inside China. Jiang also agreed that three religious leaders from the United States could visit his country, including Tibet. In October 1998, Beijing signed the International Covenant on Civil and Political Rights (it has still not ratified this treaty). The signature appeared to be tied to the initiation of a bilateral Sino-American human rights dialogue, the first meeting being held in Washington in January 1999.[13]

One goal of the dialogue was to couple the bilateral discussions with Washington's UN strategy: as Katrin Kinzelbach has noted, the United States "never dropped the threat of a [UN] resolution and did not agree to an unconditional continuation of the human rights dialogue." For example, when it tabled a CHR resolution in 2004, it argued that it was doing so because the Chinese government had not fulfilled points agreed at the 2002 bilateral human rights dialogue meeting, including inviting the UN Special Rapporteur on Torture to visit. Beijing extended that invitation in 2005, prompting the United States to refrain from tabling a UN resolution criticizing China that year.[14]

These U.S. tactics dwindled in later years, not least because of their reduced effectiveness in the context of China's growing economic power, as well as increased developing-world membership in the UNHRC, which thus became geographically more representative than the CHR. However, Washington used other, lower-profile, routes to maintain some pressure. For example, in 2016 Western delegations, together with Japan, issued a statement expressing concern at the "arrests and ongoing detention of rights activists, civil society leaders, and lawyers" inside China as well as the "unexplained recent disappearances and apparent coerced returns of Chinese and foreign citizens from outside mainland China."[15]

Thus, despite China's own sources of leverage, it could be induced, at least until the start of the second decade of this century, to undertake actions that implied an acceptance that human rights conditions inside states were rightfully a matter for international attention, and that all states were expected to become members of treaty bodies. However, the resort to mutual bargaining also demonstrated that on the U.S. side, human rights had regularly to compete with a number of other major issues in the Sino-American relationship; and on China's side, in the absence of normative socialization, this suggested that Beijing's approach might change if both its dependence on U.S. economic power and its assumption of the status benefits of maintaining a good relationship with the United States were to diminish. Not only could it consider articulating more forcefully its own beliefs on these matters, but it would also be better placed to resist the demands of others.

Indeed, China emerged as the world's second-largest economy in 2010, the leading trading nation in 2013, the leading destination for foreign direct investment (FDI) in 2012, and the second-largest source of overseas FDI. It is now the largest trading partner of about two-thirds of the world's economies and accounts for about 19 percent of global output. In these circumstances, its confidence in promoting its own politico-economic model has grown, and that confidence has spilled over into its human rights diplomacy.

President Xi Jinping has several times exhorted the country's diplomats to lead the reform of global governance, and that includes reform of human rights institutions. As with the regional organizations that Alexander Cooley references in chapter 4 of this volume, Beijing has worked to repurpose bodies such as the UNHRC, and has set up new human rights organizations that align China more closely with the Global South.[16] Moreover, the four years of the Trump administration that seriously damaged U.S. identity as a democratic and rights-protecting state provided opportunities for Beijing to advance its positions in this policy area and to point to the hypocritical nature of the U.S. posture.

The Disruptive Trump Era

It is widely accepted that the Trump presidency seriously tarnished the role of the United States as a leading, if flawed, promoter of human rights. President Donald Trump came to power having campaigned on a promise to "bring back a hell of a lot worse than waterboarding." On taking office, he issued an executive order banning citizens from seven Muslim states from entering the United States and swiftly revoked U.S. membership of the UN's HRC. Trump also attacked and sanctioned officials working for the International Criminal Court for their decision to investigate alleged abuses in Afghanistan by U.S. service personnel.

Matters were no better inside the United States. President Trump threatened the independence of the media and judiciary, regularly attacked the Black Lives Matter movement, and refused to accept the 2020 election result. The ensuing riot on January 6, 2021, when Trump supporters stormed the Capitol building in Washington was believed by many around the world to have been instigated by Trump himself.[17]

Known for his admiration of authoritarian leaders, Trump regularly heaped praise on President Xi, describing him as a "terrific guy" in 2017, shortly after the death of China's human rights activist and Nobel Peace Prize recipient Liu Xiaobo.[18] At a private meeting with Xi at the 2019 G-20 meeting, Trump evinced sympathy for the Chinese government's decision to engage in the mass internment of Muslim Uyghurs in Xinjiang, apparently describing that as "exactly the right thing to do."[19] In response to developments in Hong Kong, Trump told Xi in June 2019 that he would not condemn a Chinese crackdown on the unrest.[20] Apart from these empathetic statements, Trump revealed his overriding wish not to jeopardize the ongoing trade negotiations with Beijing, which he clearly prioritized over other elements in the relationship, even as his administration began to toughen its human rights–related China policy.

While President Trump was fixated on the trade deficit and on imposing tariffs on a range of Chinese goods, others within his administration worked to elevate the seriousness of the challenge China was said to pose to the U.S. way of life, depicting it as an existential, ideological threat. Consequently human rights issues became a core part of a "whole-of-government" approach to China. Secretary of State Mike Pompeo took the lead in highlighting, along with the national security adviser, the director of the Federal Bureau of Investigation, and the attorney general, the gravity of the challenge that China represented. Pompeo, in particular, excoriated the CCP-led authoritarian government in Beijing for its secrecy in the early stages of the outbreak of COVID-19, drew attention to its widespread human rights violations, and its use of sur-veillance technologies to control its population (indeed the Trump adminis-tration had already determined it would attempt to constrain developments in this area).[21]

Congress added its weight, passing legislation authorizing sanctions against named Chinese officials in response to mass incarcerations in Xinjiang, and removing Hong Kong's Special Trading Status after Beijing passed its National Security Law.[22] U.S. public attitudes toward China sank to a historic low, with some 73 percent of those polled in 2020 holding a negative view of the coun-try.[23] Indeed, Andrew Nathan has argued that "values shifted from an ancil-lary position in the Sino-American relationship to the unifying framework for all elements of the strategic competition between the two countries."[24] This is of signal importance because, as Jacques deLisle has noted, conflict over val-ues is more zero-sum and "less amenable to compromise than are disputes over more tangible interests."[25] Whereas previously it had proved possible to mod-ulate the divisions over human rights in Sino-American relations, it was now more difficult to set these matters aside.

By the end of the Trump presidency, the discussion of China's human rights record had been extended into an ideological battle using language reminis-cent of the Cold War. Pompeo's focus on the CCP and his characterization of the competition with China as between "freedom and tyranny" set the stage for regular references to the challenge that an autocracy like China posed to democratic forms of governance everywhere in the world.[26] Pompeo drove home an uncompromising message that implied an ultimate U.S. goal of re-gime change. The Trump administration, he said, had "exposed the nature of the Chinese Communist Party and called it what it is: a Marxist-Leninist regime that exerts power over the long-suffering Chinese people through brain-washing and brute force." He determined that the CCP had committed geno-cide against the Muslim Uyghurs residing in Xinjiang, warning that if it was "allowed to commit genocide and crimes against humanity against its own people, imagine what it will be emboldened to do to the free world, in the not-so distant-future."[27]

The problem was that Pompeo and others neglected the perspectives of many governments and peoples outside the United States: that their country had seriously damaged its credibility on these issues, not least because of the administration's assault on human rights at home. Few took seriously the idea that Trump cared about human rights inside China. As the president of Free-dom House told the *Washington Post*, although "the spread of authoritarian-ism is a phenomenon that is proceeding quite nicely on its own," the "outsize role" of the United States made a difference given what he called its status as "one of the world's oldest and most influential democracies." A report by Freedom House underlined that authoritarian states now had "ample new fodder" for their criticisms of the U.S. domestic human rights record; crucially, it added, "and the evidence they cite will remain in the world's collective memory for a long time to come."[28] Washington had all but surrendered any credibility it might have had to lead on these issues abroad, facilitating Beijing's efforts to build support for its beliefs on human rights and for the arguments it used to explain constraints on what it termed terrorists and religious extremists inside China.

The Contemporary China Challenge

As noted earlier, this loss in U.S. moral stature has coincided with the emergence of a China that is more ambitious in promoting its perspectives on human rights. In the past, Washington had had some success in building coalitions of support in the UN's human rights bodies and had kept some leverage on human rights in play in the bilateral relationship. However, that is a more difficult undertaking in a period where China has started to reshape the international human rights regime from within and has cast its authoritarian model, with its emphasis on economic development and social stability under the guidance of strong state institutions, as the best means of protecting people's rights (rather than the rights of individuals).

Thus, at the highest levels, and in domestic and international gatherings, Chinese officials make the normative argument that legal sovereign equality and noninterference in internal affairs are the most important norms governing state-to-state relations, and that the state is the best guarantor of human rights. Beijing has attacked the universality of rights, arguing that all countries "must proceed from . . . prevailing realities" and go their "own way." It claims that the CCP has "opened a new path of human rights protection, and added diversity to the concept of human rights with its own practices." Development is cast as "the key to solving all China's problems"; as having driven its progress on human rights; and, by implication, as the solution for other developing countries—as shown in Beijing's introduction of resolutions emphasizing this point at the UNHRC. Beijing has described development as a foundational right from which other human rights may flow, thus challenging the idea of the indivisibility of human rights.[29]

China has also engaged in institutional shaping. It has pressured the UNHRC to reduce attention to country-specific resolutions and attacked Special Rapporteurs for overstepping their mandates. It has worked to turn the Universal Periodic Review process into one where countries such as China are praised for their accomplishments rather than held to account for serious lapses in rights protection. It has moved to constrain the role of independent human rights nongovernmental organizations in UNHRC proceedings and attacked the concept of a "human rights defender." It has criticized the Office of the High Commissioner for Human Rights for a failure to promote a "culture of diversity" and attempted to restrict funding for human rights posts working with the treaty bodies.

Moreover, Beijing has demonstrated that it can garner support for its stance on these matters, successfully passing resolutions at the UNHRC that refer to the "contribution of development to the enjoyment of all human rights" and the promotion of "mutually beneficial cooperation in the field of human rights."[30] Letters and statements critical of Beijing's egregious behavior in Xinjiang and Hong Kong have been countered by China's supporters, who praise its "remarkable achievements in the field of human rights," its welcome efforts to counter what Beijing claims is widespread terrorist sentiment among the Muslim population in Xinjiang, and to reestablish security and stability in Hong Kong.[31]

To reinforce the message that Chinese positions receive widespread validation, Beijing has established alternative human rights organizations, such as the South-South Forum on Human Rights, which has met in Beijing in 2017, 2019, and 2021. At its first meeting this body passed a Beijing Declaration on human rights, reflecting China's vision for human rights governance, and the Chinese foreign minister advocated diversity and localization, claiming China had "blazed an oriental pathway toward modernization."[32]

Many of those in support of China are recipients of its economic largesse, dependent on a good trading relationship, or concerned that they themselves could be the target of criticism within bodies such as the UNHRC. In addition, China's achievements, especially in poverty reduction, impress many developing countries, and they too advocate there should be more support for the "right to development." That China is said to have brought some 800 million people out of poverty is frequently referenced in UN reports and elsewhere. Much as with the Millennium Development Goals, the UN's Sustainable Development Goals (SDGs) are going to rely mightily on China if the United Nations is to claim any degree of success.

Receptivity to Chinese messages also rests on a congruence of views: many former colonized states are strongly attached to the idea of the legal sovereign equality of states and noninterference in internal affairs. The asymmetrical power relations that characterize the modern international system give particular strength to these normative ideas. It is this fear of the strong imposing their conceptions of justice on the weak that motivates a number of states to support China's arguments.

A Path to U.S. Recovery?

President Biden came into office promising to do all in his power to reverse his predecessor's toxic legacy and to repair the damage the Trump administration, as well as Beijing, had inflicted on the human rights regime. The new administration pledged to reinstate U.S. support for multilateralist approaches and institutions and to repair human rights deficiencies at home. It quickly announced the return of the United States to the UNHRC as an "active observer," with the intention to seek election onto the Council for the 2022–2024 term.[33] Like previous administrations, apart from Trump's, the Biden administration, as Secretary of State Antony J. Blinken remarked to the Council, would place democracy and human rights "at the center" of its foreign policy.[34]

In those same remarks, Blinken acknowledged the damage to the U.S. standing on human rights that had to be addressed. He recognized that "any pledge to fight for human rights around the world must begin with a pledge to fight for human rights at home," referencing the prevalence of "systemic racism and economic injustice" in American society. Perhaps mindful of the June 2020 call by UN independent rights experts for the United States to address these matters, Blinken pointed to the swift action President Biden had already taken to tackle "the root causes of these inequities, including in housing, prison reform, improving the conditions of indigenous peoples, and fighting discrimination against Asian Americans."[35]

There were also some faint indications that the Biden administration better understood the need to promote economic, social, and cultural rights in rebuilding America's image as a rights-protecting country. This is important because attention to these matters will appeal to many countries represented on the UNHRC. The United States has never ratified the ICESCR and any attempt to do so now would not get U.S. Senate confirmation. However, intended compliance with these rights made it into the "Interim National Security Strategic Guidance" released in March 2021, which acknowledged that for the United States to truly "build back better" at home, and in particular to deal with systemic racism, required "aggressive action to address structures, policies, and practices that contribute to the wealth gap, to health disparities, and to inequalities in educational access, outcomes, and beyond."[36]

In a striking passage, the Interim Guidance linked many of these same goals with projected U.S. actions overseas, promising development policies that would bolster collective rights, including the provision of good-quality educational opportunities for children and youth, the advancement of gender equality, Lesbian, Gay, Bisexual, Transgender, Queer, Intersex (LGBTQI+) rights, and the empowerment of women, as part of a broad "commitment to inclusive economic growth and social cohesion."[37] The administration promised a turn away from using its military might overseas to deal with humanitarian crises or to promote democracy: as Blinken noted, U.S. military interventions "often come at far too high a cost, both to us and to others."[38]

On China, however, the change in stance has not been as stark. A tough policy toward that country stands out as one area of bipartisan consensus in a polarized political environment, and public opinion polling indicates that Americans' trust of China is at a (new) historic low, with 89 percent viewing Beijing as either a competitor or an enemy rather than a partner. Some 67 percent describe their feelings toward China as "somewhat cold" or "very cold." When both Democrats and Republicans were asked about the issues that came to mind when they thought about China, human rights came top of the list (20 percent), just above economic matters (19 percent).[39]

These findings indicate that rights have become a prominent source of tension in the relationship, aligning neatly with general U.S. concerns about China's technological development, particularly in areas of personal surveillance and on the principles of internet governance (see chapter 5 by Rana Moustafa and chapter 8 by Emily Taylor, Kate Jones, and Carolina Caeiro). The Biden administration has maintained that China's repressive policies toward the Uyghurs represent genocide, and the unfolding of the National Security Law in Hong Kong, together with further evidence of atrocities in Xinjiang, have attracted a wide range of U.S. sanctions.

While there is less emphasis than before on the fact that China is led by the Communist Party, the Biden administration has chosen to stress an essential clash of values. In a series of official statements and documents, it has depicted the world as being at "an inflection point" and "in the midst of an historic and fundamental debate" about the nature of world order—one where there exist powerful forces arguing that "autocracy is the best way forward" versus those "who understand that democracy is essential to meeting all the challenges to our changing world."[40]

Thus, while there is a desire for the U.S. relationship with China to be "collaborative when it can be," it is plain that it will also be "competitive when it should be . . . and adversarial when it must be."[41] With that "zero-sum" framing of a clash of values, it will be difficult to find points of agreement with Beijing on other major issues such as climate change, the nonproliferation of nuclear weapons, and global health crises. Moreover, past U.S. behavior has shown how difficult it is to demonstrate consistent application of policies linked to values.

A prominent emphasis on contesting values may also weaken the ability of the Biden administration to form a coalition of support behind a policy that firmly criticizes the PRC for its human rights transgressions. Beijing has found supporters within the UNHRC, and many other states do not favor a confrontational framing of relations with China, even if several remain concerned about the evidence of internal repression.

Policy Implications and Recommendations

Maintaining a human rights strategy attentive to the idea of the universality and indivisibility of rights is a particularly challenging proposition at a time of greater Chinese influence, and when powerful memories remain of Trump's egregious disregard of human rights internationally and domestically. China has built coalitions of support in part as a result of its transactional diplomacy but also through its obviously successful transition from being one of the poorest developing countries in the Maoist era to its current status as the second-largest economy in the world. Many other countries want to accord development a primary place in the human rights canon, as well as to protect a Westphalian vision of state sovereignty. Beijing can be expected to pursue these lines of argument discursively and through its diplomatic actions within the UN and elsewhere.

The United States has rightly decided that it needs to show some humility about the country's own human rights failings; as President Biden has put it, "We'll be a much more credible partner because of these efforts to shore up our own foundations."[42] It should also leverage its ability to combine the United States' own economic strength and political influence with a range of democratic states similarly concerned about the advance of authoritarian practices. Such states should swiftly make good on their offer to provide alternatives to the scholarships, training, economic investments, and aid that China has made available. A U.S. administration committed to multilateralism will also need to work through the difficulties associated with generating a consistent and united message with its partners on human rights matters, including the joint imposition of sanctions when deemed necessary and appropriate.[43]

Beyond that, Washington and other like-minded governments need to remind Beijing of the legal requirements associated with the many human rights treaties it has signed, all of which are built on the assumption that human rights are not solely of domestic concern but also a matter for international scrutiny. China similarly needs to be publicly challenged when its rhetoric threatens the notion of the universality and indivisibility of human rights, as reflected in the UN Charter that it claims to revere, in the Universal Declaration of Human Rights, and in the SDGs. Its attacks on human rights defenders and on human rights organizations in UN bodies similarly need to be confronted, and additional methods of support for civil society actors operating under heightened constraints need to be identified.

In addition, China's position on development as a foundational right could be countered, given that Beijing does not actually treat development as a right, but as a policy determined by the party-state. Moreover, a developmental approach that results in negative externalities (such as pollution and rising inequality) has been a marked feature of the Chinese model, impacts that have proved extremely difficult for its leaders to remedy. Beijing's argument that nationally determined policies provide the most effective means of dealing with the shared-fate issues that now threaten the survival of humanity is essentially outdated in our interdependent world.

Perhaps in response to some of these weaknesses and criticisms, there is some wavering in support for China in bodies such as the UNHRC and the UN General Assembly that could be exploited. For example, although China was voted back onto the UNHRC for a period of three years, the numbers in support of its application were lower than in past bids, most likely as a result of evidence regarding its harshly repressive policies in Xinjiang and Hong Kong.[44] Developments such as this suggest that an active U.S. presence within the UN's human rights institutions may appeal beyond the Western group and could lead to the building of successful supportive coalitions.

However, also vital to that success is the challenging requirement for the United States to maintain a position on human rights that attends not only to the source of the inequities within American society, but also to those that exist in so many other countries around the globe.

Notes

1. Rosemary Foot, *Rights beyond Borders: The Global Community and the Struggle over Human Rights in China* (Oxford University Press, 2000), esp. part 2.

2. Rosemary Foot, *China, the UN, and Human Protection: Beliefs, Power, Image* (Oxford University Press, 2020), ch. 6.

3. President Carter chose to do this even though Amnesty International's first damning human rights report on China was produced in 1978. See Amnesty International,

Political Imprisonment in the People's Republic of China (London: Amnesty International Publications, 1978); Katrin Kinzelbach, "Human Rights in Chinese Foreign Policy: A Battle for Global Public Opinion," in *Handbook on Human Rights in China*, edited by Sarah Biddulph and Joshua Rosenzweig (Cheltenham, U.K.: Edward Elgar, 2019), pp. 84–102, esp. p. 88.

4. Rosemary Foot, "China and the Tiananmen Crisis of June 1989," in *Foreign Policy: Theories, Actors, Cases*, 3rd ed., edited by Steve Smith, Amelia Hadfield, and Tim Dunne (Oxford University Press, 2016), pp. 334–55.

5. Rosemary Foot, "Bush, China and Human Rights," *Survival* 45, 2 (2003), pp. 167–86.

6. Quoted in Kenneth Roth, "Barack Obama's Shaky Legacy on Human Rights," Human Rights Watch, January 9, 2017, www.hrw.org/news/2017/01/09/barack -obamas-shaky-legacy-human-rights.

7. For an outline of areas of agreement, see, for example, the Obama-Xi statement in Washington, September 2015, https://obamawhitehouse.archives.gov/the-press -office/2015/09/25/fact-sheet-president-xi-jinpings-state-visit-united-states.

8. David M. Lampton, "America's China Policy in the Age of the Finance Minister: Clinton Ends Linkage," *China Quarterly* 139 (September 1994), pp. 597–621; David M. Lampton, "China Policy in Clinton's First Year," in *Beyond MFN: Trade with China and American Interests,* edited by James R. Lilley and Wendell L. Willkie II (Washington: American Enterprise Institute, 1994).

9. Jeffrey A. Bader, *Obama and China's Rise: An Insider's Account of America's Asia Strategy* (Brookings, 2012), pp. 15–16.

10. "Secretary Clinton's March 24, 2009 Conversation with Australian Prime Minister Kevin Rudd," March 24, 2009, Public Library of US Diplomacy, https:// wikileaks.org/plusd/cables/09STATE30049_a.html.

11. For one analysis of the importance of this designation, see Tiang Boon Hoo, *China's Global Identity: Considering the Responsibilities of Great Power* (Georgetown University Press, 2018).

12. Foot, *Rights beyond Borders*, pp. 183–87.

13. Ibid., pp. 213–14.

14. Kinzelbach, "Human Rights in Chinese Foreign Policy," p. 95.

15. "Joint Statement—Human Rights Situation in China, Delivered by U.S. Ambassador to the UNHRC Keith Harper," March 10, 2016, https://geneva.usmission .gov/2016/03/10/item-2-joint-statement-human-rights-situation-in-china/. Confidential interviews in Geneva in December 2018 indicated that this statement stung the Chinese delegation, and Beijing authorities castigated officials in Geneva for not having anticipated it and taken steps to derail it.

16. Foot, *China, the UN, and Human Protection*, pp. 209–12.

17. These are but a selection of the examples that show Trump's disdain for human rights and democratic practices. See Kathryn Sikkink, *Evidence for Hope: Making Human Rights Work in the 21st Century* (Princeton University Press, 2017), p. 6; Salvador Santino F. Regilme Jr., "The Decline of American Power and Donald Trump:

Reflections on Human Rights, Neoliberalism, and the World Order," *Geoforum* 102 (June 2019), pp. 157–66, esp. pp. 159–60.

18. Human Rights Watch, *World Report 2018,* https://www.hrw.org/world-report /2018.

19. The quotation on the Uyghur mass incarceration is taken from John Bolton's memoir, *The Room Where It Happened* (New York: Simon & Schuster, 2020), and was picked up in many news feeds in June 2020, as Bolton promoted the book. See, for example, David Choi and Sonam Seth, "Trump Told China's President That Build-ing Concentration Camps for Millions of Uighur Muslims Was 'Exactly the Right Thing to Do,' Former Adviser Says," *Business Insider,* June 17, 2020, www.business insider.com/trump-china-detention-camp-xinjiang-2020-6?r=US&IR=T.

20. Cited in Thomas Wright, "Pompeo's Surreal Speech on China," *Brookings* (blog), July 27, 2020, www.brookings.edu/blog/order-from-chaos/2020/07/27/pompeos -surreal-speech-on-china/.

21. "How 2020 Shaped U.S.-China Relations," Council on Foreign Relations, De-cember 15, 2020, www.cfr.org/article/how-2020-shaped-us-china-relations; Jacques deLisle, "When Rivalry Goes Viral: COVID-19, U.S.-China Relations, and East Asia," *Orbis,* Winter 2021, pp. 46–74, https://doi.org/10.1016/j.orbis.2020.11.003.

22. Leslie Vinjamuri, "US Foreign Policy Priorities: What Difference Can an Elec-tion Make?," Chatham House, October 15, 2020, https://americas.chathamhouse .org/article/us-foreign-policy-priorities-what-difference-can-an-election-make/.

23. Pew Research Center, "Unfavorable Views of China Reach Historic Highs in Many Countries," October 6, 2020, https://www.pewresearch.org/global/2020/10/06 /unfavorable-views-of-china-reach-historic-highs-in-many-countries/.

24. Andrew J. Nathan, "Getting Human Rights Right: Consistency, Patience, Multilateralism, and Setting a Good Example," Brookings, November 2020, www .brookings.edu/wp-content/uploads/2020/11/Andrew-J-Nathan.pdf.

25. deLisle, "When Rivalry Goes Viral," p. 54.

26. See Mike Pompeo, "Communist China and the Free World's Future," Speech at the Richard Nixon Presidential Library, U.S. State Department, July 23, 2020, https://2017-2021.state.gov/communist-china-and-the-free-worlds-future/index .html.

27. Mike Pompeo, "Determination of the Secretary of State on Atrocities in Xin-jiang," U.S. Embassy and Consulates in Turkey, January 19, 2021, https://tr.usembassy .gov/determination-of-the-secretary-of-state-on-atrocities-in-xinjiang/.

28. *Freedom in the World Report 2021,* Freedom House, pp. 8–9, https:// freedomhouse.org/report/freedom-world/2021/democracy-under-siege; Ishaan Thar-oor, "The 'Free World' Keeps Shrinking," *Washington Post,* March 3, 2021, https://s2 .washingtonpost.com/camp-rw/?trackId=596b63639bbc0f403f901289&s=603f16c8 9d2fda4c88fa4c90&linknum=7&linktot=69.

29. State Council of the People's Republic of China, "The Communist Party of China and Human Rights Protection—A 100-Year Quest," *Xinhua,* June 24, 2021. See also Foot, *China, the UN, and Human Protection,* pp 207–9; "Win-Win Cooperation

for the Common Cause of Human Rights," March 1, 2018, www.china-un.ch/eng/dbtyw/rqrd_1/thsm/t1538784.htm; and "A People-Centered Approach for Global Human Rights Progress, Remarks by H. E. Wang Yi," February 22, 2021, www.fmprc.gov.cn/mfa_eng/zxxx_662805/t1855685.shtml.

30. Foot, *China, the UN, and Human Protection*, pp. 207–9.

31. Foot, *China, the UN, and Human Protection*, p. 214. For a recent "dueling" statement, see Liu Xin, "More Than 90 Countries Express Support to China amid Rampant Anti-China Campaign at UN Human Rights Body," *Global Times*, June 22, 2021, www.globaltimes.cn/page/202106/1226834.shtml.

32. "Advance the Global Human Rights Cause and Build a Community with a Shared Future for Mankind," Address by H. E. Wang Yi, December 7, 2017, www.china-un.ch/eng/dbtyw/rqrd_1/thsm/t1519207.htm.

33. And "active" it immediately turned out to be: at the March 2021 session of the UNHRC, the U.S. delegation, on behalf of fifty states, rejected statements critical of Western positions put forward by Cuba and Belarus. See Marc Limon, "US-China-Russia Rivalry Spills over into the Human Rights Council," *Universal Rights* (blog), March 22, 2021, www.universal-rights.org/blog/us-china-russia-rivalry-spills-over-into-the-human-rights-council/. The United States was reelected to the Council on October 14, 2021, and started serving from January 2022.

34. "Secretary Blinken: Remarks to the 46th Session of the Human Rights Council," UN Mission in Geneva, February 24, 2021, https://geneva.usmission.gov/2021/02/24/secretary-hrc/.

35. Ibid.; "Independent Rights Experts Urge US to Address Systemic Racism and Racial Bias," *UN News*, June 5, 2020, https://news.un.org/en/story/2020/06/1065722. Human rights experts called for this again on February 26, 2021. See "Rights Experts Call for Reforms to End Police Brutality, Systemic Racism," *UN News*, February 26, 2021, https://news.un.org/en/story/2021/02/1085872.

36. "Interim National Security Strategic Guidance," The White House, March 2021, pp. 18–19, www.whitehouse.gov/wp-content/uploads/2021/03/NSC-1v2.pdf.

37. Ibid., pp. 12–13.

38. Secretary Blinken, "A Foreign Policy for the American People," United States Department of State, March 3, 2021, www.state.gov/a-foreign-policy-for-the-american-people/. However, the manner of the U.S. withdrawal from Afghanistan in August 2021 has also been costly, especially for the human rights of many Afghans.

39. Laura Silver, Kat Devlin, and Christine Huang, "Most Americans Support Tough Stance toward China on Human Rights, Economic Issues," Pew Research Center, March 4, 2021, www.pewresearch.org/global/2021/03/04/most-americans-support-tough-stance-toward-china-on-human-rights-economic-issues/.

40. President Biden's cover letter to the "Interim Guidance." See too the readout from the meeting in Anchorage, Alaska, "How It Happened," *Asia Nikkei*, March 19, 2021, https://asia.nikkei.com/Politics/International-relations/US-China-tensions/How-it-happened-Transcript-of-the-US-China-opening-remarks-in-Alaska. Rana

Moustafa's chapter 5 references China's attempts to tie its political model to its successful control of the COVID pandemic.

41. Blinken, "A Foreign Policy for the American People," p. 9.

42. "Remarks by President Biden on America's Place in the World," U.S. Department of State, Washington, February 4, 2021, www.whitehouse.gov/briefing-room /speeches-remarks/2021/02/04/remarks-by-president-biden-on-americas-place-in -the-world/.

43. As happened on March 21, 2021, when the European Union, the United States, the United Kingdom, and Canada announced sanctions on Chinese officials associated with policies toward the Muslim Uyghurs in Xinjiang. For a Chinese perspective on this move, see "It's Not a Fight about Human Rights, but about Hegemony and Anti-Hegemony," *Global Times Editorial*, March 23, 2021, www.globaltimes.cn /opinion/editorial/.

44. Rosemary Foot, "The UN High Commissioner's contentious visit to China," East Asia Forum, July 8, 2022, https://www.eastasiaforum.org/2022/07/08/the-un -high-commissioners-contentious-visit-to-china/.

THREE

Crossing the "Redline"

Engaging Russia in the Multilateral Order

NANDINI RAMANUJAM AND VISHAKHA WIJENAYAKE

Russia is clamoring to reclaim its influence over its near abroad by using its military might. As of May 2022, tensions between the West and Russia have reached a tipping point following Russia's "special military operation" in Ukraine.[1] The unabashed use of force by Russia against one of its neighbors has shifted the international legal and security order, pushing countries such as Finland and Sweden to seek NATO membership.[2] At the domestic level, the increasing crackdown on the opposition, and civil society organizations such as Memorial International, as well as the press and media outlets, leaves no doubt that the Russian regime is blatantly undermining human rights within its borders.[3] This chapter underlines the importance of holding Russia accountable for its egregious human rights violations domestically and abroad. But at the same time, the chapter argues that strategies of isolation may do more harm than good in the long term. To this end we explore avenues to prevent powerful yet authoritarian actors such as Russia from further eroding the post–World War II international order founded on liberal values and principles. The global community will need to explore strategies to ward off the emergence of parallel international orders based on anti-liberal values and principles.

The chapter provides an overview of the checkered history of post-Soviet Russia's relationship with human rights. Russia's chaotic transition to a semi-institutionalized democracy and market economy in the 1990s was marked by a brief period in which it attempted to align itself to the international liberal order and, with it, the human rights normative and institutional order.[4] However, for the past two decades, Russia's aggressive military strategy in its near abroad, allegations of cyberattacks, poisoning of political opponents and critics, and election meddling in foreign jurisdictions have strained relations with the United States and Europe.

During the presidency of Donald Trump, whose relationship with President Vladimir Putin was the subject of spirited debate and speculation, Russia's actions leading to breaches of the international order went largely unchallenged by the United States, its main geopolitical rival. But the tide has shifted since the election of Joe Biden as president. He has stated that the United States will not recognize Russia's annexation of Crimea, which was a violation of international law.[5] He has further refused to accept the results of the March 2021 referendum in which 95 percent of voters in Crimea expressed support for a union with Russia.[6] The United States imposed sanctions over Russia's treatment of Alexei Navalny, a leading political opponent of Putin and an anticorruption activist, and is reviewing its position toward Russia over cyberattacks against U.S. elections and agencies as well as bounties being offered to Taliban-linked groups to target U.S. forces.[7] Following the February 2022 Russian aggression against Ukraine, the United States, along with other G7 countries, have imposed unprecedented sanctions at the individual, sectoral, and financial levels.[8] With over 14 million people displaced and thousands of civilian casualties to date,[9] there is a real danger that the situation in Ukraine could become a protracted armed conflict, leaving Russia a pariah state in total isolation.

The U.S. shift has highlighted potentially volatile and rapidly evolving geopolitical competition and Russia's conflictual relationship with the United States and Europe over the liberal international system. There is little consensus among scholars and policy advocates on whether and how to engage Russia constructively in the multilateral global order and what consideration should be given to its failure to comply with human rights norms in such endeavors.[10] For his part, Putin has been defiant, as indicated in his April 2021 State of the Union address: "I hope that no one will think about crossing the 'redline' regarding Russia. We ourselves will determine in each specific case where it will be drawn."[11] Recently emboldened by constitutional amendments that would potentially extend his term as president, he continues to challenge standards of collective global governance and accountability, including international human rights law. Russia under Putin no longer feels the need to justify its actions to stay in line with international law; it is prepared instead to draw its own redlines boldly regarding its own domestic political and foreign policy agendas. Can the multipolar global world accommodate Russia's blatant attempt to undermine the international legal order to assert its relevance? Or can that order be reformed through Russia's inclusion in ways that strengthen and update its component elements?

The Cold War era's human rights discourse reflected the reality of a bipolar world: the USSR's narrative that privileged socioeconomic rights was engaged in an ideological battle with the liberal, individualist notion of rights focused on civil and political freedoms. Today, however, the world stage has an increasing number of diverse actors, with states such as China and India bringing their own counternarratives to human rights and development. These new actors form nuanced geopolitical relationships that do not subscribe to a bipolar world order. For example, India's abstention in the UN General Assembly vote against Russian aggression partly stems from its reliance on Russia for arms and to counterbalance "Chinese hegemony in their shared neighborhood."[12] At the same time, India is a member of the Quad, along with Australia, Japan, and the United States, showing its strategy to make allies with Western and liberal countries.[13] Amid these complex global power structures, Russia's superpower status has waned to expose a vulnerable nation with a highly undiversified, oil-dependent economy and a declining population.[14] The era of democratization following the demise of the Soviet Union is regarded by those nostalgic about the Soviet past as "the lost decades" when Russia faced embarrassment on the international stage.[15] Wild West capitalism empowered oligarchs to take over state assets, leaving Russians with a desire for stability and economic recovery.

Putin's domestic political rhetoric has capitalized on this wounded national pride and nursed it with a romanticized narrative of the Soviet legacy and an unhealthy dose of nativism. He has repressed domestic opposition instead of purging corruption, while at the same time rewarding political and economic allies with lucrative deals and himself amassing a personal fortune. Russia has turned into a kleptocracy within which an anticorruption activist such as Navalny was able to capture the imagination of Russians and become an international figure challenging Putin's regime.[16] Russia has also moved on from being regarded as a country in democratic transition to being labeled by Freedom House as "a consolidated authoritarian regime."[17] In the exercise of its authoritarian powers, Moscow mimics and taunts certain aspects of democratic governance, as and when it suits its interests.[18]

As noted earlier, it is important to hold Russia accountable for the human and economic costs of its human rights violations and international interventions. However, treating it solely as a rogue state or isolating it can lead to further deterioration in a rapidly evolving and disintegrating multipolar global order. Russia's role among the Permanent Five (P-5) in the United Nations Security Council (UNSC), as well as its nuclear arsenal and arms supply to other nations, make it imperative that the West strive to find pathways for constructive engagement that could also be extended to a post-Putin Russia. Three decades after the emergence of the Russian Federation, its political and judicial institutions retain many characteristics of the old regime. Identifying the sociopolitical and historical dimensions of Russia's reluctance to adopt the current human rights paradigm needs to be a precondition for any such engagement. To build a more sustainable and inclusive international order, and foster a democratic and rule of law-abiding institutional culture within Russia, measures to ensure the accountability of the Russian state will need to be complemented by a constructive engagement with the Russian state, civil society, and its people.

Human Rights at Home

In January 2021, over 200,000 protesters gathered across 125 cities in Russia, including in rural, agricultural regions and conservative strongholds, to demand the release of arrested opposition politician Navalny.[19] This event refocused global attention on Russia's suppression of internal dissent. Distressingly, these tactics have been used by Putin before, and often. Boris Nemtsov, a fierce critic of the Kremlin, was assassinated in 2015.[20] The relentless persecution of Navalny is similar to the 2003 arrest, subsequent trials, and prolonged incarceration of Mikhail Khodorkovsky.[21] In these cases, an already centralized, personalized power structure demonstrated its willingness to use its iron fist to secure Putin's will.[22]

Borrowing from the Soviet era, Russia has also instrumentalized laws to restrict opposing voices and democratic participation in politics. A law of July 2012 requires nongovernmental organizations (NGOs) to register as "foreign agents" if they receive donations from abroad. Later legislation adopted in May 2015 gives prosecutors the power to sanction both foreign and international organizations working in Russia that are labeled "undesirable," as well as Russian organizations and nationals involved with such "undesirable organizations."[23] Dmitry Dubrovsky states that by cutting Western funding of Russian NGOs, such laws allow the authorities to reinforce their control over civil society and fuel paranoia among Russians that the United States is interfering in Russia's internal affairs.[24] Media and academic freedoms have also been severely curtailed during Putin's regime, and strict regulations have been imposed on internet service providers and social media platforms.[25] This domestic stifling of freedom of expression casts an ominous cloud over civil society efforts to rally support against violations of human rights perpetrated by the Russian regime. The importance of local civil society activism must not be undermined if an organic culture of human rights is to take root in Russia.

Russia's relationship with the modern human rights framework, as enshrined in UN and regional treaties and implemented through UN Charter mechanisms and regional courts, is distinct and complex. Historically, the USSR played a significant role in shaping international human rights law, particularly through the promotion of socioeconomic rights. It argued that political rights become illusory when the right to work and to a decent livelihood and the right of children to an adequate education are not guaranteed.[26] Not only did the Soviet Union ensure that socioeconomic and cultural rights were enshrined in international treaties, but it also constitutionally guaranteed these rights domestically to its citizens, including the provision of free health care, education, and cultural resources.[27] Following Marxist concepts of history and economic justice, this guarantee of civil and political rights was contingent on conformity with the socialist system.[28] Accordingly, the Soviet understanding of human rights was one where the state was central in both conferring rights and imposing duties on citizens. In addition to supporting socioeconomic rights, as a matter of state principle, the USSR's rhetoric placed a high value internationally on state sovereignty and noninterference in internal affairs as cornerstones of international law.[29]

The collapse of the USSR and the ensuing transition to democracy was coupled with accepting human rights obligations under both the European and the UN frameworks, which meant Russia's de jure endorsement of the liberal human rights paradigm.[30] This precipitated a deviation from the dominance of the collective over the individual that is often noted as a key element of Russian culture.[31] The departure from the socialist form of government was manifested in the more liberal articulation of human rights, for example, through enshrining guarantees in the 1993 Constitution to protect private property rights and, along with these, a modern market economy.[32] This was mirrored in the economic reforms (shock therapy) and privatization, which in turn engendered social consequences including a drop in the standard of living for some during the "lost decades."[33] This transformation revealed how shifts in economic policies and social welfare structures can have severe impacts on human lives and security; life expectancy within Russia fell following the end of the Cold War.[34] The financial crisis of 1998 and the devaluation of the rouble only added to increasing disillusionment within the country with the promise of an open economy and liberal domestic policies.

The belief that transplanting Western laws would contribute to Russian development assumes that imitation of Western liberal democracies leads to economic and political progress. According to Brian Z. Tamanaha, the template of capitalism, democracy, the rule of law, and universal human rights that works in a given society may not work the same way in another society with different arrangements and underpinnings.[35] Transplanting foreign principles and institutions, including liberal iterations of human rights principles, cannot be expected to show immediate results in a country unless it is accompanied by appropriate shifts in legal culture and mentality.[36] Likewise, while imitation of Western norms was prevalent in post–Cold War Russia, this experience did not lead to a complete conversion of values.[37] The historical inclination toward a powerful centralized state still permeates the Russian worldview. Moreover, the failures of transplanted models led to popular distrust and even rejection of the liberal frameworks of human rights and rule of law, especially as promoted by outside powers—a sentiment Putin has used to his benefit. Therefore, the critique of Russia's performance in relation to human rights would benefit from looking beyond Putin's dominant, singular narrative and paying closer attention instead to Russia's institutional culture.[38]

The Russian Constitution and its recent amendments highlight the friction within Russia between the legacy of historical privileging of socioeconomic rights and the struggle to stop the country from sliding into authoritarianism by asserting more civil and political freedoms. In April 2021 Putin gave the final approval to legislation that would amend the Constitution. The constitutional amendments reinforce a subset of socioeconomic rights. Although surveys in general, and especially in political climates such as Russia's, have to be taken with more than just a grain of salt, a January 2020 survey of Russians noted that more than 80 percent of respondents supported the changes, consistent with the population's strong support for socioeconomic rights and the involvement of the state in the economy and society.[39] The amendments established that the minimum wage cannot be less than the poverty threshold and required that pensions and cash payments be indexed to inflation.[40] In a clever political move, the amendments were linked to the president's political ambitions to consolidate power, such as a change that would allow Putin to remain in power for twelve more years after his fourth presidency ends in 2024 and would grant the president the authority to dismiss Constitutional Court judges and other senior judges for misconduct. This does not bode well for a Russia that is already suffering from a serious erosion of the rule of law and lack of protection of human rights in a situation where the executive has unchecked power and the separation of powers is weak.

The constitutional amendments further allude to Russia's thousand-year history and its purported traditional ideals and beliefs. Moscow seems to be taking a page out of Beijing's playbook, which has also capitalized on emotionally popular, nationalist rhetoric to portray China as a victim of bullying Western powers.[41] This nativist rhetoric advocates for an exceptional position for Russia within human rights. It has also been a point of leverage, enabling popular support for 2013 "anti-LGBTQ [Lesbian, Gay, Bisexual, Transgender, Queer] laws" to be whipped up by exalting the traditional Russian family and portraying voices that advocate for civil rights and progressive values as reflecting foreign, decadent, liberal sociopolitical ideologies.[42] This regressive attitude toward the rights of the LGBTQ community has become a geopolitical symbol against Western liberalism, allying Russia with other conservative European states such as Poland.

The Kremlin's rejection of certain elements of the liberal democratic model stems from its political objective of consolidating power free from external challenges. But it is not a coherent alternative to Western liberalism.[43] The notion of "sovereign democracy" advanced by Putin's regime reverts to a Soviet narrative built around the relationship between the people and the government, united to accomplish a "national idea," thereby upholding "collective concern for national sovereignty in the guise of 'sovereign democracy.'"[44] It lacks the participatory or deliberative nature of democracy, which can truly accommodate a plural polity conducive to the respect and fulfillment of human rights.[45] The idea of sovereign democracy also comes with Slavophile undertones and endorses the view that Russians must represent themselves and seek organic change rather than having liberal values, which include civil and political rights, imposed on them by external forces.[46] In this manner, Putin has framed the universal human rights framework as Western particularism, which is portrayed as having been designed to interfere in other countries' internal affairs while imposing double standards.[47] What is needed is a robust civil society within Russia that challenges these narratives of nativism and promotes a language of multilateralism and human rights. However, with the Russian state's intensifying crackdown on the internet, media, and civil society following its aggression on Ukraine, the already constrained democratic space has further closed down.[48] While global attention stays focused on Ukraine, it is critical to finds ways to offer assistance, and lend solidarity to independent media and civil society actors in Russia to empower citizens to hold the Russian state accountable for its gross violations of international law human rights.

Europe: A Contested Relationship

Russia's entry into the Council of Europe (CoE) in 1996 ushered in an era of hope for legislative, judicial, and other institutional reforms.[49] Russia ratified the European Convention on Human Rights (ECHR) in 1998. In the five years after it joined the CoE, Russia passed more than 2,300 federal laws and carried out reforms to implement human rights guarantees and ensure conformity with international law.[50] However, the speech Putin delivered at the 2007 Munich Security Conference, which North Atlantic Treaty Organization (NATO) nations found surprising and disappointing at the time, has proved to be prophetic of Moscow's approach to international relations and signaled that Russia no longer wanted to be seen as a student of more "advanced" democracies.[51] Following its brief flirtation with liberal democratic transformation, Russia has reverted to its tradition of a strong state with no appetite for liberal human rights influences from Europe.[52] The ideological clashes that underpin its reluctant engagement with the European human rights framework can be traced back to its discontent at being subsumed into a European system while striving to reclaim its legacy as an empire in its own right.

On March 16, 2022, the CoE decided that Russia can no longer be one of its member states. On the preceding day, the Russian government had formally notified its wish to withdraw from the CoE and communicated its intention to denounce the ECHR.[53] This is not Russia's first battle with the CoE. Following Russia's annexation of Crimea in March 2014, the Parliamentary Assembly of the CoE suspended the country's voting rights. These were restored in June 2019, but not before Russia had retaliated by withholding funding and threatening to leave the CoE. These tensions are emblematic of the tangible impacts of Russia's consolidation of power in its near abroad have on its relationship with regional multilateral forums, including the European human rights framework. They also reveal Europe's powerlessness to hold Russia truly accountable for its military aggression and human rights violations.[54] Domestic support for its exploits in its near abroad has fortified Russia's confrontational practices with the European human rights framework in the past. This support is facilitated by a narrative that reinforces the need to take aggressive measures to prevent perceived threats to the "projected identity of a 'Russian world' (*Russkii Mir*)" encompassing the Russian language and culture, and a common, Russia-centric past.[55] This further highlights Russians' discontent that the end of the Communist period went hand in hand with the disintegration of the Soviet Union—a geographical and cultural space—and the legacy of a heroic Soviet identity to which the people had a sentimental attachment.

However, even while recognizing the misinformation and suppression of facts about the war within Russia, it remains doubtful whether the domestic support for nativist rhetoric will be able to withstand the impact of Western sanctions that are constantly being intensified.[56] The economic costs of sanctions and the isolation of Russians from the global space is expected to weaken support for Russia's empire-building agenda.

Russia's inclusion in the European framework had meant that its efforts to consolidate power in its near abroad have entailed vital and increasing scrutiny through a human rights lens. On March 1, 2022, prior to Russia's CoE exit, the European Court of Human Rights (ECtHR) responded positively to a request by Ukraine to issue interim measures against Russian military action by calling on Russia to refrain from targeting civilians and other protected persons and objects.[57] Russia's human rights violations had previously come under judicial scrutiny at the ECtHR. For example, in July 2004, in *Ilascu and Others* v. *Moldova and Russia*, the majority of the Grand Chamber of ECtHR found that Russia rendered support to Transdniestria amounting to "effective control."[58] The Court has also delivered judgments relating to the situation in Chechnya in the North Caucasus.[59] A recent example of the ECtHR's regulation of Russian human rights obligations in its near abroad is the *Georgia* v. *Russia (II)* decision delivered on January 21, 2021, concerning allegations by the Georgian government of administrative practices on the part of the Russian Federation, such as unlawful detention, violating the right to life, freedom from torture, and freedom of movement of displaced persons, and the obligation to carry out effective investigations, among others.[60] Moreover, *Ukraine* v. *Russia (re Crimea) (applications 20958/14 and 38334/18)*, which were declared partly admissible in January 2021, concern Ukraine's allegations of Russia's violations of the ECHR in Crimea through administrative practices that include killing and shooting, unlawful automatic imposition of Russian citizenship, and suppression of non-Russian media.[61] While Europe has attempted to rein in Russia's military muscle-flexing through these human rights–based legal maneuvers, Russia's departure from the CoE and its denunciation of the ECHR challenge the enforcement of human rights in Russia through these mechanisms. Judicial accountability of Russian actions in its near abroad has shifted from human rights forums to the International Criminal Court (ICC) with the Prosecutor of the ICC deploying investigators and forensic experts to Ukraine in order to advance its investigations into crimes under the Rome Statute.[62]

Previously, however, the scrutiny by the European human rights framework had extended not only to Russia's activities in its near abroad but also to its domestic suppression of dissent. The ECtHR has made several interventions regarding violations of Navalny's human rights by Russian authorities.[63] In February 2021, it ordered Russia to release him from jail, stating that a failure to do so would be a contravention of the ECHR.[64] The Russian Ministry of Justice has rejected what it refers to as "crude interference into the judicial system of Russia."[65] Russia has increasingly resisted complying with the ECtHR. In 2014 the latter issued its judgment in the *Yukos* case, which concerned a company managed by Mikhail Khodorkovsky; it ordered a payment of 1,866,104,634 euros, which Russia has not made.[66] In July 2015, the Russian Constitutional Court ruled that in exceptional cases Russia could deviate from its obligation to enforce an ECtHR judgment if this was the only possible way to avoid a violation of the fundamental principles and norms of the Russian Constitution.[67] This principle was also incorporated into national legislation in December 2015.[68] This is despite Article 15(4) of the 1993 Constitution, which states that where an international treaty conflicts with domestic legislation, the international treaty rule prevails. The Venice Commission, in its Final Opinion of June 13, 2016, stressed that the execution of ECtHR judgments "is an unequivocal, imperative legal obligation, whose respect is vital for preserving and fostering the community of principles and values of the European continent."[69] According to the proposed amendments to the Russian Constitution, the Constitutional Court will be able to rule on whether or not decisions contradicting the Constitution and taken by international bodies to which Russia is party can be applied.[70]

Russia has further attempted to challenge the European human rights framework by creating alternative subregional forums, a point further elaborated in chapter 4 by Alexander Cooley. The Commonwealth of Independent States was created in 1991 following the fall of the Soviet Union and was in theory intended to preserve the economic, political, and military ties of former Soviet republics. In practice, it aimed to extend Russia's hegemonic shadow within the region.[71] Europe has not reacted to such efforts positively. For example, a report finalized in 2001 by the Committee on Legal Affairs and Human Rights of the Assembly of Europe concluded regarding the compatibility of the Convention on Human Rights and Fundamental Freedoms of the Commonwealth of Independent States (CIS Convention) and the ECHR that "no regional human rights mechanism should be allowed to weaken the unique unified system of human rights protection offered by the ECHR and its Court of Human Rights." This report therefore confirmed the primacy and supremacy of both the ECHR and ECtHR, and it urged CoE member or applicant states that are also members of the CIS not to sign or ratify the CIS Convention.[72]

The establishment of the CIS and its human rights framework can be seen as a Russian effort to create a plurality of forums within the European landscape, thereby potentially challenging the universalist framework of human rights presented in the ECHR. Russia has also taken advantage of multilateral institutions such as the Eurasian Economic Union (EAEU), the Shanghai Cooperation Organization (SCO), and the Brazil, Russia, India, China, and South Africa (BRICS) group to remain relevant amidst shifting power structures in the global order.[73]

Such efforts to challenge the universal human rights order by creating parallel subregional organizations invite the question: does a multipolar world mean there have to be multiple, conflicting sets of human rights standards? International legal experts have come to accept fragmentation as an inevitable feature of an increasingly complex international legal architecture. However, are a new vision and new leadership needed for inclusive global governance, so that common ground and core ideals can be identified within plurality? Acknowledging points of ideological tension is key to fostering constructive and continuous dialogue, which is necessary for the recalibration of the international order in our multipolar world. Likewise, what is manifested through these clashes between Russia and Europe are ideological conflicts undergirding their respective understandings of human rights.[74] For example, Valery Zorkin, chairman of Russia's Constitutional Court, has stated that it is senseless to choose between freedom and security, calling security one of the main human freedoms, for the sake of which the state can restrict others.[75] These ideological tensions further demonstrate Russia's rejection of its role as belonging to the European periphery.

Within the CoE, Russia was a powerful member with a history of challenging Western notions of liberty and the importance of human rights.[76] Now, it may project instead a narrative in which it presents itself as the center of its own civilization. What has also become a theme of Putin's regime is that sovereignty has come to be equated with independence from Western influence, and with it, the liberal human rights framework.[77] A foreign policy approach toward Russia cannot ignore its self-description as "an autonomous political subject" or a "sovereign democracy."[78] However, the "unrestrained pursuit of the national interest" that comes as part and parcel of this political project is perhaps justifiably interpreted in Europe as a manifestation of Russian imperialism.[79] It is imperative that Russia's unbridled challenge to international order be checked. However, Russia's move to isolate itself does not facilitate accountability through the European Human Rights framework. Accountability through International Criminal Law forums while necessary, may not address the panoply of human rights violations of Russian policies, both within and beyond its borders. Russia's departure from the European framework closes the door, at least temporarily, to facilitating more nuanced understandings of human rights considering the economic and sociopolitical realities of those living in Russia.

Russia in the UN Security Council

The UNSC is representative of a post–World War II great-power structure, with five states that are nuclear powers capable of determining global security decisions through their vetoes. To what extent these states' power within the UNSC reflects their modern strength and influence beyond the confines of the UNSC is debatable. However, simply by virtue of their power within the Security Council, they have been given a significant platform that enables them to perpetuate their relevance and impose their interests on other states. It is a forum that deals with conflicts and security concerns that have profound human rights implications on the ground. In February 2022, the UNSC, including Russia, was able to speak in one voice through a watered-down statement calling for peace in Ukraine.[80] Despite this gesture, Russia has made it clear that it does not shy away from using its power in the UNSC to forward its own geopolitical agenda. For instance, since 2012, Russia has been increasingly involved in the Syrian conflict through both aerospace support and ground forces to combat the Islamic State and Western-backed, moderate opposition groups fighting against the Assad regime.[81] Russia has demonstrated that in the Syrian conflict it can leverage how the situation develops to its own advantage, in particular through the use of its UNSC veto power.[82] In exercising its veto it has undercut human rights on the ground by denying Syrians access to cross-border assistance,[83] to the detriment of their socioeconomic rights and human security that Russia purports to champion.

Russia's actions in multilateral institutions such as the UNSC have to be seen in light of its ambitions to restructure axes of global power away from the Euro-Atlantic space, with a view to establishing itself as a key player in the emerging multipolar system.[84] China and Russia are acting as opportunistic strategic partners exercising a soft balancing of power within the UNSC by coordinating their actions on key international issues, one of their objectives being to manage U.S. power within the Middle East.[85] Moreover, India and Russia have agreed to work closely on key issues at the UNSC, "in keeping with the special and privileged strategic partnership between the two countries."[86] Russia has also been extending its power and influence in Africa through business partnerships as well as state-to-state diplomatic and knowledge-sharing endeavors. The self-image that Russia tries to project pits itself against Western countries that have a history of colonial subjugation.[87] Accordingly, a report by the Valdai Club, a progovernment think-tank, states that "African countries still see Russia as their most likely ally in protecting their interests on the international stage and as a natural counterbalance to the hegemonic aspirations of one or several world powers."[88] While such claims may not reflect the reality of Russia's exercise of power in foreign countries, historically or at present, this narrative is indicative of the allies it is trying to build and the image it is attempting to project globally. Not unlike other P-5 countries, Russia uses its UNSC veto power to achieve greater clout, with clear implications for human rights accountability at the UN. It does so in a manner that prevents the UNSC from acting to protect human rights in countries where Moscow's foreign policy interests are at stake.

Russia's actions in the UNSC regularly demonstrate its capacity to bring instability to the international arena.[89] It has consistently vetoed resolutions on Syria, often with the backing of China. For example, in July 2020 both states vetoed a resolution proposed by Belgium and Germany, which, among other things, demanded that the Syrian authorities comply immediately with their obligations under international human rights law. In vetoing the resolution, Russia introduced its own draft resolution, which limited the number of crossing points to only one.[90] The U.S. representative has accused Russia of creating a false choice between humanitarian aid, sovereignty, and sanctions, and failing to save the lives of the Syrian people by siding with Bashar al-Assad's regime. Similarly, in 2012 Russia vetoed a resolution on Syria, claiming that the UNSC refused to take its amendments into account.[91] Beyond the Syrian context, in March 2021 Russia failed to support a resolution (which among other things expressed concern at violations of human rights) with regard to the military coup in Myanmar.[92] In 2008, it vetoed a resolution on the situation in Zimbabwe, voicing its support for diplomatic measures adopted by leaders of other African states.[93] This is a pattern that shows Russia's consistent derailing of UNSC efforts to take proactive measures that seek to address humanitarian situations affecting civilians' human rights, by alluding to alternative resolutions and the potential for diplomatic solutions that have questionable capacity to deliver practical results.

Sanctions have become a go-to tool of Western states to punish other states for human rights violations. For example, following the recent attacks on Ukraine, a series of new sanctions were issued against Russia by the EU, North American, and some Asian states.[94] The UNSC, however, remains an ill-suited forum to impose sanctions against Russian threats to international security and human rights. This is so as Russia, for its part, has used its veto power to oppose UNSC resolutions that aim to implement sanctions, especially when its interests are at stake. In doing so, Russia has raised concerns about the impact of sanctions on individuals on the ground. For instance, it has noted the impact that imposing sanctions on the Assad regime would have on the Syrian people and territories under government control, specifically stating that increased shortages "of food, medicines and basic commodities, as well as rising inflation, are their direct consequences."[95] The Syrian crisis demonstrates a fundamental aspect of Russia's public stance on international intervention, which opposes any implicit or explicit endorsement by the Security Council of the removal of an incumbent government.[96] However, in all these instances, Russia's demands for nonintervention need to be critically assessed in the context of its unequivocal pursuit of its own geopolitical and economic interests

Moreover, Russia has used language suggesting the West is pitted against state sovereignty, stating that Western members' calculations "to use the Security Council of the United Nations to further their plans of imposing their own designs on sovereign States will not prevail."[97] This rhetoric can also be seen in its labeling of France, the United Kingdom, and the United States, as "the troika of the three Western permanent members of the Security Council," and seeking to delegitimize Britain by referring to its "colonial customs."[98] Russia, therefore, has promoted a divisive narrative of two camps among the veto members, identifying itself as belonging to the camp that defends the sovereignty of the "non-West" and the Global South. These practices are eroding the basis for common understandings that are prerequisites of an international order and well-functioning multilateral institutions, while failing to offer a coherent alternative. Analyzing the language used by Russia in the UNSC is important, given that these shared understandings are generated and maintained through social interaction.[99] Jean-Marc Coicaud identifies two layers of principles that bind the international community together. The first relates to the elementary but crucial goal of securing the existence and coexistence of states—principles such as nonintervention in the internal or external affairs of other states, international cooperation, and good faith. The second layer comprises principles concerned with the democratic aspects of international relations, such as respect for human rights.[100] By accusing Western nations of infringing state sovereignty and violating norms of nonintervention, the language used by Russia in its statements in the UNSC tends to engage the first layer of principles, striking at the heart of what binds the international community together.

Recommendations

Ivan Krastev wrote in 2007 that "western policymakers are torn between their desires to 'talk tough' and 'teach Russia a lesson' and the realization that the West has limited capacity to influence Russia's policies."[101] This limitation cannot be pinned down to one root cause but rests on Russia's continuing power within major international organizations, its unabashed exercise of aggression and military might both at home and abroad, the personality cult of President Putin, and a political culture of Russian exceptionalism with regard to the liberal human rights framework. This is particularly observable with the imposition of sanctions on Russia, which has not had a high success rate in achieving the intended human rights objectives. So far, the West's tactics to hold Russia accountable, including through naming and shaming of individuals, have largely failed to yield results in improving that country's human rights record. It remains to be seen whether the recent spate of sanctions on individuals as well as on various sectors will be successfully manipulated by the regime, as done in the past, to amplify its anti-West rhetoric.[102]

On the other hand, adopting an approach of "strategic patience" in anticipation of an inevitable decline in Russian power is also not wise, especially while the security of its neighbors and well-being of threatened individuals hang in the balance.[103] Some strategies for enhancing the human rights agenda focus on Putin himself and expect that a regime change would improve the situation. While acknowledging that a different leader would bring a different style and rhythm to international and domestic human rights policy, a Putin-focused strategy ignores the reality that "the fundamentals of the Russian ideological narrative are shared across the spectrum of the political elite."[104] In any event, regime change itself remains problematic, given that Putin's suppression of opposition makes it almost impossible to gauge his popularity, and the Russian mindset that favors the status quo "reconciles Putin's supporters with his no-alternative legitimacy formula."[105] However, we do not want to advocate defeatism, offering instead three recommendations that might help turn the tide on Russia's relationship with human rights.

First, supporting local civil society remains vital, whether it is to facilitate regime change or to spread awareness of human rights and build a culture of human rights from within. Although this is not a unique or novel suggestion, it is one that is worth repeating. Attempts to transplant human rights through external imposition have been largely unsuccessful in Russia. Sally Engle Merry has compellingly demonstrated that international human rights norms are not fixed but need to grow roots through a process of "vernacularizing," which is critical if they are to be adapted and legitimized in the local context.[106] It is also important to recognize, as Cooley does in chapter 4, that civil society is not a monolith and can itself become infiltrated by government interests, whether through the Kremlin or through more transnational influences.[107] A more challenging aspect of this proposal is to identify tangible ways in which the international community can support Russian civil society amid a strict crackdown on any civil society entities that are affiliated with foreign donors, as well as constant threats to dissidents' lives and security. One very simple way to support human rights activists and scholars who are compelled to leave the country to continue their work is to provide such individuals with protection and resources abroad, as well as to facilitate mobility by making it easy for them to obtain visas to participate in international conferences and other forums. Importantly, on a more structural level, diplomatic engagement with Russia should consistently prioritize and incentivize the need to reverse the restrictions on civil society imposed through legal amendments. The recent decision of the Supreme Court of Russia to liquidate Memorial International demonstrates that the Russian judiciary cannot be trusted to act as an effective check on state repression of civil society. Therefore, any demands to protect dissenting voices and civil society should be coupled with the need for the separation of powers that facilitates independent institutions.

Second, the global community must urgently recalibrate the human rights agenda so that it reflects the interdependency of human rights norms and concerns.[108] The decades following the end of the Cold War have produced various critiques and challenges to the "one size fits all" liberal human rights agenda.[109] Its formal guarantees appear overinflated when juxtaposed with its thin de facto implementation on the ground. The current paradigm's tilt toward civil and political rights as seen through the lens of negative obligations continues to undermine the importance of positive obligations that are necessary for the realization and the interdependency of all rights, including socioeconomic rights, group rights, and third-generation rights.[110] Russia is undermining civil and political liberties by highlighting this discrepancy in the attention given by the West to economic rights. This dangerous trend must be reversed as these rights are not mutually exclusive and in fact are interdependent, operating as one "ecosystem." Such a recalibration of the human rights agenda would gain broader legitimacy and buy-in from diverse states. This is not an invitation to lower human rights standards but a plea to refocus on the core structure of human rights principles in its entirety, with a plural and diverse international society in mind.

Third, bilateral and multilateral interactions must continue. The international community has sought to punitively exclude Russia from the world stage while Russia isolates itself with the support of only a few like-minded allies. In either case, Russia's presence continues to be felt even in its absence from international forums, showing no remorse for its continued transgressions. Russia's isolation also raises the difficulties of attempting to protect the human rights interests of individual Russians while imposing sanctions whose adverse economic effects will trickle down to ordinary Russian citizens. Isolationism also shuts down bilateral and multilateral interactions that are necessary to identify core values that can be shared by and bind together a heterogeneous international community.

Despite the complexity of the issue, the existing human rights accountability measures and advocacy initiatives need to be supplemented with inclusive project-based multilateralism, which has shared values as a goal rather than as a precondition.[111] It is crucial to identify windows of opportunity where such engagement becomes possible. The 2030 Agenda for Sustainable Development is an apt example. It is an inclusive agenda in which human rights are integrated, and it acts as a forum with concrete milestones and relatively uncontroversial goals, the achievement of which would still have significant positive impacts on human freedoms and dignity.[112] The Sustainable Development Goals (SDGs) strive to overcome siloed, piecemeal approaches and therefore are seen as interdependent, each integral to achieving sustainable development.[113] Most importantly, the agenda is a global platform with which Russia voluntarily engages; this can be contrasted with its usual approach of supporting subregional organizations that fragment human rights. While Russia's performance in working toward the SDGs leaves a lot to be desired, the process of voluntary reporting by the state, in combination with civil society shadow reports, can facilitate a nuanced dialogue and engagement with Russia on contentious issues.[114] In the face of Russia's exit from the CoE, the ICC is becoming a pivotal forum to raise accountability for violations suffered by civilians' at the hands of Russia on foreign soil, even though Russia, much like China and the United States, does not accept the jurisdiction of the ICC. Future possibilities for global engagement may also have to envision forums currently not viewed as spaces for advancing human rights concerns. Such approaches may not explicitly use the language of human rights but could be more effective in achieving core human rights objectives of freedom and dignity.

Every day seems to be a new day on Russia regarding human rights within its borders and when it comes to its deployment of military forces within the borders of its neighbors. In these volatile conditions, isolationist strategies may be a helpful bargaining tool. However, they do not entirely replace dialogue and engagement, especially as a long-term strategy. Despite the violence unfolding in Ukraine, President Volodymyr Zelensky remains confident about talks between Ukraine and Russia taking place at a future date and has stated that a bilateral talk between him and Putin might end the war in Ukraine.[115] Even amid war, optimism for bilateral engagement continues. This chapter urges cautious engagement with Russia in both bilateral and heterogeneous forums to supplement the existing accountability mechanisms, with the primary objective of ameliorating the situation of civil society and individuals within Russia as well as those affected by Russian action beyond its borders.

Notes

1. "Russian Federation Announces 'Special Military Operation' in Ukraine as Security Council Meets in Eleventh-Hour Effort to Avoid Full-Scale Conflict," Security Council, 8974th Meeting (Night), February 23, 2022, https://www.un.org/press /en/2022/sc14803.doc.htm; "Russia Rejects U.S. Suggestions It's Looking for Pretext to Invade Ukraine," Associated Press, January 17, 2022, https://www.cbc.ca/news /world/russia-ukraine-tension-1.6317497; "Sanctions on Putin Would Be Step Too Far, Kremlin Warns U.S.," *Moscow Times*, January 13, 2022, https://www.themoscowtimes .com/2022/01/13/sanctions-on-putin-would-be-step-too-far-kremlin-warns-us -a76033; John Haltiwanger, "Russia Warns It Will Sever Ties with the US If It Sanctions Putin over Ukraine Crisis," *Business Insider*, https://www.businessinsider.com /russia-warns-it-will-cut-ties-with-us-if-putin-sanctioned-over-ukraine-2022-1.

2. "Finland and Sweden Submit Applications to Join NATO," *North Atlantic Treaty Organization News*, May 18, 2022, https://www.nato.int/cps/en/natohq/news_195468 .htm?selectedLocale=en.

3. Anna Chernova and Joshua Berlinger, "Russian Court Shuts Down Human Rights Group Memorial International," *CNN World*, December 28, 2021, https:// www.cnn.com/2021/12/28/europe/memorial-international-russia-intl/index.html; "Memorial: Russia's Civil Rights Group Uncovering an Uncomfortable Past," *BBC News*, January 2, 2022, https://www.bbc.com/news/world-europe-59853010; https:// www.fidh.org/en/region/europe-central-asia/russia/russian-courts-deal-a-blow-to -the-very-core-of-russia-s-civil-society.

4. In this chapter references to the liberal human rights paradigm mean the human rights framework enshrined in the multilateral human rights treaties implemented through UN Charter mechanisms as well as the European regional treaties and Court.

5. "Biden: 'We Will Stand with Ukraine' against Russia on Crimea," *Al Jazeera*, February 26, 2021, www.aljazeera.com/news/2021/2/26/biden-we-will-stand-with -ukraine-against-russia-on-crimea.

6. "Crimea Referendum: Voters 'Back Russia Union,'" *BBC News*, March 16, 2014, www.bbc.com/news/world-europe-26606097.

7. Abigail Williams and others, "U.S., E.U. Impose Sanctions on Russia over Navalny's Poisoning," *NBC News*, March 1, 2021, www.nbcnews.com/news/world/u-s -eu-set-impose-sanctions-russia-n1259249.

8. "Fact Sheet: United States and G7 Partners Impose Severe Costs for Putin's War against Ukraine", *The White House Briefing Room*, May 8, 2022, https://www .whitehouse.gov/briefing-room/statements-releases/2022/05/08/fact-sheet-united -states-and-g7-partners-impose-severe-costs-for-putins-war-against-ukraine/#:~:text =The%20United%20States%20will%20sanction,Stock%20Company%20 NTV%20Broadcasting%20Company.

9. "How Many Ukrainians Have Fled Their Homes and Where Have They Gone?," *BBC News*, May 25, 2022, https://www.bbc.com/news/world-60555472; "Ukraine: Civilian Casualty Update 22 April 2022,",News: Office of the High Commissioner for Human Rights, April 22, 2022, https://www.ohchr.org/en/news/2022/04/ukraine -civilian-casualty-update-22-april-2022.

10. See, for example, Thomas Graham, "Let Russia Be Russia," *Foreign Affairs*, November/December 2019, www.foreignaffairs.com/articles/russia-fsu/2019-10-15/let -russia-be-russia; Dylan Myles-Primakoff, "America's Russia Policy Must Not Ignore Human Rights," *Atlantic Council* (blog), March 9, 2021; Emma Ashford and Matthew Burrows, "Reality Check #4: Focus on Interests, Not on Human Rights with Russia," *Atlantic Council* (blog), March 5, 2021, www.atlanticcouncil.org/content-series/reality -check/reality-check-4-focus-on-interests-not-on-human-rights-with-russia/.

11. "Presidential Address to the Federal Assembly," Team of the Official Website of the President of Russia, April 21, 2021, http://en.kremlin.ru/events/president/news /65418.

12. Gareth Price, "Ukraine War: Why India Abstained on UN Vote against Russia," *Chatham House*, March 25, 2022, https://www.chathamhouse.org/2022/03 /ukraine-war-why-india-abstained-un-vote-against-russia; Frédéric Grare, "A Question of Balance: India and Europe after Russia's Invasion of Ukraine," *European Council on Foreign Relations*, May 16, 2022, https://ecfr.eu/publication/a-question-of-balance -india-and-europe-after-russias-invasion-of-ukraine/.

13. Vikas Pandey, "Quad: The China Factor at the Heart of the Summit," *BBC News,* May 24, 2022, https://www.bbc.com/news/world-asia-india-61547082.

14. Bethany Wright, "What the Pandemic Exposes about Russian Dependence on Oil," *World Crunch*, November 16, 2020, https://worldcrunch.com/business-finance /what-the-pandemic-exposes-about-russian-dependence-on-oil; Daniel Treisman, "Is Russia Cursed by Oil?," *Journal of International Affairs* 63, 2 (2010).

15. Vladimir Popov, "The Long Road to Normalcy," UNU-WIDER Working Paper 2010/13 (2010), p. 2.

16. Miriam Lanskoy and Dylan Myles-Primakoff, "The Rise of Kleptocracy: Power and Plunder in Putin's Russia," *Journal of Democracy* 29, 1 (2018), pp. 76–77. Also see Karen Dawisha, *Putin's Kleptocracy: Who Owns Russia?* (New York: Simon and Schuster, 2014).

17. "Russia," Nations in Transit 2021, Freedom House, https://freedomhouse.org/country/russia/nations-transit/2021.

18. William Partlett, "Can Russia Keep Faking Democracy?," Brookings, May 22, 2012, www.brookings.edu/opinions/can-russia-keep-faking-democracy/; Aryeh Neier, "The Imitation Games That Authoritarians Play," *New Republic*, March 24, 2020, https://newrepublic.com/article/156777/imitation-games-authoritarians-trump-putin.

19. "Alexei Navalny: Germany Urges EU Action over Novichok Poisoning," *BBC News*, September 3, 2020, www.bbc.com/news/world-europe-54010741; "Russian Opposition Leader Navalny Arrested upon Arrival in Moscow," *Politico*, January 17, 2021, www.politico.eu/article/russian-opposition-leader-alexei-navalny-arrested-upon-arrival-in-moscow/; Anastasia Edel, "The Berlin Patient," *Foreign Policy*, April 25, 2021, https://foreignpolicy.com/2021/04/25/navalny-protest-dissent-russia-putin.

20. "Why Was Boris Nemtsov Murdered?," *Politico*, March 5, 2015, www.politico.eu/article/why-was-boris-nemtsov-murdered/.

21. "The Khodorkovsky Trial: A Report on the Observation of the Criminal Trial of Mikhail Borisovich Khodorkovsky and Platon Leonidovich Lebedev, March 2009 to December 2010," International Bar Association's Human Rights Institute (IBAHRI), September 2011; "Russian Oligarch in London Fatalistic about His Safety from Attack," *The Guardian*, March 20, 2018, www.theguardian.com/world/2018/mar/20/russian-oligarch-in-london-fatalistic-about-his-safety-from-attack; "Russian Businessmen Declared Prisoners of Conscience after Convictions Are Upheld," Amnesty International, October 13, 2011, https://web.archive.org/web/20111013071109/http://www.amnesty.org/en/for-media/press-releases/russian-businessmen-declared-prisoners-conscience-after-convictions-are-uph.

22. Michael Waller, *Russian Politics Today: The Return of a Tradition* (New York: Palgrave, 2005).

23. "Russia: Persecution of 'Undesirable' Activists," Human Rights Watch, January 18, 2020, www.hrw.org/news/2020/01/18/russia-persecution-undesirable-activists#:~:text=The%20law%20on%20%E2%80%9Cundesirable%20organizations,%2C%20defense%2C%20or%20constitutional%20order.

24. Dmitry Dubrovsky, "Foreign Agents and Undesirable Organizations," *IWM Post* 116 (Fall 2015), p. 21.

25. "Online and on All Fronts," Human Rights Watch, July 18, 2017, www.hrw.org/report/2017/07/18/online-and-all-fronts/russias-assault-freedom-expression; "Russia: Growing Internet Isolation, Control, Censorship," Human Rights Watch, June 18, 2020, www.hrw.org/news/2020/06/18/russia-growing-internet-isolation-control-censorship. In 2018 Russia filed a lawsuit to limit access to the Telegram messaging app after the company refused to give Russian state security services access to its users' secret messages. In March 2021, Russia started suing five social media platforms for allegedly failing to delete posts urging children to take part in illegal protests concerning the detention of Navalny. See "Russia Files Lawsuit to Block Telegram Messaging App," Reuters, April 6, 2018, www.reuters.com/article/us-russia

-telegram/russia-files-lawsuit-to-block-telegram-messaging-app-idUKKCN1HD143; "Russia Sues Google, Facebook, Twitter for Not Deleting Protest Content: Report," *CTV News*, March 9, 2021, www.ctvnews.ca/sci-tech/russia-sues-google-facebook -twitter-for-not-deleting-protest-content-report-1.5339374.

26. 21 U.N. GAOR, C.3 (1396th mtg.) 109, 112, U.N. Doc. A/C.3/SR.1396 (1966).

27. In the Soviet Constitution of 1977, these are the right to work (Article 40), right to rest and leisure (Article 41), right to free health care (Article 42), right to social security (Article 43), right to housing (Article 44), right to education (Article 45), and right to cultural benefits (Article 46). See also the 1936 Constitution.

28. In the Soviet Constitution of 1977, rather than characterizing civil and political rights as negative rights requiring state nonintervention, the state's role in the positive obligations relating to civil and political rights was expressly delineated. As was the case with the 1936 Constitution, civil and political rights were guaranteed but with obvious caveats: according to Article 50, freedom of speech, of the press, and of assembly, meetings, street processions, and demonstrations are guaranteed in accordance with the interests of the people and in order to strengthen and develop the socialist system. Mary Hawkesworth, "Ideological Immunity: The Soviet Response to Human Rights Criticism," *Universal Human Rights* 2, 1 (1980), pp. 67–84.

29. Bill Bowring, "Russia and Human Rights: Incompatible Opposites," *Göttingen Journal of International Law* 1, 2 (2009), pp. 257–67.

30. Ibid.

31. Mikhail Antonov, "Conservatism in Russia and Sovereignty in Human Rights," *Review of Central and East European Law* 39, 1 (2014), p. 24.

32. See Russia's Constitution of 1993, Articles 8, 9, 35, and 36; property rights provisions received detailed regulation in the Civil Code of 1994, the Land Code of 2001, and various other specialized legislative acts.

33. Vladislav Starzhenetskiy, "Property Rights in Russia: Reconsidering the Socialist Legal Tradition," in *Russia and the European Court of Human Rights: The Strasbourg Effect*, edited by Lauri Mälksoo and Wolfgang Benedek (Cambridge University Press, 2018), pp. 295–97, 299; Felix Yurlov, "Russia—A Lost Decade," *World Affairs: The Journal of International Issues* 3, 3 (1999), pp. 80–95; Michael D. Intrilligator and others, "What Russia Can Learn from China in Its Transition to Market Economy," in *Clumsy Solutions for a Complex World: Governance, Politics and Plural Perceptions*, edited by Marco Verweij and M. Thompson (Basingstoke, U.K.: Palgrave Macmillan, 2006).

34. Stephen Holmes and Ivan Krastev, *The Light That Failed: Why the West Is Losing the Fight for Democracy* (New York: Pegasus Books, 2020), p. 84.

35. Brian Z. Tamanaha, "The Primacy of Society and the Failures of Law and Development," *Cornell International Law Journal* 44, 2 (2011), pp. 209–15.

36. Mikhail Antonov, "Philosophy Behind Human Rights: Valery Zorkin vs. the West?," in *Russia and the European Court of Human Rights*, pp. 150–57.

37. Holmes and Krastev, *The Light That Failed*, p. 79. Antonov, "Conservatism in Russia," p. 13, states that Russian judges and lawyers continue to view attempts to

advance international jurisprudence at the cost of Russian domestic law as an inadmissible encroachment upon Russian sovereignty.

38. Nandini Ramanujam, Mara Verna, and Julia Betts, "Rule of Law and Economic Development: A Comparative Analysis of Approaches to Economic Development across the BRIC Countries," Rule of Law and Economic Development Research Group, December 2012, pp. 78–79: "The Soviet Union's institutions were themselves largely a continuation of tsarist institutions, which were predicated on absolutist law and oligarchy."

39. Левада-центр»: 64% россиян готовы участвовать в голосовании о поправках в Конституцию, 72% их поддержат', 10 февраля 2020 [Levada Center: "64% of Russians are ready to vote on amendments to the Constitution, 72% will support them," February 10, 2020], https://meduza.io/news/2020/02/10/levada-tsentr-64-rossiyan-gotovy-pouchastvovat-v-golosovanii-o-popravkah-v-konstitutsiyu-72-ih-podderzhat.

40. "Russians Vote on Putin's Reforms to Constitution," *BBC News*, June 25, 2020, www.bbc.com/news/world-europe-5317606.

41. Suisheng Zhao, "China's Pragmatic Nationalism: Is It Manageable?," *Washington Quarterly* 29, 1 (2005), pp. 131–44. For a discussion on China's foreign policy and engagements with human rights, see "Exploring Public International Law Issues with Chinese Scholars—Part 4," International Law Programme Roundtable Meeting Summary, Chatham House, June 2–3, 2018, www.chathamhouse.org/2018/06/exploring-public-international-law-issues-chinese-scholars-part-four.

42. On nativism, see Benedikt Harzl, "Nativist Ideological Responses to European/Liberal Human Rights Discourses in Contemporary Russia," in *Russia and the European Court of Human Right*s, edited by Mälksoo and Benedek, pp. 355–56; on LGBT and the rights of the traditional family, see Federal Law 135-FZ, June 29, 2013, on "propaganda of non-traditional sexual relations" and Federal Law 167-FZ, July 2, 2013, on measures relating to adoptions; and Andrea Chandler, "Russia's Laws on 'Non-Traditional' Relationships as Response to Global Norm Diffusion," *International Journal of Human Rights* 25, 4 (2021), pp. 616–18.

43. Harzl, "Nativist Ideological Responses," p. 358; Holmes and Krastev, *The Light That Failed*, p. 132.

44. Antonov, "Conservatism in Russia," p. 25.

45. Nancy Fraser, "Rethinking the Public Sphere: A Contribution to the Critique of Actually Existing Democracy," *Social Text* 25/26 (1990), pp. 56–80.

46. Antonov, "Conservatism in Russia," p. 27.

47. Holmes and Krastev, *The Light That Failed*, p. 82.

48. Alicia Ceccanese, "'Disastrous for Press Freedom': What Russia's Goal of an Isolated Internet Means for Journalists," *Committee to Protect Journalists*, May 23, 2022, https://cpj.org/2022/05/disastrous-for-press-freedom-what-russias-goal-of-an-isolated-internet-means-for-journalists/.

49. Lauri Mälksoo, "Introduction: Russia, Strasbourg, and the Paradox of a Human Rights Backlash," in *Russia and the European Court of Human Rights,* edited by Mälksoo and Benedek, p. 4.

50. Yuri Ivanovich Kalinin, "The Russian Penal System: Past, Present and Future," lecture delivered at King's College London, November 2002, p. 9, www.prisonstudies .org/sites/default/files/resources/downloads/website_kalinin.pdf.

51. Louis Charbonneau, "Putin Says U.S. Wants to Dominate World," Reuters, February 10, 2007, https://www.reuters.com/article/us-russia-usa-idUSL1053774820070210.

52. Mälksoo, "Introduction," p. 10.

53. Council of Europe, "Resolution CM/Res(2022)2 on the Cessation of the Membership of the Russian Federation to the Council of Europe," adopted by the Committee of Ministers at the 1428ter meeting of the Ministers' Deputies, March 16, 2022; "Russia Quits Council of Europe Rights Watchdog," Reuters, March 15, 2022, https:// www.reuters.com/world/europe/russia-formally-quits-council-europe-rights-watchdog -2022-03-15/; Jannika Jahn, "The Council of Europe Excludes Russia: A Setback for Human Rights," EJIL: Talk!, March 23, 2022, https://www.ejiltalk.org/the-council-of -europe-excludes-russia-a-setback-for-human-rights/#:~:text=Upon%20unani mous%20request%20of%20the,to%20withdraw%20the%20preceding%20day.

54. See James Nixey, "Lavrov and Russia Outplay the European Union Yet Again," Chatham House, February 15, 2021, www.chathamhouse.org/2021/02/lavrov-and -russia-outplay-european-union-yet-again.

55. Ibid., p. 718.

56. Anna Matveeva, "Russia's Power Projection after the Ukraine Crisis," *Europe-Asia Studies* 70, 5 (2018), pp. 711–13, www.tandfonline.com/doi/full/10.1080 /09668136.2018.1479735.

57. "The European Court Grants Urgent Interim Measures in Application Concerning Russian Military Operations on Ukrainian territory," Press Release, Registrar of the European Court of Human Rights, March 1, 2022.

58. *Ilascu and Others* v. *Moldova and Russia*, 48787/99, Council of Europe: European Court of Human Rights, July 8, 2004.

59. *Abdulkhanov and Others* v. *Russia,* 22782/06, European Court of Human Rights, October 3, 2013; *Turluyeva* v. *Russia*, 63638/09, European Court of Human Rights, June 20, 2013; *Maskhadova and Others* v. *Russia,* 18071/05, European Court of Human Rights, June 6, 2013; *Sabanchiyeva and Others* v. *Russia*, 38450/05, European Court of Human Rights, June 6, 2013.

60. There is one more case relating to Georgia pending in the ECtHR. *Georgia* v. *Russia (IV)*, 39611/18, European Court of Human Rights, August 22, 2018, relates to the human rights situation along the administrative boundary lines between Georgian-controlled territory and Abkhazia and South Ossetia.

61. On November 27, 2020, the Grand Chamber of the European Court of Human Rights in interstate application *Ukraine* v. *Russia (re Eastern Ukraine),* 8019/16, decided to join to that application two interstate applications, *Ukraine* v. *Russia (II),* 43800/14, and *The Netherlands* v. *Russia*, 28525/20, which were pending before a chamber. Another case, *Ukraine* v. *Russia (III),* 49537/14, was struck off after the Ukrainian government stated that it did not wish to pursue it.

62. "ICC Prosecutor Karim A.A. Khan QC Announces Deployment of Forensics and Investigative Team to Ukraine, Welcomes Strong Cooperation with the Government of the Netherlands," International Criminal Court: News, May 17, 2022, https://www.icc-cpi.int/news/icc-prosecutor-karim-aa-khan-qc-announces-deployment-forensics-and-investigative-team-ukraine.

63. *Navalnyy* v. *Russia*, 62670/12, European Court of Human Rights, November 17, 2016; *Navalnyy* v. *Russia*, 32058/13, European Court of Human Rights, May 15, 2014; *Navalnyy* v. *Russia*, 1176/15, European Court of Human Rights, February 20, 2018; *Navalnyy* v. *Russia*, 25809/17, European Court of Human Rights, June 19, 2017; *Navalnyy* v. *Russia*, 67894/17, European Court of Human Rights, March 9, 2018; *Navalnyy and Ofitserov* v. *Russia*, 78193/17, European Court of Human Rights, December 21, 2017; *Navalnyy* v. *Russia*, 55589/17, European Court of Human Rights, January 28, 2020; *Navalnyy* v. *Russia*, 56491/18, European Court of Human Rights, January 28, 2020; and *Navalnyy* v. *Russia*, 36418/20, European Court of Human Rights, January 12, 2021.

64. "Navalny Must Be Freed, European Rights Court Tells Russia," *BBC News*, February 17, 2021, https://www.bbc.com/news/world-europe-56102257.

65. "Europe's Top Human Rights Court Demands Russia Release Alexey Navalny Immediately," *CBS News*, February 17, 2021, www.cbsnews.com/news/alexey-navalny-european-court-human-rights-demands-release/.

66. *OAO Neftyanaya Kompaniya Yukos* v. *Russia,* 14902/04, European Court of Human Rights, July 31, 2014 (just compensation).

67. Resolution of the Constitutional Court of the Russian Federation of July 14, 2015, N 21-P, St. Petersburg, https://rg.ru/2015/07/27/ks-dok.html.

68. "Russia Passes Law to Overrule European Human Rights Court," *BBC News*, December 4, 2015, www.bbc.com/news/world-europe-35007059.

69. Final Opinion on the Amendments to the Federal Constitutional Law on the Constitutional Court, Opinion 832/2015, European Commission for Democracy through Law, June 13, 2016, para. 38.

70. Martin Russell, "Constitutional Change in Russia: More Putin, or Preparing for Post-Putin?," *European Parliament Briefing*, May 2020, www.europarl.europa.eu/RegData/etudes/BRIE/2020/651935/EPRS_BRI(2020)651935_EN.pdf.

71. Paul Kubicek, "The Commonwealth of Independent States: An Example of Failed Regionalism?," *Review of International Studies* 35, S1 (2009), pp. 237–39.

72. Report: Co-Existence of the Convention on Human Rights and Fundamental Freedoms of the Commonwealth of Independent States and the European Convention on Human Rights, Committee on Legal Affairs and Human Rights, Doc. 9075, May 3, 2001, https://assembly.coe.int/nw/xml/XRef/X2H-Xref-ViewHTML.asp?FileID=9298&lang=EN.

73. Paul Stronski and Richard Solosky, "Multipolarity in Practice: Understanding Russia's Engagement with Regional Institutions," Carnegie Endowment for International Peace, January 8, 2020, https://carnegieendowment.org/2020/01/08

/multipolarity-in-practice-understanding-russia-s-engagement-with-regional
-institutions-pub-80717.

74. *Ždanoka* v. *Latvia*, judgment (Grand Chamber), appl. 58278/00, March 16, 2006, para. 98 notes that the ECHR was designed to maintain and promote the ideals and values of a democratic society. Democracy is thus the only political model contemplated by the Convention and, accordingly, the only one compatible with it.

75. Зорькин призвал добавить в правовую систему "военной суровости" [Zorkin urges the addition of "military necessity" to the legal system], *ZAKS*, November 25, 2015, https://www.zaks.ru/new/archive/view/147253.

76. Mälksoo, "Introduction," p. 11.

77. Holmes and Krastev, *The Light That Failed*, p. 13.

78. Andrey S. Makarychev, "Russia's Search for International Identity through the Sovereign Democracy Concept," *International Spectator* 43, 2 (2008), p. 49.

79. Ivan Krastev, "Russia vs Europe: Sovereignty Wars," *Open Democracy*, September 5, 2007, www.opendemocracy.net/en/russia_vs_europe_the_sovereignty_wars/.

80. "Security Council 'Speaks with One Voice for Peace in Ukraine,'" *UN News*, May 6, 2022, https://news.un.org/en/story/2022/05/1117742.

81. "Russia/Syria: Possibly Unlawful Russian Air Strikes Entire," Human Rights Watch, October 25, 2015, www.hrw.org/news/2015/10/25/russia/syria-possibly -unlawful-russian-air-strikes.

82. Nikolay Kozhanov, "Russian Policy across the Middle East," Chatham House Research Paper, February 21, 2018, www.chathamhouse.org/2018/02/russian-policy -across-middle-east/russias-pivot-middle-east-after-2012.

83. "Russia Unmoved as Security Council Again Warned of Syrian Children's Plight," *Arab News*, February 26, 2021, https://arab.news/2xprz.

84. Stronski and Solosky, "Multipolarity in Practice."

85. Mordechai Chaziza, "Soft Balancing Strategy in the Middle East: Chinese and Russian Vetoes in the United Nations Security Council in the Syria Crisis," *China Report* 50, 3 (2014), pp. 243–58, at p. 247, https://doi.org/10.1177/0009445514534126. China and Russia have also used vaccine diplomacy to expand their influence across borders, including in the Middle East, and are engaging in joint space exploration projects. Anne-Sylvaine Chassany, "The West Should Pay Attention to Russia and China's Vaccine Diplomacy," *Financial Times*, February 10, 2021, www.ft.com/content /c20b92f0-d670-47ea-a217-add1d6ef2fbd.

86. "India and Russia Agree to Work Closely on Key Issues at U.N. Security Council," *The Hindu*, February 17, 2021, www.thehindu.com/news/national/india-and -russia-agree-to-work-closely-on-key-issues-at-the-un-security-council /article33858914.ece.

87. Vadim Balytniko, Oleg Barabanov, Andrei Yemelyanov, Dmitry Poletaev, and Igor Sid, "Russia's Return to Africa: Strategy and Prospects," Valdai Discussion Club Report, October 2019, p. 35, https://valdaiclub.com/files/27418/.

88. Ibid.

89. Holmes and Krastev, *The Light That Failed*, p. 114.

90. Letter dated July 8, 2020, from the president of the Security Council addressed to the secretary-general and the permanent representatives of the members of the Security Council, UN Security Council, July 9, 2020, S/2020/661, Annex 18.

91. "The Situation in the Middle East," 6,711th meeting UN Security Council, S/PV.6711, February 4, 2012.

92. "China, Russia Stop UN Security Council Move to Condemn Myanmar Coup," *Financial Express,* March 10, 2021, https://thefinancialexpress.com.bd/world /china-russia-stop-un-security-council-move-to-condemn-myanmar-coup -1615350622. Russia also opposed a resolution in 2007 on the situation in Myanmar proposed by the United Kingdom and the United States. "The Situation in Myanmar," 5,619th meeting, UN Security Council, S/PV.5619, January 12, 2007.

93. "Peace and Security in Africa (Zimbabwe)," 5,933rd meeting, UN Security Council, S/PV.5933, July 11, 2008.

94. Minami Funakoshi, Hugh Lawson, and Kannaki Deka, "Tracking Sanctions against Russia," *Reuters,* May 24, 2022, https://graphics.reuters.com/UKRAINE -CRISIS/SANCTIONS/byvrjenzmve/.

95. Letter dated July 10, 2020, from the president of the Security Council addressed to the secretary-general and the permanent representatives of the members of the Security Council, UN Security Council, July 13, 2020, S/2020/693, Annex XVIII. Russia's approach indirectly harks back to the Soviet legacy of socioeconomic rights that are affected by the use of sanctions.

96. Samuel Charap, "Russia, Syria and the Doctrine of Intervention," *Survival* 55, 1 (2013), pp. 35–36. "The Situation in the Middle East," 6,627th meeting, UN Security Council, October 4, 2011, S/PV.6627.

97. The Western members of the Council have refused to work on the text of the draft resolution (S/2012/547, Rev.2) submitted by the Russian delegation.

98. "The Situation in the Middle East," 7,785th meeting, UN Security Council, S/PV.7785, October 8, 2016.

99. Jutta Brunnee and Stephen J. Toope, *Legitimacy and Legality in International Law: An Interactional Account* (Cambridge University Press, 2010), p. 64.

100. Jean-Marc Coicaud, "Deconstructing International Legitimacy," in *Fault Lines of International Legitimacy,* edited by Hilary Charlesworth and Jean-Marc Coicaud (Cambridge University Press, 2010), pp. 29–50.

101. Krastev, "Russia vs Europe."

102. Ashford and Burrows, "Reality Check #4."

103. Nicu Popescu, "Why the EU Should Stop Waiting for the Godot of Russian Decline," European Council on Foreign Relations, March 5, 2021, https://ecfr.eu /article/why-the-eu-should-stop-waiting-for-the-godot-of-russian-decline/.

104. Matveeva, "Russia's Power Projection," p. 714.

105. Holmes and Krastev, *The Light That Failed*, p. 100.

106. See Sally Engle Merry, *Human Rights and Gender Violence: Translating International Law into Local Justice* (University of Chicago Press, 2006). See also Sally Engle

Merry, "Transnational Human Rights and Local Activism: Mapping the Middle," *American Anthropologist* 108, 1 (2006), pp. 38–51.

107. Saskia Brechenmacher and Thomas Carothers, "Examining Civil Society Legitimacy," Carnegie Endowment for International Peace, May 2, 2018, https://carnegieendowment.org/2018/05/02/examining-civil-society-legitimacy-pub-76211; Thomas Carothers and William Barndt, "Civil Society," *Foreign Policy* 117 (Winter 1999–2000), pp. 18–24, 26–29.

108. Engle Merry, "Transnational Human Rights and Local Activism."

109. Andrey Kortunov, "Multilateralism Needs Reinventing, Not Resurrecting," Russian International Affairs Council, December 9, 2020, https://russiancouncil.ru/en/analytics-and-comments/analytics/multilateralism-needs-reinventing-not-resurrecting; Jack Donnelly, "Human Rights: A New Standard of Civilization?," *International Affairs* 74, 1 (1998), pp. 1–23; Ratna Kapur, "Human Rights in the 21st Century: Taking a Walk on the Dark Side," *Sydney Law Review* 28, 4 (2006), pp. 665–87; Makau Mutua, "Human Rights in Africa: The Limited Promise of Liberalism," *African Studies Review* 51, 1 (2008), pp. 17–39; Simon Tisdall, "Tunisia Shows That Democracy Will Struggle If It Can't Deliver Prosperity," *The Guardian*, August 1, 2021, www.theguardian.com/commentisfree/2021/aug/01/tunisia-shows-that-democracy-will-struggle-if-it-cant-deliver-prosperity?CMP=Share_iOSApp_Other.

110. Tisdall, "Tunisia Shows That Democracy Will Struggle."

111. Kortunov, "Multilateralism Needs Reinventing, Not Resurrecting."

112. Key Messages, "Transforming Our World: Human Rights in the 2030 Agenda for Sustainable Development," Office of the Higher Commissioner for Human Rights, www.ohchr.org/Documents/Issues/MDGs/Post2015/HRAndPost2015.pdf.

113. Agnello and Ramanujam, "Recalibration of the Sustainable Development Agenda," p. 89.

114. "Voluntary National Review of the Progress Made in the Implementation of the 2030 Agenda for Sustainable Development," Russian Federation, 2020, https://sustainabledevelopment.un.org/content/documents/26959VNR_2020_Russia_Report_English.pdf; "2020–2030: Decade of Action in Russia—Challenges and Solutions," Coalition for Sustainable Development of Russia, Moscow, 2020, https://action4sd.org/wp-content/uploads/2020/09/Russia-VNR-report-2020.pdf.

115. "Zelensky: Only Diplomacy Can End Ukraine War," *BBC News*, May 21, 2022, https://www.bbc.com/news/world-europe-61535353.

FOUR

Same Blueprint, New Norms

Regional Organizations, Illiberalism, and the
Rise of Contested Global Governance

ALEXANDER COOLEY

It is no secret that, over the last decade, Beijing and Moscow have become more vocal in their questioning of the value of liberal democracy and universal political rights. Once defensive about their political values following the Soviet collapse, they are now emboldened geopolitically and actively seek to undermine liberalism as part of their challenge to U.S. global leadership and the normative fabric of the U.S.-led international order. Internationally, China and Russia have promoted new counternorms that oppose universal rights by invoking sovereignty and security, the notion of civilizational diversity, and the importance of "traditional values."[1] They have used their "sharp power" to target opinion-forming institutions and spheres within the West—such as the media, academia, and think-tanks—that have criticized their actions and normative practices.[2] Moreover, they have also engaged in a far broader and deeper revisionism that seeks to disrupt, contest, and ultimately transform the multilateral governance architectures on which much of the human rights regime relies.

Policymakers and scholars alike have been conditioned to view certain institutions, networks, and global actors as inherently supporting the liberal human rights framework.[3] For example, we tend to regard international bodies as upholders—at least officially—of human rights commitments, regional groupings such as the European Union (EU) and their supranational secretariats as committed to liberal standards and values, and nongovernment organizations (NGOs) as important agents and drivers of principled advocacy. But as Dan Nexon and I have recently argued more broadly, our system of global governance is already characterized by a mix of liberal and illiberal ordering norms, institutions, and actors.[4] Many of the intergovernmental organizations and institutional forms once associated with liberal global governance have been repurposed to support illiberal policies.

This chapter identifies and discusses three key transformations of this kind, led by China and Russia, in the contemporary architecture of global governance. First, these two states have led the way in founding new security and economic regional organizations—especially across Eurasia, South Asia, and Southeast Asia—whose mission values and practices clearly conflict with, and now actively undercut, basic liberal principles and international human rights protections. Second, Beijing and Moscow have also repurposed the operations and organizational culture of major existing international and regional organizations, watering down their work on human rights–related issues or influencing them to adopt viewpoints and declarations that align with authoritarian practices. Third, China and Russia have successfully recast many of the human rights–related NGOs as "security threats" and curtailed their activities, while replacing them in regional and international forums with government-sponsored nongovernmental organizations (GONGOs). Taken together, these transformations in global governance have both challenged the efficacy and impact of traditional advocacy networks and introduced new counternetworks that promote illiberal values at the global level.

Advocates and policymakers have been slow to recognize the sustained challenge that this counterordering entails. It is a challenge that will not simply fizzle out or depend on which country gains the upper hand in this era of renewed "Great Power Competition."[5] Rather, advocates of political liberalism and the human rights regime will have to step up and confront large swaths of illiberal order, now ensconced in the fabric of global governance, that were previously neglected or just diplomatically ignored.

The New Regional Organizations

Over the last two decades Moscow and Beijing have launched a series of new regional organizations in the economic, political, and security spheres. Membership of these bodies tends to be concentrated in the immediate neighborhood of Russia and China, namely Eurasia, South Asia, and Southeast Asia, and includes the Shanghai Cooperation Organization (SCO), the Collective Security Treaty Organization (CSTO), the Quadrilateral Cooperation and Co-ordination Mechanism (QCCM), the Eurasian Economic Union (EAEU), and the Asian Infrastructure Investment Bank (AIIB).[6] Of course, the BRICS— Brazil, Russia, India, China, and South Africa—could also be counted as a joint China-Russia initiative with the more global ambition of increasing their agenda-setting capacity on global governance-related issues and enabling their voices to be heard.[7]

Although these new regional organizations were initially dismissed as mar-ginal or even mimetic actors not worthy of international recognition or West-ern engagement, their proliferation has transformed the ecology of global gov-ernance. In the wake of the Soviet collapse, the overwhelming consensus among scholars of international relations and regionalism was that regional in-tegration helped to support democratic principles and practice.[8] As both the European Union and the North Atlantic Treaty Organization (NATO) pre-pared in the late 1990s for an unprecedented expansion of membership, they developed a set of criteria and body of legislation known as "membership con-ditionality" that all aspirant countries had to adopt before entry.[9] Many of these conditions sought to promote democratic practices and promote human rights, including the rights of minorities, media freedoms, and freedom of as-sociation. Scholars remained divided over whether EU or NATO conditional-ity actually worked through genuine socialization rather than the material incentives of membership, but few expressed doubts at the time that expansion and accession would help to lock in and institutionalize democratic norms and practices.[10]

However, the last two decades have challenged the assumption that region-alism or more regional integration would inherently promote democratic val-ues and political rights, especially in non-Western settings. The SCO, CSTO, EAEU, and similar organizations appear to mimic the form of Western counterparts such as the Organization for Security and Co-operation in Eu-rope (OSCE) or the EU, but they have different practices and common norms.[11] New research and scholarship, particularly into the dynamics of regional organ-izations in the former Soviet space, have explored how regional organizations and intergovernmentalism can be used by governments to facilitate authori-tarian learning and reciprocity about undemocratic practices. The key point in much of this literature is to draw attention to the needs of authoritarian regimes. Rather than using regional organizations to facilitate gains in overall welfare for their countries' economies or particular economic sectors—such as those that result from removing barriers to trade and creating a common

economic space—autocrats use such bodies to secure themselves from domestic and external threats and the erosion of their authority, and at times
to advance authoritarian leaders elsewhere. Regime security trumps pareto-
maximizing economic agreements.[12] Regionalism not only offers material
pathways—such as facilitating side payments and the provision of public goods
from richer authoritarians to smaller states—in return for compliance, but also
creates new normative contexts that justify and promote authoritarianism.[13]
Member states of authoritarian-leaning organizations, in turn, can use regionalism and invoke regional solidarity as a basis for rejecting universal norms
that are politically disruptive, and for upholding member state sovereignty. On
point, in early January 2022, Russia dispatched troops to Kazakhstan under
the CSTO intervention mechanism at the request of Kazakhstan's president,
Kassym-Jomart Tokayev.[14] Tokayev faced mass antigovernment street protests
and an attempted power grab by allies linked to former president Nursultan
Nazarbayev; the CSTO's intervention signaled to the Kazakh security services
that Moscow backed the embattled Kazakh president and his heavy-handed
crackdown that resulted in 225 deaths and thousands of arrests.[15]

The SCO has facilitated China's security agenda, as seen most obviously
in its adoption of the Chinese-inspired security norm of combating the "three
evils" of separatism, terrorism, and extremism.[16] At the same time, as Tom Ambrosio has shown, the organization officially invokes a common norm of the
so-called Shanghai Spirit, which critiques universal understandings of political community (such as liberal democracy), promotes civilizational diversity
and respect for member state sovereignty, and calls for the democratization of
international relations—understood as a retrenchment in the role of the United
States and its liberal agenda.[17] The SCO has also actively promoted, under the
auspices of its Regional Anti-Terrorism Structure, a number of regional security practices that contravene human rights norms, including maintaining
common blacklists of extreme organizations and individuals that also ensnare
political opponents and dissidents. Not surprisingly, the United Nations Rapporteur on Human Rights and Terrorism expressed concern about the criteria
used in these listing practices and the lack of clear criteria by which individuals or groups could challenge their status or de-list themselves.[18]

In the name of security, the SCO also appears to have authorized new
regional-level legal practices and violations of international human rights obligations. Take the SCO's Anti-Terrorism Treaty, established in 2009. In combating the "three evils" denoted above, the treaty allows for suspects to be
transferred from the custody of one member state to another with minimum

evidence, denies the accused a political asylum hearing, and permits member states to "dispatch their agents to the territory" of a fellow member state for up to thirty days when conducting a criminal investigation.[19] Legal experts with the OSCE have criticized the vague and subjective designation of what constitutes "extremism" or "separatism," while noting that the convention does not give any guidance or procedures on how its provisions should be enforced in accordance with existing human rights frameworks or legal protections.[20] According to several human rights organizations, the SCO security treaty has been used to justify a number of politically motivated political renditions and abductions, including sending Central Asian dissidents back to their home countries and transferring Uyghurs and Falun Gong members from Russia and Central Asia to China.[21] These new regional laws seem to conflict openly with international obligations. For example, Kazakhstani prosecutors cited the SCO accords to justify the extradition of twenty-nine political asylum seekers to Uzbekistan, a country notorious for using torture. But a subsequent communication from the UN Committee Against Torture (CAT) found that the Kazakh authorities had violated the CAT's nonrefoulement obligation.[22]

In addition to offering a regional space and legal context to promote illiberal practices among host governments, the cooperative institutions of these regional organizations also appear to be aiding and abetting illiberal practices. One example is the Inter-Parliamentary Assembly of the Russian-led Commonwealth of Independent States (CIS), charged with fostering legal harmonization among member states. Using antiplagiarism software that compares original and disseminated texts, researchers found that the regional body has played a critical role in disseminating to the smaller Central Asian states a range of legislation adopted by the Russian Federation that restricts peaceful assembly, curtails the activities of NGOs, and broadly defines the activities and financing of terrorism and extremism.[23] Overall, the authors find that Kyrgyzstan and Tajikistan were especially likely to import whole tracts of legislation of Russian law into their own criminal codes. For example, 47 percent of Kyrgyzstan's Supreme Council's laws and 48 percent of laws passed by Tajikistan's legislative body directly copied the Russian version. The authors conclude that "Russia acts as an 'authoritarian gravity centre' defining the policy agenda and facilitating cooperation to harmonize laws through the CIS-IPA [Commonwealth of Independent States-Interparliamentary Assembly]." Unlike the international parliamentary assemblies of established democratic membership organizations, that of the CIS appears to be functioning as an agent of illiberal convergence.

Repurposing International Organizations

Beyond just establishing new regional organizations with new norms and practices that run counter to human rights standards, Beijing and Moscow are more assertively setting agendas and trying to influence the activities of existing international bodies. The COVID-19 pandemic drew attention to how Beijing successfully tipped the outcome of the World Health Organization's (WHO's) prior leadership contest toward its preferred candidate, while the WHO on multiple occasions backed off from criticizing China's own reaction to the pandemic and its information-sharing practices. China itself leads four of the UN's fifteen bodies and exerts increasing influence in nearly all of them.[24]

The United Nations Human Rights Council (UNHRC) has been an arena for these new geopolitical battles over human rights norms and agendas. Russia has been increasingly involved in transnational efforts to push back on the Lesbian, Gay, Bisexual, Transgender, Queer (LGBTQ) agenda—often in cooperation with U.S.-based evangelical movements, as explored in chapter 7 by Melani McAlister—under the guise of promoting "religious freedom" or defending traditional values. For example, the body voted in 2009 for the Russian-led effort to promote "traditional values" and in 2014 for another Russian-sponsored initiative designed to "protect the family," a clear affront to the recognition of LGBTQ rights.

In July 2019, the UNHRC revealed the extent of Beijing's new-found influence. A group of twenty-two countries drafted a letter to the UN High Commissioner for Human Rights accusing China of using its internment camp network to conduct "mass arbitrary detentions and related violations" and destroy the Uyghurs' indigenous culture and religious way of life;[25] the signatories comprised core countries and groupings usually associated with the liberal international community including the United Kingdom, the EU, the Nordic countries, Japan, Australia, and New Zealand. However, just a few weeks later, China countered by mobilizing thirty-seven countries—mostly drawn from across the Middle East, Africa, Southeast Asia, and Eurasia—to sign a letter stating: "Faced with the grave challenge of terrorism and extremism, China has undertaken a series of counter-terrorism and de-radicalization measures in Xinjiang, including setting up vocational education and training centers."[26] Their letter also commended Beijing for "its remarkable achievements in the field of human rights" and expressed appreciation for "China's commitment to openness and transparency."[27] United Nations Secretary General António Guterres was himself criticized by human rights watchdogs for his reluctance to criticize the detention centers.[28]

Even several of the international organizations associated with strong mandates promoting human rights in the immediate post–Cold War era have seemingly curtailed their activity related to human rights and norms, or have witnessed new internal divisions that have eroded unanimity and consensus on such issues. Consider the evolution of the OSCE, the post–Cold War successor to the détente-era Conference on Security and Co-operation in Europe (CSCE).[29] Comprising all of the countries of Europe and the former Soviet Union, the OSCE was founded with the "human dimension," which embodied the promotion of liberal democratic values and norms, as one of its central pillars. In the 1990s, it was involved in postconflict reconciliation and state-building in areas such as the Balkans and the Caucasus, while it actively promoted minority rights and freedom of expression across the postcommunist region. However, as Russia and many of the former Soviet states have openly moved to criticize and then reject liberal democratic values, the OSCE's human dimension has become scrutinized and its projects curtailed or defunded. Although the bureaucracy still tries to maneuver against such backlash among member countries, the organization's human dimension portfolio has become very sparse indeed, focusing mostly on countering human trafficking.

This is clear, for example, in the area of election monitoring. After the OSCE's election observation body, the Office for Democratic Institutions and Human Rights (ODIHR), criticized the quality of nearly every national election in Eurasia in the 1990s and early 2000s, Russia, along with Belarus and the Central Asian states, proposed a number of "reforms" to gut its autonomy and ability to criticize and conduct substantial long-term monitoring missions.[30] In addition, the field of election monitoring became crowded and its findings contested, as other private and public groups also began to monitor elections, with methods that were less rigorous and findings that were more supportive of authoritarian governments.[31] Indeed, many of these new observation teams come from regional organizations such as the SCO or the CIS. By 2020 the ODIHR itself appeared marginalized in its Election-Day assessments. For example, when the OSCE heavily criticized the election of Tokayev, the interim president of Kazakhstan in 2019, he responded by dismissing the OSCE as "just one of the international organisations [monitoring the vote]," and saying that "we should not focus on the assessment of this particular organisation."[32]

Even the European Union has struggled to retain consensus on the human rights record, especially regarding China. Those smaller European states that have actively courted Chinese investment, especially through the Belt and Road Initiative, appear more reluctant to issue public condemnatory statements on this issue. For example, in June 2017 Greece blocked a statement condemning

China's human rights practices, the first time, according to human rights watchdogs, that the EU has failed to issue a statement at the UNHRC.[33] The Greek foreign minister commented that the statement amounted to "unconstructive criticism of China;" the Greek government had just secured a large investment by a Chinese logistics company to upgrade the port of Piraeus. Similarly, in April 2021 Hungary blocked a planned EU statement criticizing Hong Kong's new security law, in solidarity with the United Kingdom and the United States—a move that German foreign minister Heiko Maas described as "absolutely incomprehensible."[34] After a phone call with Hungarian prime minister Viktor Orbán, Chinese president Xi Jinping lauded the controversial Hungarian leader for "safeguarding overall China-European relations."

True, a plausible case can be made that, to some extent, the United Nations has always been an arena for competing normative agendas. And despite its problems on China-related issues, the European Union has achieved consensus on maintaining sanctions on Russia following the annexation of Crimea, despite forecasts that European unity might not withstand Moscow's divide-and-rule tactics. But as a result of these geopolitical shifts, the existing multilateral organizations that we have assumed lie at the core of the international human rights regime are far more contested now than in the 1990s.

From NGOs to GONGOs

The third recent key transformation has been a shift in the types of "nonstate" actors operating transnationally. While the 1990s saw a global explosion in the number of NGOs and human rights defenders, in the following two decades, with active intervention by Moscow and Beijing, NGOs worldwide suffered a wave of new restrictions on their activities, registration, and sources of funding.[35] In the case of the Russian Federation, Moscow directly criminalized membership of a series of Western-supported "undesirable organizations."[36] The response has been the widespread rise of government-supported NGOs. Driven by savvy regimes that seek to preserve the appearance of civil society but quell actual political opposition, these GONGOs help shape narratives about the state's responsiveness to public policy by displacing civil society actors. They increasingly interface with external actors such as international organizations, donors, and the media, and even consume valuable time and resources in global spaces once reserved for NGOs, such as the OSCE's annual Human Dimension Implementation Meetings (HDIMs) in Warsaw.

GONGOs do not only present and defend viewpoints endorsed by governments, their presence overseas as emissaries of "civil society" crowds international forums designed as civil society dialogues and fuels the transnational contestation about ideas of what constitutes acceptable human rights practices and standards. These international activities appear to have intensified in recent years. Following its annexation of Crimea, Russia has flooded international events with GONGOs, such as the Foundation for Historical Perspective or Diaspora of Bulgarians in Crimea, to dispute Ukrainian-led criticisms of the legality of the annexation, the status of minority rights, and the clampdown on media freedoms enacted by the Kremlin.[37] Such vocal activists are part of a broad network of state-funded "Russian World" actors, foundations, and media and cultural groups designed to shape overseas public opinion about Russian actions within the countries of the post-Soviet states and even the West itself.[38] Similarly, Central Asian governments—especially Tajikistan's—have been criticized for "taking up space" at the OSCE's HDIM as well as actually intimidating human rights defenders, exiles, and dissidents attending or speaking at the conference in Warsaw.[39]

Within the UN's Universal Periodic Review process, China and Russia have sought to resurrect and ally with the Like-Minded Group (LMG), comprising fifty-two states of the developing world, to push back on excessive involvement by independent NGOs and promote the uncritical statements made by GONGOs in support of governments during their Universal Periodic Review. In addition, at various UN meetings and in preparation for them, China has used GONGOs to systematically harass members of civil society groups critical of Chinese human rights policies toward the Uyghurs, Tibet, or Hong Kong.[40] As Human Rights Watch notes in its report on China's subversion of the UN human rights mechanism, UN officials and staffers have responded only weakly to these intimidation tactics as China's influence within the UN continues to grow.

A World of Contested and Contending Transnational Networks

During the 1990s, scholars and policymakers identified transnational activist networks as an important phenomenon in international relations, allowing NGOs and global civil society to spread universal values via networks of like-minded allies and advocates. The liberal transnational network structure—premised both on American primacy and the uncontested hegemony of liberal norms in global governance—was also key to understanding how activism operated to mobilize allies and name and shame recalcitrant states. In their seminal book on transnational activist networks, Margaret Keck and Kathryn

Sikkink argued that the flexible structure of the network empowered activists to pressure human rights and norms violators by allowing activists to "boomerang," forging tactical coalitions with like-minded actors in international and regional organizations, other NGOs, and influential allied states in a manner that would rebound on governments and pressure them to uphold international norms such as human rights treaty commitments.[41] Even at the time, this influential theory of change was analytically challenged. Some scholars pointed to the material motivations driving the transnational sector,[42] while others astutely observed that individual gatekeepers at international organizations played an important role in deciding which rights-related issues were worthy of an international campaign.[43]

Beyond these critiques, the geopolitical trends identified in this chapter—the establishment of new regional organizations, the refashioning of traditionally liberal bodies, and the rise of GONGOs at the expense of NGOs—are transforming the ecology of international order and altering how such transnationalism operates in practice. In short, Chinese and Russian global governance is challenging and complicating the "boomerang" process once used by activists to support liberal causes, as well as introducing new transnational counternetworks that seek—much like their liberal counterparts—to disseminate norms and values across borders, but in this case illiberal ones.

Consider how such a boomerang effect might function in a situation where the target state, engaged in blatant illiberal practices such as gross human rights violations, also has allies throughout the global governance chain, including across other states, in the leadership of international and regional organizations, and among sympathetic transnational actors that support or justify their illiberal practices. "Boomeranging" would itself become competitive, as both liberal activists and illiberal governments would seek to mobilize transnational allies in support of their specific positions. Such a dynamic appears to characterize the current campaign surrounding Chinese policies in Xinjiang.

In response to the activism of transnational Uygur rights groups and their Western supporters, China has enlisted state allies to support its position (as evidenced at the HCR) and has aggressively sought to mobilize commercial allies in public opposition to a related campaign to ban the use of Xinjiang-produced cotton. In 2019 Chinese state media banned the showing of National Basketball Association (NBA) games in response to critical comments about Xinjiang made by the general manager of the Houston Rockets, while the Chinese market remains a key source of revenue for NBA players and celebrities with ties to Chinese clothing manufacturers.[44] And the recent public embrace of Xinjiang cotton by the Japanese manufacturer Muji suggests that China's significant market power and leverage have become critical sources of support for undercutting the Xinjiang boycott globally.[45]

At the same time, new transnational networks that promote illiberal values are emerging wholesale. Just like their original liberal counterparts, these networks are united in their principles (opposing universal liberalism) and seek to link activists, social groups (religious, government-sponsored youth groups and ethnonational organizations), regional organizations, and allied state governments. Consider, for instance, the evolution and current activities of the World Congress of Families (WCF) (also discussed in Melani McAlister's chapter). The WCF was initially founded in the 1990s in the United States by two organizations of the Christian right, but has since expanded and globalized its work. For the last decade, it has been especially involved in the postcommunist space and has received funding and political support from Eurasian oligarchs and government-affiliated groups.[46] It presents itself as a transnational counter to the Soros-backed Open Society and holds annual plenary conferences that seek to promote an antiliberal advocacy including an agenda that is anti-immigration, anti-LGBTQ, antireproductive rights, and "anti-globalist." The sessions held in Budapest, Hungary, and Chisinau, Moldova (both in 2018), also featured laudatory keynote speeches delivered by the host state's head of government. The WCF also actively liaises with conservative governments and campaigns for its agenda in institutions such as the HCR.

Conclusions and Policy Recommendations

A world in which we can no longer assume that networks of global governance will function to support the human rights regime requires some bold action on behalf of governments, human rights defenders, and foundations. I propose the following four approaches:

1. Pursue comprehensive engagement with new regional bodies. Rather than debating the merits of "limited engagement" with these new regional organizations, Western officials should consider the merits of comprehensive engagement. Only engaging with groups like the SCO or CSTO about specific issues (e.g., the security situation in Afghanistan) confers both status and legitimacy on these new bodies but does nothing to challenge either their dissemination of counternorms or their counterordering activities. In other words, discussion of normative issues should not be bypassed but form part of any efforts to establish dialogues and cooperation. Advocates of the liberal order should press leaders from regional organizations, in the context of interorganizational engagement, to show how certain practices (political asylum protections, election observation standards) align with international treaty commitments and best practices. Indeed, rather than refusing to engage with non-Western regional organizations such as the SCO or the EAEU, thereby allowing the expansion of illiberal networking, Western groups such as the EU or NATO should embrace comprehensive engagement with their illiberal counterparts.

2. Be prepared to pick sides domestically. The rise of new illiberal transnational networks mirrors the rise of intense political polarization in the United States and Poland and other countries where liberal and illiberal norms are now openly pitted against each other in intense new culture wars with important social policy ramifications. As a result, viewing international policy or global governance as a separate sphere, detached from domestic politics, is no longer viable. Administrations that seek to promote human rights norms and protections must actively support and network with like-minded governments and political parties in the context of routine diplomacy, while drawing attention to illiberal political platforms and practices.

3. Human rights donors should rescale globally. This recommendation flows from the nature of this new transnational contestation. It is almost a mantra that support for human rights defenders should be channeled to local organizations, activists, and legal offices; and this should remain an important priority of major human rights work and international funders. However, it is no longer possible to ignore the transnational and global dimensions in which this backlash against human rights norms is taking place. The networking of far-right movements that share illiberal values presents a fundamental challenge to the values and advocacy strategies of human rights defenders. Funders should consider providing more support for the investigation of these transnational links, including their funding ties, their elite networks, and their media and information campaigns; and they should support investigative journalism into their evolution and international conferences and meetings.

4. Reforming the UNHRC. Finally, steps should be taken to reform the UNHRC to make it less susceptible to capture by authoritarians. Membership eligibility should be tightened to exclude countries under active UN sanction, and proposed nominations should be subjected to a period of public discussion, involving expert and NGO testimony, which would include a public review of the human rights record of candidate countries prior to their election. Membership should be made conditional on avoiding interference in the activities of NGOs and civil society engaged with the body.

Notes

1. Alexander Cooley, "Authoritarianism Goes Global: Countering Democratic Norms," *Journal of Democracy* 26, 3 (2015), pp, 49–63.

2. Christopher Walker, "What Is 'Sharp Power'?," *Journal of Democracy* 29, 3 (2018), pp. 9–23.

3. For example, see Thomas Risse and Kathryn Sikkink, "The Socialization of International Human Rights Norms," in *The Power of Human Rights: International Norms and Domestic Change*, edited by Thomas Risse and Kathryn Sikkink (Cambridge University Press, 1999), pp. 1–38; and Thomas Pegram, "Diffusion across Political Systems: The Global Spread of National Human Rights Institutions," *Human Rights Quarterly* 32 (2010), pp. 729–60. For a critique of such initial optimistic post–Cold War accounts, see Stephen Hopgood, Jack Snyder, and Leslie Vinjamuri (eds.), *Human Rights Futures* (Cambridge University Press, 2017).

4. Alexander Cooley and Daniel Nexon, "The Illiberal Tide: Why the International Order Is Tilting towards Autocracy," *Foreign Affairs*, March 26, 2021, www .foreignaffairs.com/articles/united-states/2021-03-26/illiberal-tide.

5. Daniel Nexon, "Against Great Power Competition," *Foreign Affairs*, February 15, 2021, www.foreignaffairs.com/articles/united-states/2021-02-15/against-great-power -competition.

6. Alexander Cooley and Daniel Nexon, *Exit from Hegemony: The Unraveling of the American Global Order* (Oxford University Press, 2020), ch. 4.

7. Cynthia A. Roberts, Leslie Elliott Armijo, and Saori N. Katada, *The BRICS and Collective Financial Statecraft* (Oxford University Press, 2018).

8. See Jon Pevehouse, *Democracy from Above: Regional Organizations and Democratization* (Cambridge University Press, 2005); and Jon Pevehouse, "With a Little Help from My Friends? Regional Organizations and the Consolidation of Democracy," *American Journal of Political Science* 46, 3 (2002), pp. 611–26.

9. On EU and NATO conditionality and its impact on domestic politics, see Milada Vachudova, *Europe Undivided: Democracy, Leverage, and Integration after Communism* (Oxford University Press, 2005).

10. Frank Schimmelfennig and Ulrich Sedelmeier, "Governance by Conditionality: EU Rule Transfer to the Candidate Countries of Central and Eastern Europe," *Journal of European Public Policy* 11, 4 (2004), pp. 661–79; Alexandra Gheciu, *NATO in the "New Europe": The Politics of International Socialization after the Cold War* (Stanford University Press, 2005); and Judith Kelley, "International Actors on the Domestic Scene: Membership Conditionality and Socialization by International Institutions," *International Organization* 58, 3 (2004), pp. 425–57.

11. David Lewis, "Who's Socialising Whom? Regional Organisations and Contested Norms in Central Asia," *Europe-Asia Studies* 64, 7 (2012), pp. 1219–37.

12. On the peculiar logic of regional integration and patrimonial regimes, see Kathleen Collins, "Economic and Security Regionalism among Patrimonial Authoritarian Regimes: The Case of Central Asia," *Europe-Asia Studies* 61, 2 (2009), pp. 249–81.

13. See especially, Alexander Libman and Anastassia Obydenkova, "Regional International Organizations as a Strategy of Autocracy: The Eurasian Economic Union and Russian Foreign Policy," *International Affairs* 94, 5 (2018), pp. 1037–58; and Alexander Libman and Anastassia Obydenkova, "Understanding Authoritarian Regionalism," *Journal of Democracy* 29, 4 (2018), pp. 151–65.

14. Alexander Cooley, "Kazakhstan Called for Assistance. Why Did Russia Dispatch Troops so Quickly?" *Washington Post,* January 9, 2022, https://www.washingtonpost.com/politics/2022/01/09/kazakhstan-called-assistance-why-did-russia-dispatch-troops-so-quickly/.

15. Kate Mallinson, "Tokayev Faces Double Challenge in Kazakhstan," Chatham House, January 14, 2022, https://www.chathamhouse.org/2022/01/tokayev-faces-double-challenge-troubled-kazakhstan.

16. Stephen Aris, "The Shanghai Cooperation Organisation:'Tackling the Three Evils': A Regional Response to Non-Traditional Security Challenges or an Anti-Western Bloc?," *Europe-Asia Studies* 61, 3 (2009), pp. 457–82.

17. Thomas Ambrosio, "Catching the 'Shanghai Spirit': How the Shanghai Cooperation Organization Promotes Authoritarian Norms in Central Asia," *Europe-Asia Studies* 60, 8 (2008), pp. 1321–44.

18. OHCHR, UN Human Rights Council, 10th Session. A/HRC/10/3 4 February 2009, www2.ohchr.org/english/issues/terrorism/rapporteur/docs/A.HRC.10.3.pdf; para. 35.

19. Available at Shanghai Cooperation Organization Secretariat, "Convention of the Shanghai Cooperation Organisation Against Terrorism," March 2009, http://eng.sectsco.org/documents/.

20. Organisation for Security and Co-operation in Europe (OSCE), "Note on the Shanghai Convention on Combatting Terrorism, Separatism and Extremism," Office for Democratic Institutions and Human Rights, September 21, 2020, www.osce.org/files/f/documents/e/8/467697.pdf.

21. See International Federation for Human Rights (FIDH), "Shanghai Cooperation Organisation: A Vehicle for Human Rights Violations," 2012, www.fidh.org/IMG/pdf/sco_report.pdf; "Counter-Terrorism and Human Rights: The Impact of the Shanghai Cooperation Organization," Human Rights in China, March 2011, www.hrichina.org/en/search/site/SCO%20human%20rights.

22. Human Rights Watch, "Kazakhstan: Don't Extradite Uzbeks to Torture," June 7, 2011, www.hrw.org/news/2011/06/07/kazakhstan-dont-extradite-uzbeks-torture.

23. Edward Lemon and Oleg Antonov, "Authoritarian Legal Harmonization in the Post-Soviet Space," *Democratization* 27, 7 (2020), pp. 1221–39.

24. Kristine Lee, "It's Not Just the WHO: How China Is Moving on the Whole U.N.," *Politico*, April 5, 2020, www.politico.com/news/magazine/2020/04/15/its-not-just-the-who-how-china-is-moving-on-the-whole-un-189029; and Courtney J. Fung and Shing-Hon Lam, "China Already Leads 4 of the 15 UN Specialized Agencies and Is Aiming for a 5th," *Washington Post*, March 3, 2020, www.washingtonpost.com/politics/2020/03/03/china-already-leads-4-15-un-specialized-agencies-is-aiming-5th/.

25. "22 Countries Sign Letter Calling on China to Close Xinjiang Uyghur Camps," *CNN,* July 11, 2019, www.cnn.com/2019/07/11/asia/xinjiang-uyghur-un-letter-intl -hnk.

26. Joyce Huang, "UN Human Rights Council Divided over China's Xinjiang Policies," *VOA News*, July 17, 2019, www.voanews.com/east-asia-pacific/un-human -rights-council-divided-over-chinas-xinjiang-policies.

27. UN Human Rights Council, 41st Session, August 9, 2019, A/HRC/41/G/17, https://ap.ohchr.org/Documents/E/HRC/c_gov/A_HRC_41_G_17.DOCX.

28. Human Rights Watch, "UN Chief Should Denounce China's Abuses in Xinjiang," September 17, 2019, www.hrw.org/news/2019/09/17/un-chief-should-denounce -chinas-abuses-xinjiang.

29. Rick Fawn, *International Organizations and Internal Conditionality* (London: Palgrave Macmillan, 2013).

30. Rick Fawn, "Battle over the Box: International Election Observation Missions, Political Competition and Retrenchment in the Post-Soviet Space," *International Affairs* 82, 6 (2006), pp. 1133–53.

31. Judith Kelley, "The More the Merrier? The Effects of Having Multiple International Election Monitoring Organizations," *Perspectives on Politics* (February 12, 2009), pp. 59–64.

32. "Nazarbayev's Hand-Picked Successor Tokayev Elected Kazakh President," Reuters, June 10, 2019, www.reuters.com/article/us-kazakhstan-election/nazarbayevs -handpicked-successor-tokayev-elected-kazakh-president-idUSKCN1TB0JA.

33. "Greece Blocks EU Statement on China Human Rights at the UN," Reuters, June 18, 2017, www.reuters.com/article/us-eu-un-rights/greece-blocks-eu-statement-on -china-human-rights-at-u-n-idUSKBN1990FP.

34. Finbarr Bermingham, "Germany 'Has All the Tools' to Whip Hungary into Line on Hong Kong, but Does It Really Want To?," *South China Morning Post*, May 12, 2021, www.scmp.com/news/china/diplomacy/article/3133097/germany-has-all-tools -whip-hungary-line-hong-kong-does-it.

35. See Patricia Bromley, Evan Schofer, and Wesley Longhofer, "Contentions over World Culture: The Rise of Legal Restrictions on Foreign Funding to NGOs, 1994–2015," *Social Forces* 99, 1 (2020), pp. 281–304; and Darin Christensen and Jeremy M. Weinstein, "Defunding Dissent: Restrictions on Aid to NGOs," *Journal of Democracy* 24, 2 (2013), pp. 77–91.

36. Sergei Davidis, "Russia's 'Undesirable Organization' Law Marks a New Level of Repression," *Wilson Center* (blog), April 12, 2019, https://www.wilsoncenter.org /blog-post/russias-undesirable-organization-law-marks-new-level-repression.

37. See Orysia Lutsevych, "Agents of the Russian World: Proxy Groups in the Contested Neighborhood," Chatham House, April 2016, www.chathamhouse.org/sites /default/files/publications/research/2016-04-14-agents-russian-world-lutsevych -embargoed.pdf; Ron Synovitz, "Attack of the GONGOs: Government Organized NGOs Attack Warsaw Meeting," *RFE/RL*, September 19, 2019, www.rferl.org/a/attack -of-the-gongos-government-organized-ngos-flood-warsaw-meeting/30191944.html.

38. Lutsevych, "Agents of the Russian World."

39. Synovitz, "Attack of the GONGOs."

40. Rana Siu Inboden, "China at the UN; Choking Civil Society," *Journal of Democracy* 32, 3 (July 2021), pp. 124–35; Human Rights Watch, *The Costs of International Advocacy: China's Interference in United Nations Human Rights Mechanisms* (New York, 2017), www.hrw.org/sites/default/files/report_pdf/chinaun0917_web.pdf.

41. Margaret E. Keck and Kathryn Sikkink, *Activists beyond Borders* (Cornell University Press, 1998).

42. Alexander Cooley and James Ron, "The NGO Scramble: Organizational Insecurity and the Political Economy of Transnational Action," *International Security* 27, 1 (2002), pp. 5–39; and Clifford Bob, "Merchants of Morality," *Foreign Policy* (2002), pp. 36–45.

43. Charli Carpenter, "Setting the Advocacy Agenda: Theorizing Issue Emergence and Nonemergence in Transnational Advocacy Networks," *International Studies Quarterly* 51, 1 (2007), pp. 99–120.

44. Alexander Stevenson, "China's Forced Labor Backlash Threatens to Put NBA in Unwanted Spotlight," *New York Times,* April 12, 2021, www.nytimes.com/2021/04/09/business/china-nba-anta-xinjiang.html.

45. Megumi Fujikawa, "Japan's Muji Appeals to China by Advertising Use of Xinjiang Cotton," *Wall Street Journal,* May 11, 2021, www.wsj.com/articles/japans-muji-appeals-to-china-by-advertising-use-of-xinjiang-cotton-11620692294.

46. See Kristina Stoeckl, "The Rise of the Russian Christian Right: The Case of the World Congress of Families," *Religion, State and Society* 48, 4 (2020), pp. 223–38.

FIVE

Human Rights, Pandemics, and the Infrastructure of Human Rights Institutions

RANA MOUSTAFA

Multilateralism is the foundation for the promotion and protection of human rights. Reflected in the founding of the United Nations (UN),[1] the articulation and defense of human rights norms and claims are deeply embedded in the evolution of the post–World War II multilateral institutional world order, from international bodies dedicated to human rights themselves to others charged with health, and economic growth and development.

Despite the broad attention given to human rights across these institutions, states have remained reluctant to cede power or resources to fulfill these mandates, and have also often underfunded human rights bodies. The result has been that despite the lofty notions of human rights built into multilateral charters, the bodies charged with enforcing them have failed to meet expectations and mandates. This in turn has undermined the legitimacy of the human rights institutions (HRIs) and weakened multilateralism.

The decade before COVID-19 witnessed criticism of HRIs as a result of their failure to end, or even to some degree prevent serious violations of human rights in many parts of the world, particularly Syria, Myanmar, and Yemen.[2] The United States, under Donald Trump, withdrew from the UN Human Rights Council (UNHRC). Moreover, the governments of Venezuela under Hugo Chávez and Brazil under Dilma Rousseff rhetorically attacked the Inter-American Commission on Human Rights (IACHR) and the Inter-American Court of Human Rights (IACtHR), while Russia withheld funding from the Council of Europe (CoE), claiming that the institutions and norms were threats to culture, local norms, and national sovereignty.

In that context, COVID-19 had unprecedented implications for human rights worldwide, adding to preexisting skepticism of—and even assaults on—the authority and capacity of the HRIs to respond to those implications. In a press release in August 2020, the chairpersons of the ten UN treaty bodies warned that their work was at risk due to lack of funding.[3] This paralleled rising concern about the inability of HRIs to respond to vaccine nationalism, which undermines global efforts to end the pandemic. The UN Independent Expert on the Promotion of a Democratic and Equitable International Order has conducted a study examining the obstacles to an effective multilateral response to this situation.[4]

Nevertheless, states have renewed their commitment to multilateralism on different occasions during the pandemic, most notably in commemorating the seventy-fifth anniversary of the UN.[5] Despite the preexisting challenges, perhaps the pandemic and the pressures it has exposed can provide lessons for reconsidering and reconfiguring human rights institutions and procedures. This chapter starts by exploring the human rights implications of pandemics in general and the new challenges brought by COVID-19, before considering the specific capacity of the HRIs to respond to these challenges. The final section offers a set of recommendations for improving the functioning of these institutions now and in future pandemics.

Human Rights and Pandemics

COVID-19 is "a human crisis that is fast becoming a human rights crisis," warned UN Secretary-General António Guterres in April 2020, amid increasing claims that various human rights were being negatively affected by state responses.[6] But the adverse effects of pandemics on human rights are not new: states' responses to previous pandemics have always raised concern over their implications for human rights.

Conventional wisdom has long held that responding to public health emergencies through measures such as quarantine, isolation, travel restrictions, assembly restrictions, and surveillance may require limiting certain rights. The 1966 International Covenant on Civil and Political Rights (ICCPR) allows states to limit certain rights to take the necessary measures to protect public health.[7] The same understanding applies to the 1966 International Covenant on Economic, Social and Cultural Rights (ICESCR),[8] and to regional human rights instruments.[9]

However, the right of states to impose such limitations is not absolute. It is generally accepted that they shall be prescribed by law and be nondiscriminatory. It is also obligatory that limitations are imposed to pursue a legitimate aim (in this case, the protection of public health) and should be necessary and proportionate, meaning that a "state shall use no more restrictive means than are required" to secure public health.[10]

If the public health emergency rises to the level of threatening "the life of the nation and its existence," it is generally accepted that states may take measures derogating from their human rights obligations, thus suspending the enjoyment of certain rights.[11] Even so, the right to derogate from human rights is not absolute. States, in the first place, cannot derogate from nonderogable rights.[12] Here, suspension should be temporary and only imposed to the extent strictly required by the exigencies of protecting public health. Other states should be notified of derogations under the relevant provisions in the human rights conventions.

Nevertheless, successive public health emergencies have raised concerns regarding states' compliance with these limitations on their power. Responses to the human immunodeficiency virus/acquired immunodeficiency syndrome (HIV/AIDS) crisis (in the 1980s) were notorious for being discriminatory against HIV/AIDS sufferers. States isolated and quarantined those who tested positive for AIDS, even though those measures were seen as medically unnecessary because AIDS cannot spread through simple proximity.[13] The counterproductivity of those measures drew attention to the necessity of adopting a human rights–based approach to responses to health crises. Jonathan Mann, the former head of the Global Program on AIDS run by the World Health Organization (WHO) and the father of the human rights–based approach to health, made the following argument:

> As respect for human rights and dignity is a sine qua non for promoting and protecting human well-being . . . the human rights framework offers public health a more coherent, comprehensive, and practical framework for analysis and action on the societal root causes of vulnerability to HIV/AIDS than any framework inherited from traditional public health or biomedical science.[14]

The HIV/AIDS pandemic confirmed that human rights are an integral component of the response to infectious diseases.[15] Nonetheless, states still adopt measures against those living with HIV/AIDS that contravene the limitations framework of international human rights law.[16]

Measures adopted by states responding to Severe Acute Respiratory Syndrome (SARS) in 2002 and 2003 raised similar concerns.[17] As a result, the WHO revised its International Health Regulations in 2005 to include a number of provisions stressing the necessity of adopting a human rights–based approach to responses to infectious diseases.[18] Article 3(1) expressly states that "the implementation of these Regulations shall be with full respect for the dignity, human rights and fundamental freedoms of persons." However, ensuing public health emergencies on tuberculosis, swine flu, and Ebola witnessed to varying degrees measures that were again considered to be in violation of the human rights limitation and derogations framework.[19]

Given the history and the recognition of the risk to human rights posed by responses to public health emergencies, did COVID-19 bring any new challenges to civil, political, economic, cultural, or social rights?

Human Rights in the COVID-19 Pandemic

COVID-19 is no different from previous pandemics in triggering excessive, disproportionate, and even illegitimate state measures. Nevertheless, it has brought new challenges to the human rights system, primarily stemming from the implications of its unprecedented geographical spread and global political context.

By mid-April 2020, the virus had affected all states worldwide, infecting 1,918,138 people and causing the deaths of 123,126 people, as reported to the WHO.[20] In terms of human rights, the pandemic has caused restrictions on a global scale, which in turn has had unprecedented negative implications for "nearly every right across the spectrum of the Universal Declaration of Human Rights."[21] In addition to the curtailment of civil and political freedoms, the global cessation of movement between borders and within countries has had equally unprecedented socioeconomic and cultural implications. The pandemic caused a massive decline in employment, not witnessed since World War II;[22] it is estimated that more than 120 million people were forced into extreme poverty during 2020.[23] Furthermore, global school closures and job losses resulted in unparalleled declines in human development worldwide.[24]

These global challenges to human rights called for "heightened solidarity" between states.[25] However, the unprecedented geographical spread of COVID-19 was a major hurdle to reaching this level of cooperation, exposing the gap in the international legal framework concerning cooperation in situations where all states are affected.

Moreover, COVID-19 broke out in an environment of increasing populism and authoritarianism. Thus concern was expressed that this pandemic would have an enduring effect on human rights; violations would fast become the norm not only within specific states but on the international level—an effect that would be tolerated by individuals out of fear and concern over future pandemics.

The pandemic has been used as a pretext by some states to enforce measures that seek to curtail rights and freedoms beyond what is necessary to combat it. As the WHO declared COVID-19 a public health emergency of international concern,[26] many states declared a state of emergency, vesting the executive organ with expansive powers to restrict human rights although the infection rates in those countries did not necessitate such restrictions.[27] Given that states of emergency tend to outlast emergencies in authoritarian states, there is a high risk that human rights violations will go unchecked in those states.[28] COVID-19 created fertile ground for disseminating fake news, and this has given states the opportunity to adopt new laws[29] and implement existing ones that criminalize misinformation with vaguely defined provisions. This, in turn, has allowed states to prosecute those who have stood in opposition to their policies and decisions, normalizing violations of freedom of speech.[30]

In addition, the fact that COVID-19, unlike previous pandemics, hit Western democratic states hard has resulted in a convergence of some measures between these states and populist/authoritarian states in other parts of the world.[31] In consequence, there has been a growing fear that these measures would fast become the norm at the international level, given the high threat level for future pandemics.[32] For instance, the surveillance techniques adopted in both democratic and populist/authoritarian states to monitor the movement of citizens are subject to a serious risk of such normalization.[33] In other words, there is a significant risk that international consensus will be reached as to the ongoing necessity of surveillance measures to prevent future pandemics.[34] This has been the case with surveillance measures implemented in response to the events of 9/11 but that continue to be used for the purposes of counterterrorism.[35] It is also likely that these measures will be repurposed, causing further erosion not only to the right of privacy but also to freedom of expression and freedom of assembly.[36] There was growing concern that surveillance measures would be adopted not only for purposes related to COVID-19 but also during the Black Lives Matter protests.[37]

The global neglect of refugees and asylum seekers during COVID-19 has raised concerns about the long-term implications of refugee law within international law. Some states have used the pandemic as a pretext for advancing anti-immigrant policies by sending refugees back or closing the processing of applications.[38] Others have closed their borders, turning a blind eye to the rights of refugees and asylum seekers. This widespread disregard for refugees threatens the erosion of their rights under international law, especially in times of pandemics.[39]

The global political context prevailing during this pandemic represents a unique, historic challenge exaggerated by COVID-19. The United States repeatedly praised China in the early months of 2020 for its disease containment measures.[40] In March 2020, however, with the upsurge in infection and mortality rates, the United States blamed China for the spread of the pandemic worldwide, stressing the human rights violations committed in suppressing information about the virus that would arguably have halted its global spread. Conspiracy theories have traveled back and forth between the two countries.[41] As a result, COVID-19, unlike previous pandemics, turned "into a battleground in their competition for power and influence."[42] This in turn has had various negative impacts on the functionality of multilateral organizations that have a direct or indirect mandate to protect human rights, namely the WHO and the UN Security Council (UNSC).

The United States under the Trump administration accused the WHO of covering up China's human rights violations and of being biased in favor of its political agenda. In response, President Donald Trump threatened to cut U.S. funding for the WHO and to withdraw from the organization. The direct impact of those decisions on the functionality of the WHO has yet to be determined,[43] but Trump's accusations triggered calls for reform from many states.[44] They also caused individuals to become more reluctant to comply with state measures based on WHO recommendations.[45]

Increasing tensions between the United States and China have also negatively affected the UN Security Council. Owing to their disagreement on the origins of COVID-19 and the role of the WHO, the UNSC failed to adopt any resolution in the three months after the UN Secretary-General brought to its attention "the significant threats to the maintenance of international peace and security" posed by the pandemic.[46] On July 1, 2020, the Security Council adopted Resolution 2532, yet this was considered a "missed opportunity"[47] because it focused only on the security aspect of the pandemic.[48] Even in that respect, the UNSC has arguably failed to adopt a meaningful ceasefire resolution to ongoing conflicts.[49] Time has shown the limited practical significance of this resolution, with escalating violence reported in different parts of the world.

Moreover, China has used the pandemic as a catalyst for redefining human rights and promoting its approach to state control and governance. After allegedly containing the spread of COVID-19, it launched a propaganda campaign to set its own approach to human rights as a role model in controlling the pandemic and to portray the authoritarian measures it adopted as best-equipped to contain the spread of infectious diseases.[50] China also took the opportunity to promote its development-first approach by claiming that it had followed this approach in its response to COVID-19.[51] It has also taken advantage of the pandemic to pinpoint the violations and excessive measures adopted by Western states in their response to the virus to tarnish their image as guardians of human rights.[52]

In sum, the unprecedented socioeconomic implications of COVID-19, the high risk of normalizing violations of human rights, the attempted redefining of human rights, and the prevailing global political context can all be regarded as new challenges brought on by this pandemic to the human rights regime. How have human rights institutions responded to these challenges?

Human Rights Institutions in the Pandemic: Updating Practices

The new challenges to human rights brought about by COVID-19 have emphasized the necessity and urgency of ensuring the holistic protection of these rights. A timely response to human rights violations during pandemics is crucial to mitigating their socioeconomic impacts. Pandemics aggravate existing inequalities, making it more difficult to "build back better." Thus it is important to reverse unnecessary, disproportionate, and discriminatory measures during, rather than after, the pandemic. Waiting until it is over risks the loss of evidence, which can be either destroyed or manipulated by perpetrators of human rights violations.[53] Furthermore, COVID-19 has clearly demonstrated the indivisibility and interdependency of human rights, requiring a holistic and coordinated protection of civil, political, social, economic, and cultural rights.

While there is a vast literature addressing the human rights implications of states' responses to COVID-19,[54] less attention has been given to assessing the performance of the institutional structure of the human rights regime during the COVID-19 pandemic. To what extent have HRIs proved fit to protect human rights in times of pandemic?

Given the ongoing concern over the continued human rights violations under the pretext of COVID-19 protections, it is understandable that HRIs are regarded as failing in this regard. However, this compliance-based evaluation is ill-suited to assessing the impact of HRIs during the crisis because it does not capture the progress they have made and in most cases leads to their work being characterized as failing. This is because "achieving meaningful change in human rights work is difficult—particularly in the short term."[55] It took HRIs nearly three decades to achieve progress in enforcing a human rights–based approach to states' responses to the HIV/AIDS pandemic. Consequently, it would be unjust to ignore their massive efforts to protect human rights during the current pandemic.

Over the past two years, despite worldwide travel restrictions and state-imposed lockdowns, different human rights bodies have adapted their working methods to overcome mobility restrictions.[56] They have held virtual sessions, implemented remote monitoring in lieu of country visits, and virtually resumed the functioning of their individual complaints mechanisms.[57]

Furthermore, international and regional HRIs provided prompt guidance on the normative framework for the protection of human rights during pandemics. They issued general statements on the limitations and derogations framework.[58] They also adopted thematic statements to address states' obligations regarding particular rights and the extent to which those rights can be derogated from or limited,[59] and in addition issued country-specific statements.[60]

In addition, HRIs established online trackers to monitor state responses to COVID-19 that could affect various aspects of human rights. For example, the Special Rapporteur for the Protection and Promotion of Human Rights while Countering Terrorism, in partnership with the International Center for Not-For-Profit Law (ICNL) and the European Center for Not-For-Profit Law (ECNL), established an online tracker monitoring states' responses affecting civic freedoms and human rights, with a focus on emergency laws.[61] The European Union (EU) sponsored the International Institute for Democracy and Electoral Assistance (IDEA) in a similar initiative focusing on democracy and human rights.[62]

HRIs have also been sharing good practices among states to assist them in shaping their response strategies to COVID-19,[63] launching training sessions for state officials and civil society organizations to promote a human rights–based approach to COVID-19 response plans.

Human Rights Institutions in the Pandemic: Shortcomings

This is not to deny that COVID-19 has exposed the existing deficiencies in the HRIs and put the spotlight on the urgent need to reform these bodies so they can effectively fulfill their mandates in responding to the human rights implications of COVID-19 and future pandemics.

First, enforcing human rights has always been a major structural deficiency of HRIs, and COVID-19 further exposed their incapacity to provide effective, real-time responses to violations.

Concerning the UN human rights system, the lack of power to adopt binding decisions and enforce them is an admitted structural deficiency in the system. Furthermore, the reporting procedures, as highlighted by Michael O'Flaherty, have "little to offer as a contribution to the resolution of emergency situations" because "emergencies must be addressed while they occur and not according to the accidental application of a reporting cycle."[64] Nor has the individual communications procedure proven to be effective during the pandemic, primarily owing to the backlog encountered by human rights institutions. Further, UN human rights institutions lack the time and resources to follow up on the large number of recommendations adopted.

Similarly, the African system of human rights lacks the necessary enforcement measures to guarantee compliance with human rights during the pandemic. In addition, the African Court of Human Rights (ACtHR) has been facing an "existential crisis" after a number of African states decided to withdraw their acceptance of direct access to the Court by individuals and nongovernmental organizations (NGOs).[65] Although both can submit cases to the African Commission on Human and Peoples' Rights for referral to the Court, this does not seem practical given that the Commission has only referred three cases to the ACtHR out of the three hundred cases it has adjudicated.[66] Thus the ACtHR does not seem to have any effective role in enforcing human rights during the pandemic. (See also chapter 12 by Solomon Dersso in this volume.)

Nor does the European Court of Human Rights (ECtHR) seem to be sufficiently equipped to promptly enforce human rights during pandemics. This is primarily due to the fact that potential plaintiffs must first exhaust local remedies before appealing to the Court and to a large backlog of cases.[67] Even though the ECtHR has a policy that allows it to prioritize urgent cases,[68] this policy does not generally favor cases related to COVID-19.[69] The Court has emphasized that it will only allow requests for interim measures when there is an imminent risk of irreversible harm.[70] Thus it does not play a role in providing timely responses to human rights violations. (See also chapter 6 by Gerald Neuman and chapter 10 by Urfan Khaliq in this volume.)

Nevertheless, an attempt to force states to comply with their human rights obligations was made within the framework of the European Union, with a proposal to condition the reception of any funds from the EU budget on respect for the rule of law. However, Hungary and Poland, the two European states in the spotlight for their violations of human rights during the pandemic,[71] strongly opposed this proposal and threatened to block the EU's COVID-19 recovery aid.[72] A compromise was then reached to adopt the proposal, but its entry into force was conditioned on not being challenged before the European

Court of Justice (ECJ). As expected, the implementation of this conditionality mechanism was delayed as Hungary and Poland challenged it before the Court.[73] On February 16, 2022, the ECJ upheld the conditionality mechanism.[74] Although the decision was applauded by the European states,[75] there has been some doubt about its effectiveness in inducing compliance with human rights.[76] At any rate, unilateral sanctions or the conditionality of recovery funds as a viable means of enforcing compliance with human rights during a pandemic raises its own concerns.[77] Both these measures would increase tensions between states at a time when cooperation is most needed to combat the pandemic.

Furthermore, the unilateral conditionality of recovery aid is less likely to be effective in the atmosphere of rivalry that currently exists between the United States and China.[78] The United States' efforts to condition development funds sent to sub-Saharan African states to help them fight the HIV/AIDS pandemic were unchallenged by other states because, as David P. Fidler highlighted, "in a system that has a preponderant power rather than a balance of power, the hegemonic state can pursue its interests and ideas with less resistance."[79] However, as he goes on to point out, the "balance-of-power politics drives major powers to view issues, initiatives, and ideas in terms of how they might affect the distribution of power. This 'zero-sum' perspective forces the great powers to attempt to control developments to hurt competitor states or to prevent change that might benefit rivals."[80] Moreover, conditioning funds on respect for human rights will not contribute to a holistic protection of these rights in the fight against COVID-19 because states usually use this conditioning power as an instrument to advance their own perspective of human rights.[81]

Nevertheless, it is important that funding by international institutions such as the UN COVID-19 Response and Recovery Fund or the African Union Recovery Fund should be committed to the promotion and protection of human rights, in the sense that it should not be used in any programs that violate (or involve the risk of violating) human rights. These bodies could follow the example of the AIDS Global Fund—a public-private partnership dedicated to attracting and disbursing additional resources to prevent and treat HIV/AIDS, tuberculosis, and malaria—whose funding process has been devoted to the protection of human rights; the removal of human rights–related barriers is even among its strategic objectives for the years 2017–2022.[82]

The IACHR has taken its response one step further. Despite the many challenges faced by the Inter-American System of Human Rights,[83] its Commission has been praised for its response to the human rights crisis brought on by COVID-19.[84] According to its annual progress report, the IACHR succeeded in securing enough funding for all activities planned for 2020.[85] Furthermore, it established the Rapid and Integrated Response Coordination Unit for COVID-19 Pandemic Crisis Management (SACROI COVID-19, to use its Spanish acronym). This unit was created specifically to monitor states' responses to the pandemic and their implications for human rights. It issues policy recommendations on these responses, along with a follow-up mechanism to review states' compliance with those recommendations. It also has the mandate to identify requests for precautionary measures against responses that risk irreparable harm, and to follow up on their implementation.[86] And it works "with a crisis response team that will be coordinated by the Executive Secretary and will be made up of the heads of the Special Rapporteurships; and other personnel assigned by the Executive Secretary, according to needs."[87]

Although it does not have enforcement powers, SACROI-COVID-19 has been considered exemplary for protecting human rights during the pandemic. A COVID-19-centered mandate allows better monitoring of state compliance with human rights obligations. At the same time, it allows the IACHR to continue its work on non-COVID-19 violations of human rights. This unit has been also strengthened by a follow-up mechanism specifically designed to observe the implementation of COVID-19-related recommendations, thereby overcoming the difficulties of monitoring their implementation within the normal functioning of the IACHR considering the time and resources available. As in all cases of human rights monitoring, follow-ups remain the key to enhancing compliance in the absence of enforcement powers by HRIs.[88]

Moreover, SACROI-COVID-19 gives special attention to requests for precautionary measures by those prone to irreparable harm because of COVID-19 measures. These requests do not wait in line with other requests but seem to be reviewed simultaneously. Out of 344 requests for precautionary measures related to COVID-19 received in 2020, 336 (97 percent) had been evaluated by December 31, 2020.[89]

In addition to the enforcement deficiency, the chronic underfunding of HRIs that has always impeded their functioning was exacerbated by the deteriorating economic situation resulting from COVID-19. Consequently, they had to work at reduced activity levels, postponing many of their mandated activities.[90] For example, the UN human rights treaty bodies have postponed their reviews of state reports, a decision widely criticized by NGOs.[91] Insufficient funding has also prevented the UN human rights system from providing technical and practical assistance to all states that have requested it.

Before the pandemic, attention had repeatedly been drawn to the lack of cooperation between the different HRI bodies (within the UN human rights system or between the UN system and the other regional human rights bodies) and how this undermined their performance. COVID-19 has underscored the importance of such cooperation, and indeed there has now been some collaboration, as reflected in the joint statements issued during the pandemic.[92] Nevertheless, most statements and guidelines have been issued separately. This has led to overlap and duplication, which poses more of a managerial problem[93] than a cohesion problem[94] because it becomes hard to follow them. This duplication will compound existing "evaluation fatigue" in the states resulting from overlapping reporting requirements.[95] It will further complicate the work of NGOs in following up on states' compliance with their human rights obligations, and it also represents a misuse of much-needed resources.

In acknowledgment of these problems, the UN established a new committee, the UN Human Rights Treaty Bodies Working Group on COVID-19, with the objectives of "facilitating a coherent treaty bodies' voice on a crucial common challenge," and providing a joint comprehensive response to it. However, to date no further work has been done. Nevertheless, the IACHR SACROI-COVID-19 has proved exemplary in terms of coordination as it comprises heads of special rapporteurships, coordinated by the Executive Secretary.

The growth of populism and authoritarianism during the pandemic raised another urgent call to reform the HRI membership process to increase transparency, impartiality, and nonpoliticization. It is common for populist and authoritarian governments to reject compliance with HRI recommendations by claiming they are politicized. As already noted, President Trump rejected the WHO's recommendations, withdrew from the organization, and stopped funding it on the grounds that it lacked transparency and favored China. He cited China's relations with Ethiopia, the country of nationality of Dr. Tedros Ghebreyesus, the WHO executive director, and the latter's past history.[96] It is, of course, important to ensure the transparency of HRIs not only for the sake of countering populist and authoritarian arguments, which will always be raised no matter what reforms are accomplished, but to enhance the performance of these bodies.

The pandemic has exposed a new structural deficiency in the work of HRIs, reflected in their shift to working online. There is no doubt that the shift has enabled HRIs to continue functioning and to engage in the promotion and protection of human rights. Nevertheless, it has been considered an obstacle to their effective functioning. One of the challenges is accessibility. For example, HRIs had difficulty choosing an online platform that would be accessible to persons with disabilities.[97] Additionally, while enabling increased access to NGOs that previously faced travel restrictions, the shift to online working has still hampered those NGOs that lack the necessary tools to do so effectively.[98] NGOs have also emphasized the need for increased transparency in the scheduling of HRI sessions and in their participation rules.[99] Moreover, the UN treaty body members had to reduce their activity levels because they had not received their allowances for working virtually, which were only tied to traveling outside their country of residence.[100] Consequently, working online, and not at full capacity, has forced HRIs to address a reduced agenda.

In addition to these structural deficiencies, the substantive content of recommendations issued by HRIs during the pandemic has lacked sufficient legal justification for most statements and guidelines adopted.[101] As rightly noted by Lisa Reinsberg, "Many statements are merely lists of actions that States 'should' or 'can' take, in a legal vacuum."[102] COVID-19 has entailed a balancing act when it comes to human rights. Thus, in a statement about the protection of one particular right, it is not sufficient to mention the related legal provisions without mentioning how the protection of this right could be balanced with the protection of other rights under international law. States have used conflicting legal obligations under international law to justify their practices of hoarding medical equipment and vaccines during the pandemic. This conflict of norms was addressed in few, if any, of the statements made on universal access to these resources.[103] The failure to identify the normative underpinnings of these recommendations weakens their value as an advocacy tool that can be mobilized by NGOs and civil society in their protection of human rights. The lack of sufficient legal justification also undermines the effect of these recommendations in countering populist and nationalist exclusionary strategies. However, this does not mean that HRIs should advance expansive interpretations, unless they are strongly argued. Laurence R. Helfer has highlighted that "expanding legal norms and institutional competencies . . . creates easy targets for populist backlashes that may undermine decades of hard-won achievements."[104]

In sum, despite the enormous efforts undertaken by HRIs to provide timely and holistic protection of human rights during COVID-19, it is evident that the structural deficiencies of these institutions require urgent reform for these efforts to succeed. HRIs also need to strengthen their legal discourse to increase their impact in inducing better compliance with the human rights regime.

Moving Forward: Strengthening the Work of Human Rights Institutions in Pandemics

While HRIs were under fire long before COVID-19, in the midst of an ongoing push to strengthen them, the pandemic has brought new challenges to the human rights system. These challenges are compounded by the prevailing global political context and threaten to undermine decades of efforts and hard-won gains in that field. This, in turn, has shown the need for exceptional protection of human rights in a timely and holistic way, but global and regional HRIs have not proved fit to provide this, given their structural and substantive deficiencies. Therefore, the focus in the future should be on strengthening their capacity to address these shortcomings.

States should consider the creation of a committee similar to IACHR SACROI COVID-19 that would be dedicated specifically to the human rights implications of the pandemic, mandated with monitoring states' responses. Such a body would be charged with preparing general, thematic, and country-specific recommendations and policy guidelines and providing technical assistance to states, NGOS, national human rights institutions (NHRIs), and civil society on their implementation. A specialized committee would enhance HRIs' ability to provide timely protection, as well as reduce their workload, allowing them to pursue their normal mandates to address nonpandemic-related human rights issues.

This committee should, like SACROI COVID-19, be empowered to follow up on its recommendations and guidelines, and to receive and respond to requests for precautionary measures against irreparable harm caused by pandemic-related measures. The committee would be composed of experts from both international and regional human rights bodies to ensure adequate coordination. The inclusion of experts from the regional bodies would allow a better contextualization of statements and guidelines. Improved coordination would also reduce the duplication of work among the different HRIs, saving financial resources and allowing their reallocation to reduce the funding gaps between different HRIs.[105]

This pandemic-focused human rights body would also work in close collaboration with the WHO. Communications to states regarding alleged violations of human rights would need to take into consideration the specific health situation prevailing in the state in question. This in turn would contribute to the acceptance of these recommendations. Scientifically based recommendations would help to counter arguments that authoritarian measures are best suited to curbing the spread of infectious diseases. Along the same lines, the committee needs to provide a sufficient legal basis to strengthen the power of its arguments and recommendations.

The question would be where to house this initiative. The committee could be established by the UN's Office of the High Commissioner for Human Rights (OHCHR). But it would then lack the necessary powers to follow up on the adopted recommendations and guidelines and receive COVID-19-related requests for precautionary measures, as is evident in the structure of the UN Human Rights Treaty Bodies Working Group on COVID-19. Establishing the committee through the Human Rights Council would also not seem to be a viable option, given growing concerns about its members' profiles on human rights. COVID-19 has clearly demonstrated that the UN Security Council would not be suitable, given the growing rivalry between two of its permanent members, China and the United States. Therefore, establishment by the UN General Assembly seems to be the least-worst available option, in terms of overcoming the geopolitical divide among states and securing a wide consensus for the committee—a necessary prerequisite for any cooperation. Consequently, states with a good human rights agenda should use the UN General Assembly as a platform to secure consensus for the committee. Despite political divides, the General Assembly has indeed managed to issue a set of admittedly rather ineffective recommendations, reflecting states' commitment to cooperation and solidarity during the pandemic.

Recent attacks on international human rights bodies and insecurity of government support demonstrate that state funding of this pandemic rights committee would not be sufficient to carry out its mandate in full, especially in the environment of global economic recession resulting from the pandemic, which would provide a perfect justification for continued underfunding.[106] One possibility would be the creation of a trust fund with contributions from multiple sources, including foundations and business. However, in seeking funding from the private sector, the committee must be careful to preserve transparency to ensure its legitimacy, independence, and impartiality, and consequently the rate of compliance with its recommendations and statements.[107]

As the success of other human rights bodies has shown, the effectiveness of any new pandemic-related committee will require engagement with NGOs, NHRIs, and other domestic actors having a role in the protection of human rights. Their participation is vital not only for the implementation and impact of recommendations issued by HRIs, but also to their formulation, as they can contribute to an understanding of the domestic context of the state in question.[108] Therefore, the procedures of the pandemic rights committee need to ensure the wide and meaningful participation of NGOs in its meetings, whether they are held in-person or virtually. In the latter case, obstacles related to safe platforms, simultaneous interpretations, closed captions, sign language, time zone gaps, and access by NGOs with limited digital tools need to be procedurally addressed.

In conclusion, COVID-19 has clearly exposed the structural deficiency in HRIs that weakens their response, despite the massive efforts expended, to the pandemic's unprecedented implications for human rights. However, this should not be the moment to lose faith in multilateralism; rather, it should be the moment to start working to strengthen it. A pandemic rights-focused committee could be one way to ensure timely, holistic, and coordinated protection for human rights in the current and future pandemics, building back better and mitigating their long-term impacts on human rights.

Notes

1. Article 2 of the UN Charter. See also Article 55 of the Charter.

2. Surya P. Subedi, *The Effectiveness of the UN Human Rights System: Reform and Judicialisation of Human Rights* (London: Routledge, 2017), pp. 25–27.

3. "Work of Human Rights Treaty Bodies at Risk, Warns UN Committee Chairs," August 4, 2020, www.ohchr.org/en/NewsEvents/Pages/DisplayNews.aspx?NewsID =26147&LangID=E.

4. "Report of the Independent Expert on the Promotion of a Democratic and Equitable Order, Livingstone Sewanyana: In Defence of a Renewed Multilateralism to Address the Coronavirus Disease (COVID-19) Pandemic and Other Global Challenges," A/HRC/48/58, August 9, 2021.

5. See UN General Assembly, "The Declaration on the Commemoration of the Seventy-Fifth Anniversary of the United Nations," A/RES/75/1, September 21, 2020.

6. UN Secretary-General António Guterres, "We Are All in This Together: Human Rights and COVID-19 Response and Recovery," United Nations, April 23, 2020, www.un.org/en/un-coronavirus-communications-team/we-are-all-together-human -rights-and-covid-19-response-and.

7. Freedom of Expression (Article 19), Freedom of Religion (Article 18), Freedom of Movement (Article 12), Freedom of Association (Article 22), and Freedom of Assembly (Article 21).

8. Article 4 of the ICESCR.

9. See European Convention on Human Rights (ECHR): Article 8 (Right to Respect for Private and Family Life), Article 9 (Freedom of Religion), Article 10 (Freedom of Expression), Article 11 (Freedom of Assembly); Protocol 4 to the ECHR: Article 2 (Freedom of Movement); Article G of the European Social Charter. See also the American Convention on Human Rights (ACHR): Article 12 (Freedom of Religion), Article 13 (Freedom of Expression), Article 15 (Freedom of Assembly), Article

16 (Freedom of Association), Article 22 (Freedom of Movement); and Articles 11 (Freedom of Assembly) and 12 (Freedom of Movement) of the African Charter on Human Rights (AFCHR).

10. The Siracusa Principles on the Limitation and Derogation Provisions of the International Covenant on Civil and Political Rights, UN Doc. E/CN.4/1985/4, September 28, 1984, Annex.

11. Article 4 of the ICCPR; Article 15(1) of the ECHR; Article 27 of the ACHR; Article F of the European Social Charter.

12. Under Article 4 of the ICCPR, the following are nonderogable rights: the right to life, the prohibition of torture and slavery, the right not to be imprisoned on the sole basis of a contractual obligation, the principle of legality, the right to be recognized as a person before the law, and the freedoms of conscience and religion. See also the list of nonderogable rights under Article 15 of the ECHR and Article 27 of the ACHR.

13. Sharifah Sekalala and John Harrington, "Communicable Disease, Health Security, and Human Rights: From AIDS to Ebola," in *Foundations of Global Health and Human Rights,* edited by Lawrence O. Gostin and Benjamin Mason Meier (Oxford University Press, 2020), p. 223. A voluminous literature has discussed the implications for human rights of measures adopted by states in response to the HIV/AIDS pandemic. See Lawrence O. Gostin and Zita Lazzarini, *Human Rights and Public Health in the AIDS Pandemic* (Oxford University Press, 1997); Miriam Maluwa, Peter Aggleton, and Richard Parker, "HIV- and AIDS-Related Stigma, Discrimination, and Human Rights: A Critical Overview," *Health and Human Rights* 6, 1 (2002), pp. 1–18, www.jstor.org/stable/4065311?seq=1; David Patterson and Leslie London, "International Law, Human Rights and HIV/AIDS," *Bulletin of the World Health Organization* 80, 12 (2002), https://apps.who.int/iris/handle/10665/71665.

14. Jonathan M. Mann, "Human Rights and AIDS: The Future of the Pandemic," *30 John Marshall Law Review* 195 (Fall 1996), p. 204.

15. See the 2001 Declaration of Commitment on HIV/AIDS, A/RES/S-26/2, June 27, 2001; Political Declaration on HIV/AIDS, A/RES/60/262, June 15, 2006; Political Declaration on HIV and AIDS: Intensifying Our Efforts to Eliminate HIV and AIDS, A/RES/65/277, July 8, 2011.

16. See UNAIDS Explainer, "Still Not Welcome: HIV-Related Travel Restrictions," June 27, 2019, www.unaids.org/sites/default/files/media_asset/hiv-related -travel-restrictions-explainer_en.pdf; UNAIDS, "Act to Change Laws That Discriminate," March 1, 2019, www.unaids.org/sites/default/files/media_asset/2019_Zero Discrimination_Brochure_en.pdf. See also Jamie Enoch and Peter Piot, "Human Rights in the Fourth Decade of the HIV/AIDS Response: An Inspiring Legacy and Urgent Imperative," *Health and Human Rights Journal* 19 (December 2017), pp. 117–22, www.ncbi.nlm.nih.gov/pmc/articles/PMC5739363/.

17. Lesley A. Jacobs, "Rights and Quarantine during the SARS Global Health Crises: Differentiated Legal Consciousness in Hong Kong, Shanghai, and Toronto," *Law and Society Review* 2 (September 2007), pp. 511–51, www.jstor.org/stable /4623394; Huiling Ding and Elizabeth A. Pitts, "Singapore's Quarantine Rhetoric

and Human Rights in Emergency Health Risks," *Rhetoric, Professional Communication, and Globalization* 4 (October 2013), pp. 55–77, https://repository.lib.ncsu.edu /bitstream/handle/1840.2/2580/RPCG2013.pdf?sequence=1.

18. For a list of those provisions, see David P. Fidler, "From International Sanitary Conventions to Global Health Security: The New International Health Regulations," *Chinese Journal of International Law* 4, 2 (2005), p. 368.

19. For human rights concerns raised with regard to tuberculosis: Philippe Calain and David P. Fidler, "XDR Tuberculosis, the New International Health Regulations, and Human Rights" (2007), p. 463, www.repository.law.indiana.edu/facpub/463/; Andrea Boggio, Matteo Zignol, Ernesto Jaramillo, Paul Nunn, Geneviève Pinet, and Mario Raviglione, "Limitations on Human Rights: Are They Justifiable to Reduce the Burden of TB in the Era of MDR- and XDR-TB?," *Health and Human Rights in Practice* 10 (2008), pp. 121–26, www.heinonline.org. For human rights concerns raised with regard to swine flu (H1N1): "Swine Flu Measures No Excuse for Abridging Rights," Human Rights Watch, May 18, 2009, www.hrw.org/news/2009/05/18/swine -flu-measures-no-excuse-abridging-rights. For human rights concerns during Ebola, see Office of the United Nations High Commissioner for Human Rights (West Africa Regional Office), "A Human Rights Perspective into the Ebola Outbreak" (2014), www.globalhealth.org/wp-content/uploads/A-human-rights-perspective-into-the -Ebola-outbreak.pdf. See also UN Refugee Agency (UNHCR), "Considerations on the Impact of Measures Relating to Ebola Virus Disease, on Persons Who Are or May Be in Need of International Protection" (2014), www.refworld.org/pdfid/548014ce4 .pdf. See further Patrick M. Eba, "Ebola and Human Rights in West Africa" (2014), www.thelancet.com/journals/lancet/article/PIIS0140-6736(14)61412-4/fulltext; and Deisy Ventura, "The Impact of International Health Crisis on the Rights of Migrants," *Sur International Journal on Human Rights* (May 2016), https://sur.conectas.org/en /impact-international-health-crises-rights-migrants/.

20. "WHO Weekly Operational Update on COVID-19," April 15, 2020, www .who.int/publications/m/item/weekly-update-on-covid-19–15-april-2020. See WHO Coronavirus (COVID-19) Dashboard, https://covid19.who.int for the latest figures.

21. Karima Bennoune, "Lest We Should Sleep: COVID-19 and Human Rights," *American Journal of International Law* 114, 4, p. 669 (for a comprehensive study on the implications of COVID-19).

22. UN and other partner organizations of the Committee for the Coordination of Statistical Activities (CCSA), *How COVID-19 Is Changing the World: A Statistical Perspective*, vol. III (2020), pp. 20–21.

23. Ibid., pp. 32–33.

24. Ibid., pp. 54–55. For more on how COVID-19 has affected different aspects of human life and state responses to the virus, see volumes I and II of this study.

25. "COVID-19 Threatening Global Peace and Security, UN Chief Warns," April 10, 2020, https://news.un.org/en/story/2020/04/1061502.

26. "Statement on the Second Meeting of the International Health Regulations Committee regarding the Outbreak of Novel Coronavirus (2019-nCoV)," January 30,

2020, www.who.int/news/item/30-01-2020-statement-on-the-second-meeting-of-the
-international-health-regulations-(2005)-emergency-committee-regarding-the-out
break-of-novel-coronavirus-(2019-ncov).

27. For an account of those states that have declared a state of emergency, see the
COVID-19 Civic Freedom Tracker, www.icnl.org/covid19tracker/?location=&issue
=5&date=&type=.

28. Michele Collazzo and Alexandra Tyan, "Emergency Powers, COVID-19 and
the New Challenge for Human Rights," June 27, 2020, www.iai.it/en/pubblicazioni
/emergency-powers-covid-19-and-new-challenge-human-rights.

29. "Rush to Pass 'Fake News' Laws during COVID-19 Intensifying Global Media
Freedom Challenges," October 22, 2020, https://ipi.media/rush-to-pass-fake-news
-laws-during-covid-19-intensifying-global-media-freedom-challenges/.

30. IPI COVID-19 Press Freedom Tracker, https://ipi.media/covid19/?alert_type
=fake-news-regulation-passed-during-covid-19&language=0&years=0&country=0;
Human Rights Watch, "COVID-19 Triggers Wave of Free Speech Abuse," https://
features.hrw.org/features/features/covid/index.html. See also "Report of the Special
Rapporteur on the Promotion and Protection of the Right to Freedom of Opinion
and Expression: Disease Pandemics and the Freedom of Opinion and Expression,"
A/HRC/44/49, April 23, 2020.

31. Stephen Thomson and Eric C. Ip, "COVID-19 Emergency Measures and Im-
pending Authoritarian Pandemics," *Journal of Law and Biosciences* 7, 1 (January–
June 2020), pp.1–33, https://doi.org/10.1093/jlb/lsaa064.

32. Melissa Sou-Jie Brunnersum, "COVID-19 Will Not Be Last Pandemic,"
WHO, December 26, 2020, www.dw.com/en/covid-19-will-not-be-last-pandemic
-who/a-56065483. See also R. K. Obi, N. M. Orji, F. C. Nwanebu, C. C. Okangba,
and U. U. Ndubuisi, "Emerging and Re-Emerging Infectious Diseases: The Perpet-
ual Menace," *Asian Journal of Experimental Biological Sciences* 1 (2010), pp. 271–82.

33. International Center for Not-for-Profit Law (ICNL), COVID-19 Digital Rights
Tracker, www.top10vpn.com/research/investigations/covid-19-digital-rights-tracker
/#Digital-Tracking, showing that Europe comes in second place for adopting digital
tracking measures and applying contact tracing, and first place for imposing physical
surveillance.

34. See Barrie Sander and Luca Belli, "COVID-19, Cyber Surveillance, Normali-
sation and Human Rights Law," April 1, 2020, http://opiniojuris.org/2020/04/01
/covid-19-symposium-covid-19-cyber-surveillance-normalisation-and-human-rights
-law/; Yuval Noah Harari, "The World after Coronavirus," March 20, 2020, www.ft
.com/content/19d90308-6858-11ea-a3c9-1fe6fedcca75; and Alan Z. Rozenshtein,
"Government Surveillance in an Age of Pandemics," March 23, 2020, www.lawfareblog
.com/government-surveillance-age-pandemics.

35. Michele Collazzo and Alexandra Tyan, "Emergency Powers."

36. Seana Davis, "Could the Coronavirus Pandemic Lead to Mass Surveillance in
Europe?," March 31, 2020, www.euronews.com/2020/03/31/could-the-coronavirus
-pandemic-lead-to-mass-surveillance-in-europe.

37. Geoffrey A. Fawler, "Black Lives Matter Could Change Facial Recognition Forever—If Big Tech Doesn't Stand in the Way," June 12, 2020, www.washingtonpost.com/technology/2020/06/12/facial-recognition-ban/.

38. Lama Mourad and Stephanie Schwartz, "Could COVID-19 Upend International Asylum Norms?," April 9, 2020, www.lawfareblog.com/could-covid-19-upend-international-asylum-norms#.

39. Ibid.

40. Nathan McDermott and Andrew Kaczynski, "CNN, Trump Repeatedly Praised China's Response to Coronavirus in February," *CNN*, March 25, 2020, https://edition.cnn.com/2020/03/25/politics/trump-coronavirus-china/index.html.

41. K. Chen and others, "Conspiracy and Debunking Narratives about COVID-19 Origins on Chinese Social Media: How It Started and Who Is to Blame," *Harvard Kennedy School (HKS) Misinformation Review,* https://doi.org/10.37016/mr-2020-50; Helen Davidson, "China Revives Conspiracy Theory of US Army Link to COVID," January 20, 2021, www.theguardian.com/world/2021/jan/20/china-revives-conspiracy-theory-of-us-army-link-to-covid.

42. David P. Fidler, "The COVID-19 Pandemic, Geopolitics and International Law," *Journal of International Humanitarian Legal Studies* 11 (2020), p. 246. See also Yanzhong Huang, "The U.S and China Could Cooperate to Defeat the Pandemic—Instead Their Antagonism Makes Matters Worse," *Foreign Affairs*, March 24, 2020, www.foreignaffairs.com/articles/china/2020-03-24/us-and-china-could-cooperate-defeat-pandemic.

43. UN News, "WHO Reviewing Impact of US Funding Withdrawal amid COVID-19 Pandemic," April 15, 2020, https://news.un.org/en/story/2020/04/1061822. For factors to take into consideration when assessing the impact of Trump's decisions, see "U.S. Withdrawal from the World Health Organization: Process and Implications," Congressional Research Service, October 21, 2020, p. 11, https://fas.org/sgp/crs/row/R46575.pdf.

44. Those calls have resulted in the establishment of an independent panel to "review experience gained and lessons learned from the WHO-coordinated international health response to COVID-19." See WHA73.1, May 19, 2020.

45. For the effects of misinformation and disinformation, see "Article 19 Briefing, Viral Lies: Misinformation and the Coronavirus," March 2020, www.article19.org/wp-content/uploads/2020/03/Coronavirus-final.pdf.

46. Secretary-General's remarks to the Security Council on the COVID-19 pandemic, April 9, 2020, www.un.org/sg/en/content/sg/statement/2020-04-09/secretary-generals-remarks-the-security-council-the-covid-19-pandemic-delivered.

47. Ilja Richard Pavone, "Security Council Resolution 2532 (2020) on COVID-19: A Missed Opportunity?," *ESIL Reflections COVID-19 Series* February 8, 2020, https://esil-sedi.eu/wp-content/uploads/2021/02/ESIL-Reflection-Pavone.pdf.

48. The Security Council could have had a coordinating role for the response to the pandemic similar to its role during the Ebola outbreak (2014). See Marko Svicevic, "COVID-19 as a Threat to International Peace and Security: What Place for the UN

Security Council?," www.ejiltalk.org/covid-19-as-a-threat-to-international-peace-and -security-what-place-for-the-un-security-council/.

49. Pavone, "Security Council Resolution 2532;" Richard Gowan and Ashish Pradhan, "Salvaging the Security Council's Coronavirus Response," August 4, 2020, https://reliefweb.int/report/world/salvaging-security-council-s-coronavirus-response.

50. Javier C. Hernandez, "China Spins Coronavirus Crisis, Hailing Itself as a Global Leader," March 3, 2020, www.nytimes.com/2020/02/28/world/asia/china -coronavirus-response-propaganda.html.

51. Remarks by H. E. Wang Yi, State Councilor and Foreign Minister of the People's Republic of China, at the High-Level Segment of the 46th Session of the United Nations Human Rights Council, "A People-Centered Approach for Global Human Rights Progress," February 22, 2021, www.fmprc.gov.cn/mfa_eng/zxxx _662805/t1855685.shtml.

52. Chen Qingqing and Cao Siqi, "China Issues Annual US Human Rights Report amid Escalating Washington-Led Attacks on Beijing," March 24, 2021, www .globaltimes.cn/page/202103/1219366.shtml; "China, on Behalf of 26 Countries, Criticizes US, Other Western Countries for Violating Human Rights," October 6, 2020, www.globaltimes.cn/content/1202752.shtml.

53. Diane Desierto, "The Myth and Mayhem of 'Build Back Better:' Human Rights Decision-Making and Human Dignity Imperatives in COVID-19," May 25, 2020, www.ejiltalk.org/the-myth-and-mayhem-of-build-back-better-human-rights -decision-making-as-the-human-dignity-imperative-in-covid-19/; "Monitoring Anti-Democratic Trends and Human Rights Abuses in the Age of COVID-19," WOLA Advocacy for Human Rights in the Americas, April 13, 2020, www.wola.org/analysis /anti-democratic-trends-human-rights-abuses-covid-19-latin-america/.

54. For example, see Sam Zarifi and Kate Powers, "Human Rights in the Time of COVID-19—Front and Centre," April 6, 2020, http://opiniojuris.org/2020/04/06 /covid-19-human-rights-in-the-time-of-covid-19-front-and-centre/; Martin Scheinin, "To Derogate or Not to Derogate?," April 6, 2020, https://opiniojuris.org/2020/04/06 /covid-19-symposium-to-derogate-or-not-to-derogate/; "Human Rights Dimensions of COVID-19 Response," March 19, 2020, www.hrw.org/sites/default/files/supporting _resources/202003covid_report_0.pdf; Alessandro Spadaro, "Testing the Limits of Human Rights," *European Journal of Risk Regulation* 11, 2 (2020), pp. 317–25.

55. Ian Gorvin, "Producing the Evidence: First Steps towards Systematized Evaluation at Human Rights Watch," *Journal of Human Rights Practice* 1, 3 (2009), p. 478. For the shortcomings of the compliance-based evaluation in general, see Rhonda Schlangen, "Monitoring and Evaluation for Human Rights Organizations: Three Case Studies," January 2014, pp. 3–4, www.pointk.org/resources/files/CEI _HR_Case_Studies.pdf; Jasper Krommendijk, "The Domestic Effectiveness of International Human Rights Monitoring in Established Democracies: The Case of the UN Human Rights Treaty Bodies," *Review of International Organizations* 10 (2015), pp. 492–94; Catherine Corey Barber, "Tackling the Evaluation Challenge in Human Rights: Assessing the Impact of Strategic Litigation Strategies," *International Journal*

of Human Rights 16 (2012), pp. 416–17. See also Joseph J. Amon and Eric Friedman, "Human Rights Advocacy in Global Health," in *Foundations of Global Health*, edited by Gostin and Meier, pp. 148–50.

56. See International Justice Resource Center, "Human Rights Bodies: Schedule and Procedural Changes amid COVID-19 Pandemic," April 1, 2020, https://ijrcenter .org/2020/04/01/human-rights-bodies-schedule-procedural-changes-amid-covid-19 -pandemic/.

57. For a comprehensive overview of human rights institutions' schedules during COVID-19, see the monthly report published by the International Justice Resource Center at https://ijrcenter.org/category/monthly-overview/. For the work modalities of the UN human rights system during COVID-19, see UN OHCHR, "The UN Human Rights Appeal 2021," p. 25, www.ohchr.org/Documents/Publications/Annual Appeal2021.pdf.

58. For an updated compilation of general statements issued by different international and regional bodies, see International Justice Resource Center, "COVID-19 Guidance from Supranational Human Rights Bodies," https://ijrcenter.org/covid-19 -guidance-from-supranational-human-rights-bodies/#Arab_Human_Rights _Committee.

59. For an updated compilation of thematic statements issued by different international and regional bodies, see the International Justice Resource Center, "COVID-19 Guidance from Supranational Human Rights Bodies," https://ijrcenter.org/covid-19 -guidance-from-supranational-human-rights-bodies/#Arab_Human_Rights _Committee.

60. For example, UN Special Procedures has issued reports and statements focusing on Cambodia, the Central African Republic, Eritrea, the Islamic Republic of Iran, Israel and the Occupied Palestinian Territory, Myanmar, and the Democratic People's Republic of Korea. See Working Document covering information as of April 28, 2020, www.ohchr.org/Documents/HRBodies/SP/COVID19_and_SP_28_April_2020.pdf.

61. COVID-19 Civic Freedom Tracker.

62. Vince Chadwick, "EU Launches Another Tool on Pandemic Threat to Human Rights," July 8, 2020, www.devex.com/news/eu-launches-another-tool-on-pandemic -s-threat-to-human-rights-97645.

63. For example, see UNHCR, "Practical Recommendations and Good Practice to Address Protection Concerns in the Context of the COVID-19 Pandemic," April 9, 2020, www.refworld.org/docid/5ede06a94.html.

64. Michael O'Flaherty, "Treaty Bodies Responding to States of Emergency: The Case of Bosnia and Herzegovina," in *The Future of UN Human Rights Treaty Monitoring*, edited by Philip Alston and James Crawford (Cambridge University Press, 2000), p. 440.

65. "Africa: Regional Human Rights Bodies Struggle to Uphold Rights amid Political Headwinds," October 21, 2020, www.amnesty.org/en/latest/news/2020/10 /africa-regional-human-rights-bodies-struggle-to-uphold-rights-amid-political -headwinds/. See also Nicole De Silva, "A Court in Crisis: African States' Increasing

Resistance to Africa's Human Rights Courts," May 19, 2020, http://opiniojuris.org /2020/05/19/a-court-in-crisis-african-states-increasing-resistance-to-africas-human -rights-court/.

66. See African Court, ACHPR Cases, https://www.african-court.org/cpmt /statistic.

67. See Kushtrim Istrefi, "Supervision of Derogations in the Wake of COVID-19: A Litmus Test for the Secretary General of the Council of Europe," April 6, 2020, www.ejiltalk.org/supervision-of-derogations-in-the-wake-of-covid-19-a-litmus-test -for-the-secretary-general-of-the-council-of-europe/; Kanstantsin Dzehtsiarou, "What Can the European Court of Human Rights Do in the Time of Crisis?," April 14, 2020, https://strasbourgobservers.com/2020/04/14/what-can-the-european-court-of -human-rights-do-in-the-time-of-crisis/.

68. "The ECtHR Priority Policy," www.echr.coe.int/Documents/Priority_policy _ENG.pdf.

69. Istrefi, "Supervision of Derogations"; Dzehtsiarou, "What Can the European Court of Human Rights Do?"

70. "Coronavirus: Exceptional Measures at the European Court of Human Rights," March 18, 2020, www.coe.int/en/web/portal/-/coronavirus-exceptional-measures-at -the-european-court-of-human-rights.

71. See OHCHR, "Press Briefing Note on Hungary," March 27, 2020, www.ohchr .org/EN/NewsEvents/Pages/DisplayNews.aspx?NewsID=25750&LangID=E. See also "Council of Europe Secretary General Writes to Viktor Orbán regarding COVID-19 State of Emergency in Hungary," March 24, 2020, https://rm.coe.int/orban-pm -hungary-24-03-2020/16809d5f04.

72. Sandor Zsiros and Joanna Gill, "Hungary and Poland Block EU's COVID-19 Recovery Package over New Rule of Law Drive," November 18, 2020, www.euronews .com/2020/11/16/hungary-and-poland-threaten-coronavirus-recovery-package.

73. "Poland and Hungary File Complaint over EU Budget Mechanism," March 11, 2021, www.dw.com/en/poland-and-hungary-file-complaint-over-eu-budget-mechanism /a-56835979.

74. Court of Justice of the European Union, Press Release 28/22, Judgments in Cases C-156/21 *Hungary* v *Parliament* and C-157/21 *Poland* v *Parliament and Council*, "Measures for the protection of the Union budget: the Court of Justice, sitting as a full Court, dismisses the actions brought by Hungary and Poland against the conditionality mechanism which makes the receipt of financing from the Union budget subject to the respect by the Member States for the principles of the rule of law," February 16, 2022, https://curia.europa.eu/jcms/upload/docs/application/pdf/2022-02 /cp220028en.pdf.

75. Matina Stevis-Gridneff, Monika Pronczuk, and Benjamin Novak, "Top European Court Rules E.U. Can Freeze Aid to Poland and Hungary," February 16, 2022, http://www.nytimes.com/by/matina-stevis-gridneff.

76. See Rafał Mańko and Magdalena Sapała, "Protecting the EU Budget against Generalized Rule of Law Deficiencies," European Parliamentary Research Service,

July 2020, www.europarl.europa.eu/RegData/etudes/BRIE/2018/630299/EPRS
_BRI(2018)630299_EN.pdf; Kim Lane Scheppele, Laurent Peche, and Sebastien Platon, "Compromising the Rule of Law While Compromising on the Rule of Law,"
December 13, 2020, https://verfassungsblog.de/compromising-the-rule-of-law-while
-compromising-on-the-rule-of-law/.

77. There have been urgent calls to suspend unilateral sanctions during COVID-
19, championed by the UN Secretary-General and the OHCHR. See "Ease Sanctions
against Countries Fighting COVID-19: UN Human Rights Chief," March 24, 2020,
https://news.un.org/en/story/2020/03/1060092; "Unilateral Sanctions Make It Harder
to Fight COVID-19, Must Be Dropped, Says UN Expert," October 16, 2020, https://
www.ohchr.org/EN/NewsEvents/Pages/DisplayNews.aspx?NewsID=26393
&LangID=E.

78. China has been granting "rights-free" development funds, undermining human
rights conditions imposed by the United States and the European States. See Sophie
Richardson, "China's Influence on the Global Human Rights System," September 14,
2020, www.hrw.org/news/2020/09/14/chinas-influence-global-human-rights-system.

79. David P. Fidler, "Africa, COVID-19, and International Law: From Hegemonic
Priority to the Geopolitical Periphery?," *Ethiopian Yearbook of International Law 2019*,
p. 34, www.cfr.org/sites/default/files/pdf/fidler_africa_covid_int_law.pdf.

80. Ibid.

81. The United States has been criticized for using the funds sent to sub-Saharan states
as a means to advance its own approach to human rights. See David P. Fidler, "Fighting
the Axis of Illness: HIV/AIDS, Human Rights, and U.S Foreign Policy," articles by
Maurer Faculty, 2004, pp. 99–136, www.repository.law.indiana.edu/facpub/400/.

82. "The Global Fund Strategy 2017–2022: Investing to End Epidemics," www
.theglobalfund.org/media/2531/core_globalfundstrategy2017-2022_strategy_en
.pdf.

83. See chapter 11 by Santiago Canton and Angelita Baeyens in this volume.

84. Mariela Morales Antoniazzi and Silvia Steininger, "How to Protect Human
Rights in Times of Corona? Lessons from the Inter-American Human Rights System," May 1, 2020, www.ejiltalk.org/how-to-protect-human-rights-in-times-of-corona
-lessons-from-the-inter-american-human-rights-system/.

85. See the Annual Report on Implementation of the IACHR Strategic Plan 2017–
2021, February 2021, www.oas.org/en/iachr/media_center/preleases/2021/BIPE-2020
-EN.pdf.

86. For a detailed statement about the Rapid and Integrated Response Coordination Unit for COVID-19 Pandemic Crisis Management, see SACROI-COVID-19,
www.oas.org/en/IACHR/jsForm/?File=/en/iachr/sacroi_covid19/default.asp.

87. Ibid.

88. Studies have demonstrated that follow-up measures contribute to better compliance. See Darren Hawkins and Wade Jacoby, "Partial Compliance: A Comparison
of the European and Inter-American Courts of Human Rights," *Journal of Interna-*

tional Law and International Relations 6, 1 (2010), pp. 38, 61; James L. Cavallaro and Stephanie Erin Brewer, "Reevaluating Regional Human Rights Litigation in the Twenty-first Century: The Case of the Inter-American Court," *AJIL* 102, 4, pp. 768–827. See also Marcia V. J. Kran, "Following Up: The Key to Seeing States Act on Treaty Body Recommendations," November 13, 2019, www.openglobalrights.org/key-to -seeing-states-act-on-treaty-body-recommendations/.

89. See IACHR Annual Report 2020, www.oas.org/en/iachr/reports/ia.asp.

90. UN OHCHR, "The UN Human Rights Appeal 2021," p. 35.

91. Joint NGO Letter: UN Human Rights Treaty Bodies during the COVID-19 Pandemic, May 11, 2020, www.globaldetentionproject.org/joint-ngo-letter-un-human -rights-treaty-bodies-during-the-covid-19-pandemic; Civil Society Letter to the UN High Commissioner of Human Rights Council President Requesting to Supplement UPR Submissions due to COVID-19, May 21, 2020, www.aclu.org/letter/civil-society -letter-un-high-commissioner-and-human-rights-council-president-requesting; Joint Civil Society Letter on UN Human Rights Treaty Body Reviews during the COVID-19 Pandemic, October 2, 2020, www.omct.org/files/2020/10/26110/joint_civil_society _letter_2021_untbs_reviews_in_the_covid19_context_02.10.2020.pdf.

92. For example, see Joint Declaration on Freedom of Expression and Elections in the Digital Age, www.oas.org/en/iachr/expression/showarticle.asp?artID=1174&lID =1; Dialogue between the Three Human Rights Courts of the World: The Impact of COVID-19 on Human Rights, July 13, 2020, www.youtube.com/watch?v =FMWOFS4WjB0; Joint Statement on Data Protection and Privacy in the COVID-19 Response, November 19, 2020, www.who.int/news/item/19-11-2020-joint-statement -on-data-protection-and-privacy-in-the-covid-19-response; Joint Statement on the Rights and Health of Refugees, Migrants and Stateless Must Be Protected in COVID-19 Response, www.ohchr.org/EN/NewsEvents/Pages/DisplayNews.aspx?NewsID=25762 &LangID=E.

93. Lisa Reinsberg, "Mapping the Proliferation of Human Rights Bodies' Guidance on COVID-19 Mitigation," May 22, 2020, www.justsecurity.org/70170/mapping -the-proliferation-of-human-rights-bodies-guidance-on-covid-19-mitigation/.

94. The cohesion between different HRIs has not been perceived as a major problem in international literature because there are few examples of contradictory recommendations. For more on that, see Christina Cerna: "Introductory Remarks by Christina Cerna," *Proceedings of the Annual Meeting (American Society of International Law)* 105 (2011), pp. 507–9; Eric Tistounet, "The Problem of Overlapping among Different Treaty Bodies," in *The Future of UN Human Rights Treaty Monitoring*, edited by Alston and Crawford, pp. 389–94.

95. Jasper Krommendijk, "The (in)Effectiveness of UN Human Rights Treaty Body Recommendations," *Netherlands Quarterly of Human Rights* 33, 2, p. 209.

96. Simon Marks and Sarah Wheaton, "The Doctor Making Trump Queasy," May 7, 2020, www.politico.eu/article/coronavirus-tedros-who-doctor-making-donald -trump-queasy/.

97. Olivier de Frouville, "The United Nations Treaty Bodies in a Transition—Review March–December 2020 Chronicle," Working Paper, Geneva Academy of International Humanitarian Law and Human Rights, June 2021, pp. 4–7, www.geneva-academy.ch/joomlatools-files/docman-files/working-papers/The%20United%20Nations%20Treaty%20Bodies%20in%20a%20Transition%20Period.pdf).

98. This has been highlighted in the meeting with activists. See also Japhet Biegon, "Can the Virtual Sessions of the African Commission Generate More Civil Society Participation?," October 26, 2020, www.openglobalrights.org/can-the-virtual-sessions-of-the-african-commission-generate-more-civil-society-participation/.

99. Joint NGO Letter; Civil Society Letter to the UN High Commissioner; Joint Civil Society Letter on UN Human Rights Treaty Body reviews.

100. Olivier de Frouville, "The United Nations Treaty Bodies in a Transition," p. 7.

101. See Rana Moustafa, "Friends or Foes? International Law and Health Nationalism during COVID-19," December 6, 2021, www.thinkglobalhealth.org/article/friends-or-foes-international-law-and-health-nationalism-during-covid-19.

102. Reinsberg, "Mapping the Proliferation."

103. For example, see Statement by UN Human Rights Experts, "Universal Access to Vaccines Is Essential for Prevention and Containment of COVID-19 around the World," November 9, 2020, www.ohchr.org/EN/NewsEvents/Pages/DisplayNews.aspx?NewsID=26484&LangID=E.

104. Laurence R. Helfer, "Populism and International Human Rights Law Institutions: A Survival Guide," July 10, 2018, p. 237, https://papers.ssrn.com/sol3/papers.cfm?abstract_id=3202633.

105. In that context the Global Review Panel set up to review the financial spending of the Joint United Nations Programme on HIV/AIDS (UNAIDS) noted that the Programme's coordinated response had led to better deployment of its resources. See www.unaids.org/en/resources/campaigns/global_review_panel.

106. The economic situation prevailing during COVID-19 has increased the arrears in states parties' contributions to the UN regular budget, thus affecting the resources allocated to the UN human rights bodies. See UN OHCHR, "The UN Human Rights Appeal 2021," p. 34. States have also imposed cuts on human rights programs under the pretext of the economic situation prevailing in the pandemic. For example, the U.K. government has imposed cuts on funding for programs supporting human rights during COVID-19. See William Worley, "UK government quietly halves funding for major human rights program," April 1, 2021, www.devex.com/news/uk-government-quietly-halves-funding-for-major-human-rights-program-99558.

107. Funding agreements between the private sector and the HRIs raise concerns because they are not made public and are most probably earmarked. See on that the very recent report issued by European Centre for Law and Justice (ECLJ), "The Financing of UN Experts in the Special Procedures of the Human Rights Council," September 2021, https://eclj.org/the-financing-of-un-experts-report?lng=en.

108. On the role of NGOs, civil society, and NHRIs in human rights, see Ted Piccone, *Catalysts for Change: How the UN's Independent Experts Promote Human Rights* (Brookings, 2012), pp. 105–21; Alan Boyle and Christine Chinkin, *The Making of International Law* (Oxford University Press, 2007), pp. 52–93; Peter J. Spiro, "NGOs and Human Rights: Channels of Power," in *Research Handbook on International Human Rights Law*, edited by Sarah Joseph and Adam McBeth (Cheltenham, U.K.: Edward Elgar, 2011), pp. 115–38.

PART II
Domestic Politics and International Human Rights Policies

SIX

Protecting Human Rights from Exclusionary Populism

GERALD NEUMAN

Before the coronavirus pandemic disrupted everything, world politics was un-settled by a series of electoral successes of right-wing populist parties, leaders, and movements. They have not gone away. Some remain in office, and others hover in waiting. The populist project of Brexit is a reality and its tensions con-tinue. Meanwhile, in Latin America, some left-wing populists cling to power, as in Venezuela and Nicaragua, and others have been resurging, as in Bolivia.

The growing strength of populism in established democracies that have pre-viously provided key support to the international human rights regime raises special concern. It not only endangers human rights within those countries' own borders, it also threatens to weaken the international system for protect-ing human rights abroad. The harms are not greater than those created by fully authoritarian governments, but the decay of rights-respecting governance is alarming. Now that the Trump presidency has ended, one may ask how the United States and other countries that see the dangers can contribute to pre-venting them.

With this purpose in mind, the chapter begins by examining the concept of populism, which is debated among political scientists. The analysis favors the "ideational approach," which understands populism as employing an ex-clusionary notion of the people—the "real people," as opposed to disfavored groups that are unworthy—and that purports to rule on behalf of the "real people," whose will should not be constrained. I do not claim that this is the only possible understanding of populism or that it covers all the phenomena that have been characterized as "populist." Rather, this definition captures the relevant category of populism for the inquiry that it undertakes. I will sometimes specify this as "exclusionary populism," as explained later.

The chapter then sketches the negative effects that populism may produce on internationally recognized human rights, both internally and through its influence on foreign policy. This is followed by a discussion of responses to exclusionary populism and its effects, by international human rights institutions, by rights-respecting governments in general, and by the United States in particular as a country recovering from populism.

The Meaning of Populism

The leading contemporary account of populism employed by political scientists is the ideational approach. Cas Mudde has described populism as "an ideology that considers society to be ultimately separated into two homogeneous and antagonistic groups, 'the pure people' versus 'the corrupt elite,' and which argues that politics should be an expression of the *volonté générale* (general will) of the people."[1] Jan-Werner Müller further adds, "Right-wing populists also typically claim to discern a symbiotic relationship between an elite that does not truly belong and marginal groups that are also distinct from the people."[2] These accounts stress important common features: populists are antipluralist; populists have an exclusionary notion of the "real people" that they contrast with morally reprehensible elites; and populists claim to speak for the will of the "real people," which should not be constrained. This ideational conception covers a wide range of more specific forms of populism, including left-wing populists, right-wing populists, and some who are neither. But merely criticizing an elite, or invoking "the people" is not enough to make someone a populist.

Other political scientists have favored different accounts of populism, for example, as an opportunistic strategy pursued by particular leaders, or as a matter of performance or political style.[3] The political-strategic approach views populism as an electoral strategy of a personalistic leader who asserts a direct relationship with the people.[4] Other authors define populism as a form of rhetoric, communicating an identification with the people; this rhetorical approach measures the populist character of a speaker as a matter of degree.

A school of political thinkers on the left, following Ernesto Laclau and Chantal Mouffe, has theorized populist mobilization as a discursive method necessary for constructing a "people" unified in antagonism to the elites in power in order to bring about transformational change.[5] How such a transformation can develop into a stable, rights-protecting democracy, however, is very unclear, as the examples of Venezuela, Bolivia, and Nicaragua illustrate. From a human rights perspective, it is important not to overlook the risks that left-wing populism can also create.

Another contrasting usage of the term "populist" involves theorists or activists who proudly claim the label for a pluralistic, participatory empowerment of the full electorate, consistent with equal rights for all. It should be emphasized that this type of rights-respecting populism is not the subject of this chapter.

Given such variations in usage, some care is required in drawing conclusions from the academic literature on populism. Authors disagree on what "populism" means and on who counts as a populist. I will argue later that, in view of these uncertainties, populism should not be treated as an operative legal concept; rather, outside observers should derive heuristic benefit from close attention to populists' actions.

Without claiming that the ideational approach provides the best definition for all purposes, or covers the full range of individuals and groups that could reasonably be called "populist," one can justify the usefulness of that approach in identifying current dangers. First, ideational populists invoke an antipluralist understanding of "the people." Second, the ideational approach emphasizes their claim to implement the people's will without legal or institutional constraint. Third, the ideational approach applies both to personalistic leaders and to parties. Perhaps the relevant category should be called "exclusionary populism."[6]

Political scientists have offered various explanations of the causes of populism.[7] In this regard, the factors may vary from country to country and at different periods, and the studies may employ different definitions of populism. Some scholars see populist politics as appealing to voters whose identities have been destabilized by modernization or globalization.[8] Others perceive populism as resulting from failures of democratic governance, in European states where convergence among parties constricts the range of policy choices, or in Latin American states where entrenched corruption leads the established parties to neglect the basic needs of the citizenry.[9] Pippa Norris and Ronald Inglehart trace the current success of authoritarian populists to a cultural backlash produced by structural changes in economics, politics, and society.[10] Richard Heydarian has emphasized that different causes operate in emerging market democracies in Asia, where despite economic growth weak institutions have been unable to meet the rising expectations of the middle classes.[11]

It is worth noting here that some of the factors identified in the literature relate to governments that fail to serve the human rights of their population, while others involve a cultural backlash that includes the negative reaction of some citizens to improvements in the human rights of others, possibly racial minorities or women. These types of causes may also operate conjointly—as when majority group members whose economic and social rights are neglected resent attention to minority groups that may be even more disadvantaged.

Dangers for Human Rights from Exclusionary Populism

This section illustrates some of the dangers of exclusionary populism to human rights within a country, to human rights in other countries, and to the international system for protecting human rights.[12] The point is not that populism threatens human rights more than fully established authoritarianism does; China and Russia (which I would not regard as democratic enough to be populist) pose greater dangers. In fact, some of the international risks that populism creates are intensified when populist governments make common cause with autocrats.

Even before populists come to power, they may incite private discrimination or violence, and existing parties may compete with them for votes by adopting some of their exclusionary policies. However, the risks multiply once populists control governmental authority and resources.

To start with, the populists' narrowed definition of "the people," combined with unconstrained implementation of what they claim to be the will of the people, threatens the rights of the excluded groups. The victims may include the ousted elites, but also vulnerable minorities whom the populists think the elites wrongly protected. The threatened rights may involve equality, economic rights, liberties, fair trial, or even life, depending on the particular local situation.

The dangers spill over, however, to other social groups. Once in power, populism risks tipping over into authoritarianism. Political scientists have emphasized the tendency of populist leaders to claim that only they represent the popular will and to deny the legitimacy of any opposition. Thus the category of enemies of the people may expand to encompass former allies, dissenters, and critics. Populists often aim to entrench themselves in power, dismantling legal guarantees of fair electoral competition and disrespecting the political rights of everyone, including their own constituency. They also disdain checks and balances, and may attempt to take over, replace, or abolish institutions such as the judiciary and independent watchdog agencies. Meanwhile, populists may seize the opportunity to enrich themselves and their major supporters, neglecting the needs and rights of the people they purport to represent.

Populists may employ the language of individual rights and in some cases may do more for the rights of their own voters than previous governments had done. From a human rights perspective, however, the allegiance of populists to rights is generally selective and defeasible. They may favor the social rights of the poor, free speech rights of the intolerant, or religious rights of the majority, for example, but only until these interfere with the populists' other priorities. Populist governments may distribute benefits to the poor on a discretionary basis, requiring personal political loyalty in return, rather than implementing genuine social rights.

In addition to violating rights of those they govern, populists clash explicitly with international human rights institutions. Populist agitation may include a focus on how human rights law interferes with implementing the populist understanding of the general will. This conflict may predate a populist's rise to power, as with the Euroskeptics, or it may begin later, after policies have been adopted and criticized, as when the International Criminal Court began to examine Rodrigo Duterte's sanguinary drug enforcement in the Philippines. The judges or personnel of the international institution, and human rights advocates relying on that institution, may then be identified as yet another corrupt elite.

Populist governments may engage in ad hoc defiance of particular rulings or broader efforts to insulate their policy from international scrutiny and interference. Venezuela under the presidency of Hugo Chávez withdrew from the American Convention on Human Rights in 2012, and then his successor Nicolás Maduro resigned from the Organization of American States (OAS) altogether in 2017. (Venezuela also created rival forms of regional cooperation to compete with those it rejected; but as mismanagement, corruption, and the fall in oil prices produced the collapse of the Venezuelan economy, these initiatives have withered.[13]) Similarly, the Philippines withdrew from the International Criminal Court after it attracted the Prosecutor's attention.[14]

Nevertheless, populist regimes may be willing to invoke international human rights mechanisms as tools to serve their own goals, either as allies against domestic opponents or in support of their foreign policy positions, just as they selectively employ rights domestically. For example, Bolivia turned to the OAS under the Inter-American Democratic Charter in 2008 to help Evo Morales overcome resistance to his proposed constitutional reforms. The right-populist Trump administration repeatedly attempted to utilize the same Charter against left-populist Venezuela, and it pursued some country-specific resolutions before quitting the Human Rights Council.

Some populist governments seek to have impact on human rights outside their borders. Although there is no single typical populist foreign policy, certain governments have contributed to the spread of populism by assisting like-minded populists in other countries.[15] Hugo Chávez famously used Venezuela's oil wealth to support left-wing populists in other Latin American countries. Prime Minister Viktor Orbán of Hungary has openly campaigned for right-wing populist candidates in nearby countries such as Slovenia and North Macedonia and has reportedly channeled financial support to them.

Instead of withdrawing from a human rights mechanism in order to avoid its scrutiny, as described above, a populist government may remain in the system and attempt to undermine or obstruct it. The government may actively lead efforts to undermine the mechanism or it may join or acquiesce in such efforts by other populist governments or fully autocratic states. For example, left-populist governments led by Venezuela, Bolivia, and Ecuador (under Rafael Correa) protected one another from OAS sanctions and sought to constrain the Inter-American Commission on Human Rights and the Inter-American Court of Human Rights.[16] Bolivia, Nicaragua, and Venezuela have joined with Russia and China in endeavors at the United Nations (UN) to weaken the global treaty body system.[17]

The role of populist members who remain in the system has become increasingly problematic as populists gain power within key supporters of the international human rights regime. Prominent examples have included the United States under Donald Trump and the European Union (EU), as will be discussed.

Populist governments may decrease their financial support to international human rights institutions, either deliberately to weaken them or merely because they want to keep the funds for purposes they value more. They may seek to change the output of international human rights institutions directly, in political bodies where governments hold seats of their own, such as in the General Assembly and the Human Rights Council, or indirectly, by modifying the procedures of more independent expert bodies that the political bodies oversee.

The spread of populism in Europe has weakened the European Union's capacity for promoting human rights within and beyond its own region. The populist-fueled Brexit has confronted the EU with the loss of an economically and diplomatically important member with a strong rule-of-law tradition. Hungary and Poland have both defied EU human rights measures and shown their willingness to hold the EU budget hostage in order to insulate themselves from financial sanctions for violating their rule-of-law obligations.[18]

Turning to the United States, the unforeseen rise of Donald Trump may have had multiple causes, but populist appeals formed a central feature of his campaign and continued on an essentially daily basis. As Ronald Inglehart and

Pippa Norris observed, "Trump's rhetoric stimulated racial resentment, intolerance of multiculturalism, nationalistic isolationism and belligerence, nostalgia for past glories, mistrust of outsiders, sexism, the appeal of tough leadership, attack-dog politics, and racial and anti-Muslim animosity."[19] The harms that the Trump administration inflicted on human rights within the United States have received widespread attention, often expressed in terms of the subversion of democracy and U.S. constitutional principles. In addition to its domestic effects, the Trump presidency was extremely damaging to human rights globally, not only by the appalling example that it gave, but by its deliberate encouragement of other right-wing populists and autocrats, such as Hungary's Viktor Orbán, Israel's Benjamin Netanyahu, Brazil's Jair Bolsonaro, and Egypt's Abdel Fattah al-Sisi, and by its attacks on the international system. This damage persists, despite Trump's defeat in the 2020 election, and regardless of whether he later returns as a candidate.

To give a few examples, Trump was contemptuous of international cooperation, condemned the European Union, withdrew from the Paris Agreement on climate change while suppressing climate science, and announced withdrawal from the World Health Organization to distract attention from his irresponsible handling of the COVID-19 pandemic. His administration resigned from the UN Human Rights Council, withheld funds from the United Nations and UN agencies, and undermined international legal prohibitions against forcible acquisition of territory. His State Department convened a "Commission on Unalienable Rights" to weaken respect for international human rights law and then conducted a propaganda campaign for its report—translated into several languages—encouraging other countries to pursue self-serving reinterpretations of their human rights obligations.[20] Trump's refusal to accept the outcome of the 2020 election, and his incitement to attack Congress in order to prolong his reign, have offered a precedent to authoritarians around the globe.

Responses to the Populist Challenge

Given the threats that the current wave of exclusionary populism poses to human rights within national borders, to human rights outside them, and to the international human rights system itself, how should human rights institutions and rights-respecting governments—now including the United States—respond? The answer needs to be complex, just as the varieties of exclusionary populism are complex, and different actors will have different roles to play.

Ideally, respect for human rights is achieved by a well-intentioned government and domestic civil society interacting within a background of international cooperation and possibly material assistance. The creation of the international human rights system reflects the recognition that the domestic processes benefit from external attention and advice, which may include binding adjudication and sometimes require stronger incentives. When exclusionary populists come to power, they disrupt these domestic processes and produce situations requiring, at a minimum, external attention and advice.

International human rights courts and similar nonjudicial monitoring bodies have been tasked with making impartial evaluations of a state's compliance with its existing international obligations. Examples include the regional human rights courts and commissions, the global human rights treaty bodies, the International Court of Justice, and the Court of Justice of the European Union, among others—for brevity, I will refer to them all as "monitoring bodies." These independent expert bodies cannot solve the problem posed by the rise of populism, but they can assist in restraining it. They can help to preserve the rule of law and democratic alternatives to populism; they can aid in addressing underlying social causes of populism; they can identify human rights violations committed by populist governments and seek to provide remedies. They can also change their own behavior that may have contributed to populism and avoid making things worse.

Here, as in other situations, the monitoring bodies depend for success on the cooperation of actors with other powers and roles. Other international bodies, governments of other countries, international nongovernmental organizations (NGOs), and local civil society are potential allies in motivating branches of a national government to change rules and practices.

Rights-respecting governments have multiple reasons to be concerned by the misdeeds of states under populist rule. These include the general interests that states have in the rights of one another's citizens under modern international law, specific repercussions that exclusionary populism may have for their own nationals and co-ethnics, the spillover effects of populist misrule on neighboring countries, the distortion of international organizations in which they are joint members, and support that populist governments give to populist opposition movements in other states. As a result, states may seek to protect human rights either by acting through multilateral organizations such as the United Nations, the European Union, or the Organization of American States, or they may pursue bilateral responses in their relations with populist states.

This section discusses the methods by which human rights monitoring bodies and rights-respecting states address the problems caused by populism. First, it explains that monitoring bodies (and generally states) should treat exclusionary populism according to its substance rather than its name. Second, it examines how monitoring bodies (and other states) should share with local actors the task of opposing populist abuse of power. Third, it argues that they must deal with the issues of economic inequality that are often contributory causes of populism. Fourth, it focuses on the need for monitoring bodies to learn from populist critiques of their output, in order to improve their own performance, and for states to protect the independence and funding of monitoring bodies. Fifth, it argues that states need to maintain their own ability to adopt negative incentives against populist human rights violations. Finally, the section makes some specific recommendations for the United States, as a state endeavoring both to recover from populism and to support human rights abroad.

Confronting Populism as Such?

Should the international human rights system directly address populism as an operative legal category? That question is relevant both to international monitoring bodies and to rights-respecting states that cooperate with them. In particular, should they determine whether a specific politician, party, or government qualifies as "populist" and attach legal consequences to that characterization? For several reasons, they should not.

One important consideration is the context of monitoring bodies acting within a human rights law framework. "Populism" is not a legal term recognized in international law, and it has no universally accepted definition. The disputes among scholars regarding the proper understanding of the term have been sufficiently illustrated above. Despite agreement on some core examples, social scientists disagree not only on how to conceptualize populism but also on which politicians or parties should count as populist. Monitoring bodies would open themselves to delegitimating charges of bias and political selectivity if they relied on such a concept as a reason for finding violations or condemning states.

Instead, monitoring bodies can focus on the actions of populists without explicitly categorizing them as such, especially in dealing with the policies of populist governments. Abuses such as discriminatory laws, assaults on the independence of the judiciary, suppression of political competition, attacks on the press, police violence, and similar outcomes of populism are already human rights violations that come within the jurisdiction of various human rights bodies.

I am not saying that monitoring bodies should take no notice of the phenomenon of populism or should never mention it. On the contrary, they should be alert to the risks that it creates for human rights and to the special challenges of interacting with populist governments. International bodies should not, however, try to make populism as such an element of a human rights violation. And they should be conscious of the ambiguity of the term.

There should be room for monitoring bodies to keep a wary eye on populist governments, among others, in accordance with their mandates. Some of the hallmarks of populist consolidation of power include the capture of electoral commissions, takeover of judiciaries, banning of NGOs, subordination of media, and removal of term limits. Such techniques, whether deliberately diffused or merely imitated, have been recognized as elements of an authoritarian "playbook" that should be treated as warning signs of an incremental hollowing out of democracy.[21] Monitoring bodies should pay close attention to these practices individually as well as in the aggregate—at least, to the extent that these issues lie within the body's jurisdiction.[22]

Monitoring bodies could also make an important contribution by clarifying that human rights related to political participation do *not* require the absence of term limits for elected presidents and that these term limits are an important protection for responsive representative democracy. Populist leaders have sought to extend their power by eliminating rules that prevent their reelection, and sometimes subservient courts have invalidated such rules by finding that they violate human rights—either the rights of the leader or the rights of the voters.[23] Monitoring bodies should explain unequivocally that the human rights argument for indefinite reelection of presidents is specious. The Venice Commission of the Council of Europe has issued a useful report favoring nondiscriminatory term limits for presidents; and the Inter-American Court of Human Rights issued an advisory opinion in 2021 holding not only that term limits are compatible with human rights, but that the American Convention on Human Rights prohibits indefinite reelection.[24] It would be beneficial for the Human Rights Committee at the global level and the African Commission on Human and People's Rights to add their own analyses.[25]

In stressing these structural issues of civil and political rights, I do not mean that monitoring bodies that also have jurisdiction to address economic and social rights should de-emphasize them. The need to address economic inequality is discussed below.

Rights-respecting states have similar reasons for caution in using the contested concept of populism when they criticize another state, particularly when they act as members of international organizations. Actions taken in the name of the organization may need to display neutrality, and the ambiguity of the word makes it unsuitable for the articulation of generalized policies. Moreover, some regional organizations have special powers to take action in response to structural alterations in their member states that undermine democracy or the rule of law, or depart from the state's constitutional order.[26] Exclusionary populism may supply a heuristic lens for noticing occasions when such responses may be needed, but the more specific violations provide the prerequisites for action.

However, states in their bilateral relations do not face the same expectations of apolitical behavior and nonselectivity that international monitoring bodies do. Nor are they expected to articulate their foreign policies in neutral and generalizable terms. Thus there may be more room for them to invoke the term "populist" in their dealings with another state, especially when the context ensures that the intended meaning will not be misunderstood.

Counterframing against Populist Politics

Without explicitly condemning populism as such, monitoring bodies and rights-respecting states can contribute to the struggle against it by defending the contrasting ideology of universal human rights and by facilitating open political contestation at the national level, which is where the conflict of ideas must ultimately be won. In the context of discontent with the status quo, populism and human rights provide incompatible perspectives on where the problem lies and how to go about solving it.

Sociologists have emphasized the role of framing in the efforts of social and political movements to persuade citizens to accept their proposals.[27] Populists promote an account in which corrupt elites are to blame for numerous ills, and reassertion of the unconstrained popular will through the leadership of the populists will correct them. Human rights advocates and institutions offer competing accounts whose common theme is that unconstrained government power leads to invasion or neglect of universal rights of individuals.

As is often the case in the system of human rights protection, different roles are appropriate for different actors. Monitoring bodies at the universal or regional level have more generic justifications for the obligations that they enforce. Democratic governance requires rights constraints for all and judicial independence, not the unlimited pursuit of majority will; governments must accept criticism and political competition. Advocates within the national system can particularize their arguments with culturally based references and locally held values that international bodies do not, or should not, rely on. Governments of other states may have both options, depending on their relationship with the state in question.

The effectiveness of external criticism on the domestic audience may depend on how it aligns with local values. For example, in a context where populists hijack an established democratic culture, defending the right to criticize the government against suppression and retaliation may resonate with the voters and awaken them to risks to their own rights as well. National values of freedom of the press, social solidarity, or equal respect may have deeper historical roots in a country than modern treaty articulations.

Most of the work to resist ideational populism, however, must be performed by local actors—human rights defenders, journalists, political opponents, and social movements. A monitoring body can support their efforts, and their right to undertake these efforts, but it should not expect their advocacy to follow international models. Local critics of populist governments will have local discourses that they can employ instead of or alongside the international rights discourse. Local advocates are not bound by norms of neutrality and expertise that monitoring bodies profess; they are free to engage politically and to make openly emotional appeals.[28] Even where international obligations are fully reflected in domestic law, the national versions of universal norms may be more relevant in domestic political debate, especially during periods of populist rule. In the final analysis, successful opposition to populist governments requires locally credible political alternatives. Ideally these will be respectful of universal rights, but rights compliance should be coupled with a particular affirmative vision that attracts voters.

Rights-respecting states face some of the same obstacles as monitoring bodies in reaching the local population of a populist-ruled state in order to help preserve political space for a democratic opposition. The cultural distance between the assisting state and the state with a populist government is one factor that may impair the ability of the former to communicate with local resonance to the residents of the latter. Other historical and political factors in their bilateral relations may make the communication more, or less, successful, and in some situations the advocacy of another country may be considerably more influential than advocacy from global institutions.

Realizing Economic and Social Rights

Being alert to the civil and political rights that exclusionary populism attacks does not mean that either monitoring bodies or rights-respecting states should neglect economic and social rights. Economic hardship and economic inequality have been identified as causal factors in the rise of populism—both left-populism and right-populism—in various countries (though not all). It would be self-defeating to address only the symptoms and not the causes if one has the opportunity to do both. Monitoring bodies that have mandates including economic and social rights should attend to them as part of their response to populism. There are limits, however, to a monitoring body's ability to promote the transnational sharing of resources that realization of economic and social rights may require.

States have greater breadth of authority to seek new solutions than specialized human rights institutions that implement existing obligations, and rights-respecting states in the Global North have access to the resources that are needed. As the world rebuilds from the COVID-19 pandemic, it will be even more urgent to address issues of economic inequality within and among states that were pressing before its onset and have worsened since. That is not to imply that the issues are easy or that the solutions are obvious. Economic and social rights doctrines provide analyses that can justify and guide some of the efforts states make, but there are other discourses such as sustainable development and conflict prevention that can be applied in combination with them.

Meanwhile, however, rights-respecting states need to resist ongoing efforts at the global level to impose *unconditional* duties of transnational redistribution that would preclude the use of economic incentives to promote human rights compliance. As will be discussed later, extraterritorial obligations of assistance and coordination in the realization of economic and social rights, and other collective rights attributed to peoples, should not be naively or cynically twisted into an unqualified obligation of one state to subsidize the depredations by a second state's government against parts of its own population.

Improving and Protecting Human Rights Monitoring Bodies

A monitoring body should not only pass judgment on the actions and claims of populists, it should also reflect on the arguments populists make, in order to evaluate its own practice. Within a human rights framework, deliberative attention to the criticisms leveled against international institutions may help a monitoring body improve its analysis or strategy. At the same time, rights-respecting states need to protect the monitoring body's ability to deliberate appropriately and carry out its functions, defending the body against the efforts of populists and authoritarians to incapacitate it procedurally or financially.

Reflecting on Populist Critiques

International human rights institutions have important lessons to learn from the current wave of populism. Populist rhetoric often includes explicit attacks on international monitoring bodies.[29] These bodies are seen as part of the global elite or the "world government" that threatens the nation; their decisions are said to favor the rights of criminals, terrorists, migrants, prisoners, and other enemies over the rights of the people. I do not want to make claims of causation regarding the importance of human rights backlash for the success of populists; multiple factors contribute to their performance in elections and referendums. Nonetheless, there is value in examining the objections, to see what could be learned from them, to reduce the appeal of populists, or simply to improve the performance of the treaty regimes.

For example, particular claims that human rights bodies overprotect unpopular groups may merely be hateful rhetoric, but examination sometimes reveals elements of valid concern within them. Monitoring bodies should not disregard such objections to their rulings without reflection.

Members of monitoring bodies are, in fact, mostly foreign experts. Transnational monitoring enlists states mutually in protecting one another's populations, shielding current minorities against present harm and members of current majorities against future harm. Ideally states and local human rights defenders would help explain and vindicate the system, but the arrangement is susceptible to nationalist and populist attacks. This reality raises the burden of justification on the experts to show that they are not merely external elites abusing power.

The fundamental principle of international human rights law is that every human being has rights, and populist movements that seek to deny that principle are essentially rejecting the system. Not all populist critiques, however, depend on denying a right altogether. Most human rights are subject to justified limitation for the purpose of directly protecting the rights of others and also for certain more general purposes that are indirectly related to the rights of others (such as "national security").[30] Both the rights and the limitations are important.

A common populist objection to the human rights system maintains that human rights bodies give too much weight to the rights of criminals. A few human rights are and should be absolute, such as the prohibition of torture. Other acts of law enforcement may involve rights that are protected in qualified terms, or explicitly subject to limitation. In determining violations of those rights, monitoring bodies should make clear that they are not disproportionately restricting the government's response to criminal activity, and in particular that they recognize the need to protect the rights of others. As a matter of substance, this recognition should inform the reasoning that leads to a finding of violation. As a matter of exposition—and especially when faced with this type of critique—there would be value in making explicit for readers the body's attention to the rights of nonparticipating victims.

What happens if monitoring bodies conclude that some populist objections to particular decisions or doctrines may have some accuracy, and modify them? Perhaps less than we might hope. Once populist attacks have been unleashed, their rhetoric often operates at a level that can gloss over changes in factual reality. Furthermore, once exclusionary populists come to power, they are likely to acquire new reasons for quarreling with a monitoring body as they seek to entrench their power. Nonetheless, there may be lessons in particular objections that would help the monitoring bodies avoid similar errors in the future, and not supply new fuel to populist fire.

Protecting the Funding and Independence of Monitoring Bodies

Populist governments have repeatedly sought to reduce the impact of monitoring bodies by cutting their funding and limiting their independence, sometimes acting in partnership with fully authoritarian states that are also members of the bodies' sponsoring international organization (such as the UN or the OAS). Even without such deliberate punitive efforts, monitoring bodies face budgetary reductions when states shift their spending priorities or in times of austerity. The continuing economic effects of the COVID-19 pandemic may deprive the system of resources at a time when governments most need to be monitored.

Rights-respecting states need to protect the ability of the system to function, and to resist efforts to undermine monitoring bodies, especially those bodies with jurisdiction to address populist governments' characteristic abuses. Unfortunately there is a kind of egalitarian culture within the UN that disfavors judgments of quality among the various human rights mechanisms, and that facilitates dispersion of resources to less consequential projects.

If necessary, a human rights body can survive lean years when its budget shrinks, so long as the cuts are not too deep and it retains control of its spending choices within the lower amount. The more serious threats involve interference with the body's independence and direct restraint of its functions. These have included efforts to give political bodies disciplinary powers over members of monitoring bodies, to prohibit follow-up procedures or the issuance of general comments, and to limit the information that monitoring bodies can receive.[31] Proposals of that kind portend long-term impairment of the institution's mandate, and rights-respecting states should vigorously oppose them.

Sanctions and Conditional Assistance

States are in a position to do more than criticize populist governments that violate human rights; they can also impose material consequences on them. There are numerous forms of cooperation and assistance that rights-respecting states are free to withhold.[32] The basis of the withholding should be the actual violations, and not the labeling as "populist" per se. A state may have the confidence to make the judgment for itself, or it may avail itself of the findings of international courts and other monitoring bodies. These findings possess an authority and objectivity that can be combined with the political power and financial resources of states to press for change.[33]

Withholding assistance may serve several purposes. It creates countervailing incentives for a government that sees advantage in violating rights; it signals to the other government and its population the seriousness of the violations; and it avoids complicity in the violations or the responsibility for maintaining in power the government that commits them.

Rights-respecting states need to preserve their authority to pursue these goals, in the face of various initiatives aiming to redefine their international obligations in a manner that would unduly restrict or outlaw these sanctions. Authoritarian states such as Cuba, China, and Russia, with some populist allies, have led efforts within the United Nations to proscribe human rights–based sanctions that are not approved by the Security Council (and thereby subject to veto). Various arguments of a state-centered or human rights–based character have been invoked to this end, including the sovereign equality of states, the impermissibility of "unilateral coercive measures," a collective right of peoples to solidarity, and an elaboration of the right to development.[34] Some of these asserted norms are ambiguously defined, making the wrongfulness of measures dependent on an expansive definition of the transnational duties they are said to contravene; others deny the legitimacy of one state's judging the actions of another.

Rights-respecting states need to continue opposing vague and over-broad definitions of "coercive measures" that would eliminate human rights sanctions, and object to the inclusion of a prohibition of such measures in declarations and draft treaties. The human rights of those persons affected by sanctions do need to be taken into account in the operation of sanctions, but not in the exaggerated way favored by advocates of a ban.

Moreover, sanctions arise not only bilaterally but in the context of a prior agreement that authorizes the use of economic pressure to enforce compliance with human rights obligations undertaken within a regional organization. Such preconsented measures, accepted by a state for the sake of its population, should not be viewed as "coercive."

In the case of the European Union, it is disputed whether the organization needs more tools or needs more willingness to use the tools it has, to deal with open defiance of its values by Hungary and Poland.[35] The EU should have and should use the power both to condemn and to impose material consequences for systemic undermining of democracy. Although some decisional procedures give deviant states or groups of deviant states the opportunity to veto decisions, other actions can be taken by majorities. Rights-respecting EU governments should recognize how the deliberately spread contagion of right-wing populism in the EU threatens their own interests, and should resist subsidizing it.

Moreover, Europe has a particularly thick array of mutually reinforcing human rights institutions within the EU and the larger Council of Europe that diagnoses the violations. The EU's Court of Justice and the European Court of Human Rights, which can make decisions by majority, have provided leadership in judgments that are legally binding.[36] Such decisions require political support for their effective implementation, but their legitimacy and authority can reassure those who are inclined to act, and strengthen the motivation of others. The EU Court of Justice has given rule-of-law criteria in EU law greater traction against backsliding by developing a nonregression principle that invokes the state's own prior level of democratization as part of the standard for showing a violation. That criterion not only adds specificity but should assist in explaining the EU's reaction for the benefit of the state's own population, which must ultimately be persuaded to turn against the populists.

The United States as a Recovering Populist State

The United States now has a rights-respecting government at the federal level, which narrowly defeated a right-populist incumbent, and which seeks to restore and secure its liberal democratic character. Populism retains a hold on various state governments, making that task more difficult. The current administration is also seeking to reengage more cooperatively with the international system, including the human rights system. The considerations discussed above have relevance for the United States, both as a state that has suffered from populism and as a state that is trying once more to be a key supporter of the human rights regime.

The Trump years should not be contrasted with an imaginary golden age in which human rights norms provided the sole factor in U.S. foreign policy, and one should not expect such a policy to follow now. Moreover, the United

States has largely emphasized civil and political rights rather than the full range embraced by the international human rights system, including economic and social rights. Nonetheless, Trump's indifference to human rights, admiration for autocrats, and encouragement of right-wing populism in other countries represented a major departure. His administration caused significant damage to the international perception of the United States and to conditions abroad that will be difficult to repair. The danger that Trumpism or its equivalent might return to power is itself an obstacle to U.S. credibility.

At home, the United States needs to restore democratic pluralism and a sense of common purpose. The atmosphere of polarization preceded Trump, but he exacerbated it, and he and his allies and enablers are continuing to do so. The public health and economic crises resulting from COVID-19 provide both challenges and opportunities for reestablishing shared goals.

The economic insecurity that contributed to Trump's rise clearly needs to be addressed, for the good of both his supporters and those he disdained. This project relates to the international concept of economic and social rights, but that global discourse is unlikely to prove useful in the United States and would for many in the population be counterproductive. Framing the issues in terms of the country's own democratic and egalitarian values will have wider appeal to a public accustomed to American exceptionalism.[37] The government should also seek as far as possible to gain the cooperation of diverse religious voices, whose compassionate messages support its public goals—this is doubly important, both to reach their communities and to counteract the impression that right-wing populism is the proper home of religion.[38] Meanwhile, the public needs not only to benefit but to be shown that it is benefiting, in the face of determined efforts of populists to mislead.

Intensified threats to the U.S. electoral system impend as Trump and his supporters reiterate their baseless objections to his defeat, and allies in state legislatures adopt measures to suppress voting and to rewrite election outcomes.[39] Creative countermeasures will be needed if the Senate minority continues to obstruct reform.

The United States badly needs to vindicate truthfulness after four years of continuous fraud at the highest levels. This requires both candor going forward (which will not always be easy) and greater disclosure of the actions of the prior regime and their consequences. The public needs to be shown the level of self-enrichment, corruption, falsification, and conscious illegality that the Trump administration perpetrated.[40] Extreme cases may justify criminal prosecution or civil sanctions, but reputational accountability should be provided more broadly. The Trump administration terminated or suppressed some internal investigations and redacted the reports of others, while intimidating whistle-blowers.[41] Disclosure of primary internal documentation may be as important as the conclusions of independent investigations, which are likely to be dismissed by shameless loyalists as partisan "witch hunts." In some instances there may be objectively persuasive reasons of national security or related concerns for limiting disclosure, but otherwise the self-protective claims of abusive former officials should be outweighed by the public interest in setting the record straight. Regrettably, the needed process of publication may become entangled with byzantine and unsettled doctrines of executive privilege.[42]

Turning to foreign relations, the United States has much to contribute as a rights-respecting state. The Biden administration has already begun to take some of the appropriate steps. It is reengaging with neglected allies and international arrangements, including the World Health Organization and the Paris Agreement on climate change, has rejoined the Human Rights Council, and has ceased to praise autocracy. Still, it is important that these course corrections continue. Secretary of State Antony Blinken has repudiated the notorious report of the Trump administration's "Commission on Unalienable Rights," which sought to dilute U.S. human rights policy and discredit international monitoring bodies.[43] The State Department will need to make further efforts to counteract the encouragement that the wide official dissemination of the report, and private efforts to continue publicizing it, give to other populist governments.

Meanwhile, the Trump administration's mutually supportive relations with right-populist governments need to be rethought. A prime example was the Netanyahu government in Israel, which traded political favors with Trump. Among other actions, Trump proclaimed U.S. recognition of Israeli sovereignty over Syria's Golan Heights, in defiance of modern international law's prohibition of acquisition of territory by conquest, and in December 2020 he agreed to recognize Morocco's sovereignty over the former Spanish colony of Western Sahara in exchange for Morocco's recognizing Israel.[44] These disruptive moves threaten to destabilize the basic ground rules of armed conflict and to legitimate Russia's expansion across its borders by force. In Latin America, the United States needs to exert moderating influence, to the extent it can, on both left-populist and right-populist governments.

The Trump administration also established a so-called International Religious Freedom (or Belief) Alliance, enlisting primarily right-wing populist governments such as Hungary, Poland, and Brazil. The Alliance enabled religiously intolerant governments to claim attachment to religious liberty by protesting persecution of their own coreligionists, and to argue for the supremacy of religious freedom over the human rights of women and sexual minorities.[45] The new administration has continued in the Alliance, providing its Secretariat in the State Department's Office of International Religious Freedom and leading one of its working groups (on threats posed by technology).[46] The United States could resign from the Alliance, but it should consider expanding and reforming it. Rights-respecting countries reluctant to join a project of Mike Pompeo might be willing to contribute to a genuinely evenhanded approach to religious freedom that is recalibrated to be consistent with the human rights of all. Actual religious persecution is definitely a serious problem in the world, and a diverse group of governments willing to help enforce existing international standards could decrease it—particularly if they are sufficiently diverse and committed to examining their own failings as well as those of others. A reconfigured alliance could support the work of existing human rights mechanisms rather than attempting to undermine or replace them. Domestically, the effort might also draw some religious constituencies back toward shared values and away from populist divisiveness.

The problem of participation in the Alliance illustrates a disadvantage of convening states as admitted members in a standing organization to address the challenges of populism. Membership becomes a credential that may be undeserved from the outset and that is politically very difficult to withdraw, even after changes in a member's government. The same concerns apply to the idea of anointing a group of 10 democracies—the "D-10"—to defend democracy, rather than convening ad hoc meetings of countries based on their current circumstances.[47] One need only consider the real possibility of France under a future President Marine Le Pen. Whatever merit the idea might have in opposition to full-fledged autocracy, it is unsuitable at this time as a strategy against exclusionary populism.

Conclusion

Exclusionary populism threatens human rights, and rights-respecting states have both principled and self-protective reasons for responding to its spread. Autocracy poses even greater dangers, but the protection of pluralistic democracy depends on constraints that populists also disdain. Populism arises in different contexts and takes different forms, and so strategies for opposing it must be sensitive to context.

International human rights monitoring bodies should treat populism by its substance, condemning the characteristic violations that result, rather than considering "populism" itself as a violation. The international bodies should protect local opponents of populism, who add nationally resonant advocacy to the more distant universal discourse. These bodies should address the causes as well as the consequences of populism, especially the neglect of economic and social rights. Monitoring bodies should not merely dismiss populist critiques of their decisions but should examine the feedback for possible lessons about their own conclusions and explanations.

Rights-respecting states, now including the United States, should generally focus on the violations, reinforcing the efforts of monitoring bodies and the rights of local opponents. That also requires states to protect the independence and fiscal capacity of monitoring bodies. The United States needs to stabilize its own democracy to counter exclusionary populism abroad. Rights-respecting states must address the problems of economic inequality that often contribute to populist electoral success. At the same time, they need to preserve their own authority to impose appropriate sanctions on states that violate human rights; rights-respecting EU states should muster the will to sanction their own members. The United States should reckon with the abuses of the Trump years and try to enlist religious allies in projects consistent with universal human rights.

Notes

1. Cas Mudde, "Populism: An Ideational Approach," in *The Oxford Handbook of Populism*, edited by Cristóbal Rovira Kaltwasser, Paul Taggart, Paulina Ochoa Espejo, and Pierre Ostiguy (Oxford University Press, 2017), pp. 29–47.

2. Jan-Werner Müller, *What Is Populism?* (University of Pennsylvania Press, 2016), p. 23.

3. This section draws on Gerald L. Neuman, "Populist Threats to the International Human Rights System," in *Human Rights in a Time of Populism: Challenges and Responses*, edited by Gerald L. Neuman (Cambridge University Press, 2020), pp. 1–19.

4. Kurt Weyland, "Populism: A Political-Strategic Approach," in *Oxford Handbook*, edited by Rovira Kaltwasser et al., pp. 48–72; Steven Levitsky and James Loxton, "Populism and Competitive Authoritarianism in the Andes," *Democratization* 20, 1 (2013), p. 110, https://doi.org/10.1080/13510347.2013.738864.

5. See Ernesto Laclau, *On Populist Reason* (London: Verso, 2005).

6. Professors Mudde and Rovira Kaltwasser, proponents of the ideational approach, have used the term "exclusionary populism" in a narrower sense, contrasting contemporary examples in European welfare states with more "inclusionary" examples of ideational populism in Latin America that offer empowerment to long-disenfranchised economic classes. All of these, however, are ideational populists, inclusive toward some and exclusionary toward others, and thus "exclusionary" in the wider sense I am using here.

7. See Kirk A. Hawkins, Madeleine Read, and Teun Pauwels, "Populism and Its Causes," in *Oxford Handbook*, edited by Rovira Kaltwasser et al., pp. 267–86.

8. Ibid., p. 269; Kenneth M. Roberts, "Neoliberalism and the Transformation of Populism in Latin America," *World Politics* 48, 1 (1995), p. 82, www.jstor.org/stable /25053953.

9. For example, Kirk A. Hawkins, "Responding to Radical Populism: Chavismo in Venezuela," *Democratization* 23, 2 (2016), p. 242, https://doi.org/10.1080/13510347 .2015.1058783; Hanspeter Kriesi, "The Populist Challenge," *West European Politics* 37, 2 (2014), p. 361, https://doi.org/10.1080/01402382.2014.887879.

10. Pippa Norris and Ronald Inglehart, *Cultural Backlash: Trump, Brexit and the Rise of Authoritarian Populism* (Cambridge University Press, 2019).

11. See Richard Javad Heydarian, "Penal Populism in Emerging Markets: Human Rights and Democracy in the Age of Strongmen," in *Human Rights in a Time of Populism*, edited by Neuman, pp. 130–63.

12. The examples will assume that the countries or leaders mentioned are properly described as populist—I am not claiming that the facts mentioned suffice to demonstrate exclusionary populism.

13. See Asa K. Cusak, *Venezuela, ALBA, and the Limits of Postneoliberal Regionalism in Latin America and the Caribbean* (New York: Palgrave Macmillan, 2019); compare Alexander Cooley's chapter 4 in this volume, which discusses the creation of authoritarian international organizations by China and Russia.

14. See Jason Gutierrez, "Amid Inquiry of Duterte, Philippines Exits International Criminal Court," *New York Times*, March 17, 2019, www.nytimes.com/2019/03/17 /world/asia/philippines-international-criminal-court.html; Antonio F. Perez, "Democracy Clauses in the Americas: The Challenge of Venezuela's Withdrawal from the OAS," *American University International Law Review* 33 (2017), p. 391, https:// scholarship.law.edu/scholar/985/. The effectiveness of Maduro's withdrawal from the OAS is disputed.

15. Rosa Balfour, Corina Stratulat, Juliane Schmidt, et al., "Europe's Troublemakers: The Populist Challenge to Foreign Policy," European Policy Center, 2016, pp. 35–36, www.epc.eu/documents/uploads/pub_6377_europe_s_troublemakers.pdf ?doc_id=1714.

16. See Mónica Pinto, "The Crisis of the Inter-American System," *American Society of International Law Proceedings* 107 (2013), p. 127, https://doi.org/10.5305 /procannmeetasil.107.0127.

17. See Christen Broecker and Michael O'Flaherty, "The Outcome of the General Assembly's Treaty Body Strengthening Process: An Important Milestone on a Longer Journey," 2014, www.universal-rights.org/urg-policy-reports/the-outcome-of-the -general-assemblys-treaty-body-strengthening-process-an-important-milestone-on-a -longer-journey/; see also Alexander Cooley's chapter 4, on efforts by Russia and China to dilute UN oversight.

18. See Benjamin Martill and Monika Sus, "Known Unknowns: EU Foreign, Security and Defence Policy after Brexit," Dahrendorf Forum, 2018, www.dahrendorf

-forum.eu/publications/known-unknowns/; Anna Júlia Donáth, "Absolutely Corrupted: The Rise of an Illiberal System and the Future of Hungarian Democracy," *Brown Journal of World Affairs* 27, 2, p. 1, https://bjwa.brown.edu/27-2/absolutely -corrupted-the-rise-of-an-illiberal-system-and-the-future-of-hungarian-democracy/.

19. Norris and Inglehart, *Cultural Backlash*, p. 76.

20. See also chapter 7 by Melani McAlister in this volume, discussing the origin of the Commission on Unalienable Rights and criticisms of its report.

21. See César Rodríguez-Garavito and Krizna Gomez, "Responding to the Populist Challenge: A New Playbook for the Human Rights Field," in *Rising to the Populist Challenge: A New Playbook for Human Rights Actors*, edited by César Rodríguez-Garavito and Krizna Gomez (Bogotá: Dejusticia, 2018), pp. 11–53; Christopher Sabatini and Ryan Berg, "Autocrats Have a Playbook—Now Democrats Need One Too," *Foreign Policy*, February 10, 2021, https://foreignpolicy.com/2021/02/10 /autocrats-have-a-playbook-now-democrats-need-one-too/; Kurt Weyland, "Autocratic Diffusion and Cooperation: The Impact of Interests vs. Ideology," *Democratization* 24, 7, (2017), p. 1235, https://doi.org/10.1080/13510347.2017.1307823.

22. For example, the regional human rights courts and the Human Rights Committee have general authority to examine civil and political rights such as voting rights, free expression and association, and judicial independence; monitoring bodies focused on economic and social rights or on specially protected groups such as children have more limited opportunities to address these issues.

23. See Tom Ginsburg, James Melton, and Zachary Elkins, "On the Evasion of Executive Term Limits," *William and Mary Law Review* 52, 6 (2011), p. 1807, https:// papers.ssrn.com/sol3/papers.cfm?abstract_id=1683594; and David Landau, "Presidential Term Limits in Latin America: A Critical Analysis of the Migration of the Unconstitutional Constitutional Amendment Doctrine," *Law and Ethics of Human Rights* 12 (2018), p. 225, https://papers.ssrn.com/sol3/papers.cfm?abstract_id=3053521.

24. European Commission for Democracy Through Law, "Report on Term-Limits: Part I—Presidents," CDL-AD(2018)010 (2018), www.venice.coe.int/webforms /documents/default.aspx?pdffile=CDL-AD(2018)010-e; Advisory Opinion OC-28/21, Indefinite Presidential Re-Election in Presidential Systems in the Context of the Inter-American System of Human Rights (Interpretation and scope of Articles 1, 23, 24, and 32 of the American Convention on Human Rights, XX of the American Declaration of the Rights and Duties of Man, 3(d) of the Charter of the Organization of American States and of the Inter-American Democratic Charter), 28 Inter-American Court of Human Rights (ser. A) (2021) (with two dissenting opinions).

25. Admittedly, term limits for a particular office would not prevent populist leaders from guiding their governing parties from alternative posts or unofficial positions, as Jarosław Kaczyński currently does in Poland, but they do at least restrict de jure concentration of power over long periods of time and create opportunities for rivalries within a populist party to weaken its threat to competitive democracy.

26. For example, the Inter-American Democratic Charter, Articles 17–22 (2001) (addressing unconstitutional interruption of the democratic order of a member state);

and the African Charter on Democracy, Elections and Governance, Articles 23–26 (providing for sanctions against listed illegal means of accessing or maintaining power).

27. Robert D. Benford and David A. Snow, "Framing Processes and Social Movements: An Overview and Assessment," *Annual Review of Sociology* 26 (2000), p. 615, https://doi.org/10.1146/annurev.soc.26.1.611.

28. See Rodríguez-Garavito and Gomez, "Responding to the Populist Challenge," p. 39.

29. See, for example, Ángel R. Oquendo, "The Politicization of Human Rights: Within the Inter-American System and Beyond," *New York University Journal of International Law and Politics* 50, 1 (2017), p. 1, https://nyujilp.org/wp-content/uploads /2018/02/Oquendo-PDF.pdf.

30. For example, the International Covenant on Civil and Political Rights, Article 19(3)(b) (allowing restrictions on freedom of expression that are necessary for the protection of national security); and the American Convention on Human Rights, Article 13(2)(b) (same).

31. See Broecker and O'Flaherty, "The Outcome of the Treaty Body Strengthening Process"; see also Pinto, "Crisis of the Inter-American System."

32. I say "free to withhold" because there may be treaty obligations to confer certain benefits, subject to certain conditions, and there are too many variations to address them all here.

33. Moreover, within international organizations, the fact that an international court can decide by majority may make these findings a useful supplement when a political body is stymied by a veto rule.

34. See, for example, Alexandra Hofer, "The Developed/Developing Divide on Unilateral Coercive Measures: Legitimate Enforcement or Illegitimate Intervention?," *Chinese Journal of International Law* 16, 2 (2017), p. 175, https://papers.ssrn.com/sol3 /papers.cfm?abstract_id=3581655; Rosa Freedman and Jacob Mchangama, "Expanding or Diluting Human Rights? The Proliferation of United Nations Special Procedure Mandates," *Human Rights Quarterly* 38, 1 (2016), pp. 164, 189–93, https://papers .ssrn.com/sol3/papers.cfm?abstract_id=2775622; Draft Convention on the Right to Development, Article 14, UN Doc. A/HRC/WG.2/21/2 (2020).

35. Kim Lane Scheppele and R. Daniel Kelemen, "Defending Democracy in EU Member States: Beyond Article 7 TEU," in *EU Law in Populist Times: Crises and Prospects*, edited by Francesca Bignami (2020), pp. 413–56; Justyna Łacny, "The Rule of Law Conditionality under Regulation No 2092/2020—Is It All about the Money?," *Hague Journal on the Rule of Law* 13 (2021), p. 79, https://link.springer.com/article /10.1007/s40803-021-00154-6.

36. See, for example, *Repubblika* v. *Il-Prim Ministru*, Case C-896/19 (CJEU 2021) [Grand Chamber]; *Xero Flor w Polsce* v. *Poland*, App. no. 4907/18, ECHR (2021).

37. Nonetheless, international human rights framings may provide encouragement to citizens whose claims for justice are not adequately met by current U.S. constitutional doctrines. I am grateful to Gay McDougall for emphasizing this point.

38. See also chapter 7 by Melani McAlister.

39. See Jane Mayer, "The Big Money behind the Big Lie," *New Yorker*, August 9, 2021, www.newyorker.com/magazine/2021/08/09/the-big-money-behind-the-big-lie.

40. See, for example, Sam Berger, "How a Future President Can Hold the Trump Administration Accountable," Center for American Progress, August 6, 2020, https://cdn.americanprogress.org/content/uploads/2020/08/05105154/TrumpAccountability-brief.pdf?_ga=2.116672966.134675517.1617069745-695515846.1617069745.

41. Ibid.

42. See Mark J. Rozell and Michel A. Sollenberger, *Executive Privilege: Presidential Power, Secrecy, and Accountability*, 4th ed. (University Press of Kansas, 2020); Jonathan David Shaub, "The Executive's Privilege," *Duke Law Journal* 70 (2020), p. 1, https://scholarship.law.duke.edu/dlj/vol70/iss1/1/; see *Nixon* v. *Administrator of General Services*, 433 U.S. 425, 448–49 (1977) (recognizing qualified interest of a former president in limiting public access to confidential communications).

43. See U.S. Department of State, "Secretary Antony J. Blinken on Release of the 2020 Country Reports on Human Rights Practices," March 30, 2021, www.state.gov/secretary-antony-j-blinken-on-release-of-the-2020-country-reports-on-human-rights-practices/.

44. On the Golan Heights, see Jean Galbraith, "Contemporary Practice of the United States Relating to International Law—United States Recognizes Israeli Sovereignty over the Golan Heights," *American Journal of International Law* 113, 3 (2019), p. 613, https://doi.org/10.1017/ajil.2019.35; Oona Hathaway and Scott Shapiro, "Trump's Golan Policy and Its Threat to the Post-War International Legal Order," *Just Security* (blog), May 16, 2019, www.justsecurity.org/64141/trumps-golan-policy-and-its-threat-to-the-post-war-international-legal-order/; on Morocco, see Kristen E. Eichensehr, "United States Recognizes Morocco's Sovereignty over Western Sahara," *American Journal of International Law* 115, 2 (2021), p. 318, https://doi.org/10.1017/ajil.2021.11.

45. See Jeffrey Haynes, "Trump and the Politics of International Religious Freedom," *Religions* 11, 8 (2020), p. 385, www.mdpi.com/2077-1444/11/8/385; see also chapter 7 by Melani McAlister, which discusses the origins and focus of the Alliance.

46. See U.S. Department of State, International Religious Freedom or Belief Alliance, 2021, www.state.gov/international-religious-freedom-or-belief-alliance/. In 2021, President Biden chose Rashad Hussain to head that Office, as part of the effort "to build an Administration that looks like America and reflects people of all faiths." White House, "President Biden Announces Intent to Nominate and Appoint Leaders to Serve in Key Religious Affairs Roles," July 30, 2021, www.whitehouse.gov/briefing-room/statements-releases/2021/07/30/president-biden-announces-intent-to-nominate-and-appoint-leaders-to-serve-in-key-religious-affairs-roles/. Brief notes about monthly meetings of the Alliance can be found on the web page of the Danish Office of the Special Representative for Freedom of Religion or Belief; see Ministry of Foreign Affairs of Denmark, Activities, 2021, https://um.dk/en/foreign-policy/office

-of-the-special-representative-for-freedom-of-religions-or-belief/selected-activities-of
-the-office-of-the-special-representative-for-freedom-of-religion-or-belief/.

47. See, for example, Michel Duclos, "Do We Need a Global Alliance of Democracies?," *Institut Montaigne* (Blog), January 7, 2021, www.institutmontaigne.org/en
/blog/do-we-need-global-alliance-democracies.

SEVEN

Evangelicals and Human Rights

MELANI MCALISTER

U.S. evangelicals are human rights actors, although their definitions of rights and approach to international legal regimes frequently place them in conflict with global norms. The situation is even more complex globally, where evangelicals have evoked human rights claims in some situations and national contexts but actively abjure it in others. Overall, since the 1990s they have increasingly, if conditionally, embraced "human rights" as a moral language for analyzing political crises, while often sitting uneasily within—or in opposition to—international human rights institutions.

American evangelicals are leaders in this global evangelical international conversation about rights, and this chapter focuses on their history and practices, with attention to how human rights discourse also facilitates transnational connections. At the same time, evangelicals globally have increasingly operated as part of a larger coalition of conservative Christians, one that is distinctly ecumenical—bringing together Orthodox, Catholics, Mormons, and evangelical Protestants. This new transnational and ecumenical conservatism highlights religious freedom as a primary value, singles out Islam as a threat, and diminishes or denies certain rights that are central to the international human rights agenda, particularly Lesbian, Gay, Bisexual, Transgender, Queer (LGBTQ+) rights and women's reproductive rights. I highlight here three interrelated factors that shape evangelicals' relationship to human rights discourse: (1) the focus on religious freedom as a primary right; (2) a series of arguments against LGBTQ+ and women's rights as an impingement on religious freedom; and (3) the emergence of a transnational and ecumenical coalition to pursue these interlocking agendas.

One fundamental context for U.S. evangelicals' engagement in international conversations about human rights is the reality that evangelicalism is a truly global religious phenomenon—indeed, Americans and Europeans are a minority of this religious subgroup, which has grown tremendously in Asia, Africa, and Latin America over the last four decades.[1] This growth of Global South Christianity, particularly in its Pentecostal and evangelical forms, has meant that the international institutions of evangelicalism—the Lausanne Movement, the World Evangelical Alliance, the Pentecostal World Fellowship— are increasingly led by Asians, Africans, and Latin Americans, even as U.S. evangelicals maintain considerable clout, financial and otherwise. American evangelical leaders, church pastors, even ordinary believers on short-term missions—as well as anybody with an internet connection—have greater contact with like-minded believers around the world than previous generations could have imagined. American Christians have always been missionary-minded, but today's evangelicals are increasingly (but not uniformly) aware of themselves as just one part of a much larger transnational faith.

This awareness has played a key role in how and when evangelicals have directly involved themselves in U.S. foreign policy. In recent years, a number of historians have documented their role as activists on U.S. foreign policy over many decades: starting as lobbyists in response to the famine and genocide in Armenia at the turn of the twentieth century, to becoming major players fighting communism at home and abroad in the Cold War, to their significant role in pushing for U.S. support for Israel, as well as furthering anti-Muslim sentiment in recent decades.[2] U.S. evangelicals have a range of political views: among white evangelicals, a small number are quite liberal on most issues; many more are moderately conservative; and a large percentage are quite conservative on most domestic and foreign policy issues. Evangelicals of color are more liberal on almost every measure than their white counterparts.[3] Across the board, they have formed a broad range of political organizations and coalitions over the last decades (ranging from conservative groups such as Moral Majority, Stand for Israel, and Alliance Defending Freedom to the more moderate Institute for Global Engagement and the liberal-leaning Evangelicals for Social Action), which sometimes worked for specific legislation, and at other times simply advocated for awareness of signature issues.

It was within this larger context of globalization and an expansive sense of political investment that U.S. evangelicals began to take on human rights as a key issue, frequently (but not solely) through the lens of religious freedom. The impact of human rights as an increasingly accepted moral framework has been multivalent. It has undoubtedly led to a strengthening of the position of the small U.S. evangelical Left, influenced by a similar movement in Latin America, that has argued for greater attention to economic and social rights.[4] But, more significantly, a focus on human rights has also given moral authority to those who argue that Christians in particular are victims of religious persecution and in need of international protection. That focus has reshaped evangelical language and activism, as both U.S. and global evangelical institutions organize themselves around a kind of "human rights as self-defense" model. This sense of embattlement has shaped the ways in which the politics of religious freedom has become deeply embedded with the politics of sexuality and gender. That is, evangelicals across the world have taken positions in opposition to the global human rights consensus on reproductive rights, gender equality, and LGBTQ+ rights, defending their positions in the language of religious freedom and rights. They are certainly not alone in focusing more on some rights than on others, but their deep transnational networks have made them unexpectedly effective at furthering their own rights agendas, and, in the process, reshaping the global conversation to highlight religious freedom as uniquely endangered.

Historical Background

Samuel Moyn has famously argued that the modern foundations of human rights were built as much from western European Christian conservatism as from the secular Left.[5] As Christopher Sabatini describes in the introduction to this volume, there are many serious questions about this claim, and it is rightfully debated as an origin story for the modern movement. Certainly in the United States, evangelicals of the 1950s and 1960s had very little traffic with any kind of human rights language and were indeed hostile to its primary institutional home, the United Nations (UN). By the late 1970s and in the 1980s, however, conservative Christian thinkers themselves began to lay claim to the language of human rights, in part through the argument that the idea of rights has a fundamentally Christian foundation. In the 1970s, evangelical publications such as *Christianity Today* and *World Vision* often embraced the language of human rights, even as the editors occasionally worried aloud that the "unlovely" concept put people rather than God at the center of moral discourse. In 1984, the internationally regarded, theologically conservative

Protestant theologian Max Stackhouse argued that not only did belief in God require a commitment to human rights, but the very concept of human rights was built on theism.

> The first presuppositional belief—the belief in a universal moral law which stands over and above every people, every culture, and every social contract which the people construct out of their own genius—relies upon a second presuppositional belief, which is none other than the ancient Semitic insight that all humans are made in the image of God, and that all peoples—rich and poor, powerful and weak, wise and simple, well and lowly-born—are all equally under the same God and under that God's universal and equitable righteousness. Human rights are thus a gift and demand of God.[6]

Stackhouse saw in the broad moral appeal of human rights to people around the world something like a presupposition of God, so that "rights talk" was not an alternative to but an argument for monotheism in general and Christianity in particular.

These theological conversations, however, were secondary to the pragmatic ways in which U.S. evangelicals began to take up human rights issues during the Cold War. Tracing this movement requires a recognition that their political visions were never rigidly focused on domestic issues, as scholarship has previously implied. But it also highlights the ways in which they made common cause with Catholics and sometimes even liberal Protestants on a range of issues, from religious freedom to abortion. As Udi Greenberg has shown, a major rapprochement between Catholics and Protestants occurred with Vatican II in 1964, when the Catholic church reversed its policy of trying to limit Protestant evangelism in Catholic-dominated European states.[7] Both Catholics and Protestants were involved in anti-communist religious freedom crusades throughout the Cold War, developing a model of political rights that was also shared with a range of secular conservatives. In the 1970s, conservative Catholics and evangelicals developed an alliance in the anti-abortion movement. The founder of the Moral Majority, Jerry Falwell, commented that the fight against abortion had taught him to let go of his separatist tendencies and to ally with Catholics who shared his platform.[8]

After Vatican II, U.S. Catholics and Protestants (both ecumenical and evangelical) made religious freedom a signature political issue. During the 1960s and 1970s, evangelical activists were involved in a variety of anti-communist campaigns, focusing frequently on Christian communities in the Soviet bloc. Notably, they joined in supporting the 1974 Jackson-Vanik amendment that pressured the USSR over Jewish emigration. That same year, the Lausanne Congress on World Evangelism, the largest global gathering of evangelicals to date, called upon leaders of all nations "to guarantee freedom of thought and conscience, and freedom to practice and propagate religion in accordance with the will of God and as set forth in the Universal Declaration of Human Rights."[9]

This public embrace of human rights did not necessarily mean liberalizing politics. As Lauren Turek has shown, many U.S. evangelicals closely allied themselves with conservative Christian politicians guilty of profound human rights violations, particularly in South Africa and Latin America, as was the case with General Rios Montt in Guatemala in the 1980s. If they believed a given regime was good for missionary work, or if the leaders claimed to be conservative Christians, evangelical believers often whitewashed and justified their oppressive behavior, while still decrying government leaders in China, the USSR, and parts of the Middle East who disallowed evangelism or discriminated against Christians.[10]

It is a sign of the capaciousness of human rights language that the framework of human rights could also fit with an emerging liberal ethos in the diverse global evangelical community. Starting in the 1970s, Latin American, African, and Asian members moved more to the forefront of its leadership. Often much more inclined to take seriously issues such as poverty, oppression, and war, they helped expand the traditional religious freedom agenda toward a broader focus on "social concern"—including the language of human rights that now included social and economic rights.[11] In this way, some of these leaders were moved to embrace human rights more fully: there were evangelicals who supported Biafra in the Nigeria-Biafra war, opposed apartheid, fought for the southern Sudanese, and spoke out against the Contras in Nicaragua—all under the rubric of human rights, using the signature language of the human rights movement and what, by the 1970s, had become its standardized visual rhetoric of barbed wire and suffering bodies.[12]

Nonetheless, it was religious freedom that remained the signature human right for U.S. evangelicals, and this focus did not recede with the end of the Cold War. In the late twentieth century, the global movement increasingly began to concentrate on what it saw as a rising threat: Islam. The movement on behalf of "persecuted Christians" became a key form of evangelical internationalism in the 1990s. This sense of persecution was an important driver behind evangelical leadership in the 1998 International Religious Freedom Act (IRFA), which turned religious freedom into an institutionalized pillar of U.S. foreign policy.[13] A younger generation of astute political actors had become fluent in the language of Capitol Hill, as evangelicals formed think-tanks and nongovernmental organizations (NGOs) that integrated human rights activism. Some of these leaders focused only on the suffering of Christians (often at the hands of Muslims), seeing human rights as a user-friendly language for pursuing a more sectarian agenda on behalf of fellow believers. Out of the IRFA legislation there developed a new U.S. Commission for International Religious Freedom and a new ambassador for International Religious Freedom. (The roles of the commissioners and the ambassador were heavily skewed in both the Bush and Trump administrations toward white conservative Christians.) At the same time, IRFA created an opening for more genuinely capacious commitments. By the turn of the twenty-first century, a host of organizations, including think-tanks such as the Institute for Global Engagement, and older evangelical institutions such as Intervarsity Christian Fellowship and World Vision, began to speak about the imperative of support for human rights alongside, and in conjunction with, a primary call to missionary work.

Indeed, missionary work itself was changing. While many missions agencies insisted that they were interested only in furthering the gospel, not in taking any social stands, their impact in any given area almost inevitably had political consequences. This was true in the early 1960s when American missions declared themselves opposed to the Republic of the Congo's first prime minister, Patrice Lumumba, and in a different way it remained true in 2003 in Iraq, when U.S. missionaries followed behind American troops with care packages stuffed with blankets and Bible verses. Earlier generations of U.S. evangelicals had often been known for refusing to prioritize health and food services over evangelism, but by the 1980s some of the country's best-known Christian conservatives made "social concern" and human rights their calling cards: the Reverend Franklin Graham as head of Samaritan's Purse, Rick Warren as leader of a global campaign against human immunodeficiency virus/acquired immunodeficiency syndrome (HIV/AIDS), and Pentecostal T. D. Jakes of MegaCARE Ministries. In the early 2000s, both Black and white U.S. evangelicals worked politically to gain government support for the Christian population of southern Sudan during Sudan's civil war, while also sending money to support schools, church-building, and traditional missionary work.[14]

Human Rights Activism in the Twenty-First Century

In today's environment, evangelical human rights activism is fractured. Liberal or moderately conservative organizations continue to advocate for religious freedom in general, not just for Christians, in conjunction with their advocacy for other social goods such as ending poverty or empowering women. The

Institute for Global Engagement (IGE) is exemplary here. A small think-tank with a large footprint, founded by Robert Seiple, the first U.S. ambassador for religious freedom; IGE publishes a journal, *Religion and International Affairs* and hosts a range of programs that promote interreligious understanding, especially in Asia. Similarly, the humanitarian organization World Vision, which by the 1980s had begun to move from being a missionary organization with humanitarian projects into a full-fledged aid and development organization, also began to take more positions that aligned it with global human rights norms. It officially adopted the United Nations Declaration of Human Rights in 1985 and became more actively engaged on issues of social justice and development, and of basic human rights.[15] This openness to human rights norms and language is evident, for example, in the Rohingya Muslim crisis in Myanmar, where IGE, *Christianity Today,* World Vision, and a range of other evangelical organizations have all taken strong stances.[16]

It is the focus on "persecuted Christians," however, that remains perhaps the key political vision uniting a broad range of evangelical believers, across denominations, racial identities, and national borders. The idea that Christians are persecuted for their beliefs—by Muslims, by secular states, or by liberal nonbelievers—has become a central component of conservative (and often liberal) Christian political discourse. This view is trumpeted online, at church conferences, in promotional fundraising for humanitarian organizations, and through a range of groups devoted specifically to that issue, such as Persecution: International Christian Concern and Open Doors. The idea that Christians are "the most persecuted group in the world" has become standard language among evangelicals—and increasingly is taken as a given among a range of other Christians, including the Orthodox and Catholics.[17] Using a language of human rights and religious freedom, the "persecuted Christians" movement casts Christian believers as both victims and heroes in a melodrama of steadfastness against evil.[18] It traverses communities divided by denomination or politics: the "persecuted Christian" may be Orthodox or Catholic or Baptist, and the language of concern about their suffering is shared broadly, inflected differently in the liberal *Sojourners* than the far-right *World*, but often rather seamlessly eliding political boundaries. Still, those most invested in the discourse of Christian persecution tend to be part of the ecumenical conservative coalition that reemerged from the ashes of the Christian right in the 1990s—a coalition now more expansive in who "counts" as Christian, and far more transnational, than in previous generations.

The Trump administration made religious freedom into a signature issue, designed to appeal to evangelicals and other conservative Christians. The State

Department moved its Office of International Religious Freedom (which had been established with the International Religious Freedom Act in 1998) out of the human rights bureau and made it a standalone office.[19] The administration courted evangelicals, not only through its highly visible Evangelical Advisory Board, but also through the appointment of Kansas senator and anti-Shari'a warrior Sam Brownback as the U.S. ambassador for international religious freedom, and the choice of Mike Pompeo as secretary of state. Brownback and Pompeo, both from Kansas, were equally outspoken about their conservative Christian beliefs.[20]

Pompeo then hosted two Ministerials to Advance Religious Freedom in 2018 and 2019 (a third was held in Poland in 2020).[21] Although much of the work was high-minded and perhaps even useful, there were many problematic aspects to these events. They shared with the overall international religious freedom movement a tendency to mischaracterize complex political and ethnic tensions as religious conflicts. And they overtly promoted a U.S.-centric vision of religion-state relations as a global ideal.[22] The goal was to highlight religious freedom not as one important human right, but as *the* signal and signature right. For example, one concrete outcome of these Ministerials was the International Religious Freedom Alliance: twenty-seven countries committed to upholding "the right to hold any faith or belief, or none at all, and the freedom to change faith."[23] No other human right received nearly as much sustained attention in the Trump administration, and arguably the same could be said for U.S. foreign policy overall in the past twenty years.[24] Donald Trump's focus paid off, as bodies ranging from the moderately conservative, such as Institute for Global Engagement and *Christianity Today,* to the right-wing, such as the American Center for Law and Justice (associated with Pat Robertson's Virginia-based Regent University) and Family Research Council, hailed the sense that the White House was laser-focused on their issues.[25]

At the same time, Trump's appointment of three conservative Supreme Court justices was applauded by evangelicals, because it was widely believed they would support broad definitions of religious freedom, including the freedom to discriminate against LGBTQ+ patrons and to limit access to abortion. (They were proved partially correct with the narrow decision in *Masterpiece Cakeshop* v. *Colorado.*[26]) Crucially, however, none of the justices appointed by Trump is evangelical; two are Catholic and one is Catholic/Episcopal. The key is that conservative Catholics and conservative Protestants (and the much smaller community of conservative Orthodox Christians) are seen, and see themselves, as operating in coalition. This domestic project of expanding the definition and terrain of religious freedom has had a major impact on the U.S. global human rights agenda.

A dual focus on religious freedom and the politics of sexuality is by no means unique to the United States. In Latin America, Catholics and evangelicals may compete energetically for adherents, but they often work together on political issues related to gender and sexuality. In Panama, for example, an ecumenical group released a joint statement rejecting a 2017 Advisory Opinion of the Inter-American Court of Human Rights (IACHR) that promoted the right to self-define gender identity and supported same-sex marriage. "Lately," the statement proclaimed, "the idea has been forced on us that the defense of marriage and family is discrimination."[27] In Costa Rica, a ruling by the IACHR in 2018 that all countries in the region should allow same-sex marriage led to a backlash; an evangelical candidate (and Pentecostal journalist and singer) who had been low in the polls surged forward (in a country that is 75 percent Catholic) on the wave of opposition to this ruling, winning the first round of voting.[28] (In the end, Carlos Alvarado, who supports same-sex marriage, won in a run-off, and the country's Supreme Court lifted its ban on same-sex marriage in May 2020.) As I discuss below, similar political intersections—often influenced by U.S. money and leadership—have shaped human rights conversations in eastern Europe, Africa, and elsewhere.

International Human Rights Instruments: Two Approaches

In the ecumenical conservative coalition that has formed around human rights in the United States, there are two broad approaches toward engaging with international human rights discourse. The first, and far more common, is to try to narrow the conversation through a focus on religious freedom, which provides a basis for pushing back against LGBTQ+ rights, with the argument that public accommodation of these is a violation of religious freedom. This narrowing-but-not-rejecting approach resonates powerfully with a generation of Americans that has grown up on human rights as a moral vernacular.[29] The second approach, less common but with perhaps a more successful transnational reach, is to embrace the broader range of rights that have been recognized in the international community, but to define the heterosexual nuclear family as inherently necessary for ensuring those rights. The language of human thriving, the rights of the child, and a model of the family as purveyor and custodian of rights have all made an increasing impact in recent years.

First Strategy: Narrowing the Argument

The first, narrowing strategy can also include highlighting other ideas of rights; the language of the "right to life" for the unborn is central. Indeed, although I will highlight here the complexity of debates over LGBTQ+ rights among evangelicals and other Christian conservatives, it is crucial to note that there is essentially no debate around abortion. Both globally and in the United States, evangelicals have been almost uniform in their opposition. Indeed in U.S. polls on this issue, younger evangelicals are even slightly more conservative than their parents, although notably more liberal on gay marriage.[30] This is in part because evangelicals and other Christian conservatives have narrated abortion politics through a human rights lens: convinced that "life begins at conception," Christian conservatives mobilize an argument for the "right to life" for embryos and fetuses that draws heavily on the logic (even the imagery) of human rights activism and antitorture campaigns.[31] According to this logic, focusing on "fundamental rights" involves excluding LGBTQ+ rights because they are seen to conflict with religious rights, and excluding women's reproductive rights because they are believed to conflict with the right to freedom from execution.

This narrow version of rights activism was exemplified by the formation of the Commission on Unalienable Rights under President Trump in 2019. This Commission, announced by Secretary of State Mike Pompeo at the second Ministerial to Advance Religious Freedom, was designed to create a "framework" for a "proper understanding of human rights." Just before his announcement, Pompeo explained his rationale in the *Wall Street Journal*, arguing that the "cacophonous call for 'rights'" had replaced a focus on fundamental freedoms.[32] He wanted the Commission to look back at the Universal Declaration of Human Rights (UDHR) for basic rights, but also at the U.S. Declaration of Independence and Constitution, for a proper understanding of universal rights, which was, for Pompeo, also distinctly linked to U.S. norms.

Pompeo did not concoct this argument himself. Indeed, any understanding of the formation of the Commission, its makeup and agenda, or its entirely predictable final report requires attention to the coalition-building around rights talk among a range of religious conservatives over the previous decades. Starting in the early 2000s, this loose coalition of thinkers crafted a shared understanding of their key political issues: religious freedom, support for "the sanctity of life," and promotion of "traditional marriage." These agenda items were certainly not new, but the consensus-building that brought them together as the ecumenical conservative trifold agenda of the 2010s was distinctive.

This conglomeration of issues had been named and defended a decade before, with the 2009 Manhattan Declaration, a manifesto signed initially by more than 150 religious leaders, including prominent evangelicals, Catholics, and Orthodox Christians. The declaration uses the phrase "human rights" only once, but it is infused with claims about human dignity, freedom of religion, and rights of conscience. It focuses on three major topics. First, it argues that Christians are commanded to respect human dignity and that this command requires opposition to abortion and euthanasia. Second, it insists that "the impulse to redefine marriage" to include same-sex couples is just one symptom of the larger, more insidious "erosion of marriage culture." Finally, it focuses on religious liberty, as the "cornerstone of an unconstrained conscience." It decries what it claims are the contemporary norms in the United States that restrict freedom of conscience in the service of the (unjustified) freedoms of others:

> It is ironic that those who today assert a right to kill the unborn, aged and disabled and also a right to engage in immoral sexual practices, and even a right to have relationships integrated around these practices be recognized and blessed by law—such persons claiming these "rights" are very often in the vanguard of those who would trample upon the freedom of others to express their religious and moral commitments to the sanctity of life and to the dignity of marriage as the conjugal union of husband and wife.[33]

Positioning religious conservatives as victims—and heroes—the Manhattan Declaration discusses the willingness of Christians to defy the U.S. state when it demands that Catholic adoption agencies place children with homosexual couples or for being forced to provide services they deem immoral.

The Manhattan Declaration is a domestic document—that is, it does not particularly speak to or about the global institutions of human rights enforcement. But it lays out the first and most powerful of the two approaches to international human rights norms: the winnowing of rights talk to a few privileged agenda items, which at the same time includes in those rights the right to fetal life. The Declaration was crafted primarily by Catholic constitutional scholar and political philosopher Robert George, professor at Princeton and coauthor of *Embryo: A Defense of Human Life*.[34] George has served on the board of the Ethics and Public Policy Center, an interdenominational conservative think-tank that is "dedicated to apply the Judeo-Christian moral tradition to critical issues of public policy." He also served as a member of the U.S. Commission on International Freedom. George's influence is more than philosophical, however; he is said to have played a pivotal role in advising Mike Pompeo to form the Commission on Unalienable Rights and in shaping its membership.[35]

The Commission was viewed by some observers as a performative pandering to Trump's evangelical base. Indeed, since the group was announced at the beginning of the second Ministerial on International Religious Freedom, the timing was surely designed to link the Commission's work on defining "fundamental" rights to the ongoing and vibrant evangelical conversation about persecuted Christians that was evident at both Ministerials. But, as with those meetings themselves—which highlighted the suffering of Orthodox Christians, Catholics, Protestants, as well as non-Christian religious groups including Rohingya Muslims, European Jews, and Tibetan Buddhists—part of the work of the Commission was to turn religious freedom with a Christian edge into an ecumenical issue on a global scale. Chaired by Mary Ann Glendon, a former U.S. ambassador to the Vatican and professor at Harvard Law School (where she had been a mentor to Pompeo), the Commission comprised Catholics, Jews, one Mormon, and a couple of secular conservatives. The only person who could rightly be described as evangelical was also the sole African American on the panel, Jaqueline Rivers. A sociologist, founder of the Seymour Institute for Black Church and Policy Studies (housed under the conservative Witherspoon Institute), Rivers has been outspoken on all three key issues for religious conservatives: abortion, lesbian and gay marriage, and religious freedom. The Seymour Institute's open letter to Hillary Clinton in the 2016 presidential campaign tied together the last two with a rhetorical flourish that suggested that LGBTQ+ rights activists were racially motivated: "A well-financed war is now being waged by the gay and lesbian community in the U.S. and abroad on the faith of our ancestors."[36]

The formation of the Commission received pushback. More than four hundred leaders of NGOs and former government officials signed a letter to Pompeo questioning its necessity.[37] The final report, issued a year later, was entirely in line with the new norms of respectable rights-narrowing. In scholarly language, the report makes a robust argument for the moral importance of centering human rights and calls for U.S. action: "[W]e are of one mind on the urgent need for the United States to vigorously champion human rights in its foreign policy."[38] But the document also turns to the 1947 UDHR as if it were the full and final statement of the extent of human rights, reading it much as strict constitutionalists read the U.S. Constitution for the intent of the Founding Fathers. It ignores or downplays subsequent and binding human rights treaties. This was part of the larger project of opposing "rights proliferation." One Heritage Foundation panel made this point in an explicitly partisan fashion when attorney Benjamin Bull complained that "the activist left" was using "newly manufactured human rights to crush" the "traditional human rights" and "natural rights."[39] The Commission's members tended to be more circumspect but made similar arguments. Peter Berkowitz, for example, asserted that "the proliferation of rights claims has obscured the distinction between fundamental rights that are universally applicable and partisan preferences that are properly left to diplomacy and political give-and-take."[40]

What rights should be open for such political negotiation was sometimes made explicit—do we really think that people can meaningfully be said to have a "right to peace?," the Commission's rapporteur asked.[41] But many observers felt that the concern about "rights inflation" was less about too much focus on peasants or health care than about attention to LGBTQ+ issues. Ken Roth of Human Rights Watch reported that "when I testified before the commission, its members seemed less concerned with, say, the treaty on the rights of people with disabilities . . . than with interpretations of human rights law to protect reproductive freedom and the rights of LGBT people."[42] When the report was finally released in 2020, more than one hundred NGOs criticized both the report and Secretary Pompeo's strategic use of it.[43]

Second Strategy: Focusing on the Family

A second form of engagement with international rights norms by religious conservatives is in some ways the opposite of the first. Instead of downplaying social and economic rights as secondary in the way the "rights inflation" activists do, the family-first approach argues that the (heterosexual nuclear) family is a rights-bearer, building on the UDHR's plank on the family: "The family is the natural and fundamental group unit of society and is entitled to protection by society and the State."[44] The World Congress of Families and the UN Family Council are both religious conservative organizations that have transnational reach, and both claim UN norms as their mandate, even as they have engaged actual UN institutions ambivalently and sometimes with hostility. As the think tank Political Research Associates summarized it, this religious conservative agenda is "aimed at cementing a patriarchal and heteronormative family structure as the fundamental unit of society, and then using that as a tool to advance conservative, right-wing social policies through the UN and other international organizations."[45]

Buss and Herman argue that, in the 1990s, the U.S. Christian right moved away from a vilification of the United Nations, which had been its dominant stance during the Cold War, toward seeing the UN as a potentially useful and necessary forum for forwarding a conservative agenda on "the family." Beginning with the 1995 Beijing Conference on Women, where NGOs played a large role, Christian activists began to see a possibility of countering what they saw as the institutional bias of the UN toward secularism, feminism, and reproductive freedom. A relatively small number of conservative Christian groups, deeply opposed to the inclusion of homosexual rights or reproductive rights as part of the UN agenda, nonetheless believed that the United Nations itself could become a vehicle for protecting and promoting a more conservative vision of the family.[46]

At the same time, the end of the Cold War brought a rush of American (along with European, African, and South Korean) Christian missionaries into the territories of the former Soviet Union. Campus Crusade, Focus on the Family, and a range of other missionary organizations saw an unprecedented opportunity not only to evangelize in the former communist world but also to shape conversations about social and political issues. In the last twenty years, U.S.-based Christian organizations have spent a great deal of money in Europe—approximately $51 million, according to openDemocracy—including in Bulgaria, the Czech Republic, Italy, and Russia. How much of this money is for traditional church-building and evangelism, how much for social services, and how much for political activism is unclear, since organizations are not required to report these specifics for funds spent abroad. But some of the largest spenders are also activist groups operating at the nexus of religious freedom and sexuality: the American Center for Law and Justice, the Alliance Defending Freedom, Focus on the Family, and the Acton Institute for the Study of Religion and Liberty, as well as the Catholic Human Life International.[47]

Russia has been of particular interest, despite the fact that official representatives of the Russian Orthodox Church were frequently wary of, or showed outright hostility to, Protestant evangelism. Nonetheless, the break-up of the USSR brought a broad range of new transnational Christian connections. Out of these emerging networks, the World Congress of Families was born. In 1995, American professor Alan Carlson, then head of the Howard Center for Family, Religion, and Society (Rockford, Illinois) began meeting with several Russian partners, including one Orthodox priest.[48] According to Casey Michael, their meeting led to the earliest iteration of the World Congress of Families (WCF) in 1997. In time, WCF would host American conservatives in Russia and Russian officials in the United States and would also rope in Russian oligarchs—including at least one who is now sanctioned—as reported funders. It would also become the most wide-ranging organization dedicated to rolling back LGBTQ+ rights and, in the final years of the Obama administration, Russia's main entrée to American social conservatives.[49]

The WCF developed ties with a number of U.S. organizations on the religious Right, including the Alliance Defense Fund, Concerned Women for America, Focus on the Family, and the Catholic Family and the Human Rights Institute. It went on to host a number of meetings in Russia (and elsewhere) focused on the demographic "threat" posed by lower birth rates in the former USSR and the United States. At first the Russian Orthodox church leadership was not particularly interested in networking with American conservatives on political issues, focused instead on revitalizing and defining the church's identity in the postcommunist era. Over time, however, the WCF's Russian supporters made close contacts with the Moscow Patriarchate. As Putin became increasingly invested in an anti-LGBTQ+ agenda, passing one antigay law after another in the 2000s, the WCF continued to encourage support for the "natural family," "protecting children," and "traditional values."[50]

As Alex Cooley discusses in chapter 4 of this volume, the WCF also reached out more broadly, helping to construct a coalition "for the family" that went well beyond U.S. evangelicals and the Russian Right. Its second congress, held in 1999, brought two thousand delegates together in Geneva; sponsors included the Mormon NGO Family Voice, and the opening speaker was Cardinal Lopez Trujillo, president of the Vatican's Council for the Family.[51] As Carlson described it, the group aimed to "forge a truly international profamily movement . . . embrac[ing] all religiously grounded family morality systems around the globe, without descending into the banal."[52]

In 2003, the WCF's parent body obtained Economic and Social Council (ECOSOC) consultative status at the UN. There, it became part of a rapidly expanding network of primarily religious organizations aimed at changing or eliminating UN positions on human rights that they believe are in opposition to the "natural family." These included not only American and transnational Protestant organizations (including the American Family Association, Concerned Women for America, Focus on the Family, and the Family Research Council) but also Catholic Women for Faith and Family, Family Watch International, and the Doha Institute for Family and Development. The vast majority were based in the United States.[53] But many members of the network believed that they had natural allies in the countries of the Global South. At a follow-on in 2000 to the Beijing conference on women, an anonymous flyer circulated stating: "If the West would stop pushing homosexual and abortion 'rights' on unwilling countries, the document would be done. Don't blame the developing countries with the courage to defend their values and their right to self-government!"[54]

In 2004, the Doha International Conference on the Family was held to mark the tenth anniversary of the International Year of the Family. The coordinating committee, including the Brigham Young University's World Family Policy Center (Latter Day Saints [Mormon]), the Family Research Council (evangelical), and the Catholic Family and Human Rights Institute, all convened "under the patronage and generosity" of the Sheikha of Qatar, Moza bint Nasser Al-Missned.[55] The conference was designed to have the hallmarks of international human rights and humanitarian conferences: it was endorsed by a UN resolution, with regional meetings to prepare in advance for the agenda, including hundreds of attendees. Its final document, the Doha Declaration, quoted the UDHR on the "right of men and women" to marry and the family as the natural unit of society.[56]

The UN Family Rights Caucus pursues a similar strategy of bringing together diverse religious constituencies into UN-style meetings to issue declarations that borrow human rights language for anti-LGBTQ+ ends. The Caucus is sponsored by Family Watch International, a Mormon-led organization that holds an annual invitation-only global policy forum that often includes testimonials from people "cured" of homosexuality. The Caucus claims to have 160 individual and organizational members (which it does not name), and it is expert at drawing upon the "positive" rights that are part of the UN mandate:

> One of the most basic human rights recognized in the Universal Declaration of Human Rights is the right to found a family. In the UN Convention on the Rights of the Child, the right of children to grow up in a family environment and to know and be cared for by their parents is specifically recognized. How can these rights be realized if the family is not protected? To protect the institution of the family is to protect one of the most basic human rights known to mankind.[57]

In 2014, at the Palais des Nations, the Caucus organized a ceremony in which children read aloud "A Declaration on the Rights of Children and Their Families." Designed to echo, but very much to dissent from, the Convention on the Rights of the Child, this new declaration argued, again quoting from the UDHR, that the family is the natural unit of society, and went on to state that the child has the right to be protected, "including appropriate legal protection before, as well as after birth." It goes on to say that children have the "right to a married father and mother."[58] This expansive statement of "positive" rights is worlds away from the claims of the rights narrowers, who focus on political and civil rights, but in one key way it has a similar impact: LGBTQ+ people are treated as beyond rights norms.

These efforts came to fruition in 2015 when the UN Human Rights Council (UNHRC) adopted a resolution on the protection of the family (HRC/RS/29/22) that was initiated by some of the members of the UN Group of Friends of the Family, which includes Bangladesh, Egypt, the Holy See, Qatar, and Russia, among others. The previous day, the UNHRC had created an independent expert position charged with investigating and reporting on violence against LGBTQ+ people. Then, immediately afterward, it voted on the family protection resolution that rejected efforts to ensure inclusive language about diverse forms of family.[59]

Under President Trump, this vision of "the family" had U.S. sanction. Valerie Huber, senior policy adviser at the U.S. Department of Health and Human Services, spoke at the event "It Takes a Family" in May 2019, which was cosponsored by the UN Family Rights Caucus. A few weeks later, UN Women issued its report *Families in a Changing World* that embraced broad definitions of family and outlined the ways in which heterosexual marriage often reinforces traditional gender roles for women.[60]

Uganda: A Case Study

The complex workings of transnational and interdenominational religious networks can be seen in the fight over LGBTQ+ rights in Uganda over the last twenty years. In that context, American evangelicals were deeply involved in a debate over the 2009 Anti-Homosexuality Bill in Uganda, which called for the death penalty for any Ugandan convicted of "aggravated homosexuality," meaning homosexuals who "recruited" young people or HIV-positive people who had homosexual sex. Lesser sentences, such as life imprisonment, could be meted out for merely engaging in homosexual activity. Supported strongly by Ugandan pastor Martin Ssempa, the bill was decried by human rights activists globally.

The debate over the proposed law was indicative of the precarious status of LGBTQ+ people in Uganda, but it also showed how U.S.-based evangelicals adopted disparate positions on the law, with some implicitly or explicitly supportive and others strongly opposed. In Uganda, itself, a coalition around conservative sexual politics brought together an otherwise disparate and even competitive range of religious leaders.

Some observers blamed the antigay environment in Uganda on U.S. influence. They noted, correctly, that for years American evangelicals had been holding antigay workshops and conferences in the country. Dr. Kapya Kaoma, a Zambian cleric who has published widely on LGBTQ+ rights, was one of the first people to analyze the ties between conservative American evangelicals and conservative Christians in Uganda and elsewhere in Africa.[61] The World Congress of Families, for example, had an active presence in East Africa in the early 2000s. According to the Human Rights Campaign, at the WCF's first official event in the region in 2009, its communications director Don Feder "urged activists to do the opposite of whatever the West suggested."[62] In this way, anti-gay activists—including those from the United States—often positioned themselves as anti-imperialist spokespersons, helping to shore up "tradition."[63] One of the most notorious of these American anti-LGBTQ+ activists was Scott Lively, a Far-Right militant; head of Abiding Truth ministries; and author of *The Pink Swastika*, which blamed the Holocaust on gay men.[64] Lively, although not well-known in the United States at the time, also had ties with the World Council of Families: he seems to have done a speaking tour of Russia associated with the WCF in 2006–2007, took some credit for Russia's 2013 law outlawing "homosexual propaganda," and later claimed to have had a role in planning the 2014 WCF meeting in Moscow.[65]

Lively's claims for his role and influence are notoriously unreliable,[66] but there is no question that he traveled to Uganda in 2009 for a conference on the "Gay Agenda" organized by the Reverend Ssempa. This three-day event, with an audience numbering in the thousands, was hosted by Ssempa and Stephen Langa of Uganda's Family Life Network. The three speakers were Lively and two evangelical advocates of "conversion therapy." With Ssempa's support, Lively also managed to get an invitation to speak for several hours to Uganda's Parliament. He later described the visit as a "nuclear bomb against the gay agenda in Uganda."[67] There were other examples, including Lou Engle, the right-wing Pentecostal pastor of the International House of Prayer (based in Oklahoma), who preached a strong antigay message in Uganda while the Anti-Homosexuality Bill was under consideration.[68] In 2009 and 2010, these were only a few American pastors who spoke enthusiastically to Ugandans about the importance of their "righteous" stance. Indeed, at first it can seem hard to argue with the summary offered by National Public Radio: "U.S. Exports Cultural War to Uganda."[69]

In reality, however, the debates over homosexuality and human rights in Uganda had far more complex histories; they were not created by injections from the U.S. evangelical Right. Indeed, Ugandans were quite sensitive to any claim that they were being tutored in either theology or politics by Westerners. By 2009, a number of Ugandan church leaders had already been involved for over a decade in the debates over homosexuality that fractured the global Anglican community in the 1990s. At the 1998 Lambeth meeting—a once-in-a-decade conclave for deciding Anglican policies and positions worldwide—the evangelical wing of the Anglican church, based largely in Africa and Asia, with strong support from conservative U.S. Episcopalians, had supported a strongly worded resolution that defined marriage as "between a man and a woman in lifelong union" and rejected "homosexual practice as incompatible with Scripture."[70] The Church of Uganda joined several other African churches in boycotting the Lambeth meeting ten years later over a perceived upsurge in support for gay ordination. American pastor Rick Warren spoke out in favor of the boycott. Though a Southern Baptist, he had developed a number of ties with conservative Anglican bishops in Uganda and felt no compunction about opining on Anglican politics. Declaring homosexuality an unnatural way of life, he stated that "the Church of England is wrong, and I support the Church of Uganda."[71]

Rather than injecting U.S. positions into "unsuspecting" Ugandans, the 2009 Anti-Homosexuality Bill was the result of years of networking and connections among a denominational range of global Right activists in multiple locations. Uganda had been deeply shaped by the infusion of funds from the U.S. PEPFAR (President's Emergency Program for AIDS Relief), starting in 2005. These funds were skewed toward supporting abstinence and chastity as AIDS-prevention strategies, thanks largely to activism by U.S. Christian conservatives, both evangelical and Catholic.[72] In addition, the money itself created an environment in which activists such as Ssempa promoted a vision of the devastation caused by HIV/AIDS as a call to radical moral reform. In 2007, Ssempa led hundreds of people through the streets in Kampala to demand arrest and punishment of gay activists (or, as Ssempa described them, "homosexual promoters").[73] The rush of money for fighting AIDS went to a broad range of organizations in Uganda, including a number of Christian conservative groups, as well as transnational groups that set up shop. As anthropologist Lydia Boyd has argued, the flood of new NGOs and the influx of money also fueled anxiety about the presence of American and European humanitarians, many of whom were assumed to hold the same liberal positions on homosexuality that Ugandan Anglicans had countered in the Anglican community.[74]

The 2009 Anti-Homosexuality Bill proposed a seven-year jail term for homosexual acts and the death penalty for "aggravated homosexuality," which included having sex with a minor or a person with disabilities if the offender was HIV-positive. Ssempa led marches in favor of the bill, and President Yoweri Museveni's government immediately embraced it. The international outcry began immediately. The Swedish government threatened to withhold $50 million in aid. Human Rights Watch and the international news media produced one withering condemnation after another.[75] Rick Warren, who had supported the boycott of the Anglicans' Lambeth meeting, spoke out against the bill, calling it "unchristian."[76] Even the head of Exodus International, the U.S.-based organization that claimed it was possible to "recover" from homosexuality, wrote to President Museveni opposing the proposed law.[77]

The external pressure against the bill in some ways only strengthened its support in the Ugandan Parliament. This is not surprising, given the populist and nationalist tenor of the debates (see Gerald Neumann's discussion in chapter 6). Indeed, the calls for cuts in funding or the denunciations by groups such as Human Rights Watch, although appropriate and necessary from a human rights perspective, provided another opportunity for supporters to show their independence; anti-LGBTQ+ activists had been using the claim of colonialism since at least the distribution of the flyer at the Beijing+5 follow-on event in 2000. The sense among some Ugandans was that the West was launching an offensive, "with the tip of the spear being NGOs and human rights activists."[78]

Uganda's churches had a mixed view of the bill. Its supporters claimed to have the mass of Christians on their side, and there was evidence of that. A meeting of two hundred members of the Interreligious Council of Uganda, which included Catholic, Protestant, and Muslim representatives, came out in support of the bill, urging Parliament to resist foreign pressure to abandon or moderate it. Ssempa organized his Pastors' Task Force, which included Anglican, Pentecostal, Orthodox, Catholic, and Muslim leaders. Uganda's Catholic Church remained notably quiet. "They may not like the harsher elements of the bill," one observer commented, "but they also share the suspicion that Western forces are trying to cram a liberal social agenda down Africa's throat, and they don't want to discourage efforts to defend African values."[79] The Anglican Church of Uganda issued a statement opposing the use of the death penalty and also expressing concern at the provision that required clergy, doctors, and teachers to report homosexuality. It agreed, however, that homosexuality should not be a human right, and it commended the law's objective of defining marriage as between a man and a woman.[80]

Ultimately, international pressure did have an impact. Representative David Bahati withdrew the original Anti-Homosexuality Bill and introduced a revised version in February 2012. This removed the death penalty but added a clause that would prohibit any organization that supported gay rights from working in Uganda. That clause could potentially shut out the development arms of many foreign governments.[81] A revised bill was passed by Parliament and signed into law on February 24, 2014. Almost immediately, the tabloid *Red Pepper* published a list of Uganda's "Top Gays."[82] In the following months, attacks on LGBTQ people once again increased.

In June 2014, President Barack Obama enacted largely symbolic sanctions, which banned individual Ugandans who had been involved in human rights abuses against the LGBTQ community from entering the United States. The sanctions also provided for discontinuing or redirecting funds for a few of the programs that had been planned with the Ministry of Health and other agencies. But administration officials made it clear that Uganda was one of the most important military allies the United States had in Africa, and that both countries would continue to work together to fight the Lord's Resistance Army, along with al-Shabab in Somalia, and in coordinating antiterrorism strategies for East Africa in general. The sanctions did not prevent Sam Kutesa, Uganda's foreign minister, from traveling to the United States to take up his position as president of the UN General Assembly.[83]

In August 2014, the Anti-Homosexuality Law was nullified by the Ugandan Supreme Court on procedural grounds. The ruling happened just as President Museveni was about to lead a delegation to the United States, and many observers thought the ruling was a political maneuver designed to save him from embarrassment. On his return, Museveni promised to reintroduce the law yet again, but perhaps without penalties for consenting adults. This, he hoped, would be a law that would escape international outrage. "We agreed to come up with a new version," said one supporter, something that "protects" Ugandans but "that doesn't hurt our Western friends."[84]

For several years afterward, nothing much happened. Queer people in Uganda continued to suffer great oppression, but, legislatively, there was no serious attempt to reintroduce the bill. In the fall of 2019, some members of Parliament threatened to reintroduce legislation, even as several LGBTQ+ activists were attacked in their homes; four people died. One of those killed, Brian Wasswa, worked for the Human Rights Awareness and Promotion Forum, a Ugandan NGO that advocates for marginalized and at-risk populations. In the midst of the COVID-19 pandemic, however, the calls for new legislation quickly fell by the wayside.

Conclusions and Recommendations

Human rights language and commitments have deep and broad resonance among American Christians, including conservatives. It is a sign of the resiliency and potency of that language that so much of the discussion—about religious freedom, U.S. foreign aid, LGBTQ+ rights, and even abortion—is conducted in terms that resonate with the fundamental statements about the dignity of the human person that form the basis of human rights politics globally.

Evangelicals have taken human rights concerns seriously in Sudan, South Africa, China, as well as in various parts of Latin America and the Middle East, and there is a strong moderate contingent among American evangelicals whose input and insight should be cultivated. Indeed, work on global religious freedom issues has generally increased the awareness that Americans have about the *other* issues faced by individuals beyond U.S. borders. For an American believer, learning about religious freedom issues for Copts in Egypt might also involve learning about challenges of poverty or environmental degradation. Advocating for Christians in Myanmar can teach Americans about the situation of Rohingya as well. We see this cross-fertilization in a great deal of the work done by organizations such as World Vision, the Institute for Global Engagement, the Lausanne Movement, and Intervarsity Christian Fellowship. These organizations do not always get the headlines, but they are integrating global visions that include a sense of respect and dignity for all people. If the human rights community aims to advance a universal agenda that also reaches a broad population, including evangelicals, it needs to recognize this diversity and engage those who already see themselves as advocates of rights that go beyond (but include) religious freedom.

Even among the most conservative wing of evangelicals (and Catholic and Orthodox adherents), there are principled differences that the human rights community should be aware of. There are serious differences of opinion about LGBTQ+ rights, for example. Pew Research has shown that almost every religious group in the United States, including evangelicals, is growing more accepting of such rights.[85] Younger generations are distinctly more comfortable with gay marriage and queer politics, and there is every reason to believe that U.S. Christian organizations will shift over time as younger generations take leadership. One indication of the split was the 2014 crisis at evangelical-led World Vision, one of the world's largest charities. In March that year, its president announced that the nonprofit organization would begin hiring Christians who were in same-sex marriages, saying that gay marriage, like divorce, was a matter that Christians could reasonably disagree over. After an outcry from funders, this decision was reversed just two days later, only for a key board member to resign in protest at the reversal.[86] All of this indicates that there is far less evangelical consensus on LGBTQ+ rights than can be revealed by narratives focusing only on the global Right.

There is, however, a global divide over homosexuality that has serious consequences for any policymaking. Public opinion about whether it should be "accepted by society" is sharply divided, with the Americas and western Europe noticeably more positive than countries in eastern Europe, Africa, or most of Asia and the Middle East. The Philippines is an exception, with 73 percent of those polled saying homosexuality should be accepted. And yet in many parts of the world, the rise in acceptance over the last ten years is striking. In Kenya, only 1 percent of people in 2002 said homosexuality should be accepted; in 2020, it was 14 percent. This is still a stunningly low number, but it speaks to a trend that is repeated in countries rich and poor, in the Global North and Global South. In general, wealthier countries are more welcoming than poorer ones, which suggests that economic development and human rights agendas are profoundly intertwined.[87] The reality remains, however, that neocolonialism continues to be a powerful argument *against* the global human rights institutions, and the strange bedfellows of recent years mean that those who argue for "the family" as a rights-bearer are often able to draw on anticolonial arguments that present LGBTQ+ or women's rights as a foreign imposition. It is important, then, for supporters of these rights to highlight that *all* parties to the debate have transnational ties, and Christian conservatives are as likely to be "funded by the West" as are liberal secular NGOs; equally, liberal expansions of rights are supported by many people around the world, as the ultimate victory for gay marriage in Costa Rica indicated. That said, there is far less room to navigate the politics of abortion, which has itself been framed in the language of human rights by a large swath of Christian conservative movements.

The rise of the right-wing populist movements across the world suggests strongly that, while there are important links between religious conservatives and populist uprisings (as in the case of the attack on the Capitol in Washington on January 6, 2021 or the evangelical support for the populist Brazilian president Jair Bolsonaro), there is also significant fracturing of views. Some reports in the United States indicate that the number of people who identify as evangelical is declining notably (although this focuses only on white evangelicals, and not on the significant percentage of American evangelicals who are Black, Latinx, or Asian).[88] It is also important to recognize that the language of human rights *does* have meaningful traction among a broad swath of evangelicals, in the United States and beyond. There are important distinctions—indeed, wide differences—among evangelical communities, and focusing only on those who inhabit the Far Right ignores the potential openness among others. As the Biden administration develops its own human rights policy, it will do well to attend to the recommendations of a recent Brookings report by E. J. Dionne and Melinda Rogers, which highlighted the importance of listening carefully to the concerns of religious communities in forming U.S. policy. It is vital, they point out, not to assume an absolute divide between "people who support religious freedom" and "people who support LGBTQ+ rights," since many people in the LGBTQ+ community are religious, and many religious people, whatever their orientation, support their rights. The conversation has become difficult, but it is clear that one way forward *is* conversation: the more people know an out LGBTQ+ person, the more open they are.[89] The same is true at the institutional level: both the Biden administration and international human rights NGOs need to include evangelicals in the conversation, without assuming their inevitable hostility. There are no easy answers to the dilemma of fundamental differences in moral frameworks, but cultivating an awareness of the points of common ground among stakeholders, and recognizing the moral power of human rights discourse across a broad spectrum of Christian conservatives, can help construct approaches that are both principled and consensus-seeking.

Notes

1. Conrad Hackett and Brian J. Grim, "Global Christianity: A Report on the Size and Distribution of the World's Christian Population," Pew Forum on Religion and Public Life, December 2011, www.pewforum.org/christian/global-christianity-exec .aspx; Pew Research Center, "Religion in Latin America: Widespread Change in a Historically Catholic Region," November 13, 2014, www.pewforum.org/2014/11/13 /religion-in-latin-america/; Melani McAlister, "American Evangelicals, the Changing Global Religious Environment, and Foreign Policy Activism," *The Review of Faith & International Affairs* 17, 2 (April 3, 2019), pp. 1–12, https://doi.org/10.1080/15570274 .2019.1608652.

2. Andrew Preston, *Sword of the Spirit, Shield of Faith: Religion in American War and Diplomacy* (New York: Knopf, 2012); Heather D. Curtis, *Holy Humanitarians: American Evangelicals and Global Aid* (Harvard University Press, 2018); Melani McAlister, *The Kingdom of God Has No Borders: A Global History of American Evangelicalism* (Oxford University Press, 2018); Lauren Frances Turek, *To Bring the Good News to All Nations: Evangelical Influence on Human Rights and U.S. Foreign Relations* (Cornell University Press, 2020); Mark R. Amstutz, *Evangelicals and American Foreign Policy* (Oxford University Press, 2014); William Inboden, *Religion and American Foreign Policy, 1945–1960: The Soul of Containment* (Cambridge University Press, 2008).

3. Janelle S. Wong, *Immigrants, Evangelicals, and Politics in an Era of Demographic Change* (New York: Russell Sage Foundation, 2018).

4. David C. Kirkpatrick, *A Gospel for the Poor: Global Social Christianity and the Latin American Evangelical Left* (University of Pennsylvania Press, 2019); David R. Swartz, *Moral Minority: The Evangelical Left in an Age of Conservatism* (University of Pennsylvania Press, 2012).

5. Samuel Moyn, *Christian Human Rights* (University of Pennsylvania Press, 2015).

6. Max L. Stackhouse, "Theology, History, and Human Rights," *Soundings: An Interdisciplinary Journal* 67, 2 (1984), pp. 191–208.

7. Udi Greenberg, "Catholics, Protestants, and the Violent Birth of European Religious Pluralism," *American Historical Review* 124, 2 (April 1, 2019), pp. 511–38.

8. Daniel K. Williams, *God's Own Party: The Making of the Christian Right* (Oxford University Press, 2010), p. 173.

9. "The Lausanne Covenant," in *Let the Earth Hear His Voice*, edited by J.D. Douglas (Minneapolis, Minn.: World Wide Publications, 1975), pp. 3–9.

10. On evangelicals and human rights in this period, see Turek, *To Bring the Good News to All Nations*; Preston, *Sword of the Spirit*; Andrew Preston, "Evangelical Internationalism: A Conservative Worldview for the Age of Globalization," in *The Right Side of the Sixties: Reexamining Conservatism's Decade of Transformation*, edited by Laura Giffod and Daniel Williams (New York: Palgrave Macmillan, 2012), pp. 221–42; McAlister, *Kingdom of God*. Preventing evangelism was a serious issue of contention between U.S. evangelicals and Israel at several points in the 1960s and 1970s.

11. Kirkpatrick, *A Gospel for the Poor*; Swartz, *Moral Minority*.

12. On human rights rhetoric in this period, see Mark Philip Bradley, *The World Reimagined: Americans and Human Rights in the Twentieth Century* (Cambridge University Press, 2016); Sarah B. Snyder, *From Selma to Moscow: How Human Rights Activists Transformed U.S. Foreign Policy* (Columbia University Press, 2018); Barbara Keys, *Reclaiming American Virtue: The Human Rights Revolution of the 1970s* (Harvard University Press, 2014).

13. McAlister, *Kingdom of God*, ch. 9; Elizabeth Castelli, "Praying for the Persecuted Church: US Christian Activism in the Global Arena," *Journal of Human Rights* 4, 3 (September 2005), pp. 321–51.

14. Melani McAlister, "US Evangelicals and the Politics of Slave Redemption as Religious Freedom in Sudan," *South Atlantic Quarterly* 113, 1 (Winter 2014), pp. 87–108.

15. David P. King, *God's Internationalists: World Vision and the Age of Evangelical Humanitarianism* (University of Pennsylvania Press, 2019), pp. 191–215.

16. For example, Morgan Lee, "Love Thy Neighbor: South Asia Christians Advocate for Rohingya Muslims," *Christianity Today*, October 27, 2017, www.christianitytoday.com/news/2017/october/christians-aid-rohingya-muslims-myanmar-bangladesh-pakistan.html; "Rohingya Refugee Crisis: Facts, FAQs, and How to Help," *World Vision* (blog), June 12, 2020, www.worldvision.org/refugees-news-stories/rohingya-refugees-bangladesh-facts; Institute for Global Engagement (IGE), "IGE Co-Convenes 'Peace, Security and Co-Existence' Conference in Myanmar," https://globalengage.org/updates/view/ige-co-convenes-peace-security-co-existence-conference-in-myanmar.

17. Melani McAlister, "The Persecuted Body: Evangelical Internationalism, Islam, and the Politics of Fear," in *Facing Fear: The History of an Emotion in Global Perspective*, edited by Michael Laffan and Max Weiss (Princeton University Press, 2012), pp. 133–61; Candace Lukasik, "Human Rights and Persecution Economies," *Public Orthodoxy* (blog), October 13, 2020, https://publicorthodoxy.org/2020/10/13/human

-rights-and-persecution-economies/; Amy Fallas, "Religious Liberty Shouldn't Come at the Expense of Human Rights," *Sojourners*, July 24, 2019, https://sojo.net/articles /religious-liberty-shouldn-t-come-expense-human-rights.

18. On the political work of melodrama as a genre, see Elisabeth Robin Anker, *Orgies of Feeling: Melodrama and the Politics of Freedom* (Duke University Press, 2014).

19. The Trump administration actually closed another office started under Obama, the Office of Religion and Global Affairs, and folded its staff slots into the new Office of International Religious Freedom. Shaun Casey, "How the State Department Has Sidelined Religion's Role in Diplomacy," *Religion and Politics*, September 5, 2017, https://religionandpolitics.org/2017/09/05/how-the-state-department-has-sidelined -religions-role-in-diplomacy/.

20. For years, Pompeo attended a Presbyterian church in Wichita that was part of the ecumenical Presbyterian Church (USA). In 2011, his home church left the denomination and joined the Evangelical Presbyterian Church, a relatively new evangelical and Reformed denomination. Brownback, on the other hand, grew up as a Methodist but converted to Catholicism in 2002. However, he now attends the nondenominational Topeka Bible Church.

21. On the Trump administrations IRF policy, see Jeffrey Haynes, "Trump and the Politics of International Religious Freedom," *Religions* 11, 8 (August 2020), pp. 1–20, https://doi.org/10.3390/rel11080385. On the Ministerials, see Sarah Posner, *Unholy: How White Christian Nationalists Powered the Trump Presidency, and the Devastating Legacy They Left Behind* (New York: Random House Trade Paperbacks, 2021), p. 240; Fallas, "Religious Liberty Shouldn't Come at the Expense of Human Rights"; Jacob Lupfer, "The Politics of Religious Freedom under the Trump Administration," *Religion and Politics*, August 14, 2018, https://religionandpolitics.org/2018/08/14/the-politics-of -religious-freedom-under-the-trump-administration/. On the Evangelical Advisory Board, Rob Boston, "All the President's Men and Women: Members of President Trump's Evangelical Advisory Board Are Hard at Work Changing Public Policy—But They'd Rather You Not Know about It," *Church and State* (Silver Spring, Md.: Americans United for Separation of Church and State, October 2018).

22. Elizabeth Shakman Hurd, *Beyond Religious Freedom: The New Global Politics of Religion* (Princeton University Press, 2015); Elizabeth Shakman Hurd, "What's Wrong with Promoting Religious Freedom?," *Foreign Policy* (blog), June 12, 2013, http://mideast.foreignpolicy.com/posts/2013/06/12/whats_wrong_with_promoting _religious_freedom?wp_login_redirect=0.

23. "Declaration of Principles for the International Religious Freedom Alliance," *United States Department of State* (blog), February 5, 2020, www.state.gov/declaration -of-principles-for-the-international-religious-freedom-alliance/; Judd Birdsall, "Will Biden Demote Religious Freedom in US Foreign Policy?," ChristianityToday.com, November 17, 2020, www.christianitytoday.com/ct/2020/november-web-only/religious -freedom-biden-trump-ministerial-rights-article-18.html.

24. Gregorio Bettiza, *Finding Faith in Foreign Policy: Religion and American Diplomacy in a Postsecular World* (Oxford University Press, 2019).

25. Melani McAlister, "Evangelical Populist Internationalism and the Politics of Persecution," *Review of Faith and International Affairs* 17, 3 (September 2019), pp. 105–17.

26. Mark Satta, "Why You Can't Sell Your Cake and Control It Too: Distinguishing Use from Design in Masterpiece Cakeshop v. Colorado," *Harvard Civil Rights-Civil Liberties Law Review*, July 10, 2019, https:// harvardcrcl.org/why-you-cant-sell-your -cake-and-control-it-too-distinguishing-use-from-design-in-masterpiece-cakeshop-v -colorado/.

27. María Angélica Peñas Defago, José Manuel Morán Faúndes, and Juan Marco Vaggione, "Religious Conservatism on the Global Stage: Threats and Challenges for LGBTI Rights," Global Philanthropy Project, November 4, 2018, p. 22, https:// globalphilanthropyproject.org/2018/11/04/religious-conservatism-on-the-global- stage-threats-and-challenges-for-lgbti-rights/; "Inter-American Court of Human Rights Affirms Rights Related to Sexual Orientation, Gender Identity and Gender Expression," ESCR-Net, www.escr-net.org/caselaw/2018/advisory-opinion-gender-identity -equality-and-non-discrimination-same-sex-couples-2017.

28. Gustavo Fuchs, "Is Costa Rica on the Path to Evangelical Theocracy?," *New Internationalist,* February 9, 2018, https://newint.org/features/web-exclusive/2018/02/09 /costa-rica-theocracy.

29. Mark Philip Bradley, "American Vernaculars: The United States and the Global Human Rights Imagination," *Diplomatic History* 38, 1 (January 1, 2014), pp. 1–21.

30. Jeff Diamant, "Young Evangelicals Are More Liberal Than Their Elders on Some Issues" (Washington: Pew Research Center), May 4, 2017, www.pewresearch .org/fact-tank/2017/05/04/though-still-conservative-young-evangelicals-are-more -liberal-than-their-elders-on-some-issues/.

31. Rosalind Pollack Petchesky, "Fetal Images: The Power of Visual Culture in the Politics of Reproduction," *Feminist Studies* 13, 2 (1987), pp. 263–92, https://doi .org/10.2307/3177802; R. Marie Griffith, *Moral Combat: How Sex Divided American Christians and Fractured American Politics* (New York: Basic Books, 2017).

32. Michael R. Pompeo, "Opinion | Unalienable Rights and U.S. Foreign Policy," *Wall Street Journal*, July 7, 2019, www.wsj.com/articles/unalienable-rights-and-u-s -foreign-policy-11562526448.

33. "Manhattan Declaration: A Call of Christian Conscience," November 20, 2009, https://www.manhattandeclaration.org/.

34. Robert P. George and Christopher Tollefsen, *Embryo: A Defense of Human Life* (New York: Doubleday, 2008). George is profiled in David D. Kirkpatrick, "The Conservative-Christian Big Thinker," *New York Times*, December 16, 2009, www .nytimes.com/2009/12/20/magazine/20george-t.html.

35. Pranshu Verma, "Pompeo's Human Rights Panel Could Hurt L.G.B.T. and Women's Rights, Critics Say," *New York Times*, June 23, 2020, www.nytimes.com /2020/06/23/us/politics/pompeo-state-human-rights.html.

36. Anita Little, "Sexist, Homophobic Representatives of 'The Black Church' Just Want to Make Black America Great Again," *Religion Dispatches* (blog), November 3,

2016, https://religiondispatches.org/sexist-homophobic-representatives-of-the-black-church-just-want-to-make-black-america-great-again/. The text of the letter is archived at https://www.seymourinstitute.com/open-letter.html. The organization's site is now at https://thedesignorator.wixsite.com/seymourinstitute.

37. Aleandra Schmitt, "5 Questions about the Commission on Unalienable Rights," Center for American Progress, October 31, 2019, www.americanprogress .org/issues/security/news/2019/10/31/476632/5-questions-commission-unalienable -rights/.

38. Commission on Unalienable Rights, "Report of the Commission on Unalienable Rights" (U.S. Department of State, 2020), p. 7.

39. Posner, *Unholy*, 240.

40. Peter Berkowitz, "Criticisms Illustrate Need for State Dept. Human Rights Panel," *Real Clear Politics*, September 15, 2019, www.realclearpolitics.com/articles /2019/09/15/criticisms_illustrate_need_for_state_dept_human_rights_panel _141238.html.

41. Cartwright Weiland, "Pompeo's Critics Misrepresent the Commission on Unalienable Rights," *Foreign Policy*, September 22, 2020, http://foreignpolicy.com/2020 /09/22/critics-misrepresent-commission-unalienable-rights/.

42. Kenneth Roth, "Pompeo's Commission on Unalienable Rights Will Endanger Everyone's Human Rights," *Foreign Policy* (blog), August 27, 2020, http:// foreignpolicy.com/2020/08/27/pompeos-commission-on-unalienable-rights-will -endanger-everyones-human-rights/.

43. Center for Justice and Accountability, "United States: Human Rights Coalition Rejects Report Issued by State Department's Commission on Unalienable Rights— CJA," July 30, 2020, https://cja.org/united-states-human-rights-coalition-rejects -report-issued-by-state-departments-commission-on-unalienable-rights/.

44. Universal Declaration of Human Rights, Article 16, https://www.un.org/en /about-us/universal-declaration-of-human-rights.

45. Cole Parke, "Whose Family? Religious Right's 'Family Values' Agenda Advances Internationally," Political Research Associates, July 16, 2014, www.politicalresearch.org /2014/07/16/whose-family-religious-rights-family-values-agenda-advances -internationally.

46. Doris Buss, *Globalizing Family Values: The Christian Right in International Politics* (University of Minnesota Press, 2003).

47. Claire Provost and Adam Ramsay, "Revealed: Trump-Linked US Christian 'Fundamentalists' Pour Millions of 'Dark Money' into Europe, Boosting the Far Right," openDemocracy, March 27, 2019, www.opendemocracy.net/en/5050/revealed -trump-linked-us-christian-fundamentalists-pour-millions-of-dark-money-into -europe-boosting-the-far-right/. This study is useful in terms of providing an accounting of absolute dollars spent by a range of organizations, but it does not explain how the money was spent, and lumps together groups that are explicitly activist (the Alliance Defending Freedom, ADF, for example) with groups that likely spent most of their money on traditional evangelism, such as the Billy Graham Evangelistic Asso-

ciation, which had by far the largest spending in Europe—almost half of the total—at \$23.3 million. A more recent study by openDemocracy provides a broader global picture but is marred by its inclusion of groups that are clearly not Christian, such as the libertarian Cato Institute, the Federalist Society, and the Heritage Foundation. Claire Provost and Nandini Archer, "Revealed: \$280m 'Dark Money' Spent by US Christian Right Groups Globally," openDemocracy, October 27, 2020, www .opendemocracy.net/en/5050/trump-us-christian-spending-global-revealed/.

48. The WCF began as the Howard Center for Family, Religion, and Society, but since 2016 has become the International Organization for the Family. The World Congress of Families is its signature event and the most commonly used name for the organization as a whole. Kristina Stoeckl, "The Rise of the Russian Christian Right: The Case of the World Congress of Families," *Religion, State and Society* 48, 4 (2020), pp. 223–38, https://doi.org/10.1080/09637494.2020.1796172.

49. Michael Casey, "Russians and the American Right Started Plotting in 1995. We Have the Notes from the First Meeting," *ThinkProgress* (blog), June 19, 2018, https:// archive.thinkprogress.org/history-of-christian-fundamentalists-in-russia-and-the-us -a6bdd326841d/.

50. Stoeckl, "The Rise of the Russian Christian Right," pp. 227–29. Hannah Levintova, "These US Evangelicals Helped Create Russia's Anti-Gay Movement," *Mother Jones* (blog), February 21, 2014, www.motherjones.com/politics/2014/02/world -congress-families-russia-gay-rights/; Melani McAlister, "Why Putin Is an Ally for American Evangelicals," *The Conversation*, September 4, 2018, http://theconversation .com/why-putin-is-an-ally-for-american-evangelicals-101504; James Kirchick, "Why American Conservatives Love Anti-Gay Putin," *Daily Beast*, August 1, 2013, www .thedailybeast.com/articles/2013/08/01/why-american-conservatives-love-anti-gay -putin; UNHRC, "Exposed: The World Congress of Families" Human Rights Campaign, August 2014, http://assets2.hrc.org/files/assets/resources/ExposedTheWorld CongressOfFamilies.pdf.

51. Alexander Cooley, "Same Blueprint, New Norms: Regional Organizations, Illiberalism, and the Rise of Contested Global Governance," ch. 4 above; Gordon Urquhart, "That's Not Faith, That's Provocation," *The Guardian*, November 12, 1999, www.theguardian.com/world/1999/nov/12/catholicism.religion.

52. Allan Carlson, "A History of 'the Family' in the United Nations," 2000, quoted in Clifford Bob, *The Global Right Wing and the Clash of World Politics*, Cambridge Studies in Contentious Politics (Cambridge University Press, 2012), p. 42.

53. For a list of the major religious conservative organizations working on family issues at the UN, see María Angélica Peñas Defago, José Manuel Morán Faúndes, and Juan Marco Vaggione, *Religious Conservatism on the Global Stage: Threats and Challenges for LGBTI Rights*, Global Philanthropy Project, November 2018, https:// globalphilanthropyproject.org/religiousconservatismreport/.

54. Scott Long, "Anatomy of a Backlash: Sexuality and the 'Cultural' War on Human Rights," Human Rights Watch, 2005, p. 14, www.hrw.org/legacy/wr2k5 /anatomy/anatomy.pdf.

55. Physicians for Life, "Report on the Doha International Conference for the Family (11/2004)," APFLI, September 15, 2005, www.physiciansforlife.org/report-on -the-doha-international-conference-for-the-family-112004/.

56. Bob, *Global Right Wing*, p. 55.

57. "About Us," U.N. Family Rights Caucus, 2014, http://unfamily.wpengine.com /about/.

58. Austin Dacey, "At the UN, Conservative Christian Agenda Cloaked in Human Rights Language," *Religion Dispatches*, September 23, 2014, https://religiondispatches. org/at-the-un-an-attempt-to-re-cast-childrens-rights-as-family-rights/.

59. Peter Montgomery, "International Backlash," Political Research Associates, Fall 2016, www.politicalresearch.org/2016/11/14/international-backlash-the-religious-right -at-the-un.

60. Anne Marie Goetz and Jenaina Irani, "Is the UN Taking a Position in Today's 'Culture Wars'?," OpenDemocracy, June 25, 2019, www.opendemocracy.net/en/5050 /is-the-un-taking-a-position-in-todays-culture-wars/; Shahara Razawi, "Progress of the World's Women," UN Women, June 25, 2019, www.unwomen.org/en/digital-library /progress-of-the-worlds-women.

61. Kapya Kaoma, "Globalizing the Culture Wars: US Conservatives, African Churches, and Homophobia," Political Research Associates, November 2009; Kapya Kaoma, "How US Clergy Brought Hate to Uganda," *The Gay and Lesbian Review Worldwide* 17, 3 (June 2010), pp. 20–23.

62. UNHRC, "Exposed: The World Congress of Families."

63. Lydia Boyd, "The Problem with Freedom: Homosexuality and Human Rights in Uganda," *Anthropological Quarterly* 86, 3 (2013), pp. 697–724.

64. Scott Lively and Kevin Abrams, *The Pink Swastika: Homosexuality in the Nazi Party* (Springfield, Mass. Veritas Aeterna Press, 2017).

65. Jeremy Hooper, "Scott Lively Stirring Russia's Pot: A Timeline," GLAAD, May 5, 2014, www.glaad.org/blog/scott-lively-stirring-russias-pot-timeline; "Anti-LGBT Activist Scott Lively Returns to Russia," Southern Poverty Law Center, October 13, 2013, www.splcenter.org/hatewatch/2013/10/18/anti-lgbt-activist-scott-lively -returns-russia; Scott Lively, "Report from Moscow," *Scott Lively Ministries* (blog), October 18, 2013, www.scottlively.net/2013/10/18/report-from-moscow/.

66. For example, the WCF press release does not include Lively in its list of members of the International Planning Committee for the 2014 meeting. Don Feder, "International Planning Committee Meets in Moscow to Plan World Congress of Families VIII (September 10–12, 2014)—Christian Newswire," *Christian Newswire*, October 23, 2013, http://www.christiannewswire.com/news/7114773046.html.

67. Lively and Abrams, *The Pink Swastika*; Abby Ohlheiser, "Uganda's New Anti-Homosexuality Law Was Inspired by American Activists," *The Atlantic*, December 20, 2013, www.theatlantic.com/international/archive/2013/12/uganda-passes-law-punishes -homosexuality-life-imprisonment/356365/; Jeffrey Gettleman, "After US Evangelicals Visit, Ugandan Considers Death for Gays," *New York Times*, January 4, 2010; Kapya Kaoma, "The US Christian Right and the Attack on Gays in Africa," Political Research

Associates, October 2009, www.publiceye.org/magazine/v24n4/us-christian-right
-attack-on-gays-in-africa.html.

68. Michael Wilkerson, "Lou Engle's 'The Call Uganda' Rallies Support For Anti-
Homosexuality Bill," *Religion Dispatches*, May 4, 2010, http://religiondispatches.org
/american-supports-ugandan-anti-gay-bill/. See also Josh Kron, "In Uganda, Push to
Curb Gays Draws U.S. Guest," *New York Times*, May 2, 2010; Waymon Hudson, "The
Call Uganda: Anti-Gay American Evangelical Going to Inflame Hate in Uganda,"
Huffington Post, June 30, 2010, http://www.huffingtonpost.com/waymon-hudson
/thecall-uganda-anti-gay-a_b_558890.html. This analysis is drawn from my longer
discussion of the Ugandan case in chapter 14 of *Kingdom of God*.

69. Barbara Bradley Hagerty, "U.S. Exports Cultural War to Uganda," *NPR*, January 15, 2010, http://www.npr.org/templates/story/story.php?storyId=122572951.

70. Anglican Consultative Council, The Lambeth Conference: Resolutions Archive
from 1998 (London: Anglican Communion Office, 2005), p. 9, http://www.anglican
communion.org/. Miranda Hassett, *Anglican Communion in Crisis: How Episcopal Dissidents and Their African Allies Are Reshaping Anglicanism* (Princeton University Press,
2007), pp. 95–98.

71. Evelyn Lirri, "Uganda: Gay Row—Pastor Rick Warren Supports Country on
Boycott," *Virtue Online: The Voice for Global Orthodox Anglicanism*, March 28, 2008,
www.virtueonline.org/uganda-gay-row-us-pastor-rick-warren-supports-country
-boycott. See also Kaoma, "Globalizing the Culture Wars," p. 10.

72. John Dietrich, "The Politics of PEPFAR: The President's Emergency Plan for
AIDS Relief," *Ethics and International Affairs* (Fall 2007), p. 277–92.

73. Waymon Hudson, "Uganda's 'Kill the Gays' Bill Goes XXX?," Bilerico Project, January 26, 2010, http://www.bilerico.com/2010/01/ugandas_kill_the_gays_bill
_goes_xxx.php; Max Blumenthal, "Rick Warren's Africa Problem," *Daily Beast*, January 7, 2009, www.thedailybeast.com/blogs-and-stories/2009-01-07/the-truth-about
-rick-warren-in-africa/; Epstein, "God and the Fight against AIDS"; Xan Rice, "Gay
Activists Attack Ugandan Preacher's Porn Slideshow," *The Guardian*, February 18,
2010; "Uganda Gay-Porn Stunt 'Twisted,'" *BBC News*, February 18, 2010, http://news
.bbc.co.uk/2/hi/africa/8522039.stm.

74. Boyd, "The Problem with Freedom"; Lydia Boyd, "What's Driving Homophobia in Uganda," *The Conversation*, November 20, 2019, http://theconversation.com
/whats-driving-homophobia-in-uganda-126071.

75. Sarah Pulliam Bailey, "Intercontinental Divide: Global Pressure Mounts for
Uganda to Defeat Anti-Gay Bill," *Christianity Today*, February 1, 2010, 17–19;
Human Rights Watch, Press Statement, "Uganda: 'Anti-Homosexuality' Bill Threatens Liberties and Human Rights Defenders," www.hrw.org/news/2009/10/15/uganda
-anti-homosexuality-bill-threatens-liberties-and-human-rights-defenders; Human
Rights Watch, Press Statement, "UN: Landmark Meeting Denounces Rights Abuses
Based on Sexual Orientation, Gender Identity," www.hrw.org/news/2009/12/11/un
-landmark-meeting-denounces-rights-abuses-based-sexual-orientation-gender
-identity.

76. Rick Warren, "Letter to the Pastors of Uganda," December 2009, www.youtube
.com/watch?v=1jmGu9o4fDE.

77. Bailey, "Intercontinental Divide."

78. John L. Allen Jr., "Why Catholics Aren't Speaking Up in Uganda about Anti-
Gay Bill," *National Catholic Reporter*, December 16, 2009, www.ncronline.org/blogs
/ncr-today/why-catholics-arent-speaking-uganda-about-anti-gay-bill.

79. Lillian Kwon, "Uganda Pastors Chide Rick Warren; Defend Anti-Gay Bill,"
Christian Post, December 21, 2009, www.christianpost.com/news/uganda-pastors
-chide-rick-warren-defend-anti-gay-bill-42372/. The task force had members from the
National Fellowship of Born Again Churches, Seventh-Day Adventist Church, Orthodox Church in Uganda, Roman Catholic Church in Uganda, Islamic Office of
Social Welfare in Uganda, and Born Again Faith Federation. On the Catholic response, see John L. Allen Jr., "Anti-Gay Bill in Uganda Challenges Catholics to Take
a Stand," *National Catholic Reporter*, November 27, 2009, www.ncronline.org/blogs
/all-things-catholic/anti-gay-bill-uganda-challenges-catholics-take-stand.

80. Sarah Pulliam Bailey, "Church of Uganda Recommends Amending Anti-
Homosexuality Bill," *Christianity Today*, February 9, 2010, www.christianitytoday
.com/news/2010/february/church-of-uganda-recommends-amending-anti-homo
sexuality.html.

81. Josh Kron, "Resentment toward the West Bolsters Uganda's New Anti-Gay
Bill," *New York Times*, February 29, 2012.

82. Deadly Intolerance," *The Economist*, March 1, 2014, p. 42.

83. Peter Baker, "Uganda: Anti-Gay Law Draws Sanctions," *New York Times*,
June 19, 2014; Ty McCormick, "Is the US Military Propping Up Uganda's 'Elected'
Autocrat?," *Foreign Policy*, February 18, 2016, http://foreignpolicy.com/2016/02/18/is
-the-us-military-propping-up-ugandas-elected-autocrat-museveni-elections/.

84. Elias Biryabarema, "Uganda's Museveni Wants to Water Down Anti-Gay
Law," Reuters, August 9, 2014, http://uk.reuters.com/article/uk-uganda-gay/ugandas
-museveni-wants-to-water-down-anti-gay-law-lawmaker-idUKKBN0GC0YG
20140812.

85. Caryle Murphy, "More U.S. Christians OK with Homosexuality," Pew Research Center, December 18, 2015, www.pewresearch.org/fact-tank/2015/12/18/most
-u-s-christian-groups-grow-more-accepting-of-homosexuality/.

86. Celeste Gracey and Jeremy Weber, "World Vision: Why We're Hiring Gay
Christians in Same-Sex Marriages," ChristianityToday.com, March 24, 2014, www
.christianitytoday.com/ct/2014/march-web-only/world-vision-why-hiring-gay
-christians-same-sex-marriage.html; Eyder Peralta, "Two Days Later, World Vision Re-
verses Policy That Allowed Hiring Of Gays," *NPR*, March 26, 2014, www.npr.org
/sections/thetwo-way/2014/03/26/294945076/two-days-later-world-vision-reverses
-policy-that-allowed-hiring-of-gays; Associated Press, "World Vision Board Member
Quits over Gay Marriage Hiring Ban," *The Guardian*, April 3, 2014, www.theguardian
.com/society/2014/apr/03/world-vision-board-member-quits-gay-marriage-hiring.

87. Jacob Poushter and Nicholas Kent, "Views of Homosexuality around the World," *Pew Research Center's Global Attitudes Project* (blog), June 25, 2020, www .pewresearch.org/global/2020/06/25/global-divide-on-homosexuality-persists/.

88. Aaron Blake, "Analysis: The Rapid Decline of White Evangelical America?," *Washington Post*, July 8, 2021, www.washingtonpost.com/politics/2021/07/08/rapid -decline-white-evangelical-america/; Janelle S. Wong, *Immigrants, Evangelicals, and Politics in an Era of Demographic Change* (New York: Russell Sage Foundation, 2018).

89. Melissa Rogers and E. J. Dionne, "A Time to Heal, A Time to Build," *Brookings* (blog), October 21, 2020, https://www.brookings.edu/research/a-time-to-heal -a-time-to-build/.

PART III

New Technologies and Human Rights

EIGHT

Technical Standards and Human Rights

The Case of New IP

EMILY TAYLOR, KATE JONES, AND CAROLINA CAEIRO

Western governments are paying increased attention to technical standards and the ethical and human rights implications of emerging technologies. In their 2021 Digital and Technology Ministerial Declaration, Group of Seven (G7) member countries created the "Framework for Collaboration on Digital Technical Standards," which was subsequently endorsed by G7 leaders.[1] The framework referred to internet protocols (IP) and technical standards for emerging technologies as areas that "could affect shared values as open and democratic societies."[2] Likewise, the U.K. government pledged to work with partners "to ensure the rules and standards governing digital technologies are rooted in democratic values."[3] Standards development—previously a niche field reserved for engineers—is taking a leading role in government strategies.

This new-found attention appears directly linked to a set of proposals that China submitted for consideration within the Standardization Unit of the International Telecommunications Union (ITU), the Geneva-based United Nations (UN) agency tasked with overseeing country-led international cooperation in the telecom sector. Introduced by Chinese delegations as "New IP," the proposals would have resulted in the creation of a series of technical standards underpinning a new, centralized internet architecture. Although China's original New IP proposals were rejected at the ITU, New IP has not gone away.[4]

China's efforts to push for the standardization of New IP reveal a lot about the country's ambitions and strategy. China has openly stated that the rise of new technologies provides it with the opportunity to "seize the commanding heights of standards innovation."[5] Standards-setting enables it to build its own ideological tenets into the design and architecture of new technology in ways that until recently were largely beneath the radar of human rights bodies. By leading standardization processes, China is looking to reshape the architecture of the Internet and set the rules that will govern the technologies of the future.

Although perceived as neutral, standardization implicitly embodies values. Just as the development of the internet was shaped by the social values of engineers, governments, and companies from the West,[6] China's New IP has an authoritarian flavor. It is designed to capture large amounts of data and enable centralized controls that could be harnessed for government surveillance. Regardless of whether New IP is successfully standardized or adopted at scale, China's efforts illustrate how the standardization processes themselves have the potential to protect technologies that are not rights-respecting. Standardization can legitimize the use of new technologies and garner the protection of international trade rules for them, irrespective of existing human rights norms.

This chapter looks at the standards journey and design features of New IP as a case study to illustrate the increasing ethical and human rights implications of the development of technical standards. The analysis of New IP will build on available evidence and depictions of its building-block technologies to infer how these alternative networking architectures may be used to enable surveillance and network controls. The chapter also contributes to the existing body of scholarship on New IP by analyzing how this alternative networking model would result in domestic violations of human rights. It shows that, whether implemented by China within its territory or deployed by third countries, New IP would interfere with the right to privacy, freedom of expression and opinion, and freedom of association and assembly of network users. In the specific case of China, the chapter argues, New IP could strengthen social control programs that make implementation of some human rights conditional on good behavior, which is directly contrary to the principle of the universality of human rights. The concluding section offers a series of recommendations for human rights organizations, the technical community, and governments to incorporate human rights into technology standardization processes and protect the global and open nature of the Internet.

Push to Standardize a New Internet Architecture

New IP is an attempt to build an alternative internet. The proposal, first unveiled by Huawei in 2018 at the ITU, proposes a new model for connecting devices and sharing information and resources across networks.[7] Advocacy for New IP leverages two central Western policy concerns—internet security and growing control over internet infrastructure and applications by a few large technology companies—and claims to solve them through the application of decentralized technologies and the heightened use of identification methods for establishing trust on the network. In practice, this alternative internet infrastructure would introduce new controls at the level of the network connection and enable bulk data collection and the option to track users and contents through the use of blockchain and permanent identifiers. These features could convert New IP into an instrument for social control and state surveillance.

New IP can be described as an upgrade from the "Great Firewall." Controls over online content in China have relied heavily on interventions at the level of internet architecture. The Great Firewall, however, has been a patchwork solution to rein in the internet. The upgrade of network controls through the creation of New IP would enhance digital contention already practiced in China.[8] Under New IP, data collection and control mechanisms would become more sophisticated as they would be built into the network architecture itself. New IP would streamline additional data and feed them into existing social monitoring initiatives such as the Social Credit System—a profiling program designed to influence behavior, scoring individuals according to their compliance with specific social norms—and Chinese surveillance programs. This alternative version of the internet designed to enable greater controls and surveillance would lend itself to human rights abuse.

Ongoing efforts to standardize New IP are a sobering example of the potential impact of technical standards on human rights, and in this specific case, on the future of internet governance. New IP has the potential to fragment the global, open internet, creating a parallel architecture that allows centralized government control. Depictions of the technology indicate that this parallel architecture would not be fully interoperable and therefore, in a best-case scenario, could potentially split the internet, with one part structured so as not to respect fundamental values and norms of open societies. Such a fragmentation would both contribute to and reflect the changing international world order and its normative underpinnings.[9]

ITU as a Home for Multilateral Standards Development

A wide range of organizations are developing technical standards. These are generally divided between those that follow a multilateral model in which consensus is developed among national delegations, and those with an open standards model with pluralistic, voluntary, bottom-up participation, driven by industry and innovation needs.[10] The open standards paradigm has been instrumental in driving the internet's success. Within this paradigm, the industry-led, multistakeholder Internet Engineering Task Force (IETF) is widely regarded as the primary standards developing organization (SDO) for defining protocols.[11]

While the natural home for introducing any updates to internet standards would be the IETF, China instead opted to push for New IP's parallel architecture within the ITU standardization unit (ITU-T). Unlike the IETF's open standardization model, the ITU-T follows a multilateral model in which member states are the only participants to have a final say on approving recommended standards—or casting a vote when there is no consensus. This choice is unsurprising. ITU's multilateral, state-centric diplomacy gives China and its international allies a better shot at setting standards than multistakeholder SDOs would.[12] While other stakeholders can take part in deliberations at the ITU-T, participation costs are onerous and subject to the approval of the applicant's member state.[13] As a result, nonstate participation in ITU study groups is dominated by private sector members who can afford the hefty fees to become "sector members," while dissident voices are unlikely to be represented. In the case of China, its national delegation is not only the largest, it has also integrated representatives from Chinese technology and telecommunications companies who spearhead proposals and advance specific agenda items.[14] This participation model has led to human rights and consumer protections being widely overlooked within the ITU's standards development space.[15]

Standardizing at ITU also represents a means to secure international trade protections for new technologies, giving approved standards a market edge.[16] The World Trade Organization's (WTO's) Agreement on Technical Barriers to Trade (TBT) encourages member states to adopt existing international standards from multilateral SDOs such as ITU.[17] Members are then required to use these standards to prove product compliance with WTO regulations.[18] In other words, ITU-recommended standards become the gold standard for the import and export of technology. For China, standardizing at the ITU legitimizes the deployment of technologies domestically and, perhaps more importantly, it provides the country with a green card to export them.[19] WTO rules also prioritize adopted standards without consideration of human rights. While the TBT contemplates exceptions to the application of established standards, potential threats to human rights are not listed as a reason for departing from those standards. In this way, the international adoption of standards is unconcerned with human rights, yet protected by trade rules.

Although a detailed discussion of the role and mandates of other standards bodies is beyond the scope of this chapter, apart from the IETF and ITU there are several organizations active in the technical standards landscape, such as the International Organization for Standardization (ISO), whose membership comprises 160 national standards bodies (such as the British Standards Institution, BSI) (see figure 8-1). Like the ITU, the ISO's standards are protected under WTO rules. There are also several industry-led standards bodies such as the Institute of Electrical and Electronics Engineers (IEEE) and the World Wide Web Consortium (W3C), all of which play a prominent role in standardizing emerging technologies with a wide societal impact.

The Chinese proposals have come at a time when the ITU is looking more keenly to move beyond its original mandate, expanding from telecommunications into internet standards and policy development. This unfolding trend has opened the door for New IP and its related technologies to be discussed within multiple ITU-T Study Groups (SGs) under the guise of related applications or technologies such as blockchain, artificial intelligence (AI), and holographic communications.[20] The attempt to shift internet standards development to the ITU risks transforming this dimension of internet governance from a multistakeholder effort into a multilateral process.

China: "Tech Superpower" and Exporter of Cybernorms

The development of New IP has not happened in isolation. China's intent to become a "tech superpower" has led the country to invest heavily in smart and emerging technologies, including areas such as 5G, big data, and cloud computing.[21] New IP's proposed architecture would synchronize with telecommunications and networking technologies currently being promoted by China. If successfully standardized—entirely or partially through its various building blocks—it is likely to become an integral part of the Chinese suite of products for export.

While the economic incentives behind standards-setting efforts are clear, the internationalization of Chinese technology also represents a means to export Chinese cybernorms.[22] Through design choices, China embeds alternative approaches to human rights in the technologies it is developing and exporting.

FIGURE 8-1: **Ecosystem of Technology Standards Development Organizations***

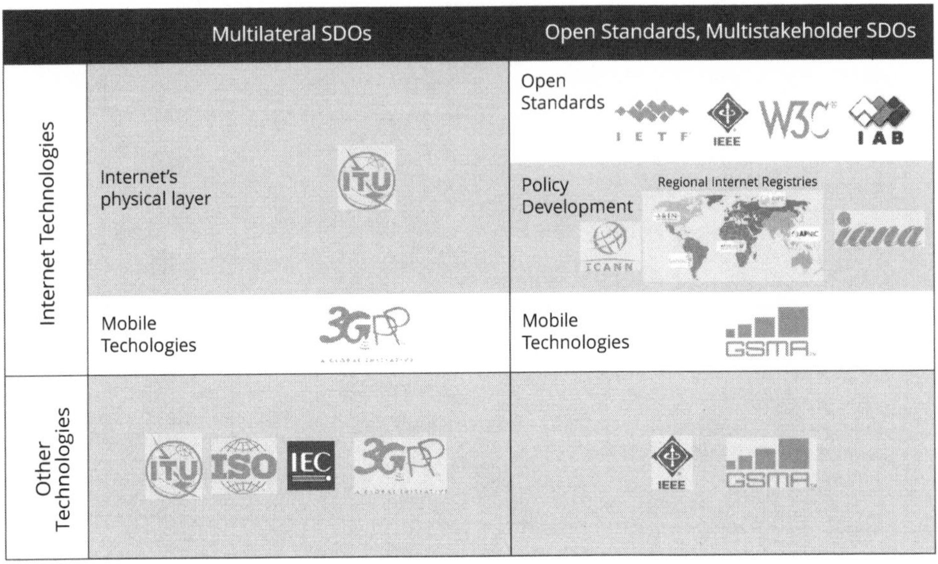

	Multilateral SDOs		Open Standards, Multistakeholder SDOs	
Internet Technologies	Internet's physical layer	ITU	Open Standards	IETF IEEE W3C IAB
			Policy Development	ICANN Regional Internet Registries iana
	Mobile Techologies	3GPP	Mobile Technologies	GSMA
Other Technologies	ITU ISO IEC 3GPP			IEEE GSMA

* Listed organizations are ITU (International Telecommunications Union, https://www.itu.int/en/ITU-T/Pages/default.aspx); ISO (International Organization for Standardization, https://www.iso.org/home.html); IEC (International Electrotechnical Commission, https://www.iec.ch/homepage); IETF (Internet Engineering Task Force, https://www.ietf.org/); IRTF (Internet Research Task Force, https://irtf.org/); IEEE (Institute of Electrical and Electronics Engineers, https://www.ieee.org/standards/index.html); W3C (World Wide Web Consortium, https://www.w3.org/); IAB (Internet Architecture Board, https://www.iab.org/); ICANN (Internet Corporation for Assigned Names and Numbers, https://www.icann.org/); RIRs (Regional Internet Registries congregated under the Number Resources Organizations, https://www.nro.net/about/rirs/); IANA (Internet Assigned Numbers Authority, https://www.iana.org/); GSMA (Global System for Mobile Communications Association, https://www.gsma.com/); and 3GPP (3rd Generation Partnership Project, https://www.3gpp.org/).

Weak privacy protections, disregard for anonymity, and tolerance for surveillance are normally the distinctive features.

China's primary strategy to secure new markets has been the Belt and Road Initiative (BRI), where the export of technology and digital infrastructure has featured prominently. Sometimes referred to as the Digital Silk Road, China's export of digital infrastructure has created concrete opportunities to internationalize standards that are built into Chinese technologies. If the technology becomes available for implementation, pitching New IP to BRI participant countries would be likely to follow. In countries where Chinese equipment is already installed, deployment of New IP may only require software updates.

Beyond BRI trade partners, natural adopters of Chinese technology include authoritarian regimes that are enticed by the potential for social control through use of Chinese products.[23] These include some countries in Africa, the Gulf, and Latin America. Others are either attracted by price or captured through aid. Beyond offering competitive prices, Chinese companies are known to underbid to secure key contracts and expand the adoption of its technology—normally with the help of state subsidies.[24] In other cases, lending schemes are leveraged to secure concessions, including agreements to purchase and deploy Chinese technology. Several BRI participating countries have already agreed to such deployment for 5G networks.[25] These strategies are affording China a growing role in developing countries where it has sought to influence communications infrastructure plans for decades. Developing countries also host large segments of the 2.7 billion people who are yet to come online.[26] This represents a huge market potential that China is well-positioned to capture with its lower-priced technology.[27]

Through China's sizable domestic market of 1.43 billion people, the leverage over BRI partners, and the commercial power of Huawei, New IP could well become a de facto standard. In other words, domestic adoption and export of New IP do not necessarily hinge on international standardization. The clincher, however, lies in the legal protections and legitimation that Chinese technologies acquire once standardized. This has made China's pursuits within ITU increasingly central to the country's strategy for technology dominance.

Where Is New IP Today?

Huawei publicly declared in September 2020 that New IP had already undergone gap analysis and conceptual research, as well as testing, and that the idea was "solid, viable, and feasible in implementation."[28] Company leadership also confirmed Huawei's intent to move ahead with the standardization of New IP within the ITU.[29] China has even conducted a live demonstration of New IP at the ITU as part of the controversial focus group Network 2030, which was tasked with scoping technology needs for the future of networks.[30]

China's standards strategy—reflected in both its Standards 2035 blueprint and its most recent Five-Year Plan—suggests that deployment of New IP is likely to start domestically, while the country works to legitimize national standards internationally through the ITU and other SDOs amenable to discussing them.[31] Large-scale piloting appears to have started in April 2021, with the announcement of a backbone network that will connect forty leading universities to test what has been advertised as the "Internet of the Future."[32] This test-bed exercise is expected to verify the performance and security of the network prior to commercial deployment. Given its sizable domestic market, China could achieve deployment of New IP at scale. Domestic deployments alone would serve to get New IP past proof of concept, improving its chances of uptake elsewhere.

In 2020, as red flags were raised around China's efforts to standardize New IP, multiple country delegations and sector organizations voiced their concerns at the ITU-T, including the United Kingdom, Norway, twenty-one European Union (EU) member states, the European Commission, the Regional Internet Address Registry (Réseaux IP Européens Network Coordination Centre [RIPE NCC]), the IEEE, and the IETF itself.[33] Leading associations within the telecommunications industry have also spoken against New IP, indicating that the sector does not support the proposal.[34]

While this signals that Western organizations are taking notice, Chinese efforts are unlikely to relent. Following the rejection of the original New IP proposal within the ITU, Chinese delegations have emerged with a new strategy: standardizing New IP piecemeal. This has manifested in proposals to kickstart the standardization process of its building-block technologies such as the use of blockchain to modify the nature of identification systems used on the internet, or the transformation of networking protocols to incorporate identifiers and expose information from data packets traveling on the net.[35] This new approach of breaking the proposal into smaller building blocks, accompanied by more specific examples of practical, industrial uses of the technology, addresses a key criticism of the original New IP: the lack of compelling use cases. In this way, the new proposals are less likely to be simply dismissed out of hand within the standards development environment. Despite the new presentation, New IP's building blocks, if put together, could still deliver a parallel internet with unmatched surveillance capabilities.

As part of its efforts to influence standards, China has also resorted to forum shopping. The China Internet Network Information Center, for instance, has filed a U.S. patent application (published on May 6, 2021) for decentralized blockchain domain name systems (DNS).[36] China's 14th Five-Year Plan, released in March 2021, indicates that intentions to embed blockchain technologies into internet architecture for enhanced centralization and tracking, as well as to step up the social credit system, are still firm objectives of the Chinese Communist Party (CCP).[37]

Similarly, Russia is challenging the existing procedures to manage the internet globally. In January 2021, it presented a proposal at the ITU calling into question the status of the global governance system for internet domain names, addresses, and critical internet infrastructure.[38] The Russian request did not stick, and the specific New IP proposals may not eventually be standardized, but both examples speak to China and Russia's joint and separate determination to challenge the internet's governance model.

The World Telecommunication Standardization Assembly (WTSA) 2020 was postponed owing to the pandemic and is currently scheduled to take place in March 2022. It will reveal whether China and its allies have been able to build sufficient consensus to move New IP proposals—or reconfiguration of the building-block technologies—ahead. Whatever the outcome of the WTSA, China is likely to continue reinforcing narratives around decentralization and trust that draw on legitimate policy concerns from the West to justify New IP, perhaps across other standards bodies or international forums.[39]

Human Rights Implications of New IP

Huawei has presented the development of New IP as a purely technical proposal to enable evolution of the network layer of the internet stack—the suite of communication protocols that make up the internet. It has also defended its attempt to standardize internet technologies outside the multistakeholder SDOs, alleging that organizations that have successfully contributed to the growth of the internet, such as the IETF, are "too slow to keep up with innovation."[40] While technology development and standardization may be expressed merely in terms of an engineering exercise, New IP and its supporting technologies would have a significant impact on fundamental human rights.

Understanding How New IP Enables Surveillance

At its core, New IP would render the internet an instrument for government control. From a technical standpoint, it proposes a restructuring of the internet architecture that modifies how the various internet layers operate (see figure 8-2). The internet's original design foresees a model in which layers operate independently and are largely unaware of one another. This design has enabled the speed and affordability that have made the internet the success it is. New IP's principal change is transformation of the network layer—how information packets travel—by incorporating new capabilities that grant those

FIGURE 8-2: **Internet Layers—Open Systems Interconnection (OSI) Model**

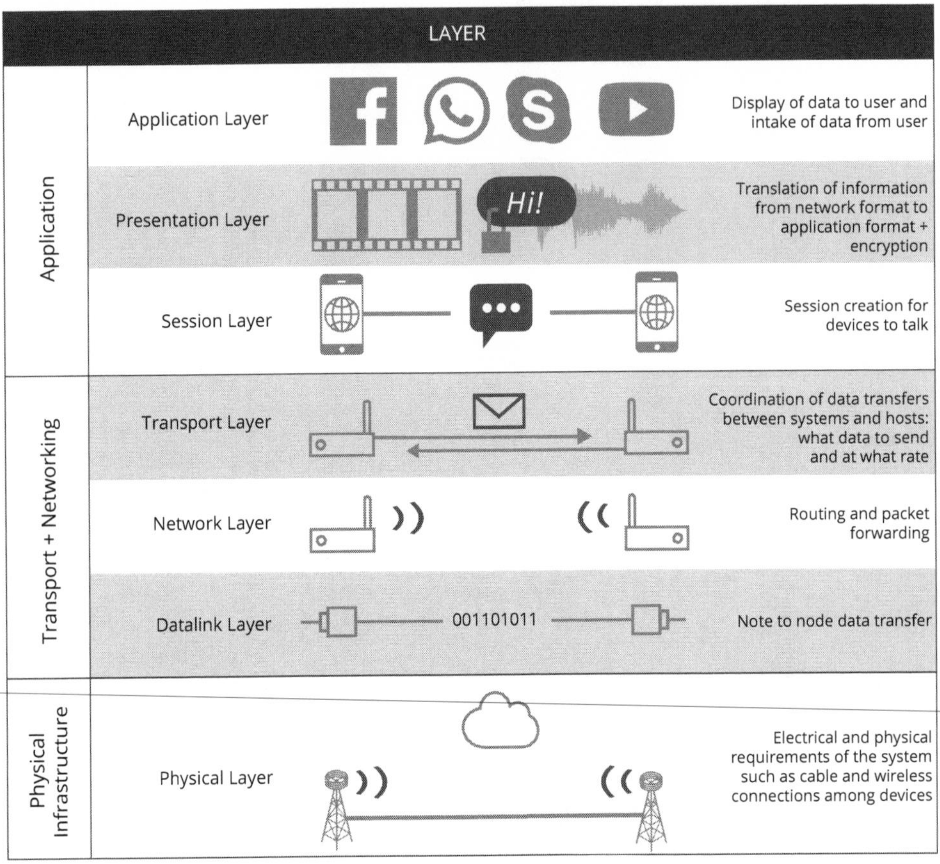

LAYER		
Application	Application Layer	Display of data to user and intake of data from user
	Presentation Layer	Translation of information from network format to application format + encryption
	Session Layer	Session creation for devices to talk
Transport + Networking	Transport Layer	Coordination of data transfers between systems and hosts: what data to send and at what rate
	Network Layer	Routing and packet forwarding
	Datalink Layer	Note to node data transfer
Physical Infrastructure	Physical Layer	Electrical and physical requirements of the system such as cable and wireless connections among devices

* Keith Shaw, "The OSI Model Explained and How to Easily Remember Its 7 Layers," *Networkworld*, October 14, 2020, www.networkworld.com/article/3239677/the-osi-model-explained-and-how-to-easily-remember-its-7-layers.html.

entities involved in managing networks and nodes greater control over internet traffic and users.

The network layer is often referred to as the "dumb pipes" of the internet, as it is tasked with the transport of data packets while being unconcerned about the content of those packets. This simplicity in design was adopted intentionally to keep internet standards lightweight and interoperable.[41] Traditionally, a line was drawn between the application layer and the core architectural layers. The application layer is the interface between humans and technology, where communications become visible and where content is created and consumed by people. The application layer is inherently political: it is where the human rights of freedom of expression, privacy, freedom of thought and opinion are most obvious. By contrast, the core architectural layers, including the network layer, offer the means for transporting information and constitute what could be described as the neutral foundations of the internet.

Chinese delegates proposing New IP claim that the dumb network layer is inadequate for the deployment of future technologies such as holograms and self-driving cars that will require very low latency—meaning minimal delays when processing high volumes of data—and guaranteed data delivery.[42] While it is unclear whether New IP could truly deliver on those promises,[43] its proposed enhancement of the network layer would render networking a new locus for control.

Under New IP, the network layer would become more complex. Specifically, New IP proposes to embed information from the application layer into the no longer "dumb pipes" of the network layer.[44] This would generate a degree of vertical integration, undermining the principle of layer independence that characterizes the internet's original design. Under this new networking model, the packet header—the label on the packet that establishes where it is headed—would be modified to include a description of the contents (see figure 8-3). With this information so readily available, the upgraded, intelligent network layer would become a proxy for control, and policy issues previously restricted to the application layer would move down the internet stack.[45] Infrastructure providers that supply networking equipment such as routers, and internet service providers (ISPs) that operate the networks would become key players in managing "services, access controls, and application of policy and regulation that would now take place at the point of connection."[46]

FIGURE 8-3: **Internet and New IP Networking Models**

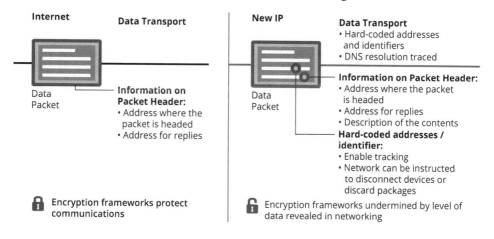

Beyond transforming the networking layer, New IP also sets out to reconceptualize the unique identifier systems that underpin the internet.[47] This is done through the incorporation of immutable identifiers and "burned in" addresses throughout the networking process and the introduction of decentralized ledger technologies (DLTs)—more commonly known as blockchain—into the networking architecture. These technologies would significantly alter the nature of the internet, introducing new tracking capabilities, facilitating access to data and information controls, and also undermining the governance models of current internet identifiers such as domain names and addresses.

Identifiers are used to locate and retrieve information by assigning unique, permanent names to "things" on the internet (such as users, content, routers, servers, devices). Within New IP proposals, these identifiers have been described as bit strings that are centrally administered and immutable. The reliance on persistent, one-to-one relationships between an identifier and an object would enable unparalleled tracing over the internet through the creation of permanent records, for example, on users' browsing history. Additionally, using these identifiers, the network could be instructed to discard packets or disconnect devices that are deemed illegitimate, through what New IP depictions describe as the "shut off" protocol.[48]

DLTs are also being proposed for standardization in ways that would transform the internet's existing identifiers systems, primarily the domain name system.[49] Huawei's descriptions of New IP include a blockchain layer that would operate at the point of networking connection to provide what Huawei representatives have described as the "decentralized trustworthiness of the Internet name spaces."[50] This claims to solve DNS security issues through the verification of IP address ownership and tracking of DNS resolution (the process of translating an IP address into a domain name). Presented as a security feature, in practice this allows unparalleled tracing over the internet.

The distributed nature of DLTs and their reliance on encryption means the technology is normally associated with being decentralized and secure. However, these features are dependent on how the technologies are implemented. If applied to the internet architecture as proposed within New IP, DLT would generate opposite effects.[51] Its use would allow for centralized control, streamline data collection, and further facilitate individualized tracking of users and content. It would also automatically collect and share data with designated entities.[52] This means it could be employed by governments to share, gather, aggregate, and analyze data. These features are likely to be supported and further enhanced by 5G's edge computing, a technology that brings information processing closer to devices and end-user, and that is expected to boost data generation and collection.[53]

Lastly, the secured implementation of this technology depends largely on who controls the DLT (and the data it processes). In China, this is likely to be state-owned entities; other governments that import these technologies could facilitate similar arrangements. Combined with immutable identifiers as described in some New IP proposals, every action and transaction thus becomes traceable and allows for surveillance and scrutiny. This would further erode anonymity online and open the door to mass surveillance. In other words, the distributed nature of DLT does not prevent centralization, and the mere use of blockchain encryption does not guarantee privacy or protection from surveillance.

There are a number of additional concerns about the integration of blockchain into a large-scale network, such as its high power consumption and environmental impact, and the latency on routing decisions, which would erode the user experience. These considerations, though valid, are beyond the scope of this chapter.

How New IP Fails to Respect Human Rights

The capture, transfer, and use of personal data envisioned by New IP would violate states' obligations in the International Bill of Rights to respect and ensure human rights and corporate actors' responsibilities, reflected in the UN Guiding Principles on Business and Human Rights, to respect human rights in their activities.[54]

As shown above, New IP would be significantly more intrusive than current forms of online surveillance. Under this model, surveillance would not happen through hacking or interfering with the network; surveillance capabilities would be built into the internet architecture itself. If adopted, New IP's data gathering, individual tracking, and user and content control capabilities would threaten multiple human rights. This section discusses the impact that a New IP network model would have on the right to privacy and other human rights that are essential for the health of open and free societies. The impacts would be felt not only on civil and political rights, but also on economic, social, and cultural rights. The section also addresses how New IP would contribute to China's social control and surveillance ecosystem and undermine the principle of universality of human rights by facilitating systems where access to rights is contingent on the fulfillment of responsibilities.

New IP would place surveillance data in the hands both of corporate actors—ISPs and infrastructure providers—and of the governments with which they collaborate. In the case of China, the companies that would hold the information yielded by New IP are either government-controlled or have close links with the government.[55] It is commonplace in China for the government to capture and use data generated by the private sector. The requirement for such data-sharing is often built into local regulations and is likely to be broadened in the years to come.[56]

IMPACTS ON PRIVACY

The right to privacy is protected in Article 12 of the Universal Declaration of Human Rights (UDHR) and Article 17 of the International Covenant on Civil and Political Rights (ICCPR), as well as regional human rights treaties. At its heart, this right seeks to defend individuals' private sphere—an area for autonomous development, interaction, and liberty that is free from state intervention.[57] The right to privacy includes informational privacy—that is, privacy in information that exists, or that can be deduced, about a person. This includes information from online communications and metadata.

While technology-mediated, mass data collection by both private and public actors is increasingly common, it must not unduly interfere with privacy. International human rights law and standards set out clear rules on the circumstances under which interferences with the right to privacy are permissible. In broad terms, any interference must be provided for by clear and publicly accessible law, pursue an objectively legitimate aim, and be necessary and proportionate to achieving that aim.

The precise parameters of acceptable interferences with the right to privacy in the collation, retention, and use of online data are being discussed in parallel with ongoing developments in information-gathering technologies and artificial intelligence. David Kaye, when UN Special Rapporteur on freedom of opinion and expression, called for an immediate moratorium on the global trade and use of surveillance technologies until "rigorous human rights safeguards are put in place to regulate such practices."[58] The statement was made with reference only to targeted surveillance. When considering mass surveillance, the challenge becomes even more severe and raises the question whether safeguards can ever be robust enough to mitigate such risk. The European Union's proposed regulation on artificial intelligence is one example of an effort to develop a legal framework to ensure respect for human rights, including through the creation of robust safeguards that would mitigate potential threats to rights from mass surveillance.

Wherever the parameters of acceptable mass collection of data and surveillance lie, it is clear that New IP would fall far short of compliance with the right to privacy. Both case law and commentary from international organizations relate to privacy infringements far less intrusive than those enabled by New IP. They show clearly that New IP would violate the right to privacy in four distinct ways.

(a) Data collection: The right to privacy stipulates that any collection of personal data must be fair, lawful, and transparent.[59] Laws permitting the collection of personal data must guarantee that such information can only be accessed by those who need it, ensure that it is only processed for purposes compatible with international human rights law, and enable individuals to ascertain what data are held about them, and by whom. Laws should also enable individuals to request the correction and deletion of those data. In practice, many states have sought to translate these requirements through data protection laws, such as the General Data Protection Regulation in the European Union.

Much debate has taken place about whether "bulk" data collection constitutes an act of surveillance. Recent analysis by the United Nations High Commissioner for Human Rights indicates that data collection relating to "a person's identity, family or life" interferes with the right to privacy.[60] Data do not need to be examined by a person or an algorithm for privacy to be impacted; the mere collection of information means that "an individual loses some control over information that could put his or her privacy at risk."[61] The European Court of Human Rights (ECtHR) too has reinforced these standards in its recent Big Brother Watch decision, which set a new precedent against indiscriminate data collection for Council of Europe (CoE) member states.[62]

New IP would not meet privacy standards on data collection. Its reliance on DLT would allow the gathering of data such as browsing history and online habits and, through immutable identifiers, those data could be attributed to specific users or devices. In addition, any metadata collected through the deployment of DLT that when aggregated could give an insight into an individual's "behavior, social relationships, private preferences, and identity" would constitute an interference with or violation of the right to privacy.[63]

(b) Surveillance: Surveillance is only permissible if—in addition to the general requirements relating to interferences with the right to privacy—it is limited in scope and duration, targeted, and subject to independent authorization and oversight.[64] According to UN Human Rights Council (UNHRC) Resolution 42/15, arbitrary surveillance, interception of communications, and collection of personal data are all violations or abuses of the right to privacy.[65]

Similarly, in the context of the COVID-19 pandemic, UNHRC Resolution 47/23 of July 2021 highlights how response measures to the pandemic have "reinforced the need to address arbitrary surveillance not in accordance with States' obligations under international human rights law and inconsistent with the principles of necessity, proportionality and legality."[66]

New IP would not meet privacy standards on surveillance. Its alternative networking model would enable mass surveillance at an unprecedented scale. The Mercator Institute for China Studies (MERICS) reports that China has rolled out surveillance initiatives such as Golden Shield, Skynet, Safe Cities and Police Clouds, and Project Sharp Eyes, yet these currently face challenges of lack of digitization and harmonization across states.[67] New IP would have the capacity to offer streamlined access to data and profiling mechanisms for the benefit of such surveillance programs. Even if, as some liberal democracies argue, mass surveillance can sometimes be justified on the grounds of national security, New IP goes far beyond being a proportionate response to any conceivable threat. Its enabling of mass-scale, long-term monitoring of the population in all circumstances would clearly not be compatible with the right to privacy.

(c) Erosion of anonymity: As assessed by the former UN Special Rapporteur on freedom of opinion and expression, anonymity online is necessary for the exercise of this right, and any restrictions on it must be strictly limited to measures that are lawful, necessary, proportionate, and in furtherance of a legitimate objective.[68]

The erosion of anonymity contemplated by New IP would meet none of these conditions. New IP would undermine anonymity by weakening encryption frameworks used in the Internet. The proposed reconfiguration of the networking layer would expose a great deal of information on users and contents. With this information so readily available, the ability of existing encryption efforts to prevent content inspection and censorship would be severely curtailed. Using burned-in identifiers, no longer anonymous users could be effectively blocked from the network. Unprotected communications would also be exposed to inspection and content blocking.

New IP would in addition co-opt existing trust mechanisms such as blockchain encryption and incorporate them into its surveillance architecture. Proponents of New IP maintain that blockchain and DLTs will render the network safe. However, as conceived under New IP, DLTs actually give great control to whoever manages their implementation—most likely government authorities or state-owned operators.[69] The erosion of mechanisms that help protect anonymity could have a significant negative impact on dissidents, human rights defenders, journalists, and activists, all of whom rely on these tools to communicate freely.[70] It would also jeopardize all internet users by rendering them vulnerable to state interference.

(d) Permanent user profiles: New IP could enable the creation of permanent profiles on individuals. The adoption of permanent user profiles would amount to a gross violation of the right to privacy and have a chilling effect on other rights. New IP's combined use of DLT and identifiers would enable individuals' online activity to be recorded on permanent ledgers. This level of individualized tracking offered by New IP would threaten, if not eliminate, anonymity online. It would potentially feed private activities online into social control or surveillance programs, such as China's social credit system, which makes financial credit and other social advantages contingent on socially acceptable behavior, and the Golden Shield Project (the Great Firewall), which controls accessible internet content.

The interest in applying DLT to tracing individuals is not new for the Chinese authorities; in 2018, the Chinese Central Internet regulator proposed legislation to require blockchain companies to sign up users by means of their national ID numbers.[71]

COMPARISON WITH WESTERN DATA COLLECTION AND SURVEILLANCE PRACTICES

Mass surveillance is certainly not unknown in the West. The Edward Snowden revelations uncovered unlawful practices of domestic and foreign surveillance emerging from the United States.[72] The amount of data amassed and used by social media and technology companies too is increasingly perceived as infringing on privacy.[73] While the mass surveillance undertaken by Western governments is arguably disproportionate, New IP and related social control would embody different surveillance objectives—control of behavior, rather than for an aim recognized as legitimate by international human rights law, such as national security or the prevention of crime. Surveillance under New IP would also happen at a wholly different scale, being the norm rather than the exception whenever the internet is used. Moreover, being all-pervasive and invisible, New IP and related measures would not be restrained by checks and balances, such as transparent rules with the opportunity to seek redress for breach through the courts, opportunities to highlight and protest against poor practice publicly and in the media, or the potential for investor scruple that restricts investment in rights-violating systems.

IMPACTS ON OTHER RIGHTS THAT ENABLE OPEN AND FREE SOCIETIES

There would be impacts in three important areas: civil and political rights; economic, cultural, and social rights (ECS); and discrimination.

Civil and political rights: New IP's surveillance capabilities would not only have an impact on individuals' right to privacy, but would also interfere with other civil and political rights that are essential for democratic societies. These include the right to freedom of opinion and expression, and the right to freedom of peaceful assembly and association. As with the right to privacy, international human rights law is clear that any restrictions on these rights must be provided for by clear and publicly accessible law, must pursue an objectively legitimate aim, and must be necessary and proportionate to achieving that aim.

New IP would affect freedom of opinion and expression in multiple ways. First, data collection and surveillance can lead to self-censorship.[74] New IP would exert an overt form of surveillance, as network users would very likely be aware of the possibility of individualized tracking of online activity. This would set off a Panopticon effect, meaning that New IP users might adjust their online behavior and particularly their communications and the information they search for and share.[75] Second, if users know that its surveillance mechanisms may entail consequences such as restricted access to social credit, New IP could serve as a mechanism to silence dissent and enforce control. Lastly, New IP could interfere with users' ability to seek, receive, and impart information and to inform opinions without interference. Specifically, entities in charge of managing DLT could block both users and content.

Similarly, New IP could have chilling impacts on the right to freedom of peaceful assembly and association. It could be leveraged by governments to disable organization through online channels by blocking specific users, such as dissidents or perceived troublemakers; specific sites and platforms that bring protesters together; or specific content related to the purpose of mobilization. These actions could be interpreted as microtargeted shutdowns, which would in turn help governments avoid the unpopular, complete network shutdowns that are commonplace today. These types of interference would undermine the right of assembly by restricting the ability to mobilize effectively.[76] New IP would also enhance the ability of governments to keep track of protesters, either through mass surveillance mechanisms enabled by data collection or through targeted surveillance enabled by user profiles. New IP's undermining of encryption and anonymity would thus have negative impacts on freedom of peaceful assembly and association.

Economic, social, and cultural (ESC) rights: Lack of access to an open, free, and global internet may impede the realization of ESC rights and of the sustainable development goals. For example, lack of free access to health information during a pandemic may prevent individuals from becoming aware of appropriate prevention and remedies and may obscure the effects of the pandemic in their communities.[77] Lack of access to a global internet may have an adverse impact on education, by reducing the sources of information available to individuals. It may reduce employment opportunities, particularly internationally. More generally, by creating barriers between communities and countries, lack of a global, open internet may reduce prospects for economic growth and development and may thereby operate to perpetuate conditions of poverty. This in itself would hinder the implementation of a wide range of ESC rights.

Discrimination: Article 2.1 ICCPR requires states not to discriminate in their implementation of rights, and Article 26 entitles all persons to equality before the law and protection against discrimination on any grounds. Similarly, Article 2.2 of the International Covenant on Economic, Social and Cultural Rights (ICESCR) requires states to implement economic, social, and cultural rights without discrimination.

The enhanced individualized tracking and profiling enabled by New IP would facilitate the discriminatory treatment of individuals and groups. For example, individualized tracking through New IP may place minorities at risk. States would have the tools to single out target groups, track their online activity, persecute them, or coerce them into adopting desired behaviors. China's well-documented surveillance of the Uyghurs through the Integrated Joint-Operations Platform (IJOP) in Xinjiang indicates that these potential uses are not far-fetched. These efforts would run in parallel with other efforts to reinforce discriminatory practices through technology such as in AI, with several Chinese firms filing patents and seeking to standardize facial recognition software that claims to be able to identify religious or ethnic minorities by their features.[78]

Risks of Conditional Implementation of Human Rights

New IP would enable the creation of data logs and collection of information at an unprecedented scale. If deployed domestically within China, government agencies in charge of managing New IP's blockchain logs could easily share collected data with the purpose of implementing or strengthening profiling, scoring, and ranking mechanisms that render access to rights and benefits conditional on meeting specific criteria. In other words, they could make human rights contingent on meeting conditions or responsibilities. Such mechanisms could penalize and impose consequences on those monitored. Social benefits and freedoms such as freedom of movement could be denied as a form of punishment to control behavior. Such consequences could be imposed not only on groups linked by a characteristic, which would constitute a form of discrimination, but also on individuals by reference to their behavior.

Conditionality is already evident in China's social credit system. First formalized as a national objective in 2014, this system is still being developed and features as a priority in the country's most recent Five-Year Plan. At its heart, it is a reward and punishment mechanism designed to render entry into various market transactions contingent upon scoring of behavior, applied to both individual and corporate actors. Unlike financial credit scoring systems in the West, this system takes account not only of financial information but also of nonfinancial information such as travel, health, and police data gathered from a multiplicity of agencies and sources.[79] The system operates not through the imposition of new obligations, but rather as a strict enforcement mechanism for existing regulations, including those that may lead to discriminatory treatment of individuals.[80]

Multiple reports indicate that China's social credit system pursues primarily financial and commercial goals, yet it has troubling effects in the enjoyment of rights. China is reported to have banned millions of citizens from buying plane or train tickets, and some local governments are also experimenting with additional limitations, barring those deemed untrustworthy from access to financial services and real estate transactions.[81]

In practice, China's rollout of the social credit system appears to have been challenging and far from uniform. There are diverse social credit regimes across various units of government, with varying assessment criteria and scope.[82] The creation of separate systems across the country has resulted in a marked fragmentation.[83] In addition, they are not fully digitized, relying heavily on nonsystematized data and human analysis.[84]

New IP would largely resolve these implementation challenges and enable further systems of contingent access to rights. New IP's reliance on DLT would facilitate nationwide data collection and data sharing with designated entities, such as government agencies and corporations that participate in social credit schemes.[85] The combined use of DLT and identifiers would further strengthen the creation of fully digital, permanent records on individuals. By significantly increasing the data-driven analytical power of the Chinese state, New IP would align very closely with China's data governance priorities to create a cohesive information ecosystem across regions and administrative levels.[86]

Contingency systems for the implementation of human rights can entrench discrimination and undermine a cardinal tenet of international human rights law: the principle of universality of human rights. This principle establishes that everyone is entitled to the benefit of human rights without discrimination. In other words, the entitlement to human rights cannot be made contingent on the performance of responsibilities.[87] While China is not a party to the ICCPR, it is to the ICESCR and numerous other instruments that stress the universal nature of human rights. By making rights contingent on responsibilities, China would breach both civil and political rights, such as the right to freedom of movement (Article 13 UDHR, Article 12 ICCPR) and economic, social, and cultural rights such as the right to social security (Article 22 UDHR, Article 9 ICESCR), as well as nondiscrimination provisions (Article 2 UDHR, Article 2 ICCPR, Article 2 ICESCR).[88]

In sum, the creation of a system that gives states the tools to make human rights and social benefits contingent on each person's individual, closely monitored behavior has deeply worrying potential for human and societal control. It would facilitate discrimination and run directly contrary to the principle of universality of human rights.

Reinforcing Human Rights in Standards Development

Historically, standardization was perceived as ethically neutral. However, as the example of New IP demonstrates, standardization processes can have important ethical and human rights implications.

Building human rights awareness into standardization is becoming ever more pressing, particularly in the field of emerging technologies. If standardization processes approve technologies that undermine human rights, the norms and processes of human rights law do not offer a robust defense against implementation of those technologies. As in other fields, human rights norms fare poorly when competing against adopted technical standards. Trade protections afforded to ITU recommended standards provide a useful example. Under WTO rules, technologies standardized within the ITU get immediate clearance to be traded internationally; the TBT agreement further encourages the adoption of approved standards. These WTO rules take precedence over human rights norms, even when standardized technologies may directly challenge human rights. Moreover, human rights norms and processes do not offer teeth to challenge technical standards. Not only is there no normative mechanism to embed human rights into standardization, but, once adopted, standards cannot be set aside on human rights grounds. On the contrary, WTO rules support standardized technologies without consideration of their compliance with human rights.[89]

If human rights continue to be overlooked in the development of technical standards, the standardization of surveillance-enabling technologies such as New IP has the potential to sweep away large swaths of the protections afforded by the Universal Declaration of Human Rights and the UN human rights treaties. Yet the government representatives, civil society, international organizations, and academic community devoted to human rights may all be oblivious because they are not aware of or engaged in standardization processes.

It is therefore vital that participation in SDOs be diversified to include those concerned with human rights. While standards development processes are expert-led processes and should remain a sphere of technical and engineering expertise, they should reinforce ongoing efforts to build a sufficiently open and diverse participation to ensure a realistic prospect of human rights issues being raised and considered in technology design. A recent ethnographic analysis of the IETF pointed to a cultural resistance among technical experts to including human rights considerations in standardization, rooted in shared views of technology as largely apolitical and "non-prescriptive" in nature.[90] In spite of the work of IETF's Human Rights Protocol Considerations Research Group, which has proposed human rights guidelines for protocol development, the organization has been slow to incorporate human rights considerations into standards.[91] Similarly, within the ITU, proposals to introduce privacy assessments and human rights impacts reviews have encountered pushback.[92] Moving toward a greater integration of human rights into standardization processes will require the removal of barriers to participation such as prohibitive costs, as well as enhanced support to newcomers to reach the level of expertise needed to participate meaningfully, and creative thinking to institutionalize human rights thinking in technical processes.

Recommendations

Like-minded governments should continue to increase their efforts to uphold the core values of a global, open, and free internet, and to oppose ongoing efforts to standardize New IP and related technologies.

The case study of New IP in this chapter illustrates how, in the light of developments in technology and artificial intelligence, a growing range of technical standards processes have ethical and human rights implications. Consequently, we make several specific recommendations with the aim of better integrating human rights into standards development.

- The human rights and diplomatic communities should, whenever possible, increase their participation in standardization processes. Multilateral bodies such as the ITU should lower the barriers to participation for nonstate members. Additional funding should be directed to enhance the participation of human rights organizations and consumer protection agencies. At the same time, governments should consider bringing human rights expertise into national delegations to multilateral bodies, including by involving nongovernmental organizations (NGOs), as some are already beginning to do.

- The UN should set up a unit on standards and human rights within the Office of the High Commissioner for Human Rights (OHCHR), tasked with advising technology SDOs on human rights issues and alerting the international human rights community to standardization developments that require attention. The OHCHR and standards bodies based in Geneva, such as the ITU, should take advantage of their proximity to share knowledge and participate in one another's meetings.

- Human rights capacity and roles should be enhanced within the Secretariats and working groups of the SDOs. Existing groups, such as the IETF's Human Rights Protocol Considerations Research Group, should be empowered to offer thorough scrutiny and advice on controversial technologies. Human rights analysis should be more thoroughly integrated into the workstream of technical working groups developing specifications and guidelines.

- Capacity-building should be enhanced to bridge the gap between technical and human rights communities. Technical experts participating in SDOs should develop greater understanding of existing human rights standards and latest human rights guidance on surveillance technologies. Likewise, human rights and diplomatic communities should strengthen their awareness of technology development, internet infrastructure, and how SDOs operate. Events organized by SDOs could offer opportunities for both communities to interact through a combination of training sessions, workshops, and panels.

- The UN Human Rights Council should commission a clear articulation of human rights standards regarding collation of data and surveillance, derived from Article 17 ICCPR and other relevant norms, and building on OHCHR's existing work on privacy in the digital age. This should aim to delineate more clearly the distinction between technology that is and is not compatible with international human rights law.

- Consideration could be given to an international statement of commitment to human rights from standards development organizations, such that no standard is to be read as legitimating practices contrary to the human rights obligations of any state. Similarly, consideration could be given to revising the WTO rules so that their advantages do not apply to technology whose use would entail mass violation of human rights.

- Coordination efforts at the national level (e.g., through standards hubs) offer accessible entry points for human rights groups to participate in standardization debates. When national standards hubs coordinate positions for standardization discussions, they should encourage diverse participation, particularly in debates about technologies that have wide societal impact. Standards hubs should then feed those inputs into international standards development. Similarly, to encourage diverse participation, government delegates responsible for monitoring technology standards should act as an early warning system to alert civil society organizations when standards that affect human rights are first proposed.

Notes

1. Cabinet Office, "Carbis Bay G7 Summit Communiqué," 2021, https://assets. publishing.service.gov.uk/government/uploads/system/uploads/attachment_data /file/1001128/Carbis_Bay_G7_Summit_Communique__PDF__430KB__25 _pages_.pdf.

2. G7 Information Center, "G7 Digital and Technology—1," 2021, www.g8 .utoronto.ca/ict/2021-annex_1-framework-standards.html.

3. U.K. Government, "Global Britain in a Competitive Age: The Integrated Review of Security, Defence, Development and Foreign Policy," July 2, 2021, www.gov .uk/government/publications/global-britain-in-a-competitive-age-the-integrated -review-of-security-defence-development-and-foreign-policy/global-britain-in-a -competitive-age-the-integrated-review-of-security-defence-development-and -foreign-policy.

4. Sheng Jiang, "New IP Networking for Network 2030," Fifth ITU Workshop on Network 2030, International Telecommunication Union, October 15, 2019, www .itu.int/en/ITU-T/Workshops-and-Seminars/2019101416/Documents/Sheng_Jiang _Presentation.pdf.

5. China Electronics Standardization Institute, "Original CSET Translation of 'Artificial Intelligence Standardization White Paper,'" Center for Security and Emerging Technology, Georgetown University, May 12, 2020, https://cset.georgetown.edu /research/artificial-intelligence-standardization-white-paper/.

6. Stacie Hoffmann, Samantha Bradshaw, and Emily Taylor, "Networks and Geopolitics: How Great Power Rivalries Infected 5G," Oxford Information Labs, 2019, https://oxil.uk/publications/geopolitics-of-5g/Geopolitics_5G_Final.pdf.

7. Initially referred to as "Decentralized Internet Infrastructure." See "Decentralized Internet Infrastructure (DII)," Light Reading (video), November 20, 2018, www .lightreading.com/blockchain/decentralized-Internet-infrastructure-(dii)/v/d-id /747708. The technology was introduced as "New IP" at the ITU-T Telecommunication Standardization Advisory Group (TSAG) in 2019. See Huawei, "New IP: Shaping the Future Network," presented at the ITU-T TSAG, Geneva, September 2019, www.ietf.org/lib/dt/documents/LIAISON/liaison-2019-09-30-itu- t-tsag-ietf-iab-l s-on-new-ip-shaping-future-network-attachment-3.pptx.

8. Ying Miao, "Managing Digital Contention in China," *Journal of Cyber Policy* 5, 2 (April 7, 2020), pp. 218–38.

9. Nick Merrill and Konstantinos Komaitis, "The Consequences of a Fragmenting, Less Global Internet," Brookings, December 17, 2020, www.brookings.edu /techstream/the-consequences-of-a-fragmenting-less-global-Internet/.

10. Konstantinos Karachalios and Karen McCabe, "Standards, Innovation, and Their Role in the Context of the World Trade Organization," International Centre for Trade and Sustainable Development (ICTSD) and World Economic Forum, December 2013, https://e15initiative.org/wp-content/uploads/2015/09/E15-Innovation-KarachaliosMcCabe-FINAL.pdf.

11. Other relevant entities include ICANN, the regional internet registries,W3C and IEEE, which lead the development of policies for name and numbering resources, web standards, and physical and data link layers standards, respectively. Internet standards are also shaped by mobile industry associations, such as 3GPP and GSMA, and by regional bodies such as ETSI.

12. Stacie Hoffmann, Dominique Lazanski, and Emily Taylor, "Standardising the Splinternet: How China's Technical Standards Could Fragment the Internet," *Journal of Cyber Policy* 5, 2 (August 2020), pp. 239–64.

13. International Telecommunications Union, "Terms and Conditions," 2021, www.itu.int/en/myitu/Membership/Become-a-Member/Terms-and-Conditions.

14. Hoffmann et al., "Standardising the Splinternet," p. 246.

15. Anna Gross, Madhumita Murgia, and Yuan Yang, "Chinese Tech Groups Shaping UN Facial Recognition Standards," *Financial Times,* December 1, 2019, www.ft .com/content/c3555a3c-0d3e-11ea-b2d6-9bf4d1957a67.

16. According to the WTO, "Technical regulations in accordance with relevant international standards are rebuttably presumed 'not to create an unnecessary obstacle to international trade.'" See World Trade Organization, "Technical Information on Technical Barriers to Trade," n.d., www.wto.org/english/tratop_e/tbt_e/tbt_info_e.htm.

17. Ibid., Article 2.4. The TBT considers as "international standards" those standards developed by organizations such as the ITU, International Standardization Organization (ISO), the International Electrotechnical Commission (IEC). See Karachalios and McCabe, "Standards, Innovation, and Their Role in the Context of the World Trade Organization."

18. See World Trade Organization, "Technical Information on Technical Barriers to Trade," TBT Agreement, Article 5.4.

19. Hoffmann et al., "Standardising the Splinternet," p. 246.

20. To date, New IP-related work at the ITU has been raised in multiple Study Groups including those dealing with protocols and test specifications (SG11), future networks and cloud (SG13), multimedia (SG16), security (SG17), and IoT and smart cities (SG20); see Hoffmann et al., "Standardising the Splinternet," p. 264.

21. Max J. Zenglein and Anna Holzmann, "Evolving Made in China 2025: China's Industrial Policy in the Quest for Global Tech Leadership," Mercator Institute for China Studies (MERICS), July 2, 2019, https://merics.org/en/report/evolving -made-china-2025.

22. "The Digital Side of the Belt and Road Initiative Is Growing," *The Economist*, February 6, 2020, www.economist.com/special-report/2020/02/06/the-digital-side-of -the-belt-and-road-initiative-is-growing.

23. Hoffmann et al., "Standardising the Splinternet," p. 254.

24. Stuart Lau and Reuters, "EU Seeks to Curb Investment by State-Backed Buyers from China and Other Countries," *South China Morning Post*, June 17, 2020, www.scmp.com/news/world/europe/article/3089474/eu-wants-curb-company -takeovers-state-backed-buyers-china-other; and Lindsay Maizland and Andrew Chatzky, "Huawei: China's Controversial Tech Giant," Council on Foreign Relations, August 6, 2020, www.cfr.org/backgrounder/huawei-chinas-controversial-tech -giant.

25. Maizland and Chatzky, "Huawei: China's Controversial Tech Giant."

26. Internet World Stats, www.Internetworldstats.com/stats.htm.

27. *The Economist*, "The Digital Side of the Belt and Road Initiative."

28. "'New IP' and Global Internet Governance," Georgia Institute of Technology, Internet Governance Project and Internet Society (video), September 23, 2020, www .Internetsociety.org/events/new-ip-and-global-Internet-governance/.

29. Ibid.

30. ITU-T, "Technical Report: Network 2030—Description of Demonstrations for Network 2030 on Sixth ITU Workshop on Network 2030 and Demo Day, 13 January 2020," June 2020, www.itu.int/en/ITU-T/focusgroups/net2030/Documents /Description_of_Demonstrations.pdf?csf=1&e=D7M69p.

31. Alexander Chipman Koty, "What Is the China Standards 2035 Plan and How Will It Impact Emerging Industries?," China Briefing, July 2, 2020, www.china -briefing.com/news/what-is-china-standards-2035-plan-how-will-it-impact-emerging -technologies-what-is-link-made-in-china-2025-goals/; "Original CSET Translation of

'Outline of the People's Republic of China 14th Five-Year Plan for National Economic and Social Development and Long-Range Objectives for 2035,'" Center for Security and Emerging Technology, Georgetown University, May 13, 2020, https://cset.george town.edu/publication/china-14th-five-year-plan/.

32. Stephen Chen, "China Starts Large-Scale Testing of its Internet of the Future," *South China Morning Post,* April 20, 2021, www.scmp.com/news/china/science/article /3130338/china-starts-large-scale-testing-its-Internet-future.

33. See TSAG Contribution 135 entitled "Response to "New IP, Shaping Future Network" Proposal" (RIPE NCC, January 28, 2020); TSAG Contribution 139 entitled "New IP" (Austria and others, September 7, 2020); TSAG Contribution 156 (IEEE, September 8, 2020); and ITU-T TSAG Liaison Statement entitled "LS on New IP, Shaping Future Network" (IETF, March 20, 2020).

34. These include the European Telecommunications Network Operators' Association (ETNO) and the Global System for Mobile Communications Association (GSMA). See ETNO, "ETNO Position Paper on the New IP Proposal," November 5, 2020, https://www.etno.eu/library/positionpapers/417-new-ip.html, and ITU-T SG13 Contribution 1069 entitled "New IP, Future Vertical Communication Networks or Similar Proposals" (Austria and others, November 18, 2020).

35. See, for example: recommendation entitled "Scenarios and Requirements of Network Resource Sharing Based on Distributed Ledger Technology," presented by China Telecom, China Unicom, ZTE, Huawei scheduled for Q4 2022; recommendation entitled "Scenarios and Requirements of Intent-Based Network for Network Evolution," presented by China Telecom and the Ministry of Industry and Information Technology of China scheduled for Q4 2022; and IETF submission entitled "Gap Analysis in Internet Addressing," July 12, 2021. All at www.itu.int/ITU-T/workprog /wp_item.aspx?isn=17181.

36. Andrew Allemann, "China Wants to Patent a Decentralized Blockchain DNS," *Domain Name Wire,* May 10, 2021, https://domainnamewire.com/2021/05/10/ china-wants-to-patent-a-decentralized-blockchain-dns/.

37. Xinhua News Agency, "Original CSET Translation of 'Outline of the People's Republic of China 14th Five-Year Plan for National Economic and Social Development and Long-Range Objectives for 2035,'" Center for Security and Emerging Technology, Georgetown University, May 13, 2020, https://cset.georgetown.edu/publica-tion/china-14th-five-year-plan/.

38. David Ignatius, "Russia Is Trying to Set the Rules for the Internet. The U.N. Saw through the Ruse," *Washington Post,* February 1, 2021, www.washingtonpost.com /opinions/2021/02/01/russia-Internet-rules-united-nations/.

39. For discussion on Chinese narratives on decentralization and "decentralized trust," see Hoffmann et al., "Standardising the Splinternet," pp. 249–50.

40. Georgia Institute of Technology, "'New IP' and Global Internet Governance."

41. See, for example, IETF RFC 1958 entitled " Architectural Principles of the Internet" (June 1996), https://datatracker.ietf.org/doc/html/rfc1958.

42. Anna Gross and Madhumita Murgia, "China and Huawei Propose Reinvention of the Internet," *Financial Times*, March 27, 2020, www.ft.com/content/c78be2cf-a1a1-40b1-8ab7-904d7095e0f2; Jon Fingas, "China, Huawei Propose Internet Protocol with a Built-In Killswitch," *Engadget,* March 30, 2020, www.engadget.com/2020-03-30-china-huawei-new-ip-proposal.html.

43. Marco Hogewoning, "Do We Need a New IP?," RIPE NCC, April 22, 2020, https://labs.ripe.net/author/marco_hogewoning/do-we-need-a-new-ip/.

44. Just as intelligence from the application layer is integrated into the networking layer, the network may signal information back to the application layer.

45. There are other areas where standards are raising human rights concerns. DNS over HTTPS (DoH) and Transport Layer Security (TLS) 1.3 are two such examples. These standards seek to protect privacy and surveillance threats but can potentially generate unintended effects that weaken the stability and security of the internet.

46. Hoffmann et al., "Standardising the Splinternet," p. 245.

47. Unique identifiers include domain names, internet protocol addresses, Autonomous Systems Numbers, and Port Numbers; these identifiers are central for current internet protocols to function. See the Internet Corporation for Assigned Names and Numbers, "ICANN Acronyms and Terms," n.d., www.icann.org/en/icann-acronyms-and-terms/unique-identifier-en.

48. Huawei, "New IP: Shaping the Future Network."

49. Chinese delegations are already working through the ITU to standardize the use of DLT in Internet architecture. Chinese companies first submitted Contribution 693 at SG13 in 2019 to discuss the creation of a decentralized DNS root based on blockchain. According to SG13's work program, conversations on DLTs are set to continue during 2022. See, for example, recommendation entitled "Framework and Requirements of Decentralized Trustworthy Network Infrastructure," scheduled for Q3 2021.

50. Light Reading, "Decentralized Internet Infrastructure (DII)."

51. One main feature of DLTs is that transactions are immutable. From a security perspective, replacing the DNS with blockchain means that threats such as fraud become almost permanent as they are hard, if not impossible, to undo.

52. Hoffmann et al., "Standardising the Splinternet," p. 250.

53. Ibid., p. 244.

54. The Universal Declaration of Human Rights (UDHR); International Covenant on Economic, Social and Cultural Rights (ICESCR); and International Covenant on Civil and Political Rights (ICCPR). China is not a party to the ICCPR, but arguably many of its obligations reflect customary international law. It is a party to the ICESCR. According to ICCPR Article 2 (1), states are required to respect and ensure the rights recognized in the Covenant, including the right to privacy.

55. For instance, there are few Chinese ISPs and they are all state-owned: China Unicom, China Telecom, and China Mobile.

56. Upcoming updates to cybersecurity regulations, namely the Multi-Level Protection Scheme 2.0 and the Cryptography Law, are expected to require companies that hold sensitive data to undergo "cybersecurity monitoring" connected to the public security agency and to adopt Chinese algorithms for encryption. See Samm Sacks, "Data Security and U.S.-China Tech Entanglement," *Lawfare*, April 2, 2020, www .lawfareblog.com/data-security-and-us-china-tech-entanglement.

57. United Nations Human Rights Council, "The Right to Privacy in the Digital Age. Report of the United Nations High Commissioner for Human Rights," UN doc A/HRC/39/29, August 3, 2018.

58. United Nations Human Rights Council, "Surveillance and Human Rights. Report of the Special Rapporteur on the Promotion and Protection of the Right to Freedom of Opinion and Expression," UN doc A/HRC/41/35, May 28, 2019.

59. UNHRC, "The Right to Privacy in the Digital Age," para. 29.

60. Ibid.

61. Ibid.; United Nations Human Rights Council, "The Right to Privacy in the Digital Age: Report of the Office of the United Nations High Commissioner for Human Rights," UN doc A/HRC/27/37, June 30, 2014.

62. The ECtHR ruled that the U.K. government's bulk data collection practices revealed by Edward Snowden in 2013 breached citizens' right to privacy. See Big Brother Watch Team, "UK Mass Surveillance Found Unlawful by Europe's Highest Human Rights Court," Big Brother Watch, May 25, 2021, https://bigbrotherwatch .org.uk/2021/05/uk-mass-surveillance-found-unlawful-by-europes-highest-human -rights-court/.

63. United Nations Human Rights Council, Resolution 42/15, UN doc A/HRC/ RES/42/15, September 26, 2019.

64. UNHRC, "The Right to Privacy in the Digital Age" (2018?).

65. UNHRC, Resolution 42/15.

66. United Nations Human Rights Council, "New and Emerging Digital Technologies and Human Rights," UN doc A/HRC/47/L.12/Rev.1, July 13, 2021.

67. Katja Drinhausen and Vincent Brussee, "China's Social Credit System in 2021," Mercator Institute for China Studies (MERICS), March 2021, p. 19, https://merics .org/en/report/chinas-social-credit-system-2021-fragmentation-towards-integration.

68. "Report of the Special Rapporteur on the Promotion and Protection of the Right to Freedom of Opinion and Expression," David Kaye, May 22, 2015 (A/HRC/29/32). See para. 56.

69. Hoffmann and others, "Standardising the Splinternet," p. 250.

70. UNHRC, "The Right to Privacy in the Digital Age." See para. 20.

71. Zheping Huang, "China Requires Blockchain-Based Information Service Providers to Register Users Using Real Names, Censor Postings and Store User Data," *South China Morning Post*, October 22, 2018, www.scmp.com/tech/blockchain/article /2169613/china-requires-blockchain-based-information-service-providers; Article 19, "Blockchain: Technology Alone Cannot Protect Freedom of Expression," July 1, 2019,

www.article19.org/resources/blockchain-technology-alone-cannot-protect-freedom-of
-expression/.

72. Raphael Satter, "U.S. Court: Mass Surveillance Program Exposed by Snowden Was Illegal," Reuters, September 2, 2020, www.reuters.com/article/us-usa-nsa-spying -idUSKBN25T3CK.

73. Bennett Cyphers and Cory Doctorow, "Privacy without Monopoly: Data Protection and Interoperability," Electronic Frontier Foundation, February 12, 2021, www.eff.org/wp/interoperability-and-privacy.

74. UNHRC, "Surveillance and Human Rights."

75. Paul Bernal, "Data Gathering, Surveillance and Human Rights: Recasting the Debate," *Journal of Cyber Policy* 1, 2 (September 16, 2016), pp. 243–64.

76. UNHRC, "Surveillance and Human Rights."

77. Harriet Moynihan and Champa Patel, "Restrictions on Online Freedom of Expression in China," Chatham House, March 2021, https://www.chathamhouse .org/2021/03/restrictions-online-freedom-expression-china/chinas-domestic -restrictions-online-freedom.

78. Leo Kelion, "Huawei Patent Mentions Use of Uighur-Spotting Tech," *BBC News*, January 13, 2021, www.bbc.co.uk/news/technology-55634388; and Anna Gross and others, "Chinese Tech Groups Shaping UN Facial Recognition Standard," *Financial Times*, December 1, 2019, www.ft.com/content/c3555a3c-0d3e-11ea-b2d6 -9bf4d1957a67.

79. Fan Liang and others, "Constructing a Data-Driven Society: China's Social Credit System as a State Surveillance Infrastructure," *Policy & Internet* 10, 4, (2018), pp. 415–53; Democratic Staff Report, "The Big Brother: China's Digital Authoritarianism," Committee on Foreign Relations, United States Senate, July 21, 2020, www .foreign.senate.gov/download/2020-sfrc-minority-report_-the-new-big-brother— -china-and-digital-authoritarianism.

80. Drinhausen and Brussee, "China's Social Credit System in 2021."

81. He Huifeng, "China's Social Credit System Shows Its Teeth, Banning Millions from Taking Flights, Trains," *South China Morning Post*, February 18, 2019, www .scmp.com/economy/china-economy/article/2186606/chinas-social-credit-system -shows-its-teeth-banning-millions.

82. Liu, Chuncheng, "Multiple Social Credit Systems in China," *Economic Sociology: The European Electronic Newsletter* 21, 1 (2019), pp. 22–32, Max Planck Institute for the Study of Societies, http://hdl.handle.net/10419/223109.

83. Ibid.; see also Drinhausen and Brussee, "China's Social Credit System in 2021," p. 13.

84. Drinhausen and Brussee, "China's Social Credit System in 2021," p. 12.

85. Hoffmann et al., "Standardising the Splinternet," p. 250.

86. Drinhausen and Brussee, "China's Social Credit System in 2021," p. 12.

87. See UN Charter, Art 55(c), UDHR Art 2, ICESCR Art 2, and ICCPR Art 2.

88. See Committee on Economic, Social and Cultural Rights (CESCR), General Comment 19 (2008), para. 9.

89. Of course, a country's implementation of a standard could be challenged through conventional domestic or international systems of human rights accountability such as litigation and treaty body review.

90. Corinne Cath, "The Technology We Choose to Create: Human Rights Advocacy in the Internet Engineering Task Force," *Telecommunications Policy* 45, 6 (2021), www.sciencedirect.com/science/article/pii/S0308596121000483.

91. To date, only one protocol has been subject to a human rights review, and solely for informational purposes. See IETF Memo entitled: "QUIC Human Rights Review," October 22, 2018. Beyond the cited guidelines, human rights considerations at IETF are mostly raised by individual participants through mailing lists and meetings.

92. As reported by an anonymous source familiar with the ITU standardization environment.

NINE

Autonomous Weapon Systems

Accountability Gaps and Racial Oppression

THOMPSON CHENGETA

The problem of impunity—the lack of accountability—when gross human rights violations by states, nonstate entities, and individuals go unpunished and victims are left without remedy is a serious threat to the human rights system. Given the foundational idea that those who violate human rights must be held responsible and that victims have a right to remedy, various national, regional, and international mechanisms have been created to ensure such accountability in times of both war and peace.

Nevertheless, some perpetrators of gross human rights violations still go unpunished and victims are left without remedies. In recent years, particularly, in countries like the United States, there has often been a concerning lack of accountability in law enforcement or the unlawful use of force against people of color. In the context of counterterrorism, there is a similar lack of accountability for the disproportionate use of force in Muslim communities, for example, in the killing of hundreds of civilians in drone strikes. Against this backdrop, states are currently developing autonomous weapon systems (AWS) whose potential use in both these areas may aggravate the problem.

This chapter examines the challenge presented by the AWS accountability gap from a racial justice perspective. It argues that any discussion of the use of such weapons must be contextualized, acknowledging first that, like many technologies powered by artificial intelligence (AI), AWS are not neutral; they are racialized and as such can easily become tools of racial oppression.

AWS—also known as killer robots—are robotic weapons that, once activated, are able to "decide" whom to target, harm, or kill without any further human intervention or control.[1] But if machines, computers, or robots have this decision-making capability, it may be impossible to establish responsibility for unlawful acts they commit. First, since there is no human control after activation, AWS are unpredictable and may act in a manner that was not anticipated or intended by the person who activated them.[2] In the event of AWS violating international human rights law (IHRL) or international humanitarian law (IHL), it may therefore be impossible to establish the mens rea (that is, intentionality) of the person who activated them, thereby affecting the important notion of individual responsibility.[3] Second, AWS may be used in an untraceable manner that may make it impossible to hold states and non-state entities accountable.[4] This is the accountability gap challenge, which can have an adverse effect on the right to remedy. However, it is not the only concern that is raised by AWS, which have far-reaching consequences for fundamental human rights such as the right to life, physical security, dignity, and nondiscrimination.

In the context of racial justice, this chapter focuses on the impact of AWS on the right to nondiscrimination and the right to remedy. The right to non-discrimination is a norm of customary international law and a norm of jus cogens (from which no derogation is allowed). Discrimination on grounds of race, nationality, religion, region, or indeed any other grounds violates human dignity and is therefore internationally prohibited. The right to nondiscrimination on the grounds of race is provided for in the International Convention on the Elimination of All Forms of Racial Discrimination (CERD),[5] as well as in the International Covenant on Civil and Political Rights[6] and other regional human rights treaties.[7] CERD also provides that in cases where there has been a violation of the right to nondiscrimination—including where state agents use violent force in violation of this right—victims are entitled to a remedy, including prosecution of the offender.[8] If the current discussions on AWS continue without sufficient regard to their potential negative impact on racial justice, the consequences for the fundamental rights of Muslims, people of color, and other ethnic minorities will be far-reaching. Indeed, in the Preamble of CERD, it is noted that racial oppression is not favorable for stable geopolitics because discrimination is "capable of disturbing peace and security among peoples and the harmony of persons living side by side."[9]

Furthermore, scholars have already begun to note the link between geo-politics and emerging AI technologies such as AWS. More importantly, some have cautioned that "the relentless pursuit of AI militarization does not protect us" as "proliferating military artificial intelligence will leave the world less safe."[10] Rather, it has been strongly recommended that states should "stop the emerging AI cold war" and "focus on ethics and global cooperation."[11] To this, one would add that the weaponization of AI creates an even more precarious situation for people of color and civilians in the Muslim world who are already on the receiving end of unlawful violence. Yet, although these groups have been disproportionately affected by the use of lethal force in law enforcement and counterterrorism operations, the current United Nations (UN) discussions on AWS have not sufficiently considered the implications for racial oppression.[12] The AWS accountability gap challenge has only been discussed in general terms without specifying likely victims.[13]

Drawing on legal, ethical, and sociological theories, the following sections discuss the impact of AWS use on responsibility, accountability, and racial justice specifically in relation to the violation of fundamental human rights of people of color and civilians in the Muslim world.

Background on UN Discussions on AWS

The UN discussions on AWS have been ongoing since 2013, when the UN Special Rapporteur on extrajudicial executions (UN Special Rapporteur) submitted his annual report to the UN Human Rights Council (UNHRC).[14] At this point, AWS were yet to be deployed, and their use may have seemed a distant prospect, but in June 2021, a UN report indicated that they were deployed in Libya, noting:

> Logistics convoys and retreating HAF [Haftar-affiliated forces] were subsequently hunted down and remotely engaged by the unmanned combat aerial vehicles or the lethal autonomous weapons systems such as the STM Kargu-2 and other loitering munitions. The lethal autonomous weapons systems were programmed to attack targets without requiring data connectivity between the operator and the munition: in effect, a true "fire, forget and find" capability.[15]

The UN Special Rapporteur further noted that the development and deployment of AWS posed challenges to IHL and IHRL, and that they might violate fundamental human rights such as the right to life and human dignity.[16]

Along the same lines, UN Secretary General António Guterres' described AWS as one of the four major threats to world peace and security, saying they were "morally repugnant, politically unacceptable and should be banned by international law."[17] Nevertheless some states[18] and scholars have argued that AWS will perform better than humans and that consequently their development and use may ameliorate the suffering of civilians on the battlefield and elsewhere where force is used.[19]

In view of the seriousness of the challenges raised by AWS, in 2014 the UN established a Group of Governmental Experts (UNGGE) on Lethal Autonomous Weapon Systems (LAWS), whose mandate is to formulate appropriate recommendations on how states should respond to AWS technology.[20] In 2021, the International Committee of the Red Cross (ICRC), an organization that is internationally regarded as the guardian of IHL, noted that states needed to adopt new laws to govern AWS.[21]

For the past eight years, the UNGGE has been involved in intensive multidisciplinary discussions on AWS, examining the issue from various standpoints, including gender perspectives. Between 2014 and 2019, it produced six reports.[22] While the concern that the use of AWS may perpetuate and/or exacerbate racial oppression has been raised by some delegates, and while it is clear that racial socialization influences their development,[23] not once were the words racism, racial oppression, racial bias, or racial discrimination mentioned in any of these six reports between 2014 to 2019—despite the fact that the 2013 UN Special Rapporteur's report highlights that AWS may be used in law enforcement situations where people of color are disproportionately affected. Furthermore, research has already shown that existing racial prejudice and bias may end up being programmed into AWS, either intentionally or unintentionally.[24]

Understanding AWS as Racialized Technology

From a racial justice perspective, any discussion of the problem of the AWS accountability gap—particularly accountability for violation of the right to nondiscrimination—and any formulation of policy on emerging related AI technologies is incomplete without acknowledging the racial identity of both perpetrators and victims. Indeed, in fighting for racial justice for victims of police brutality and unlawful killings of Black people in the United States, activists started a hashtag #saytheirnames.[25] They state that, just as the U.S. government vowed "never to forget" the victims of the September 11 terrorist attacks, they will "never forget the lives lost to the terror of racism, excessive force and countless injustices" and "never forget the Black lives taken unjustly."[26]

In all the intensive discussions about AWS' potential to violate human rights and create this accountability gap, the identities of the potential perpetrators and victims are rarely specified. The argument is that the nonspecification of the likely victims of AI technologies like AWS is neither accidental nor inconsequential—it unfortunately functions to further white supremacy and racial oppression. Racial justice practitioners have long noted that although white supremacy has shaped a system of geopolitics and global domination, influencing white moral theory and moral psychology for hundreds of years, it remains an unnamed political system.[27] The AWS technology can be located right at the center of the politics of white supremacy and domination if one considers where AWS are currently being developed, the identity of those who are developing AWS, and the people and regions where AWS are likely to be deployed. Unlike other political systems such as socialism, capitalism, or fascism, which are openly named, studied, and critiqued, "White supremacy's power is drawn from its invisibility, the taken-for-granted aspects that underwrite all other political and social contracts."[28] It is for these reasons that in the current AWS discussions, the associated racial politics is "invisible," regardless of its presence. Charles Mills has argued that despite its being ignored in many important discussions, the Racial Contract of white supremacy exists[29] and functions to create global policies and geopolitics that favor white interests at the expense of those of other peoples.[30]

Further, the nonspecification of the potential perpetrators and victims also stems from the current mistaken approach of stakeholders to AWS technology as if it were neutral. It is important to examine the issue through the lens of social and cultural theories such as decolonial theory[31] and critical race theories. These aim to dig beneath the surface to uncover and challenge power structures that shape not only our society and geopolitics but our technological inventions, including AWS. Indeed, science has been instrumental in creating systems that are oppressive to certain peoples, reproducing social structures of authority, hierarchies of race, and oppressive geopolitics. Thus it is crucial to understand that AWS and other AI technologies are neither a simple matter of algorithms nor a mere case of great human imagination in pursuit of science; rather, such technologies are shaped by specific political and ideological projects of the powerful that permeate geopolitics as we know it today.[32] As such, adopting a noncontextual and ahistorical approach when discussing AI technologies such as AWS is a dangerous pitfall. Who's developing what, and where will it be deployed and against whom? What has been the historical experience on use of force through emerging technologies such as armed drones? Where have they been deployed? It is essential for stakeholders to address these questions. Failure to do so will result in an incomplete discussion about rights that will be violated or victims who will be deprived of the right to remedy when AWS are used. Say their names. Acknowledge the identity of the potential or likely victims.

Studies have already noted that racialized AI military technologies will lead to algorithmic coloniality, algorithmic oppression, exploitation, and dispossession of those who have been historically oppressed.[33] It is therefore important to emphasize the social context of AWS and confront what amounts to epistemic forgeries, where AI technologies such as AWS are presented as if they are neutral technologies, free from social context. On the contrary, such technologies "come from a rather specific, White, and privileged place. They are racialised, gendered, and classed models of the self."[34]

The power of AI whiteness and the associated racial oppression is often concealed by a myth of color-blindness on such technologies. This purported color-blindness is particularly prevalent in Silicon Valley's tech-culture, where it "serves to inhibit serious interrogation of racial framing."[35] In his 2020 report and comments on emerging technologies, the UN Special Rapporteur on contemporary forms of racism noted that "States must reject a 'colour-blind' approach to governance and regulation of emerging technologies, one that ignores the specific marginalization of racial and ethnic minorities and conceptualizes problems and solutions relating to such technologies without accounting for their likely effects on these groups."[36] In the interest of racial justice, states and other stakeholders must therefore adopt approaches from critical theory to strip the cloak of invisibility from any AI whiteness associated with AWS development and deployment.[37] Thus, when discussing how AWS may violate rights and create an accountability gap, the identity not only of the likely victims but also of the perpetrators must be clearly acknowledged.

Contextualizing the Use of AWS and the Accountability Gap Problem

In the ongoing discussions on AWS, many stakeholders have approached the technology as if these were typical conventional weapons that will basically be used in armed conflict. Indeed, part of the UNGGE's eleven Guiding Principles is that the UN Convention on Conventional Weapons (UNCCW) is the appropriate forum for AWS discussions.[38] But by definition the mandate of the UNCCW is restricted to conventional weapons of war.[39] As such, the potential use of AWS in the context of law enforcement and counterterrorism operations outside armed conflict is ordinarily excluded from its discussions. Yet such use is highly likely.[40] With these concerns in mind, the scenario in Box 1, originally presented by the author at a workshop titled "Malign Uses of Artificial Intelligence/Autonomous Weapon Systems" organized by the UN Institute for Disarmament Research, may provide an instructive hypothetical case study.

Box 1: Malign Uses of Artificial Intelligence/Autonomous Weapon Systems—A Scenario

Zura is the capital city of the Republic of Moria. It has the highest rate of violent crime in Moria, particularly in Doomlee, a county whose residents are largely people of color. Following government approval, the Zura Police Department (ZPD) started using AWS for policing and counterterrorism operations, notwithstanding critical reports from scientists indicating that these systems perform badly when it comes to identifying people with dark skin tones or shades.

So far, ZPD has only deployed AWS in Doomlee. In many cases, their use resulted in fatal shootings of suspects. ZPD has reported that since their deployment, no police officer has been killed in the line of duty in Doomlee and the crime rate has decreased considerably.

A local television network interviewed Doomlee residents regarding ZPD's use of AWS in Doomlee. Mr. Jones, the owner of a small grocery shop, said: "I think AWS are really effective. For the first time in a very long time, I haven't had a robbery in my shop."

Dontè, a teenager whose sixteen-year-old friend was killed by an AWS, said: "The killing of my friend was racially motivated. But when I say this, they look at me like I am crazy, they tell me race has nothing to do with it as machines see no color. AWS have increased deniability of racially motivated use of force by ZPD."

Mrs. James, a victim of domestic violence, said:

When I called the ZPD emergency number telling them that my life was in danger, I expected police officers at my door. Sending AWS to police the situation made me feel a less valued citizen of Moria and less human. How come AWS are largely deployed in our poor communities, but in rich neighborhoods the ZPD sends human police officers? It appears the ZPD is saying that some communities deserve policing by human police officers while others are only fit for machines, iron and steel policing.

Local and international human rights organizations have described un-lawful and violent acts committed by AWS in Doomlee as crimes against humanity as they consider such acts to be purposeful, wide-spread, and part of a systematic ZPD policy directed against residents of Doomlee.

While the case in Box 1 is fictitious, the scenario demonstrates a potential future that is anchored in the realities faced by people of color and those living in the Muslim world when lethal force is used by state agents. On the one hand, it reveals the concerns that have been noted on the potential of AWS to exacerbate racial bias and other forms of discrimination in society. On the other hand, some scholars take the view that AWS may improve the situation of the innocent whenever and wherever states use force.[41]

As emphasized above, contextualization is essential to fully under-stand the challenges posed by the use of AWS. The hypothetical case shows that, when evaluated in the context of law enforcement and coun-terterrorism operations, AWS deployment brings to the fore histories of racial bias and of impunity when lethal force is used unlawfully in the Muslim world and in communities of people of color, and reveals, more generally, a lack of moral responsibility over institutional racism associated with law enforcement. These three issues are addressed in turn in the following sections.

A History of Racial Bias in the Use of Lethal Force

The UN CERD Committee is the body of independent international experts who monitor the implementation of the CERD by its state parties.[42] In its 2020 report, particularly relating to the United States—one of the countries cur-rently developing AWS—the CERD Committee noted various concerns re-garding racial bias and the use of lethal force. It particularly noted "the con-tinuing practice of racial profiling, the use of brutality and the excessive use of force by law enforcement officials against persons belonging to racial and ethnic minorities."[43] Similar concerns have been noted regarding other coun-tries such as France, Israel, and the United Kingdom. In cases where people of color are involved, the CERD Committee has noted the disproportionate use of lethal force regardless of whether the target is armed.[44] It also expressed con-cerns that those who attempt to demonstrate peacefully against the racist use of lethal force are often met with brutal and disproportionate use of force by state agents.

Crucially, the CERD Committee noted that the racist use of lethal force cannot be categorized as sporadic incidents committed by errant bad white police officers; rather, it is a matter of "systemic and structural discrimination [that] permeates State institutions and disproportionately promotes racial disparities against [people of color and ethnic minorities]."[45] The CERD Committee has thus noted that in all UN institutions—including the UNGGE that is currently discussing AWS—there should be condemnation of "modern day racial terror lynchings and calling for systematic reform and justice, and their statement on the protests against systemic racism."[46]

The CERD Committee has also expressed deep concerns over the lack of "appropriate accountability for and sanctions imposed [on] those responsible."[47] Thus even before the deployment of AWS, there exists an accountability gap when it comes to remedying violations of the rights of people of color and certain ethnic minorities. Yet with AWS on the horizon, things could get even worse in terms of obtaining racial justice.

The intense discussions and demand for racial justice that followed the murder of George Floyd were partly attributable to the fact that the public could see Minneapolis Police Officer Derek Chauvin committing the act. What if, as highlighted in the scenario above, Floyd had been killed by AWS? How would one even begin to characterize such an incident as constituting a racist use of lethal force when there is "no soul to damn" and "no body to kick?"[48] How easy will it become to dismiss racist use of force as machine error? Already, as will be discussed below regarding moral distancing from responsibility over institutional racism, sociologist Robin DiAngelo has expressed concern that "white fragility" not only leads many members of the white community to distance themselves from racist acts as a way of preserving their own moral character and standing, but also involves vigorous attempts to explain away violent racist acts by law enforcement officials—often by blaming the victim instead.[49] Likewise, political scientist John Emery has noted that reliance on emerging AI military technologies in the West's wars in the Middle East has created a distance between a morally wrongful act and its perpetrator.[50]

A History of Impunity in the Use of Lethal Force

In the United States and other countries where unlawful use of force by state agents against people of color has been prevalent, there have been complaints that such unlawful acts often go unpunished or entail no serious repercussions for those responsible. Indeed, one of the grievances in the worldwide Black Lives Matter protests that followed the killing of George Floyd was that police officers had been and still were killing Black people with impunity.

On the global scale, history is replete with examples of Western governments and militaries committing war crimes in Africa, the Middle East, and elsewhere without accountability. Where offenders were prosecuted, there was no transparency, leaving victims unsatisfied. Calls for the prosecution of those who authorized the 2003 Iraq invasion have been ignored, even though the parties involved admitted that the justification proffered to the international community for such an invasion was proved to be false.

In another form of impunity for human rights violations, some Western governments have refused to fully account for slavery or compensate its victims, particularly people of color. In fact, many current governments have sought to maintain all the privileges that came with slavery. In 2021, the U.S. White House published a report that defended and sought to sanitize slavery.[51] The point is that refusal to account for violations, past and present, perpetrated against peoples from certain regions in itself perpetuates racial and religious oppression.

This history of impunity in accounting for violations of the human rights of people of color or those in the Muslim world is an important pretext that needs to be recognized and challenged when discussing the potential accountability gap created by the use of AWS, given their likely use in law enforcement and in counterterrorist operations in the Middle East.

Moral Distancing from Accountability and Responsibility

The impunity challenge relates not only to legal responsibility but also to moral responsibility for such violations. AWS will introduce yet another dynamic in the defenses that are often mounted when societies refuse to take moral responsibility for institutional racism associated with the use of force. In relational ethics, moral responsibility and accountability for violations or wrongdoing must be accepted. According to DiAngelo, the desire to distance oneself from moral blameworthiness, particularly from the negative effects of racism, is part of white fragility.[52]

White supremacy has undergirded colonialism, and it can be argued that the indiscriminate use of AWS in the Middle East, Africa, and other nations in the Global South is an extension of the historical legacy of discrimination against people of color and Muslims. From a sociological standpoint, refusal to take moral responsibility for both historical and current oppression of certain peoples is part of the corpus of whiteness and white privilege. Yet white people, particularly those who see themselves as "progressives," who seek to distance themselves from moral responsibility over violations—or from not being part of the violators—are contributing to the continued oppression of people of color. White fragility explains away the targeting of people of color by attributing it to causes other than racism or racial prejudice. In other words, the moral stress to whiteness, particularly among "progressives," caused by indications that certain actions contribute to racial oppression, leads to a feeling of moral harm. Thus white fragility contributes to the current perception of racial oppression as something that can only be perpetrated intentionally and by bad white people. White fragility has led to a response to the George Floyd murder that this was a single case and not representative of a racialized society. Yet racism is not binary: even the good may be entangled in it.

The implications of DiAngelo's theory on this aspect of white fragility can also be applied to states' use of force against people of color, both domestically and abroad. In this context, the question arises: when AWS are used, what is the impact on the moral responsibility of the white general public in terms of the racist uses of force? The use of AWS may lead to a further distancing or erasure of moral responsibility. Racial oppression may no longer manifest itself visibly in the form of a white person. A machine killing a Black person will not only make it even easier to deny racism but will take the discussion about racism off the table. AWS, in this regard, may give racism a thicker cloak of invisibility. The argument may no longer be about "bad apples" in the police force but rather about machine error, making it difficult to address racism and the use of force by state agents.

The use of algorithms to kill displaces humans' moral responsibility for death by distancing them from the act of killing. In discussing the United States' use of two algorithms, bugsplat and SKYNET, in Iraq and Pakistan, Emery observes:

> The algorithmic logics of SKYNET and bugsplat both enable what they seek to constrain; namely making killing more palatable to the liberal conscience while deferring accountability for killing. . . . The systematic outsourcing of human judgement to algorithmic computation has the effect of absolving decision-makers of accountability for killing and justifying existing practices. These empirical probabilities towards death provide a cautionary tale for future military development in the field of AI. A techno-ethics that divorces us from the weight of taking lives in virtuous chaoplexic war is fraught with peril because it relinquishes due care to morally flawed coding. . . . What is at stake in these techno-practices of war is nothing less than the erosion of effective constraints on the

use of lethal force because the techno-rationalization of risk assessment has supplanted genuine ethical deliberation in contemporary conflicts.[53]

Further, as has been recognized by some sociologists, one powerful tool in racial and religious oppression is language construction. For example, DiAngelo explains that formulating discussions on racial oppression in terms of bad versus good people and intentional versus unintentional only serves to undermine discussions on racial oppression. Equally, in the case of emerging AI technologies like AWS, the construction and formulation of language have a sinister power in holding "that non-combatant deaths caused by Western militaries are only ever 'accidents' because we could never intentionally target civilians. The question of intention is brought to light by an overreliance on a techno-logic of algorithmic programming that not only rationalizes civilian deaths as a priori accidental but also raises the deeper question that these acts may be 'beyond intention.'"[54]

In documents on AWS submitted to the UNGGE, the U.S. government notes that in order to ensure that AWS help effectuate the intention of commanders,[55] it will take "practical steps to reduce the risk of unintended engagements."[56] It further posits that such an approach is consistent with the rules of international humanitarian law.[57] But its notion of reducing or minimizing unintended engagements is not found in IHL and human rights language. The United States defines "unintended engagements" as "the use of force resulting in damage to persons or objects that human operators did not intend to be the targets of [U.S.] military operations."[58] The United States further notes that such "unintended engagements" include "unacceptable levels of collateral damage beyond those consistent with the law of war, [rules of engagement], and commander's intent."[59]

Furthermore, the United States has submitted to the UNGGE that unintended engagements include accidental attacks on civilians[60] and attacks against targets whose factual context as it relates to participation in hostilities has significantly changed between the time of authorization and the point of engagement.[61] It has also referred to circumstances where there may be failures in AWS, meaning that resulting harm would not be part of the intention of persons deploying AWS. It has since defined a failure in a weapon system as "an actual or perceived degradation or loss of intended functionality or inability of the system to perform as intended or designed." Such "failures can result from a number of causes, including, but not limited to, human error, human-machine interaction failures, malfunctions, communications degradation, software coding errors, enemy cyber-attacks or infiltration into the industrial supply chain, jamming, spoofing, decoys, other enemy countermeasures or actions, or un-anticipated situations on the battlefield."[62]

Here too, these approaches by states must be examined with real victims in mind. For example, when a state talks of "unintended engagement," one ought to ask the question: unintended engagement with whom? Equally, when it talks about "accidental attacks on civilians" through AWS, one ought to ask: accidental attack on which civilian population? Contextualizing the situation and noting the identity of the likely victims can help explain why certain issues may be taken lightly or seriously. As has been noted by Peter Lee, "The greatest bias that a person might have—if they are even aware of the human propensity for bias—is the sense that it does not affect them."[63] As such, some may take lightly discussions about "unintended engagement" and "accidental attacks on civilians" by AWS because such engagements and accidents do not affect them or those close to them.

U.S. language construction on AWS goes to the root of fundamental and customary IHL rules on distinction and proportionality. The IHL rule of distinction prohibits indiscriminate attacks and is the basis of protection of the right to life in armed conflict. The obligation of belligerents is to refrain from indiscriminate attacks, not merely to reduce or minimize them. Likewise, regarding the IHL rule on proportionality, the obligation on belligerents is to refrain from conducting attacks that have disproportionate collateral damage, not merely to reduce or minimize disproportionality. In the use of new technologies such as AWS—weapons that are likely to be used in certain regions and against certain peoples—care must therefore be taken not to adopt or acquiesce in the construction of language that is irreconcilable with IHL provisions and fundamental human rights norms relevant to the use of force.

It is even more crucial to note, with regard to racial and religious oppression, that the United States is placing emphasis on AWS making mistakes and therefore not carrying out the intentions of those deploying them. There is thus already an attempt to distance those deploying AWS from responsibility or accountability for the harm that AWS may cause. Scientists have already warned that AWS will make mistakes, particularly in unstructured environments. Some of the algorithms, such as the abovementioned bugsplat, have already been deployed and caused immense suffering among the civilian population in the Middle East. To seek to continue deploying similar, or worse, technologies is not only to abandon the ethics of due care but, given the targets as described above, amounts to racial oppression. Yet there are already policies detailing issues of "unintended engagements" in a way that diffuses both legal and moral responsibility over unethical uses of AWS.

These legacies and gaps in our understanding and oversight of the roots and effects of AWS on human rights and the differential effects based on race and religion call for a new set of international norms and protections. One possibility, elaborated below, is an international compact on principles against discrimination and oppression. The norms and protections embodied in the internationally sanctioned concept must be extended to the inherent gaps embodied in the application of AWS in international warfare. But this requires, first, a recognition of the discriminatory implications of modern technology in warfare.

Conclusions and Recommendations: New Principles for Engagement

The use of AI military technologies such as AWS is among the critical factors that will influence geopolitics in the years to come. If AWS are not grounded in the human rights framework, they can contribute to an oppressive geopolitical system that is unfavorable to peoples who have been historically oppressed and dominated. As noted above, such a situation is not conducive to stable geopolitics.[64] Human history has repeatedly shown that racial and ethnic oppression begets the worst forms of violence that disturbs global peace and security. States should therefore carefully address questions of racial oppression and injustice associated with the development and deployment of AWS. This not only important for the sake of global peace and security but also for the protection of fundamental human rights. Human rights are always better protected during peacetime; measures that guide society away from the path of violence and war are therefore critical. Furthermore, racial oppression cannot be reconciled with the fundamental right to nondiscrimination.

It is important to contextualize the uses of AWS and identify the potential victims and perpetrators. When AWS are used in the context of law enforcement and counterterrorism operations, people of color and civilians in the Muslim world will be disproportionately affected. In formulating policy on the issue, states should therefore be aware that the AWS accountability gap has far-reaching consequences for racial justice: these groups of people may be denied the right to a remedy when state agents use force unlawfully through AWS.

In order to effectively address the racial oppression associated with AWS, in the discussion on this technology, stakeholders should start by acknowledging that it is not necessarily neutral but is racialized. As such, discussions on the racial implications of AWS should always be part of the agenda. Just as the African Commission for Human and Peoples' Rights recommended that states should adopt the emerging notion of maintaining human control over AWS as a human rights principle, states should adopt a set of principles against discrimination and oppression as part of the international community's governance tools on AI technologies such as AWS.

Those principles would draw on fundamental human rights principles relating to human rights and customary norms of nondiscrimination. Their main tenet would be that in the development, use, and governance of AI technologies and in maintaining accountability for human rights violations related to AI technologies, robotics, and emerging technologies, states must commit to actively seek to eliminate all forms of unlawful discrimination such as those based on race, gender, or religion. In formulating these principles, states should take account of intersectionality, and decolonial and critical race theories, among others, that critique society, culture, and geopolitics to reveal and challenge power structures affecting inventions such as AWS within a historical context of racism and the endemic refusal to recognize its legacy effects. Under this conception, it should be possible to declare a weapon illegal per se if its development, use, and implications for accountability after use are inconsistent with the right to nondiscrimination. The concept of such principles—aimed at addressing the racial oppression and other forms of unlawful discrimination associated with certain AI technologies—is critical for the human rights project across the globe. If liberal democracies and advocates for human rights fail to recognize and address the challenges described above, the already attenuated international consensus around the objectivity and universality of human rights in the world today will be weakened even further.

Finally, for many states and stakeholders who have been calling for a new legally binding instrument on AWS, it is important to realize that the UNCCW, whose mandate is limited to situations of armed conflict,[65] is not an appropriate forum where all concerns—particularly those relating to racial oppression—can be addressed. AWS are likely to be used, in the context of law enforcement and counterterrorism, in situations where it is often the rights of people of color and civilians in Muslim communities that are violated. Insisting that an institution that cannot fully address the historically loaded impact of racial injustice on specific populations is the appropriate forum to discuss technologies such as AWS runs against the interest of racial justice and contradicts the idea of the principles proposed above. There needs to be a new, international covenant to defend those very rights. Such a commitment among states—through the UN or other multinational bodies—embodying the principles of nondiscrimination and addressing the accountability gap between those who design and decide on AWS and the implications of their use in the field is a key step in the extension of human rights in the modern era. It could help raise awareness within the global community of concerned states and civil society, and move forward a much-needed debate on the human rights and discriminatory implications of modern techniques of warfare and surveillance.

Notes

1. While there is no agreed definition of AWS, this is the definition that is generally used. See, for example, A/HRC/23/47, Report of the United Nations Special Rapporteur on extrajudicial, summary, or arbitrary executions on lethal autonomous weapon systems (2013), www.ohchr.org/Documents/HRBodies/HrCouncil/Regular session/session23/A-HRC-23-47_en.pdf.

2. See International Committee of the Red Cross, "ICRC Position on Autonomous Weapon Systems," May 12, 2021, https://www.icrc.org/en/document/icrc-position -autonomous-weapon-systems.

3. Thompson Chengeta, "Accountability Gap: Autonomous Weapon Systems and Modes of Responsibility in International Law," *Denver Journal of International Law & Policy* 45, 1, April 2020, https://digitalcommons.du.edu/cgi/viewcontent .cgi?article=1011&context=djilp; Human Rights Watch, "Mind the Gap: Lack of Accountability for Killer Robots," April 19, 2015, www.hrw.org/report/2015/04/09/mind -gap/lack-accountability-killer-robots.

4. Chengeta, "Accountability Gap"; Human Rights Watch, "Mind the Gap."

5. See the International Convention on the Elimination of All Forms of Racial Discrimination, adopted and opened for signature and ratification by General Assembly Resolution 2106 (XX) of December 21, 1965; entry into force January 4, 1969, in accordance with Article 19 (CERD).

6. Article 26 of International Covenant on Civil and Political Rights, adopted and opened for signature, ratification, and accession by General Assembly Resolution 2200A (XXI) of December 16, 1966; entry into force March 23, 1976, in accordance with Article 49 (ICCPR).

7. See Article 14 of the European Convention on Human Rights; Article 24 of the Inter-American Convention of Human Rights; Article 2 of the African Charter on Human and Peoples' Rights; Article 2 of the Arab Charter on Human Rights.

8. Article 6 of CERD.

9. Preamble of CERD.

10. Denise Garcia, "Stop the Emerging AI Cold War," *Nature* 593 (7858), p. 169.

11. Ibid.

12. See A/75/18, Report of the Committee on the Elimination of Racial Discrimination, Ninety-ninth session (August 5–29, 2019), 100th session, (November 25–December 13, 2019), para. 22.

13. Chengeta, "Accountability Gap;" Human Rights Watch," Mind the Gap."

14. A/HRC/23/47, 2013.

15. See S/2021/219, Letter dated March 8, 2021, from the Panel of Experts on Libya established pursuant to Resolution 1973 (2011), addressed to the President of the Security Council, para. 63, https://documents-dds-ny.un.org/doc/UNDOC/GEN /N21/037/72/PDF/N2103772.pdf?OpenElement.

16. A/HRC/23/47, 2013.

17. See United Nations, "Machines Capable of Taking Lives without Human Involvement Are Unacceptable, Secretary-General Tells Experts on Autonomous Weapons Systems," March 25, 2019, www.un.org/press/en/2019/sgsm19512.doc.htm.

18. Australia, Israel, Russia, and the United States, among others.

19. Ron Arkin, "Lethal Autonomous Weapon Systems and the Plight of the Non-Combatant," *AISB Quarterly* 137 (2013), pp. 1–8.

20. See UNGGE, Background on LAWS in the CCW, n.d., www.un.org /disarmament/the-convention-on-certain-conventional-weapons/background-on -laws-in-the-ccw/.

21. ICRC, "ICRC Position on Autonomous Weapon Systems."

22. See CCW/MSP/2014/3, Report of the 2014 Informal Meeting of Experts on Lethal Autonomous Weapons Systems (LAWS), June 11, 2014; CCW/MSP/2015/3, Report of the 2014 Informal Meeting of Experts on Lethal Autonomous Weapons Systems (LAWS), June 2, 2015; Advanced Version of Report of the 2016 Informal Meeting of Experts on Lethal Autonomous Weapons Systems (LAWS), Submitted by the Chairperson of the Informal Meeting of Experts; CCW/GGE.1/2017/CRP.1, Report of the 2017 Group of Governmental Experts on Lethal Autonomous Weapons Systems (LAWS), November 20, 2017; CCW/GGE.1/2018/3, Report of the 2018 session of the Group of Governmental Experts on Emerging Technologies in the Area of Lethal Autonomous Weapons Systems, October 23, 2018; CCW/GGE.1/2019/3, Report of the 2019 session of the Group of Governmental Experts on Emerging Technologies in the Area of Lethal Autonomous Weapons Systems, September 25, 2019.

23. Robin DiAngelo, *White Fragility: Why It Is So Difficult for White People to Talk about Racism* (New York: Penguin, 2018), p. 14.

24. See the 2019 Report of the United Nations Working Group of Experts on People of African Descent, "Data for Racial Justice," https://undocs.org/en/A /HRC/42/59.

25. See #Saytheirnames, https://sayevery.name/.

26. Ibid.

27. Charles W. Mills, *The Racial Contract* (Cornell University Press, 1997), p. 122.

28. DiAngelo, *White Fragility*, p. 29.

29. Mills, *The Racial Contract*, p. 122.

30. Ibid., p. 40.

31. Shakir Mohamed, Marie-Therese Png, and William Isaac, "Decolonial AI: Decolonial Theory as Sociotechnical Foresight in Artificial Intelligence," *Philosophy and Technology* 33, 4 (2020), p. 659.

32. Yarden Katz, *Artificial Whiteness: Politics and Ideology in Artificial Intelligence* (Columbia University Press, 2020), pp. 3–13.

33. See Abeba Birhane, "Algorithmic Colonisation of Africa," *Scripted* 17, 2 (2020); Mohamed et al., "Decolonial AI," p. 659.

34. Katz, *Artificial Whiteness*, pp. 6–7, 8–9.

35. Stephen Cave and Kanta Dihal, "The Whiteness of AI," *Philosophy and Technology* 33, 4 (2020), p. 687; See also Safiya Noble, *Algorithms of Oppression: How Search Engines Reinforce Racism* (NYU Press, 2018); Jessie Daniels, "Race and Racism in Internet Studies: A Review and Critique," *New Media & Society* 15, 5, pp. 695–719; Jesse Daniels, "'My Brain Database Doesn't See Skin Color:' Color-Blind Racism in the Technology Industry and in Theorizing the Web," *American Behavioural Scientist* 56, 11, pp. 1377–93.

36. UN Special Rapporteur on contemporary forms of racism, Report, A/HRC/44/57, (2020), para. 48.

37. See Steve Garner, *Whiteness: An Introduction* (London: Routledge, 2007) p. 5.

38. See 2019 UNGGE Report, CCW/GGE.1/2019/CRP.1/Rev 2, p. 13.

39. Article 1(2) of the UN Convention on Conventional Weapons.

40. A/HRC/23/47, 2013.

41. See Arkin, "Lethal Autonomous Weapon Systems."

42. See the Committee on the Elimination of Racial Discrimination, www.ohchr.org/en/hrbodies/cerd/pages/cerdindex.aspx.

43. See A/75/18, CERD Report, 2019, para. 22.

44. Ibid.

45. Ibid.

46. See also CERD General Recommendations No. 31 of 2005 on the prevention of racial discrimination in the administration and functioning of the criminal justice system, No. 34 (2011) on racial discrimination against people of African descent, and No. 35 on combating racist hate speech (2013).

47. CERD General Recommendation No. 31.

48. See Peter Asaro, "A Body to Kick but Still No Soul to Damn: Legal Perspectives on Robotics," in *Robot Ethics: The Ethical and Social Implications of Robotics*, edited by Patrick Lin, George Been, and Keith Abney (MIT Press, 2010).

49. DiAngelo, *White Fragility*, pp. 9–38.

50. See John R. Emery, "Probabilities towards Death: Bugsplat, Algorithmic Assassinations, and Ethical Due Care," *Critical Military Studies* (October 2020), pp. 2–19.

51. Michael Crowley, "Trump's '1776 Report' Defends America's Founding on the Basis of Slavery and Blasts Progressivism," *New York Times*, January 18, 2021, www.nytimes.com/2021/01/18/us/trump-1776-commission-report.html.

52. DiAngelo, *White Fragility*.

53. Emery, "Probabilities towards Death," p. 16.

54. Ibid., p. 6. See also Patricia Owens, "Accidents Don't Just Happen: The Liberal Politics of High-Technology 'Humanitarian' War," *Millennium: Journal of International Studies* 32, 3 (December 1, 2003), pp. 595–616; M. Zehfuss, "Targeting: Precision and the Production of Ethics," *European Journal of International Relations* 17, 3 (October 1, 2010), pp. 543–66; J. Marshall Beier, "Short Circuit: Retracing the

Political for the Age of 'Autonomous' Weapons," *Critical Military Studies* 6, 1 (2008), pp. 1–18.

55. CCW/GGE.2/2018/WP.4, para. 1.

56. Ibid. Emphasis added in this and subsequent quotations.

57. CCW/GGE.2/2018/WP.4, para. 2.

58. United States Department of Defense Directive 3000.09, Glossary, p. 15.

59. Ibid.

60. CCW/GGE.2/2018/WP.4, para. 6.

61. Ibid.

62. Ibid.

63. Peter Lee, "Armed Drone Systems: The Ethical Challenge of Replacing Human Control with Increasingly Autonomous Elements," in *Ethics of Drone Strikes: Restraining Remote-Control Killing,* edited by Christian Enemark (Edinburgh University Press, 2020), p. 159.

64. Preamble of CERD.

65. See Article 1 (2) of the United Nations Convention on Conventional Weapons (UNCCW).

PART IV

Regional Human Rights Systems

TEN

Populism and the Protection of Human Rights in Europe

The Challenge from Within

URFAN KHALIQ

Populism in Europe, as is the case with all parts of the globe, is nothing new. The ebb and flow of political beliefs and fortunes are cyclical, and it was only a matter of time before populism, in its various forms, reared its head again and entered the mainstream.[1]

There are various European right-wing parties and equally some with a radical left-wing ideology that can be described as populist. Populist movements holding, sharing, or influencing the agendas of domestic regimes in power are no longer aberrations among European states.[2] Populism can be seen as a movement that puts the partial interests of the mobilized above the interests of others, while claiming to represent the entirety of society. It is, as Jan-Werner Müller explains, "a way of perceiving the political world that sets a morally pure and fully unified people against elites who are deemed corrupt or in some other way morally inferior."[3] Some European populist parties have a very strong aversion to immigrants, in particular Muslims, and this is especially the case in northern Europe (Denmark, Sweden, and Germany, for example), and central, eastern, and southern Europe (Poland, Hungary, and Serbia, for example). This aversion stems ostensibly from a stated desire to preserve national identity and culture. Human rights courts—in particular, international ones—are thus presented as an impediment to the fulfillment of the populist manifesto and the right of the state and its populace to make their own decisions. The Council of Europe (CoE) and above all its European Court of Human Rights (ECtHR) is now caught up in this vortex of forces.

The Council of Europe was established to enforce the relationship between democracy, the rule of law, and human rights in Europe, three pillars that are specified in its statute.[4] The Council's great contribution to human rights protection has been the European Convention on Human Rights (ECHR) in 1951 and the subsequent establishment of the European Court of Human Rights in 1953.[5] Importantly in this context, the Court's function has been to deal with human rights; it is not best suited to upholding democracy, or to a lesser extent the rule of law. The rise of populism in Europe has led to the erosion of confidence in politics, government, courts, and the mainstream media. Some citizens certainly feel that democracy, the rule of law, and human rights have not worked for them and are actually working against them.

Where the European experience is distinct from other regions of the globe, however, is that in the past when populism and its manifestations came to the fore in Europe, the repercussions were felt globally. The "World Wars" of the twentieth century were of course European conflicts in origin, but tensions between European states had consequences in many parts of the globe, owing to the expansive colonial empires these states possessed. The suffering in World War II was a primary impetus for the adoption of the Universal Declaration of Human Rights (UDHR) in 1948. It is worth stressing, however, that no matter how "globally diverse" the nine key drafters of that Declaration were in terms of the states they represented, the dominance of European cultural heritage among them is clear.[6] The adoption of the 1948 Declaration has been the basis for the legally oriented global and regional human rights edifice that has been steadily constructed ever since, and those cultural and other assumptions have continued to hold sway.

Broadly speaking, European states since 1948, notwithstanding their actual domestic legislation and colonial practices, have rhetorically been fervent supporters of the adoption of global human rights treaties. This was the case throughout the Cold War and subsequently.[7] How that dynamic played out within Europe, in terms of regional developments, was, of course, determined by politics. European states that were under the yoke of the Soviet Union or a part of its empire were not party to any legally binding human rights obligations and arrangements solely of their own.[8] They preferred to support global treaties addressing human rights issues adopted under the auspices of the United Nations (UN). By contrast, the statute of the Council of Europe, which was established in 1949, had by the end of 1950 been ratified by four-teen states.[9]

The end of the Cold War led to a very significant expansion of the member-ship of the Council of Europe, which effectively doubled in the 1990s.[10] In this trajectory, the resurgence of populism and the adoption of populist policies in a number of member states—policies that selectively support some human rights but seek to undermine others—are important for a number of reasons. As noted above, since the adoption of the UDHR, European states—more specifically Council of Europe members—have broadly been vocal supporters of human rights treaties at the global level. Member states that are skeptical, if not out-right hostile, in global and regional forums relating to the protection of human rights have proved a more novel proposition. If we further consider that legally binding human rights, despite protestations about their universality, essentially reflect a European cultural philosophy, then European states undermining that philosophical basis through their words and actions present more of a threat to the theoretical and philosophical basis of all global human rights instruments than if this undermining occurred in other states.

The current challenges to the consensus that undergirded the European human rights system should, however, be placed in a broader historical con-text that reinforces two central tenets of this chapter.

First, the protection of human rights must be a long-term strategy infused with pragmatism in the interpretation and application of human rights norms and their implications for collective policies. The adoption and expansion of human rights norms among member states of the Council of Europe occurred because this was not solely an ideological project but equally one of adapta-tion, mutation, reflection, and evolution. Populism, no matter how pressing a challenge, is simply one of many challenges.[11] The European Court in this context is seen as part of a corrupt and morally inferior elite, who further are "foreign" and thus represent the antithesis of "native" values. For example, Viktor Orbán, president of Hungary and a notorious populist, has attacked the European Court of Human Rights, saying that it should be urgently re-formed because its judgments were a "threat to the security of Europeans" and an "invitation for migrants," whom he referred to as a "Trojan horse of terrorism."[12] While some member state governments are, as noted, openly hostile to the European Court, others are increasingly skeptical and very few are fully supportive of the Court and Convention system. In recent years, dealing with more assertive, skeptical, hostile, and authoritarian regimes has become unavoidable for the Court.[13] Tensions around its interpretation of the

Convention are nothing new, but they have taken on a new urgency with the rise of populist governments and related movements, heightening the challenges to the checks and balances that are key to the domestic protection of human rights. These themes are developed later in the chapter.

The second main tenet of this chapter is that the European Union (EU) may assist in limiting the impact of some of the most pressing challenges to the Council of Europe's human rights system, in particular from populist regimes.

The (Relative) Success of the ECHR over Time

The view that the European Court of Human Rights is the most successful international human rights court has persisted, despite its failings. In 2008, Michael O'Boyle, then deputy registrar of the European Court and coauthor of the leading English-language treatise on the Court and its jurisprudence, best expressed this perception, noting that there "seems to be unanimous agreement in Europe today that the European Convention on Human Rights . . . is one of the major developments in European legal history and the crowning achievement of the Council of Europe."[14] This is remarkable given that the Court, "is overwhelmed with cases and takes so long to produce its judgments and decisions in deserving cases."[15]

The assessment of the Court as so successful has always been relative to the performance of other regional human rights courts in the Americas and Africa. (See chapter 11 by Santiago Canton and Angelita Baeyens, and chapter 12 by Solomon Dersso for discussion of these respective regional human rights systems and the historical and current challenges they have faced.) But on what basis was it the most successful? The European Court has undeniably been a leader in terms of detailed jurisprudence despite the slow pace of judgments in its early years. Can we measure success by compliance? Possibly, but even so, the context was and is important. The European Court did have a "golden era" in the 1970s and 1980s, and arguably in the early 1990s, but by then commentators often noted that it was becoming a "victim of its own success."[16] It was always suggested that the Court had too many cases to deal with because it was so good at what it did—not because structural problems were endemic in some states and there were egregious and systematic breaches of the Convention in others. Any problems were portrayed as being related primarily to delays within the European Commission on Human Rights and the Court itself, and these became the impetus for Protocol 11, which amended the Convention's institutional machinery. Entering into force in 1998, Protocol 11 revised the European Convention system, abolishing the Commission and making acceptance of the Court's jurisdiction and thus the right to individual petition compulsory for all contracting states. Protocol 11 was an important and necessary streamlining of the process for determining a complaint but was never going to be enough.

With the exception of Turkey, which ratified the Council of Europe's Statute in 1950—and perhaps to a lesser extent Greece, which withdrew before it was expelled in 1969, when it was under military rule, but returned in 1974—the membership of the Council of Europe during the Cold War consisted only of a small group of West European, capitalist states. Throughout the 1950s and 1960s membership of the Council of Europe grew, but slowly, and only extended to like-minded states.[17] Notably, at its founding and until well into the 1960s, member states Belgium, France, the Netherlands, and the United Kingdom still had colonial empires in which they perpetrated gross and systematic violations of human rights, under regimes that perpetuated egregious economic, social, and racial inequalities. The contradictions between those member states having empires and then their relationships with the European Court of Human Rights were elided by Article 1 of the Convention, which (in)famously limits the extraterritorial jurisdiction of the Convention and thus any member state's responsibility outside the physical territory of that state to exceptional circumstances.[18]

At the end of the Cold War, as the Council of Europe's membership expanded rapidly, it encompassed a number of new member states that were not well-established democracies. From the outset, protecting human rights at the regional European level was a means to an end, with member states of the Council of Europe remaining nonauthoritarian and democratic. The "common ground" among the member states in the context of the Cold War was defined by considering who and what those states were united against, namely communism and fascism.[19] With expansion, the broader political context in which the Court and Convention functioned changed fundamentally. There were not only the historical abuses within the territories of those new member states, but also their lack of suitable domestic mechanisms and processes as well as the absence of a broader culture that respected individual rights.

By the end of the Cold War, the European Convention system had been evolving—institutionally and jurisprudentially—for the best part of forty years. Prospective member states in the early 1990s were presented with a fully-fledged, mature system, with its own established approach, history, and way of doing things, into which the new members had no input or influence and to which they were compelled to adapt. This was in notable contrast to the UN human rights treaties to which those same primarily central, eastern, and southern European states had from the outset been keen signatories, contributing significantly to their drafting, and to the establishment, and functioning of the treaty bodies.

This is an often-overlooked point. The Council of Europe is a regional human rights system, which, like all such systems, should be finely attuned to the specific vagaries and cultures of that particular region in the context of human rights. Yet, eventually half of all member states from that same geographical region joined the Council of Europe many years after its establishment, not as equals but as the vanquished, and as outsiders still finding their feet in a recalibrated geopolitical environment. Membership of the Council of Europe was a clear goal for many central, eastern, and southern European states as an indicator of a break from their past. Furthermore, membership of the European Union necessitated accession to the European Convention and respect for the rule of law and democracy.[20] Equally, the Council of Europe did not have the means to prevent any backsliding to authoritarianism in these or other member states. The earlier episode with Greek military rule had already highlighted that expulsion from or suspension of membership of an international organization for systematic human rights violations was not an effective method for upholding respect for human rights and the rule of law. This is a point to which the discussion returns later in the chapter.

The Pushback against the European Court

The European Court of Human Rights and its methods of interpreting the Convention have long been strongly contested, but that contestation has been overlooked for far too long. In the seminal case of *Marckx* v. *Belgium*, decided in 1979, these tensions were laid bare. Sir Gerald Fitzmaurice, a British doyen of international law, noted in his Dissenting Opinion that the Convention was interpreted by the Court in a manner that was never intended by those who had drafted it.[21] This is a classic issue—original intention or contemporary context—and familiar to scholars of constitutional systems around the world. What Sir Gerald was identifying is what has subsequently become known as the *pro homine* methodology of interpretation of human rights treaties.[22] This requires that human rights treaties are interpreted in the way that is most favorable to the individual and the protection of human dignity.[23] That can be far removed from what contracting parties actually thought they agreed to.[24] It is related to the European Court's long-established view of the Convention as a "living instrument" to be interpreted in the light of how society has progressed.[25] This issue becomes particularly important with the rise of populist sentiments among Council of Europe states.

While methodologically complex and not always predictable in its approach in practice, the Court has always argued that the "living instrument" approach has informed the evolution of substantive rights, and that these rights must be seen in the light of the approaches taken by the majority of member states. Thus, in interpreting the Convention, the Court can consider the approaches taken by other member states in determining whether a particular member state is in compliance with its obligations or not. This is the so-called European consensus.[26] If a broadly similar approach to a matter is adopted by some or many other Council of Europe states, then that may require the respondent state in a particular case to come into line with that approach. If there is no such broad identifiable approach, then the respondent state has more discretion in its own approach. This "scope of discretion" is another technique, referred to in the Court's jurisprudence as the "margin of appreciation." The margin of appreciation essentially recognizes that states' parties are sovereign and thus have discretion as to how they protect a right. The Court's role is to identify the minimum threshold, and if the respondent state's approach is below that threshold, that will equate to a violation of the right in question. But that minimum threshold will evolve upward over time if society becomes more progressive.[27] Between these various techniques, the Court has arguably overreached its mandate.[28]

Populist regimes may play a disproportionate role in the context of the "margin of appreciation" and "European consensus" in that they are less likely to approach certain rights in a progressive way. Using the "living instrument" approach, the European Court has read rights and obligations into the Convention that simply could not have been envisaged at the time of its drafting. It has done so on the basis of how the laws have progressed in contracting states. It is important to stress that the Court is reactive, as the evolution must have taken place in some states for the Court to be able to justify its approach toward recalcitrant states that are not keeping up with the trend and approach of others. If some or most contracting states have taken a certain approach to a particular matter, then those that are out of line with this approach will have less discretion (margin of appreciation) and may be obliged to comply with the more "progressive" approach. This was precisely the approach used by the Court in *Hirst* v. *United Kingdom*, where the Court found, to the U.K. government's great irritation, that a blanket ban prohibiting all prisoners from voting did not align with the approach taken by most other European states, which allowed many prisoners to vote. Thus, the United Kingdom had a narrow margin of appreciation and was consequently in breach of its Convention obligations.[29] Successive British Conservative governments have refused to comply with the European Court's judgment. In sum, this means that the Court has less scope to be progressive in certain areas, in particular where some regimes—namely, populist ones—are more socially and culturally conservative. That reticence may prevent a similar approach developing among all Council of Europe states and consequently affording greater discretion among member states on particular matters.

Since the turn of the millennium, there has also been a thorough ongoing review of the activities and functions of the Convention system, and it has been more closely scrutinized than in earlier times.[30] Denmark, for example, is a founding member of the Council of Europe and traditionally portrayed itself as a strong supporter of the European Convention system and human rights instruments globally. Yet in recent years, domestic politics, in particular relating to immigration, and indeed some decisions of the Danish Supreme Court, have seen Danish governments at loggerheads with the Convention system and sometimes stridently critical of it.[31] The Danish chairmanship of the Council of Europe in 2017 was thus an opportunity to act on these frustrations. This manifested itself in an agenda that emphasized a strong desire to reform the Court and Convention system, although there was little tangible change in practice. Some commentators have talked of "principled resistance" to the Court and its jurisprudence—on the basis that the Court has not acted legitimately in certain instances.[32] But the Convention system has wider problems than those articulated above.[33]

The Court now has thousands of applications before it relating to the consequences of Russia's invasion of Crimea in 2014. This is in addition to the many thousands of petitions already outstanding and stemming from other situations in Russia and a handful of other states.[34] Interstate complaints are also now being used in different ways than previously.[35] The Court and its future legitimacy and viability are continually being challenged. The Brighton Declaration of April 2012, adopted at the initiative of the United Kingdom's chairmanship of the Committee of Ministers (of the Council of Europe), has had the greatest long-term effect, in its emphasis on the importance of subsidiarity.[36] Subsidiarity in this context is about states parties having the discretion they wish for and thus a recognition of their sovereignty as to how they protect rights. Protocol 15 to the Convention came into force in August 2021.[37] Its Article 1 seeks to rebalance the relationship between the states party to the Convention and the Court by reaffirming that states have "the primary responsibility to secure the rights and freedoms defined . . . and that in doing so they enjoy a margin of appreciation, [namely, discretion] subject to the supervisory jurisdiction of the European Court of Human Rights established by this Convention."[38] This is a reassertion of sovereignty, under the guise of subsidiarity. The call for a return of sovereignty—whatever it actually means—is, of course, common to many populist regimes.

As is obvious from the above, challenges to the Court by the member states have been apparent for quite some years. Protocol 15, crafted by the member states, reminds the Court that they are the masters of the Convention, and the Court is there to fulfill the role the member states have assigned to it. Yet, it did not take the Protocol for the Court to turn to conservatism when it came to the "other"—the target of many a populist's opprobrium. In a series of (in)famous cases, the Court's regressive attitudes toward the autonomy and rights of Muslim women who choose to wear the hijab are laid bare.[39] In these cases, in particular Leyla Şahin and *S.A.S.* v. *France*, the Court upheld national bans on the voluntary wearing of the hijab, as it deemed such dress to be compelled by Islam and pressure from (Muslim) men, and the antithesis of European secular values. In the equally infamous Lautsi judgment, however, the Court's sensitivities and awareness of certain limits are more than apparent.[40] The Lautsi case raised an objection to the mandatory presence of a crucifix in Italian classrooms; Italy is formally a secular state. The notion that a mandatory crucifix in a classroom is a "passive symbol," which "cannot be deemed to have an influence on pupils comparable to that of didactic speech or participation in religious activities" lacks credibility, but the Court's awareness of the vituperative reaction from numerous states meant it had to find a way to ensure crucifixes were permissible in "secular" Italy. The judgments in Leyla Şahin, SAS, and Lautsi highlight in their own ways that while the Court pushes the boundaries of the rights in the Convention, there are limits to what the member states will tolerate. The Court knows not to test those limits. All three cases should have been decided in favor of the applicants if the Court was to uphold the individual rights it had long espoused and to be consistent with its prior jurisprudence. But in each case the Court found for the state—knowing that siding with the petitioners would have been unacceptable to Turkey, France, and Italy, respectively, and that those states simply would not have accepted its judgments.

Pushing Back against Populist Regimes?

While populist regimes pose one of several challenges to the European Court, it has pushed back against some of their practices and policies. Article 18 of the Convention, which had lain dormant, has sprung to life in more recent years. It stipulates that "The restrictions permitted under this Convention to the said rights and freedoms shall not be applied for any purpose other than those for which they have been prescribed." The Court's leading judgment on Article 18 was *Merabishvili* v. *Georgia*, which shed light on how it views the application of the article.[41] The decision, however, rings some alarm bells in terms of holding populist regimes to account. In this case, Irakli Merabishvili, a former Georgian prime minister, was accused of a number of crimes and argued that his pretrial detention had the purpose of ensuring that his political presence and standing were curtailed. In 2014, the applicant was found guilty by a Georgian court of the majority of charges against him. This outcome was challenged before the European Court of Human Rights, which drew distinctions between the ulterior purpose of a restriction from an assessment of measures based upon a plurality of purposes. Here the Court was seeking to examine all the possible motives for imposing restrictions and then to assess the predominant purpose of the measures being contested. This would be done by evaluating all of the circumstances as they evolve over time. If the predominant purpose is deemed illegitimate, then Article 18 is violated.[42] The Court also noted that "the nature and degree of reprehensibility of the alleged ulterior purpose" and the fact that "the Convention was designed to maintain and promote the ideals and values of a democratic society governed by the rule of law are key."[43] In terms of temporality and circumstances, assuming the restrictions stay in place (even if they change in scope), the reasons behind the restrictions may change over time provided their primary purpose remains legitimate.[44]

The obvious associated issues are the burden of proof, and how the predominant reason should be identified and on what basis. The Court, giving itself maximum flexibility and states parties limited clarity, held that it can rely on "information about the primary facts, or contextual facts or sequences of events which can form the basis for inferences about the primary facts;" this could be corroborated and reinforced by third-party reports and judicial decisions, and inferences could be properly drawn from this information.[45] However, the predominant purpose test lacks objective criteria. Equally problematic is the notion that the Court's approach considers illegitimate purposes tolerable as long as they do not outweigh the predominant purpose, which must at all times be legitimate.

The recourse to Article 18 in *Merabishvili* v. *Georgia* is critical as the provision was initially included in the Convention to prevent states from curtailing freedoms and regressing to totalitarianism, thereby limiting the democratic nature of the state. Subsequently, the Court has considered Article 18 in *Navalnyy*

v. *Russia*. Here matters directly related to the conduct of another populist and repressive regime were again under scrutiny. In this case the Court found it had

> established beyond reasonable doubt that the restrictions imposed on the ap-
> plicant . . . pursued an ulterior purpose within the meaning of Article 18 of
> the Convention, namely to suppress that political pluralism which forms part
> of "effective political democracy" governed by "the rule of law", both being
> concepts to which the Preamble to the Convention refers.[46]

How the Court will determine "ulterior purpose" in future petitions remains to be seen. But the reference to pluralism and tolerance as hallmarks of
a democratic society cuts both ways, as the hijab cases, for example, have illustrated. What is different in the balance relating to Article 18 and democratic governance is that mainstream opposition parties are more likely to be
protected as they are indicative of tolerance. Equally, more unpopular views,
especially those associated with the "other," are likely to be marginalized and
unprotected by Article 18, even though they are part of the plurality of views
indicative of a tolerant society.

Dealing with the Challenges from Within

Populist movements that are influential at the domestic level, as noted above,
are not aberrations among Council of Europe members. Some states are showing all the hallmarks of regressing toward totalitarianism. Then there are
others that have never been liberal democracies but have still been admitted
to the Council of Europe. It was widely acknowledged that Russia did not meet
the criteria for membership, yet it was still admitted in 1996.[47] At the end of
the Cold War, the successor state to the Soviet Union was ostensibly subscrib-
ing to democracy, the rule of law, and human rights under a capitalist model.
The opportunity to engage with it as a member of the Council of Europe and
seeing it as a "work in progress" was clearly preferable to keeping it at arm's
length. Belarus, a repressive authoritarian regime, which is not a member of
the Council of Europe, is a case in point here. The Council of Europe has minimal influence in relations with this state. If once there had been the Helsinki
effect, through engagement with what became the Organisation for Security
and Co-operation in Europe (OSCE), it was plausible that membership of the
Council of Europe could equally lead to positive developments in terms of the
protection of rights and democracy in Russia. Russia clearly has not developed
in terms of liberal democracy, the rule of law, or human rights protection in the
hoped-for way.[48] It remains within the fold, however, notwithstanding various

measures such as sanctions and suspensions of voting rights in the Parliamentary Assembly.[49]

Equally, one could say that Turkey has not developed as was hoped. It has been a member state since 1950 and has engaged in egregious breaches of the Convention relating to its Kurdish minority, as well as the invasion of Cyprus in 1974. The approach toward Turkey (certainly between 1950 and 1988) was informed by Cold War politics; the membership of central, eastern, and southern European states was at that time not even a remote possibility.

Russia is, however, different from all other Council of Europe members. It is enormous in terms of territory, has by far the largest population, is militarily formidable, and has immense natural resources. It was inconceivable that it could become a member of the Council of Europe (which had, of course, originally been a club for a small number of Western liberal capitalist democracies) without fundamentally destabilizing that body in some way and changing its culture and way of doing things.[50] But Russia is now a key actor in the Council of Europe. Its influence and importance are obvious and the choices made to include not just a nondemocratic state but one that has actively attempted to subvert democracy without and outside its borders need to be managed. Significantly, it has always been clear that the European Court, as a retrospective mechanism, cannot compel change in states. It can only fine-tune existing liberal democracies; it has never been able to establish and then sustain them—especially in such a large, powerful, and recalcitrant state as Russia.

With regard to those Council of Europe states that are sliding toward repression, there is greater hope that the European system of human rights can serve as a brake, but what exactly the Court can do is not clear. The careful dismantling of the rule of law in Poland or Hungary suggests that there are no straightforward solutions.[51] In Poland the matter primarily revolves around the independence of the judiciary. A number of judgments have been handed down.[52] In May 2021, for example, a judgment of the European Court considered the unlawful election of a judge to the Polish Constitutional Tribunal to violate Article 6 of the Convention.[53] The appointment of members of the judiciary and the "sovereignty" of governments to appoint judges is a well-known lightning rod for populists. The European Union is also taking a lead here, given that both Poland and Hungary are EU member states. The EU's mechanisms allow it to use its financial and political levers to ensure that Poland and Hungary uphold the values articulated in Article 2 of the Treaty on European Union (TEU), which refers to respect for human dignity, freedom, democracy, equality, the rule of law, and respect for human rights.[54]

As concepts, neither democracy nor the rule of law is clearly articulated in international law, nor do they exist as rights per se.[55] Moreover they are distinct from human rights, although related. The EU references democracy and the rule of law in its international relations with third states, and the hazy, indeterminate, and subjective nature of what is meant is more than apparent in its practice.[56] Quite how it will define those terms internally when dealing with a member state necessitates entry into new terrain.[57] Article 2 TEU (all EU states must uphold values such as democracy, human rights, and the rule of law) was inserted precisely because it was foreseen that there might be (back) sliding toward totalitarianism and repression among EU member states (presumably only newer ones). Article 7 TEU outlines the procedure to be followed where it is considered Article 2 TEU has been violated. In December 2017, the European Commission initiated proceedings against Poland, and in September 2018 the European Parliament initiated proceedings against Hungary. At the time of writing, it is still difficult to determine where the Article 7 TEU procedure may be.[58] Much like Article 18 ECHR, Article 7 TEU was designed to provide a bulwark against authoritarianism and must be used in a consistent and coherent manner to be credible.

Conclusions and Recommendations

Many of the problems confronting the European Court and Convention are long-standing, masked for over forty years by the geopolitical context—namely the Cold War. Since the turn of the millennium, their pressing nature has become much more acute and visible. Any established international organization that doubles its membership over a short space of time would face serious issues. One that doubles to accommodate vastly different perspectives, histories, trajectories, and cultures was never going to find it easy. This, compounded by the proliferation of potential applicants, meant the system was never going to cope when there was already a significant problem with delays. Moreover, this crisis in the functioning and efficacy of the European Court, coinciding with already strongly expressed concerns around judicial overreach and legitimacy, was an unhealthy state of affairs. These crises have now coincided with routine and widespread questioning of the legitimacy of all international human rights courts and tribunals. Populists have fed off this energy and narrative. The Brexit slogan in the United Kingdom of "taking back control" was in part aimed, erroneously, at the European Court of Human Rights (and human rights more generally), as well as at the European Union.

But the Court and Convention systems now need to look back at their own past experiences. The Convention system was always informed by a long game, as indicated by the slow building of confidence over time through the 1960s and 1970s, in particular. What is striking is that there is no longer a robust political consensus across Europe around the value and necessity of regional human rights protection for all. This lack of consensus and a perceived lack of legitimacy have had a pernicious effect and may cause the longest-term damage. The hostility toward the Court on the part of some states has not led to stronger support from others; rather, some of the other states have joined the ranks of the skeptical and cynical, if not downright hostile. The hostility to the Court should serve as the canary in the coal mine, warning of the creeping repression in some member states. It is not that populist regimes per se are hostile to international courts and tribunals that protect human rights; rather, it is the narrowness of their views as to which human rights should be protected, for whom, and what the limits of pluralism should be.

Populism and the selective approach to human rights is, of course, not confined to Europe. Owing to the dominance of "European cultural thinking" in the global human rights edifice, a European retreat will be damaging to that international edifice as well as at the regional level. While this may seem alarmist, the risk should not be underestimated. It must be stressed, however, that human rights courts cannot address many of the issues raised by populist regimes. If one considers some of the populist Klaxon calls in European states around immigrants "taking our jobs and houses" or "diluting the Christian nature of Europe," then what protective role can a human rights court actually play? Key to limiting the pernicious policies of many populist regimes is ensuring that the rule of law is respected and that a vibrant, diverse, pluralist society is maintained. The protection of human rights, democracy, and the rule of law is what will prevent the (back)slide to authoritarianism. That will allow the time—however long it takes—for the challenges presented by populism to pass. The European Court can protect the rule of law in a narrow, technical sense only in terms of the independence of the judiciary. In terms of protecting democracy, it is effectively marginal, although a number of Convention rights do lend themselves to ensuring pluralistic societies in certain contexts. These are shortcomings about which little can be done by the Convention system. The Council of Europe as a whole, however, working with the European Union, may be able to buttress the rule of law and democracy across its member states, and such cooperation and coordination may, therefore, provide a fruitful way forward.

The European Union has a variable record on human rights, democracy, and promotion of the rule of law, but there is a synergy here with the Council of Europe in terms of tackling populism. A clear distinction must be drawn between the two bodies, however. The EU's powers and influence in dealing with its twenty-seven member states are vastly different from its capacity to influence those twenty-one Council of Europe states that are not also EU members. The EU has the economic, political, and financial clout to compel certain of its twenty-seven members to roll back some of their more flagrant measures such as undermining or inhibiting the rule of law. The Article 7 TEU process was mentioned above, although the strength of the EU's appetite for invoking it and following it up with effective measures remains to be seen. With regard to the Council's non-EU member states, the Union's influence in compelling reform is vastly reduced. Persuasion is key, but that requires engagement in good faith on both sides and should certainly not be taken for granted. Economic and other sanctions are part of the EU's external armory but it is not known for taking effective and meaningful measures against neighboring states. Less confrontational measures may achieve much more. It has long sought to promote, protect, and fund civil society to safeguard pluralism and vibrant democracies. There is significant scope for the European Union to complement more broadly the work of the Council of Europe, which also promotes democracy and the rule of law, so as to protect and fund the activities of relevant civil society groups. This cooperation will not be a panacea, but it will ensure the viability of pluralism in societies, which is essential for the respect of human rights. We are back to the long game, this time though the players are more diverse and complex.

Notes

1. The literature on populism is now voluminous, but for various definitions and approaches, see the opening chapters of *The Oxford Handbook of Populism*, edited by Cristóbal Kaltwasser, Paul Taggart, and Paulina Espejo (Oxford University Press, 2019); Jan-Werner Müller, *What Is Populism?* (New York: Penguin, 2017); and Roger Eatwell and Matthew Goodwin, *National Populism: The Revolt against Liberal Democracy* (New Orleans: Pelican, 2018). See also chapter 6 by Gerald Neuman in this volume.

2. Such movements can arguably be seen to be strongly influential in domestic politics—at the time of writing—in, among others, the Czech Republic, France, Greece, Hungary, Italy, the Netherlands, Poland, Russia, Serbia, Turkey, and the United Kingdom.

3. Müller, *What Is Populism?*, pp.19–20.

4. ETS No. 1, Statute of the Council of Europe, entry into force August 3, 1949.

5. The European Convention on Human Rights was adopted under the auspices of the Council of Europe and the Convention established the Court. ETS No. 5,

European Convention for the Protection of Human Rights and Fundamental Freedoms, November 4, 1950, entry into force September 3, 1953.

6. Eleanor Roosevelt (United States), William Hodgson (Australia), René Cassin (France), Hernan Santa Cruz (Chile), Charles Dukes (United Kingdom), John Humphreys (Canada), and Alexandre Bogomolov (USSR) can all be considered to be of European cultural heritage. The other members were Dr. Peng-chun Chang (China) and Dr. Charles Malik (Lebanon).

7. Reasoning and perspectives differed, of course, but this is in reference to the nine "core" UN human rights treaties. In each of these, the individualistic approach to human rights is clear.

8. Ukraine (Ukrainian SSR) and Belarus (Byelorussian SSR) were founder member states of the UN and alongside the USSR were among those that abstained from signing the Universal Declaration. The three Soviet states and their allies were strong supporters of universal human rights treaties during the Cold War and keen activists with regard to the seven core UN human rights treaties adopted to the end of 1990.

9. See note 4 above. Belgium, Denmark, France, Ireland, Italy, Luxembourg, the Netherlands, Norway, Sweden, and the United Kingdom all signed and ratified in 1949. Greece, the Federal Republic of Germany, Iceland, and Turkey ratified in 1950.

10. The notable exceptions are Portugal and Spain, which joined in 1976 and 1977, respectively, and Finland, which did not join until 1989. Eighteen states joined in the 1990s and a further six after the turn of the millennium. There are currently forty-seven member states.

11. See *European Populism and Human Rights,* edited by Jure Vidmar (Leiden: Brill/Nijhoff, 2020).

12. Sarantis Michalopolous, "Orban Attacks the European Court of Human Rights," *Euractiv,* March 30, 2017, www.euractiv.com/section/global-europe/news/orban-attacks-the-european-court-of-human-rights-at-epp-congress/.

13. It is widely considered in Strasbourg circles that many advocates on behalf of Russia before the Court are openly contemptuous of it.

14. Michael O'Boyle, "On Reforming the Operation of the European Court of Human Rights," *European Human Rights Law Review* 1, 1 (2008), citing Richard S. Kay, "The European Convention on Human Rights and the Control of Private Law," *European Human Rights Law Review* 5 (2006). Also see Laurence R. Helfer, "Redesigning the European Court of Human Rights: Embeddedness as a Deep Structural Principle of the European Human Rights Regime," *European Journal of International Law* 19, 1 (2008), https://doi.org/10.1093/ejil/chn004, stating that the European Court is the "world's most effective international human rights tribunal."

15. O'Boyle, "On Reforming the Operation of the European Court of Human Rights."

16. For one example from many, see Lynne Turnbull, "A Victim of Its Own Success: The Reform of the European Court of Human Rights," *European Public Law* 1, 2 (1995), p. 215.

17. Notably, Austria in 1956, Cyprus in 1961, Switzerland in 1963, and Malta in 1965.

18. The literature on the rather convoluted jurisprudence relating to extraterritoriality is enormous, but the most useful historical discussions behind the relevant provisions are Alfred W. B. Simpson, *Human Rights and the End of Empire: Britain and the Genesis of the European Convention* (Oxford University Press, 2001); and Ed Bates, *The Evolution of the European Convention on Human Rights: From Its Inception to the Creation* (Oxford University Press, 2010).

19. See Esra Demir-Gursel, "For the Sake of Unity: The Drafting History of the European Convention on Human Rights and Its Current Relevance," in *The European Court of Human Rights: Current Challenges in Historical Perspective,* edited by Helmut Phillip Aust and Esra Demir-Gursel (Cheltenham, U.K.: Edward Elgar, 2021), pp. 109 and 123. Demir-Gursel notes that the Council of Europe was against fascism, communism and "Hitlerism."

20. These were the so-called Copenhagen criteria—as adopted by the European Council held in Copenhagen, June 1993. For these purposes they consisted of stable political institutions and the guarantee of human rights—namely accession to the European Convention—and the rule of law. What the latter, in particular, requires is open to debate. The decision on whether candidate states for membership fulfilled the Copenhagen criteria has always been a political one.

21. Application 6833/74, *Marckx* v. *Belgium*, June 13, 1979, para. 7 of Dissenting Opinion. Sir Gerald had expressed similar views in an earlier key case, Application 4451/70, *Golder* v. *United Kingdom*, February 21, 1975. See para. 40 onwards of his Opinion.

22. For a useful overview of the issues, see Steven Wheatley, *The Idea of International Human Rights Law* (Oxford University Press, 2019), pp.109ff.

23. Ibid.

24. There is a much wider issue here, as to the inflation and expansion of human rights in treaties and by courts and tribunals, which was first flagged in Philip Alston, "Conjuring Up New Human Rights: A Proposal for Quality Control," *American Journal of International Law* 78, 3 (1984), p. 607, https://www.jstor.org/stable/2202599.

25. Notably set out in Application 5865/72, *Tyrer* v. *United Kingdom*, April 25, 1978, para. 31.

26. Although the term is actually a misnomer as there is no consensus per se. See broadly Kanstantsin Dzehtsiarou, *European Consensus and the Legitimacy of the European Court of Human Rights* (Cambridge University Press, 2015), and further *Building Consensus on European Consensus,* edited by Panos Kapotas and Vassilis Tzevelekos (Cambridge University Press, 2019).

27. For an example of the Court's evolutionary approach over time to a particular issue, consider its approach to transgender (referred to in the cases as transsexual) rights in a series of cases against the United Kingdom. In *Rees* v. *United Kingdom* [1986] ECHR 11, for example, a female-to-male "transsexual" complained that British law did not allow him to have his birth certificate issued (at the time of birth) amended

to show his new gender. The Court did not find a violation of the Convention. By 2002, however, in *Christine Goodwin* v. *United Kingdom* [2002] ECHR 588, the Court held, in a broadly similar case, that there had been a violation of Article 8 (right to respect for private and family life) of the Convention, "owing to a clear and continuing international trend towards legal recognition of the new sexual identity of postoperative transsexuals."

28. Meetings with legal advisers from various European foreign ministries suggest that even twenty years ago it was commonplace to hear that State X or Y would never have ratified the Convention and accepted the system and limitations on its own powers, if it had known the eventual outcome. On the "margin of appreciation" and how it has been deployed by the Court over time, see George Letsas, *A Theory of Interpretation of the European Convention on Human Rights* (Oxford University Press, 2009), as well as the citations in note 27 above.

29. Application 74025/01, *Hirst* v. *United Kingdom* (No. 2) judgment, Grand Chamber, October 6, 2005.

30. See Steven Greer, *The European Convention on Human Rights: Achievements, Problems and Prospects* (Cambridge University Press, 2006), pp.136ff.; and further, Steven Greer, Janneke Gerards, and Rose Slowe, *Human Rights in the Council of Europe and the European Union: Achievements, Trends and Challenges* (Cambridge University Press, 2018), pp. 90ff.

31. See Jacques Hartmann, "A Danish Crusade for the Reform of the European Court of Human Rights," https://www.ejiltalk.org/a-danish-crusade-for-the-reform-of -the-european-court-of-human-rights/ and the so-called Elsinore Reform Process, as set out at the conclusion of the Chairmanship.

32. See *Principled Resistance to ECtHR Judgments—A New Paradigm?*, edited by Marten Breuer (Berlin/Heidelberg: Springer, 2019) for an excellent set of essays with many national reflections. Also see *The European Court of Human Rights and Its Discontents*, edited by Spyridon Flogaitis, Tom Zwart, and Julie Fraser (Cheltenham, U.K.: Edward Elgar, 2013) for a variety of perspectives on the Court.

33. For a much broader view, see Aust and Demir-Gursel (eds.), *The European Court of Human Rights*.

34. At the end of 2020, there were over 13,000 cases pending for Russia, just under 12,000 for Turkey, over 10,000 for Ukraine, and over 7,500 for Romania. These four states represented over 70 percent of all pending cases. See further "The ECHR in Facts and Figures—2020," https://www.echr.coe.int/Pages/home.aspx?p=reports /factsfigures&c=.

35. See, for example, App. 38263/08, *Georgia* v. *Russia* (II), Judgment Grand Chamber January 21, 2021, and Apps 20958/14 and 38334/18 *Ukraine* v. *Russia* (re Crimea). In August 2020 the Netherlands also brought an interstate application against Russia over the downed Malaysia Airlines flight MH17 over Ukraine in 2014. On how the interstate application system had been used until recently, see Isabella Risini, *The Inter-State Application under the European Convention on Human Rights* (Leiden: Brill/Nijhoff, 2018).

36. European Court of Human Rights, "Brighton Declaration," High Level Conference on the Future of the European Court of Human Rights, 2012, www.echr.coe.int/Documents/2012_Brighton_FinalDeclaration_ENG.pdf. The Brighton Declaration built upon earlier conferences, namely the High-Level Conference on the Future of the European Court of Human Rights, organized by the Swiss Chairmanship of the Committee of Ministers, Interlaken, Switzerland, February 18–19, 2010; and a further High-Level Conference on the Future of the Court, organized by the Turkish Chairmanship of the Committee of Ministers at Izmir, Turkey, April 26–27, 2011.

37. Protocol 15, amending the Convention on the Protection of Human Rights and Fundamental Freedoms, ETS 213. Protocol 15 makes a few small changes to the Convention relating in the main to the age of judges and the period of time within which petitions must be submitted.

38. Ibid. Emphasis added.

39. Namely, Application 42393/98 *Dahlab* v. *Switzerland* ECHR 2001-V; Application 44774/98 *Leyla Şahin* v. *Turkey*; and Application 43835/11 *SAS* v. *France* [2014] ECHR 695. The Court's regressive approach in *SAS* can be contrasted with that of the Human Rights Committee in Communication 2807/2016, *Hebbadj* v. *France*; and Communication 2747/2016, *Yaker* v. *France*, views of July 17, 2018, where on almost identical material facts the HRC found that France was in breach of its obligations under the ICCPR.

40. Application 30814/06, *Lautsi & Ors* v. *Italy*, Grand Chamber, March 18, 2011.

41. Application 72508/13, *Merabishvili* v. *Georgia*, November 28, 2017.

42. Ibid., para. 305.

43. Ibid., para. 307

44. Ibid., para. 351.

45. Ibid., para. 317.

46. Application 29580/12, *Navalnyy* v. *Russia,* Grand Chamber, November 15, 2018, para. 175.

47. Article 3 of the Statute of Council of Europe identifies these as accepting: "The principles of the rule of law and of the enjoyment by all persons within its jurisdiction of human rights and fundamental freedoms, and collaborate sincerely and effectively in the realization of the aim of the Council." In practice a detailed analysis is undertaken of the conditions in a state that seeks membership but there is significant scope for subjective assessment and political considerations to play a role. On Russia's entry, see Council of Europe, Doc. 7463, January 18, 1996 and Opinion 193 (1996) of rapporteur Mr. Binding at http://assembly.coe.int/nw/xml/xref/xref-xml2html-en.asp?fileid=13932&lang=en.

48. See Parliamentary Assembly, Council of Europe. AS/Jur (2020) 05, February 4, 2020 ajdoc05 2020 Committee on Legal Affairs and Human Rights Implementation of the Judgments of the European Court of Human Rights, 10th Report: Russian Federation, which highlights serious concerns about the situation in Russia.

49. See Resolution 1990 (2014), "Reconsideration on Substantive Grounds of the Previously Ratified Credentials of the Russian Delegation," Council of Europe, http://

www.assembly.coe.int/LifeRay/APCE/pdf/Communication/2014/20140410 -Resolution1990-EN.pdf. Russia is one of the five largest contributors, at €33 million per year, and its suspension created a considerable budgetary challenge, as it responded by ceasing its payments to the Council in June 2017. This interruption in financial contributions cost the Council of Europe around €90 million over the period 2017– 2019, forcing it to propose severe budgetary cutbacks in 2020–2021.

50. Russia has, of course, played the role of a spoiler by refusing to agree to certain initiatives. See further, *Russia and the Council of Europe: 10 Years After*, edited by Katlijne Malfliet and Stephan Parmentier (London: Palgrave, 2010).

51. On the limits of rule of law in terms of the ECHR, see Geranne Lautenbach, *The Concept of the Rule of Law and the European Court of Human Rights* (Oxford University Press, 2013).

52. For example, Application 43447/19, *Reczkowicz* v. *Poland* 22 July 2021.

53. Application 4907/18, *Xero Flor w Polsce sp. z o.o.* v. *Poland*, May 7, 2021. Article 6 of the European Convention protects the right to a fair hearing and also seeks to ensure tribunals and courts are independent and impartial.

54. The Treaty on European Union (TEU) is the foundational treaty establishing the EU. More generally see Laurent Pech and Kim Scheppele, "Illiberalism Within: Rule of Law Backsliding in the EU," *Cambridge Yearbook of European Legal Studies* 19 (2017), p. 3, https://papers.ssrn.com/sol3/papers.cfm?abstract_id=3009280.

55. For overviews of both concepts, see, respectively, Jure Vidmar, "Judicial Interpretations of Democracy in Human Rights Treaties," *Cambridge Journal of International and Comparative Law* 3 (2014), p. 532, https://papers.ssrn.com/sol3/papers .cfm?abstract_id=2426318; and Robert McCorquodale, "Defining the International Rule of Law: Defying Gravity?," *International and Comparative Law Quarterly* 65, 2, p. 277, doi:10.1017/S0020589316000026.

56. For an overview, see Urfan Khaliq, *Ethical Dimensions of the Foreign Policy of the European Union: A Legal Appraisal* (Cambridge University Press, 2008).

57. The process is set out in Article 7 of the TEU.

58. See General Affairs Council, 3674th Council meeting, Brussels, February 19, 2019, Doc. 6547/19. Also see Interinstitutional File: 2018/0902(NLE) Brussels, September 20, 2018 (OR. en) 12266/1/18 REV 1. Also see *2021 Rule of Law Report: The Rule of Law Situation in the European Union*, Brussels, 20.7.2021, COM(2021) 700 final, which is scathing about the situation in a number of member states.

ELEVEN

Polishing the Crown Jewel of the Western Hemisphere

The Inter-American Commission on Human Rights

SANTIAGO CANTON AND ANGELITA BAEYENS

They knew that what they were doing was not an ordinary task. Transforming a world of horror into a world of dignity and peace was not going to be easy. But the founders of the modern human rights architecture were aware of the groundbreaking mission they were undertaking, and the words they chose to describe that moment in history attest to that belief. In signing the Universal Declaration of Human Rights (UDHR) on December 10, 1948, Eleanor Roosevelt had declared: "We stand today at the threshold of a great event both in the life of the United Nations and in the life of mankind." René Cassin, the principal drafter of the UDHR, had compared the document to a Greek temple that would lead to a better world. Twelve years later, at the regional level, in the inaugural speech of the sessions of the Inter-American Commission on Human Rights (IACHR) in 1960, its president, Rómulo Gallegos, made a similar declaration: "There is a thirst for justice in various parts of the American continent. It is suffered by conscious peoples, possessors of the inviolable right to obtain material and spiritual well-being. And our Commission, obedient to the purpose of protecting and defending the constitutive rights of human dignity, cannot be destined to fail."

The optimistic words of these human rights champions were an appropriate prologue to the extraordinary advance of human rights that would follow. For more than seven decades, the impact of the UDHR reached every corner of the world through the development of national laws and international treaties, multilateral institutions, and civil society organizations. A new consensus had emerged on the centrality of human dignity following the horrors of the war.

The first step of the new consensus was to move from the aspiration of the "common standard of achievement for all peoples and for all nations" of the UDHR, toward stronger mechanisms of rights enforcement. This came with the entry into force of the European Convention on Human Rights in 1953, modeled on the UDHR.[1] The European Convention established two institutions to supervise compliance with its precepts: the European Commission of Human Rights (1954), and the European Court of Human Rights (1959). In addition, it entrusted the Committee of Ministers of the Council of Europe with the role of monitoring the execution of the Court's judgments.

In the Americas, the member states of the Organization of American States (OAS) quickly followed the development of a regional human rights system with the creation in 1959 of the Inter-American System of Human Rights (IASHR). Modeled after the European system, the IASHR consists of two bodies, the Inter-American Commission on Human Rights (IACHR), established in 1959, and the Inter-American Court of Human Rights (IACtHR), established in 1979.

Decades later, the model initiated by the European system would also reach the African continent with the adoption of the African Charter on Human and Peoples' Rights (African Charter) in 1982, and the consequent establishment of the African Commission on Human and Peoples' Rights (ACHPR) in 1986, followed eighteen years later by the establishment of the African Court on Human and Peoples' Rights (ACtHPR). Other regional systems, which have not been fully developed to the same degree as the European, African, or inter-American ones include the ASEAN Intergovernmental Commission on Human Rights (AICHR), established in 2009 by the Association of Southeast Asian Nations, and the Arab League's Human Rights Charter and future Court of Human Rights.[2] The ripple effects of the UDHR can still be felt seventy years later as international norms and institutions continue to advance.

The Inter-American Human Rights System in Times of Dictatorships

The historical context that gave birth to the IACHR was not ideal for the creation of a body that must be able to act independently from governments to be successful. The IACHR was created during one of the tensest periods of political turmoil in Latin America's history. In January 1959, Fidel Castro's "26th of July movement" took down the dictatorship of Fulgencio Batista, and while initially well-received by many governments, Castro's attempt to expand the revolution to other corners of the Americas immediately turned into a hemispheric crisis. In July, the OAS Permanent Council called for a meeting of the foreign ministries to discuss the maintenance of peace in the Americas, particularly in the Caribbean region, as well as the "effective exercise of representative democracy and respect for human rights."[3] The final act of the meeting, held in Santiago de Chile in August 1959, created the IACHR and other institutions. One of its aims was "to condemn the methods of every system tending to suppress political and civil rights and liberties, and in particular the action of international communism or any other totalitarian doctrine."[4]

In spite of its origins marked by the Cold War and a strong U.S. governmental influence over the OAS, thanks to the integrity of its members, the IACHR was able to develop as an independent institution driven to uphold the inter-American human rights norms irrespective of the region's ideological divide.

Right from the start, the IACHR had to deal with a very complex political reality in Latin America. The pendulum constantly swung between democracy and human rights on one side, and military dictatorships and authoritarian leaders on the other. In its inaugural year, the renowned *New York Times* journalist Tad Szulc started his book *Twilights of the Tyrants* with an optimistic sentence: "The long age of dictators in Latin America is finally in its twilight." Over the previous decade, country after country in Latin America had moved from dictatorship to democracy. With the end of Rafael Trujillo's dictatorship in the Dominican Republic in May 1961, most countries in the region had governments elected by the popular will of the people. In the United States, President John F. Kennedy initiated the Alliance for Progress to support economic development and social justice in Latin America. Szulc's optimism seemed well-founded, and the region was on track for progress and democracy. But the pendulum always swings back, and democracy would soon lose ground once again. By the end of the decade, fifteen of the twenty-one Latin American countries were ruled by military governments.

In such a turbulent political environment, the role of the IACHR in those early years had a very strong political component. Visits by the Commission to the Dominican Republic during the crisis of 1961, to Augusto Pinochet's Chile in 1974, to Anastasio Somoza's Nicaragua in 1978, and to Argentina's military junta in 1979 all attest to the relevance of the IACHR's political role. In some instances, those visits helped to diminish the massive and systematic human rights violations or facilitated mediation between the government and the insurgent movements. This includes the role played in the hostage crisis at the Embassy of the Dominican Republic in Bogotá in February 1980, when the IACHR helped to negotiate the release of more than fifty people who were held captive by the guerrilla movement M-19.[5] Whether or not it was fully the intention of the OAS member states at the time to provide the IACHR with such broad authority to publicly examine the human rights situations in their countries, especially when so many of them were under authoritarian regimes, the IACHR did construe its mandate as such. In the words of former IACHR president Tom Farer, the Commission became some sort of "Hemispheric Grand Jury," filling the void that was left by weak and co-opted judiciaries around the region and the complacent eye of the West.[6]

During this decade, while its political role was clearly the most visible, the Commission's judicial role was not at all dormant. Very early on, the IACHR received thousands of complaints from individuals across Latin America and the Caribbean who claimed their rights had been violated.[7] Notably, the on-site visit to Argentina in 1979 enabled it to receive 4,153 new complaints in addition to the 596 cases already submitted.[8] The individual petition system was used then by the IACHR more as a thermometer to assess the human rights situation than as a strict legal proceeding followed by a final decision on the merits of the case. And it also served as a warning to the governments that the international community was closely observing the human rights situation in their countries.

However, over the next decades, two main factors would strengthen the IACHR's judicial role: the entry into force of the American Convention on Human Rights (ACHR) in 1978, followed by the establishment of the Inter-American Court, and the return to democracy in most Latin American countries during the 1980s.

The establishment of the Inter-American Court of Human Rights (IACtHR), with its own procedural rules, put pressure on the Commission as the "entry door" to the system to ensure that its procedures followed the same or similar standards.[9] The amendments to the IACHR's Rules of Procedure are indicative of the changes implemented to strengthen its judicial mandate. Nine out of ten such amendments were made after the establishment of the Court, which slowly started to receive cases referred by the IACHR in 1986. The first case, *Velásquez-Rodríguez* v. *Honduras*, was submitted by the IACHR to the Inter-American Court on April 24, 1986. Thereafter the IACHR submitted on average only one or two matters per year to the Court.

The Inter-American System in Times of Democracy

The return of democracy across the Americas by the end of the 1980s also had an impact on the functioning of the Commission. The new democracies, in many instances grateful to the IACHR for its role in denouncing the human rights violations of the past, started to cooperate and engage with it in a more systematic way. Argentina, Chile, and Uruguay ratified the American Convention and accepted the Court's jurisdiction.[10] Mexico and Brazil accepted the IACHR's jurisdiction toward the end of the 1990s and invited it for the first time to conduct on-site visits to evaluate the human rights situations in their countries.[11] In addition, the new freedom helped human rights organizations at the national level to become more active in publicly denouncing human rights violations committed under the new democratic regimes.

The judicial role of the IACHR continued to strengthen significantly over the next decades. This can be clearly observed from the gradual increase in the number of individual petitions received by the Commission since 1997, when it started to record them systematically. By 2019, the number had increased by 597.5 percent.[12]

Arguably, the precautionary measures are the Commission's most important tool to respond quickly and preemptively to particularly serious human rights situations. This mechanism, whereby the IACHR requests a state to adopt urgent measures to protect rights at a great risk of irreparable harm, has been instrumental in protecting the lives of thousands of people across the region.[13] Its quicker nature, and the fact that it does not involve an adversarial process, as well as its use in sometimes highly sensitive situations, has irked some states more than once. While the precautionary measures started to be implemented during the 1980s, they became more widely used during the 1990s. In regard to Colombia, for example, the issuance of precautionary measures became a critical part of the Commission's efforts to protect the lives of hundreds of human rights activists, union leaders, journalists, and members of Indigenous or Afro-Colombian communities who were under serious threat in the context of the internal armed conflict.[14] Since 2005, when the Commission started to keep track of the number of requests for precautionary measures it received, these had increased by 341.5 percent.[15]

Starting in the 1990s, but particularly in the following decade, the IACHR strengthened existing mandates and developed new functions to better protect human rights. For example, the thematic focus through the establishment of rapporteurships (coordinated with similar efforts at the UN level) became a significant tool during this period. From an initial role mainly limited to promotional activities, from the 1990s the rapporteurships became very active in denouncing human rights violations, promoting precautionary measures, advancing cases at the Commission and Court, and furthering inter-American standards. In addition, the creation of the Special Rapporteur on Freedom of Expression in 1998 represented a significant change from the traditional thematic rapporteurships: while all the others are led by one of the seven Commissioners, the Special Rapporteur on Freedom of Expression was conceived to be independent from the Commission and is headed by a full-time independent expert. This structure proved to be very successful, and the Special Rapporteur accomplished significant results in the protection of freedom of expression in the Americas, including the repeal of defamation laws and progress in specific protections for the press. A similar model was established in 2014 with the creation of the office of the Special Rapporteur on Economic, Social, Cultural, and Environmental Rights,[16] although an independent expert was not selected until 2017.[17]

As part of its monitoring mandate, the IACHR also used a specific chapter of its annual report to highlight a list of countries with particularly serious human rights situations and democratic backlashes. This "Chapter IV" list was established in the 1970s, but it only started to gain significant attention from the international community and the media during the 1990s and 2000s, particularly during the OAS General Assembly—the annual meeting of the foreign ministries of the Americas. This mechanism played a critical role in alerting the international community of the most serious human rights concerns, for example, in countries such as Colombia, Cuba, Haiti, and Venezuela.

The members of the IACHR and the judges of the Inter-American Court do not serve on a full-time basis; only their respective Secretariats do. Likewise, the members do not necessarily have the capacity or, sometimes, the technical expertise to respond to all human rights demands and tasks. For this reason, more exceptionally at first and more frequently in recent years, the IACHR has also designated other independent experts to investigate critical human rights cases or situations.

One of these special expert mechanisms set up by the IACHR was prompted by the disappearance of forty-three students from the Ayotzinapa Rural Teachers' College in 2014, which became a symbol of the human rights crisis in Mexico, where more than 85,000 people have been reported as disappeared since the launch of the "war against narcotrafficking" by President Felipe Calderón in 2006.[18] In response to a request from civil society organizations representing the students' relatives, and with the consent of the Mexican government, the IACHR created an interdisciplinary group of five independent experts, GIEI (for its acronym in Spanish).[19] Its mandate was to undertake a technical assessment of the actions implemented by the Mexican state regarding the students' disappearance.[20] The GIEI ended its second term with a detailed report that discredited the official version of the facts fabricated around the Ayotzinapa students and forced the state to reopen and drastically redirect the investigation.

The IACHR had adopted a similar approach on earlier occasions, for instance, in the investigation of the death of prominent Mexican human rights defender Digna Ochoa in 2001,[21] and the trial observation of the case on the terrorist attack on the Mutual Israel-Argentina Association (AMIA) case in Argentina.[22] However, since the Ayotzinapa GIEI, it has created new GIEIs to address the 2018 Nicaragua crisis and the human rights abuses that took place in 2019 in Bolivia.[23] Similar mechanisms, albeit staffed by members of the IACHR and its Secretariat instead of external independent experts, have been put in place to investigate the killing of members of the Ecuadorian newspaper *El Comercio* on the border with Colombia in 2018, as well as the more general situation in Nicaragua and Venezuela, or the impact of COVID-19 across the region.[24] All these mechanisms have allowed the IACHR to be much more "hands-on" in regard to high-profile cases or critical human rights situations, but at the same time imply significant resources and political support from OAS member states.

The Inter-American Court of Human Rights

While the transformation of the IACHR has been more remarkable, given the broad nature of its mandate, the Inter-American Court has also evolved considerably over time, increasing its impact and the far-reaching nature of its decisions and opinions.

The American Convention on Human Rights took almost a decade to gather enough ratifications to enter into force, and as a result it was not until 1979 that the Court started functioning. As mentioned earlier, it took a while for the IACHR to start referring cases, and in the two decades after its establishment, the tribunal only ruled on the merits of twenty cases. Meanwhile, however, the Court made good use of its advisory jurisdiction, having issued sixteen out of its twenty-seven advisory opinions by 1999.

With jurisdiction over a majority of Spanish-speaking countries, the Court has developed a small (compared to its European counterpart) but rich caseload with far-reaching implications for its jurisprudential standards and reparations.[25] A well-known example of its impact can be found in the judicial affirmation of the Commission's position that amnesty laws are contrary to international law, as decided in the Barrios Altos case against Peru: this affirmation prompted Argentina to repeal its Due Obedience and Full Stop laws.[26] Other relevant examples include the standards of reinforced due diligence duty of states to prevent and investigate gender-based violence, and the need to adopt transformative reparations, as concluded in the Cotton Field case against Mexico;[27] decisions on equality and nondiscrimination against Chile, Colombia, the Dominican Republic, and Peru (to name a few); or the more recent cases dealing with the right to health or social security, and the right to a healthy environment.[28]

Another important tool developed by the Inter-American Court is the "conventionality control theory."[29] This was first explicitly used by the Court in 2006 in the *Almonacid Arellano* v. *Chile* case and has been further reaffirmed in subsequent cases.[30] The Court initially extended the obligation to apply the American Convention to all judges at the domestic level in countries that are party to the treaty, but it has gone further by stating that this obligation includes following the interpretation of the Convention by the Court, regarded as its ultimate interpreter.

The evolution of the Court has been not only substantive but also procedural. In this regard, one of the most significant changes to its rules was made in 2000, when the victims were granted direct standing before the Court (*locus standi in judicio*).[31] This was a major departure from previous proceedings, which contemplated the Commission as the representative of the victims before the Court. States reacted by complaining that this broke the principle of "equality of arms," as they considered that they were forced to litigate against two parties instead of one.[32] Consequently, in a new amendment of the rules in 2009, the IACHR's role in the proceedings before the Court became relegated to that of a "guarantor of the Inter-American public order of human rights."[33]

Undoubtedly, the overall impact of the IASHR has been extraordinary. During several decades it has played a critical role in confronting dictatorships, supporting transitions to democracy, and consolidating new democracies. The IACHR's and Court's decisions regarding the incompatibility of amnesty laws with international human rights, the creation of critical standards regarding access to information and freedom of expression, and their progressive decisions regarding the rights of women, Indigenous peoples, and Lesbian, Gay, Bisexual, Transgender, Queer (LGBTQ) people are only a few examples of the inter-American system's many contributions in the Americas, which have earned it the nickname of the "crown jewel" of the OAS, an organization that has little to show besides the work of its human rights system and its observation of elections. Nevertheless, the success of the IASHR has not come without a high cost, and the "lack of polishing" of this jewel may make it lose its brightness.

The Inter-American Human Rights System in Times of Division

The relationship between the governments and the organs of the Inter-American System of Human Rights always had a degree of tension, with occasional accusations against the IACHR (in particular) of abusing its mandate and disrespecting state sovereignty. This was clear with regard to military governments and also during the 1990s in Alberto Fujimori's Peru. Indeed, Peru led several initiatives to "strengthen" the regional body, which in reality sought to "dramatically curb, if not gut, the supervisory powers of the Commission."[34] But it was during the first decade of this century that governments of the region developed more coordinated efforts to undermine the work of the IACHR. Several states started more vocally affirming the narrative that the IACHR treated the "new" democracies in the same way it had treated dictatorships during the 1970s, that it was exceeding its powers, and that it did not act as a subsidiary organ to the national justice systems in the region. This narrative did not come only from countries such as Colombia, Ecuador, or Venezuela, which had been under great scrutiny from the Commission during the first part of the 2000s; it also arose in countries that had traditionally defended the Commission or had maintained a neutral position, such as Argentina or Brazil.

In addition, a group of countries with "populist leaders," including Argentina, Bolivia, Ecuador, Nicaragua, and Venezuela worked in coordination to undermine the work of the Commission. A number of proposals to transform the IASHR were vociferously proclaimed by these leaders during the OAS General Assembly and other inter-American gatherings. The proposals to "strengthen" the system went from completely abolishing the Commission, to establishing a new human rights body controlled by the governments, to relocating the Commission's headquarters away from Washington in order to remove it from U.S. influence.[35]

The public attention that these proposals attracted created a perception that Latin America's populist movement was the only force behind the efforts to undermine the work of the Commission. However, a simple review of the calls by states for reforms shows that behind every criticism there was always a specific decision that the governments disliked, independently of their own particular ideology: a report after a visit, or a precautionary measure, a decision to refer a case to the IACtHR, or a press release of the Special Rapporteur on Freedom of Expression. The arguments were thus a reaction to concrete actions by the IACHR in support of human rights. Criticism by the states was not limited to expressions of discontent or complaints during formal meetings of the political bodies of the OAS, as had traditionally been the case. On the contrary, under the cynical euphemism of "strengthening" the IASHR, many states initiated processes within the OAS to undermine the work of the IACHR. In particular, the 2012 "strengthening process" supported mainly by Argentina, Brazil, Colombia, Ecuador, and Mexico, specifically targeted the precautionary measures, Chapter IV of the Commission's Annual Report, and the independence of the Special Rapporteur on Freedom of Expression.

One of the triggers for these renewed coordinated efforts to limit the powers of the IACHR was the issuance of precautionary measures to protect Indigenous populations living near the Belo Monte Dam construction in Brazil's Xingu River Basin.[36] The IACHR initially requested Brazil to halt the construction of the hydroelectric plant. This prompted a furious reaction by the Brazilian government, which recalled its ambassador to the OAS, formally announced its decision not to present a Brazilian candidate to the Commission, and suspended its financial contributions to the IACHR and the OAS as a whole.[37]

Ecuador's source of resentment against the IACHR was especially related to the workings of its Special Rapporteur on Freedom of Expression and the vocal criticism of the government's efforts to silence the press and any other critical voices.[38] The defamation case against two journalists and four executives of the newspaper *El Universo* for a publication related to alleged acts of corruption by President Rafael Correa's brother, and in which the IACHR granted precautionary measures,[39] sparked a very personal vendetta by the president against the Commission.[40]

In the case of Venezuela, the relationship with the Commission under Hugo Chávez's presidency started very positively. In September 1999, only months after his inauguration, Chávez became the first sitting president to visit the IACHR's headquarters. During his meeting with the Commission, the president expressed his support for its work and invited it to conduct an "on-site" visit to Venezuela. The relationship soon turned bitter, however, particularly after the Commission's highly critical post visit report was published in 2003.[41] Since then, Venezuela under Chávez and later under Nicolás Maduro has taken an openly hostile stance toward the IACHR.

Colombia had been placed under Chapter IV in the Commission's annual reports for twelve consecutive years (2000–2011) alongside Cuba, Venezuela, and certain others. Colombia was also consistently listed among the three top countries, both for the number of individual complaints received by the Commission and for cases in admissibility or merit stages. Additionally, for over a decade the IACHR had issued dozens of precautionary measures a year on behalf of social and political leaders at risk, and many of the cases decided by the Commission and eventually by the Court exposed the strong links between paramilitary units and the Colombian security forces.

Each for its own reasons, various countries in the region coincided in their desire to restrict the reach and powers of the Commission and also to send a warning signal to the Court, leading to the so-called strengthening process mentioned above. Unfortunately, instead of engaging in a high-level dialogue with governments to defend the integrity of IACHR's mandate and of its practices, as they had done in the past, the Commissioners yielded to the pressures from the states and responded by significantly amending their Rules of Procedure. Not surprisingly, one of the most significant changes involved the criteria for granting precautionary measures. The impact of the amendments is reflected in the dramatic fall in the number of precautionary measures granted since the reform in 2013. From 2005, when the IACHR started keeping track of the requests for precautionary measures, until 2013, when the rules were amended to appease the criticisms from many states, the IACHR granted 13 percent of the measures requested. But from 2013 until 2020, under the amended rules, it only granted 5.2 percent of such requests: a stark decrease in the use of the most important tool to protect human rights throughout the Americas. Unfortunately, this trend continues to date; between 2018 and 2020, the Commission only granted 3.7 percent of the precautionary measures requested.

The mandate of the Special Rapporteur on Freedom of Expression was another critical target of the OAS member states. Created with the strong support of the heads of state of the Americas during a summit in Chile in 1998, this rapporteurship was established by the IACHR as a new mechanism to protect the right of freedom of expression. The Special Rapporteur, though selected by the members of the Commission, was conceived as capable of executing this mandate very independently in the shape of an expert based full-time at headquarters in Washington. During its first decade, the rapporteurship had its own agenda and enjoyed little or no influence from the members of the IACHR in its execution. However, under pressure from the governments of Ecuador, Mexico, and Venezuela, among many others, the IACHR started to exert more control over the work of the Special Rapporteur, including through the Commission's Executive Secretariat.

In addition to exerting direct threats and pressure on the Inter-American System of Human Rights, states have also exerted pressure through the OAS

General Secretariat. While a source of constant tension between the IACHR and successive OAS general secretaries is embedded in the Commission's Statute and particularly the appointment of the IACHR executive secretary, there have been some attempts to directly control the Commission. During his short-lived tenure as secretary general, Miguel Ángel Rodríguez tried to create a position directly dependent on him that would control its workings outright, and without any notice or due process, he attempted to cancel the contract of Eduardo Bertoni, the Special Rapporteur on Freedom of Expression appointed by the IACHR. Similarly, one of the first things Chilean secretary general José Miguel Insulza tried to do was to remove Santiago Canton (coauthor of this chapter) from his position as executive secretary.[42] In both instances, thanks to the quick and strong unified reaction of the members of the IACHR, these attempts were unsuccessful. However, they did represent a new threat to the independence of the IACHR that had not previously existed. Also, not surprisingly, both positions, the Special Rapporteur on Freedom of Expression and the executive secretary of the IACHR, were constant targets of attacks by Venezuela during the Chávez presidency.

Historical and Emerging Challenges

In addition to the changes and practices that affected the work of the IACHR, other aspects of the system have historically represented a challenge to its overall effectiveness: its lack of universality, the lack of compliance with its decisions and recommendations, the chronic underfunding of its institutions, the significantly small number of complaints it receives, and the time it takes to resolve them.

While the number of countries that make up the OAS is relatively low in comparison with its regional counterparts, the IASHR operates with four different levels of protection for the people of the region, depending on the country from which they are seeking protection. The lowest level of protection applies to the twelve member states, including the United States, that have not ratified the system's main source of law, the American Convention on Human Rights (ACHR). The practical implication is that victims of human rights violations in these countries can only seek the protection of the IACHR and do so under the American Declaration of the Rights and Duties of Man, whose binding force is under continuous discussion. The next level of protection operates in the three OAS member states that have ratified the ACHR but have not accepted the jurisdiction of the IACtHR. Victims in these states therefore cannot have access to the regional system beyond the IACHR. The third level, covering the majority (twenty-three) of member states, relates to those that have ratified the ACHR and accepted the jurisdiction of the IACtHR. Therefore victims could in theory see their cases referred by the IACHR to the Court, provided they comply with the necessary admissibility and merits requirements. Only a handful of OAS member states have ratified most or all of the ten basic inter-American human rights treaties, in addition to accepting the jurisdiction of the IACtHR. It is unacceptable that more than sixty years after the creation of the IASHR, so many countries in the region have not yet ratified all regional human rights treaties.

The second endemic problem that has affected the impact of the Inter-American System of Human Rights is the lack of significant compliance with the decisions and recommendations of its two constitutive organs. While this is hardly a challenge that is exclusive to the IASHR, the low levels of compliance expose its structural weakness, but also the obvious need to engage in a major reform of the OAS itself. Even during the most critical exercises of reform and so-called strengthening of the IASHR, OAS member states have consistently failed to evaluate their own behavior in ensuring its effectiveness, as well as in holding other member states accountable for failing to comply with the decisions of its organs. Today, states do not even make use of the presentations of the annual reports by the IACHR and the Court during the OAS General Assembly to evaluate state compliance with the decisions of these bodies. Neither of them has much more than its follow-up mechanism to ensure states' compliance with its decisions. While it could be argued that this serves as some sort of "naming and shaming" mechanism, it puts the burden back on civil society and the victims themselves to continue advocating for compliance with a decision years after it was issued. Indeed, the IACtHR has closed only 35 out of 421 cases for reasons of compliance.

A third major challenge for the IASHR has historically been the lack of adequate funding. In particular, the Commission—which, as discussed above, has a wide and varied mandate that includes political, monitoring, advisory, and adjudicatory functions—has suffered from chronic underfunding for decades. Even though in 2018 both the Commission and the Court started receiving a significant and gradual increase in regular funds from the OAS, this still only represents 19 percent of its overall budget.[43] At the close of 2020, the IACHR had a budget of $15,964,800, of which 57 percent came from the regular OAS budget and 43 percent from voluntary contributions by member states or through international cooperation.

The fourth critical aspect of the system that seriously undermines its impact and relevance is the limited number of petitions received by the IACHR and the length of time it takes to decide on their merit. While the number of individual petitions has increased significantly since 1997, in comparison with similar systems it is still extremely low. The Inter-American System of Human Rights is set to afford access to international justice to approximately one billion people in a region where the domestic judiciary systems face abundant challenges. Yet in 2020 the Commission received only 2,448 cases, while the European Court of Human Rights, with jurisdiction over 750 million people, received 41,700 cases. Indeed, the European system received more cases in one year than the IACHR did in twenty-three years (35,509). Further, the increase in the number of cases filed with the IACHR does not seem to show a significant upward trend, and in 2020 it actually received almost 20 percent fewer cases than in 2019.

It could be argued that the impact of the IACHR should not be measured by the number of cases received, as long as the quality and reach of the decisions address important issues and human rights challenges in the region. And that is partially true. But the combination of this relatively low number of petitions and the other part of this critical challenge, the protracted proceedings, show the weaknesses and shallow reach of the system. On average, from the moment of filing to the publication of a decision on the merits or its referral to the IACtHR, the process of an individual case before the IACHR takes seventeen years. The procedural delays are certainly a consequence of the great underfunding of the Commission, but also of competing demands and activities undertaken that stretch it very thin.

This also has an impact on the Court. Given that the Commission is the necessary gateway to access the IACtHR, it is not surprising that the latter receives very few cases: an average of fifteen per year in the past twenty years. For the most unequal region of the world, with a tradition of police brutality and military interventions, and a population of one billion, this is a staggeringly low figure.

In addition to the "traditional" challenges that have affected the IASHR for decades, there are new or emerging human rights concerns to which it is not well-equipped to respond, including corruption, the climate crisis, and the impact of businesses on human rights. It is recognized that these issues have an impact on the enjoyment of human rights, and the international human rights bodies have been asked to intervene on many occasions, but it is not yet clear what they can do and how much they can accomplish. When the human rights system was established, these issues were not part of the human rights agenda, but they present pressing challenges today. The international norms and supervisory human rights bodies are not in a position to address them effectively, but civil society is urging them to do so.

One can certainly recognize that corruption is nothing new, but it is only recently that the international community has started to acknowledge its impact on human rights. To live free from corruption is not yet recognized as a right, but reducing it is fundamental to the realization of other human rights. Further, as Schulz and Raman highlight, it is not a coincidence that the most corrupt countries in the world are also those with widespread human rights abuses, inadequate rule of law, and in some even active conflict.[44] The first time that the IACHR referred to corruption as a phenomenon with human rights implications was in a country report in 2001 after an on-site visit to Paraguay. Since then it has made many references to the impact of corruption on human rights, the most significant of which comprised a thematic report published in 2019.[45] But beyond these declarations carried out through its monitoring and promotional mandates, not much has been achieved.

Similarly, environmental degradation and the negative impact that large-scale business activities can have on the enjoyment of human rights were not considered when the human rights systems were established. Today, the international community has set important limitations for addressing these issues and ensuring powerful private actors abide by the same rules as states, and the intergovernmental human rights organizations are repeatedly asked by civil society organizations to get involved. However, they lack the relevant expertise and institutional capacity to do so in a comprehensive manner.

Finally, it is important to note that there are other contemporary challenges to the work of human rights mechanisms and their progressive interpretation of rights, challenges that are not limited to the Americas. One is the increased pressure from radical conservative groups and their influence on governments, which has at times also imposed practical restraints on the IACHR's ability to work on sensitive issues, such as women's sexual and reproductive rights.[46] In 2019, for example, the U.S. State Department, prompted by evangelical groups and U.S. senators, announced a reduction in its contributions to the OAS, accusing the Inter-American Commission and the Inter-American Commission on Women of allegedly lobbying for abortion. The effect was to weaken the capacity of the IACHR Rapporteurship on the Rights of Women and thus its work on important issues beyond reproductive rights. Similarly, evangelical opposition to the 2018 Inter-American Court's decision in support of marriage equality[47] launched a previously unknown evangelical pastor's presidential candidacy that same year; he reached the second round.[48]

Although the IASHR's positive impact in the Americas cannot be denied, after more than sixty years, it is also clear that this impact has fallen short of the great expectations reflected in the optimistic words of its architects. Rómulo

Gallego's words about how the Commission would resolve the thirst for justice for the people of the Americas seem to be too far away from today's reality. In most Latin American countries, the rule of law is crumbling, poverty and inequality are increasing, and insecurity and police brutality continue to be a permanent feature of society. Unless governments and intergovernmental organizations reignite the flame and spirit of 1948 with significant structural changes in the functioning of the system, the IASHR could become marginal and less relevant.

Both member states and the OAS have to adopt reforms to strengthen the system from the outside; this will reverberate in the inner strengthening of the IACHR and the Court. Previous reform processes have failed to address the traditional challenges because they have focused on the IASHR bodies, particularly the IACHR, instead of the structure that houses it, the OAS, and one of its main pillars, the states themselves. The so-called strengthening processes were initiated by the states with the purpose of exerting a stricter control over the IACHR, but none aimed at advancing the protection of human rights and their own role in ensuring this. Apart from establishing the role of the Special Rapporteur on Freedom of Expression in 1997, the states have adopted no significant change to advance human rights since 1979, with the creation of the Inter-American Court. The governments, the OAS, and the inter-American human rights institutions must all take drastic measures to reinvigorate the regional system and to make it truly responsive to the needs and challenges of today.

When the internationalization of human rights was envisaged more than seventy years ago, the founders dreamed of a system that would bring peace and prosperity to all humankind. While that was clearly not accomplished, the human rights systems have been at the forefront in the fight for dignity all over the world. With great successes as well as failures, the human rights institutions have proved to be the main mechanisms with the independence and strength needed to confront the worst atrocities on a daily basis. The most important lesson of the last seven decades is that the international human rights systems are not only necessary but perhaps the only alternative to continue the fight for dignity. But we have also learned that these systems need to be redesigned and strengthened to address endemic problems and new challenges that were not envisioned at their founding.

As the experience of past reforms shows, at the outset of any discussion to reform the IASHR it is important to recognize that the main challenge in strengthening the system is the real possibility that some governments will try to use reform as a way to weaken it. That is the main reason why some governments and most human rights civil society organizations over the last two decades have avoided the issue. However, the status quo cannot be an option. The massive violations of human rights that are affecting millions of people all over the region must be countered more aggressively. The consensus built for decades around the American Declaration and Convention, as well as the Commission and the Court, while extraordinary in many respects, has also highlighted many old and new shortcomings that can no longer be ignored. To do so would only intensify the IASHR's serious limitations in reaching out to the hundreds of millions of people who fall outside the margins. In attempting to reach a new consensus to improve our human rights systems, we need to keep in mind the ideals that guided the founders of the modern human rights system. They focused on universal values and human dignity. Sovereignty, nonintervention, international bureaucracies, and budgets did not overshadow their dream of setting the dignity of the individual as the ultimate goal of any state action. The concluding section presents some proposals in that direction.

Recommendations

While there are important changes that should be made by the two organs of the Inter-American Human Rights System, most of the necessary reforms that would allow the system to really reach its full potential lie in the OAS and the member states themselves.

Given that implementation is one of the major challenges and the biggest impediment to the effectiveness and relevance of human rights, an OAS mechanism to ensure compliance with the recommendations of the IACHR and the decisions of the IACtHR is long overdue. Improving upon the model of the Council of Europe and its Committee of Ministers, the OAS should create a kind of Special Rapporteur to follow up and advise member states on how to comply with the decisions of these two bodies. The Special Rapporteur should be able to act with complete independence from the OAS General Secretariat and to present a detailed report to the OAS political bodies. The rapporteurship's advisory role on compliance should not include the interpretation of the decisions of the Commission or the Court but could help systematize their recommendations and decisions, thereby lifting a huge burden from the overstretched IACHR, and supporting the Court as well.

Replicating in some way the model of the Office of the UN High Commissioner for Human Rights, the IACHR should have a more permanent presence in the countries of the region, or at least in subregional hubs. While this might initially entail a significant investment of resources, it could reduce some costs in the longer term, and more importantly, it would facilitate closer interaction with the people of the Americas and increase the IACHR's influence and accessibility. This could allow for more regular and timely monitoring and gathering of key information for IACHR reports, and increase the number of individual petitions and precautionary measures filed. In addition, it could help with friendly settlements and compliance with the decisions and recommendations of both the IACHR and the Court. Of course, if stronger measures are not adopted to speed up the processing of cases at the IACHR, opening the door to a higher number of cases might lead to its complete collapse.

The OAS should create an independent High Commissioner of Human Rights to complement the work of the Commission in areas in which this body cannot intervene. For instance, a high commissioner could play an advisory role to the states in instances when the Commission has a pending case and cannot do so, and could advise the OAS secretary general on human rights issues. Over the years, the relationship between the Commission and the secretary general has proved difficult, with the former unable to play any sustained advisory role. A high commissioner could provide a space for civil society to engage more effectively on human rights with the political bodies of the OAS. For this mandate to really play a positive and constructive role that would complement the organs of the IASHR and not directly compete with them, the high commissioner should be bound to strict adherence to the principles and standards developed by the IACHR and the Inter-American Court, as the principal OAS organs and human rights authorities of the system. Additionally, the selection process for this post should be subject to the highest standards of transparency and should include the active participation of both the Commission and the Court, as well as civil society. This would avoid any real or perceived politicization of the role and ensure that the same qualities of human rights expertise and high moral authority required for a commissioner or a judge are met.

Like the Council of Europe, the OAS should redefine its goals to focus mainly on human rights and democracy. Although it has started to do so over recent years, there is still capacity in the OAS's budget to improve and allocate most of its funds to human rights and democracy work. This would enable it, among other things, to appoint full-time judges and commissioners, establish a subregional IACHR presence throughout the inter-American system, increase the number and capacity of Special Rapporteurs, and create the role of OAS Special Rapporteur on Compliance with the recommendations and decisions of the IASHR, and even the role of a High Commissioner for Human Rights to complement the work of the system.

For the inter-American system to reach its full potential, states must become full parties to all regional human rights treaties and pass national laws to implement the decisions of its organs, as needed. This should include new binding legal instruments on business and human rights, corruption, and the impact of climate change on human rights, which should also be part of the inter-American human rights framework.

The bodies of the IASHR, and particularly the Commission, also need to implement serious changes to maximize their impact and effectiveness. The IACHR should prioritize the areas of its work that have more impact on the protection of human rights in the region and that are unique to its mandate. Areas such as human rights education could be undertaken by other existing bodies, for example, the Inter-American Institute for Human Rights, or by potential new mechanisms, such as the office of the OAS High Commissioner for Human Rights proposed above.

To make the individual petition system truly more efficient and significantly increase its use throughout the region, more radical measures should be taken to speed up the processing of cases, including by systematically joining the analysis and decision on admissibility and merits instead of treating the decision to join both procedural stages as an exceptional measure, as is currently the case.

To address the lack of capacity and technical expertise on some important issues, the IACHR could consider adapting the working group model of the African Commission on Human and Peoples' Rights (ACHPR), as some commentators have suggested.[49] These working groups, led by one or more commissioners, also include a number of independent experts who share their technical expertise at no or very low cost to the ACHPR, thus expanding the pool of knowledge available to the Commission, ensuring a multidisciplinary approach to critical issues, such as the environmental impact of the extractive industries or the conditions of Indigenous populations and minorities, while alleviating the strain on the commissioners themselves.

Making these improvements to the Inter-American System of Human Rights and the way in which states engage with it might help calm the "thirst for justice" that Gallegos evoked in his inaugural speech at the head of the Commission. That thirst is stronger than ever.

Notes

1. Universal Declaration of Human Rights, Preamble, www.un.org/en/about-us /universal-declaration-of-human-rights.

2. ASEAN Intergovernmental Commission on Human Rights, https://aichr.org /about-aichr-2/; League of Arab States, Arab Charter on Human Rights, May 22, 2004, reprinted in 12 Int'l Hum. Rts. Rep. 893 (2005), entered into force March 15, 2008.

3. Fifth Meeting of Consultation of Ministers of Foreign Affairs, Organization of American States, August 12–18, 1959, Final Act, p. 3, www.oas.org/council /MEETINGS%20OF%20CONSULTATION/Actas/Acta%205.pdf.

4. Fifth Meeting of Consultation of Ministers of Foreign Affairs, Organization of American States, August 12–18, 1959, Final Act, The Declaration of Santiago, p. 4, www.oas.org/council/MEETINGS%20OF%20CONSULTATION/Actas/Acta%205 .pdf.

5. IACHR, Report on the Human Rights Situation in Colombia, 30 June 1981, chapter C, *The Commission and the Solution of the Problem Posed by the Seizure of the Dominican Embassy,* June 30, 1981, www.cidh.org/countryrep/Colombia81eng/TOC.htm.

6. Tom Farer, "The Rise of the Inter-American Human Rights Regime: No Longer a Unicorn, Not Yet an Ox," *Human Rights Quarterly* 19, 3 (1997), p. 512.

7. During the first six years of its existence, the Commission received 3,776 cases. The numbers of petitions would later drop, and between 1969 and 1973, it received only 421 communications pertaining to a total of 205 cases. In 1974 there was a significant increase in the number of individual petitions, with 626 communications received, which referred to 617 cases. See IACHR Annual Reports of the years 1969–1974, www.oas.org/en/iachr/reports/ia.asp, and the reports submitted by the IACHR to the Second Inter-American Conference, October 15, 1965. www.corteidh.or.cr /tablas/Informe%20sometido%20por%20la%20CIDH%20a%20la%20se gunda%20conf%20interam%20extraordinaria.pdf.

8. IACHR, "Annual Report 1979," ch. II, www.cidh.org/annualrep/79.80eng/toc .htm.

9. American Convention on Human Rights, Art. 60, www.oas.org/dil/treaties_b -32_american_convention_on_human_rights.pdf.

10. Argentina in 1984, Uruguay in 1985, and Chile in 1990.

11. Brazil adhered to the American Convention on Human Rights in September 1992 and only accepted the jurisdiction of the Inter-American Court in December 1998. While Mexico adhered to the American Convention in 1981, it took almost twenty years, until 1998, for it to accept the jurisdiction of the Court.

12. The number of individual petitions received by the Commission in 1997 was 435. In 2019 the number of petitions received had increased to 3,034. See https:// www.oas.org/en/iachr/multimedia/statistics/statistics.html.

13. IACHR, Rules of Procedure, Art. 25. See also IACHR, "Precautionary Measures," www.oas.org/en/IACHR/jsForm/?File=/en/iachr/decisions/mc/about-precaut ionary.asp.

14. Robert K. Goldman, "History and Action: The Inter-American Human Rights System and the Role of the Inter-American Commission on Human Rights," *Human Rights Quarterly* 31, 4 (2009), p. 876, https://www.jstor.org/stable/40389979.

15. IACH, Statistics, www.oas.org/en/iachr/multimedia/statistics/statistics.html.

16. "IACHR to Create an Office of the Special Rapporteur on Economic, Social, and Cultural Rights," Press Release 34/14, IACHR Media Center, April 3, 2014, www .oas.org/en/iachr/media_center/PReleases/2014/034.asp.

17. "IACHR Chooses Soledad García Muñoz as Special Rapporteur on Economic, Social, Cultural, and Environmental Rights (ESCER)," Press Release 090/19, IACHR Media Center, July 5, 2017, www.oas.org/en/iachr/media_center/PReleases/2017/090.asp.

18. Stephanie Brewer, "Militarized Mexico: A Lost War That Has Not Brought Peace," Washington Office on Latin America, May 12, 2021, www.wola.org/analysis/militarized-mexico-a-lost-war/.

19. IACHR, Follow-Up Mechanism to the Ayotzinapa Case (MESA), www.oas.org/en/iachr/activities/giei.asp.

20. "IACHR Makes Official Technical Cooperation Agreement about Ayotzinapa Students in Mexico," Press Release 136/14, IACHR Media Center, November 18, 2014, www.oas.org/en/iachr/media_center/PReleases/2014/136.asp.

21. "IACHR Mission to Mexico," Press Release 1/03, January 10, 2003, www.cidh.org/Comunicados/English/2003/1.03.htm.

22. IACHR, Press Release 19/01, August 8, 2001. Dean Claudio Grossman, current president of the IACHR, was named as its observer for the trial in the criminal case concerning the bombing of a Jewish community center, the Asociación Mutual Israelita (AMIA), in Buenos Aires, www.cidh.org/Comunicados/English/2001/Press19-01.htm.

23. For Nicaragua, see "IACHR to Create Interdisciplinary Group of Independent Experts to Help Investigate Recent Violence in Nicaragua," Press Release 121/18, IACHR Media Center, May 30, 2018, www.oas.org/en/iachr/media_center/PReleases/2018/121.asp. For Bolivia, see "IACHR announces integration of Interdisciplinary Group of Independent Experts for Bolivia," Press Release 13/20, IACHR Media Center, January 23, 2020, www.oas.org/en/iachr/media_center/PReleases/2020/013.asp.

24. For Colombia, see "IACHR and Its Office of the Special Rapporteur Installed in Quito Special Follow-Up Team for the Murder of Members of El Comercio's Journalistic Team," Press Release 165/18, IACHR Media Center, July 26, 2018, www.oas.org/en/iachr/media_center/PReleases/2018/165.asp. For Nicaragua, see IACHR Special Monitoring Mechanism for Nicaragua (MESENI), www.oas.org/en/iachr/jsForm/?File=/en/iachr/meseni/default.asp. For Venezuela, see IACHR Special Follow-up Mechanism for Venezuela (MESEVE), www.oas.org/en/iachr/jsForm/?File=/en/iachr/meseve/default.asp. On COVID-19, see IACHR, SACROI-COVID Rapid and Integrated Response Coordination Unit, www.oas.org/en/iachr/jsForm/?File=/en/iachr/sacroi_covid19/default.asp.

25. Out of twenty-five countries that have (at some point) accepted the jurisdiction of the Inter-American Court, the only non-Spanish–speaking countries are Barbados, Brazil, Haiti, Suriname, and Trinidad and Tobago.

26. In 2005, and largely based on the jurisprudence of the Inter-American Commission and Court, the Argentine Supreme Court of Justice ruled the amnesty laws inapplicable. See Julio Héctor Simón et al. Case 17,768, Argentine Supreme Court of Justice, June 14, 2005. On the incompatibility of amnesty laws with international law, see Case of *Las Hojas Massacre* v. *El Salvador* (Report 26/92, Case 10.287, September 24, 1992),

Uruguay (Report 29/92, Cases 10.029, 10.036, 10.145, 10.305, 10.372, 10.373, and 10.375, October 2, 1992); and Argentina (Report 28/92, Cases 10.147, 10.181, 10.240, 10.262, 10.309, and 10.311, October 2, 1992). Law 23.492 enacted on December 24, 1986, and Law 23.521 enacted on June 8, 1987, respectively. For the Peru case, see I/A Court H.R., Case of *Barrios Altos* v. *Peru*. Merits. Judgment March 14, 2001. Series C No. 75.

27. I/A Court H.R., Case of *González et al. ("Cotton Field")* v. *Mexico*. Preliminary Objection, Merits, Reparations and Costs. Judgment of November 16, 2009. Series C No. 205.

28. I/A Court H.R., Case of *Poblete Vilches* v. *Chile*. Merits, Reparations and Costs. Judgment of March 8, 2018. Series C No. 349; I/A Court H.R., Case of *Cuscul Pivaral et al.* v. *Guatemala*. Preliminary Objection, Merits, Reparations and Costs. Judgment of August 23, 2018. Series C No. 359; I/A Court H.R., Case of the *National Association of Discharged and Retired Employees of the National Tax Administration Superintendence (ANCEJUB-SUNAT)* v. *Peru*. Preliminary Objection, Merits, Reparations and Costs. Judgment of November 21, 2019. Series C No. 394. I/A Court H.R., Case of the *Indigenous Communities of the Lhaka Honhat (Our Land) Association* v. *Argentina*. Merits, Reparations and Costs. Judgment of February 6, 2020. Series C No. 400.

29. See Silvia Serrano Guzmán, "El control de convencionalidad en la jurisprudencia de la Corte Interamericana de Derechos Humanos, Comisión Nacional de los Derechos Humanos" (2013). See also Ariel Dulitzky, "An Inter-American Constitutional Court? The Invention of the Conventionality Control by the Inter-American Court of Human Rights," *Texas International Law Journal* 50, 1 (2015), pp. 45, 93.

30. In this decision, the Court asserted that "when a State has ratified an international treaty such as the American Convention, its judges, as part of the State, are also bound by such Convention. This forces them to see that all the effects of the provisions embodied in the Convention are not adversely affected by the enforcement of laws which are contrary to its purpose and that have not had any legal effects since their inception. In other words, the Judiciary must exercise a sort of 'conventionality control' between the domestic legal provisions which are applied to specific cases and the American Convention on Human Rights. To perform this task, the Judiciary has to take into account not only the treaty, but also the interpretation thereof made by the Inter-American Court, which is the ultimate interpreter of the American Convention." See I/A Court H.R., Case of *Almonacid Arellano et al.* v. *Chile*. Preliminary Objections, Merits, Reparations and Costs. Judgment of September 26, 2006. Series C No. 154, para. 124.

31. Rules of Procedure of the Inter-American Court of Human Rights. Approved by the Court at its Forty-Ninth Regular Session held from November 16 to 25, 2000, Art. 23.

32. See, for example, Cecilia Medina Quiroga, "Modificación de los reglamentos de la Corte Interamericana de Derechos Humanos y de la Comisión Interamericana de Derechos Humanos al procedimiento de peticiones individuales ante la Corte," in Universidad de Chile, *Anuario de Derechos Humanos* 7 (2011), p. 120.

33. See, for example, IACtHPR, Rules of Procedure (2010), Art. 35.1.f., which refers to the ability of the Commission to request the appointment of an expert witness only when "the Inter-American public order of human rights is affected in a significant manner." Also, under Art. 52.3 the IACHR can only interrogate expert witnesses proposed by the other parties in the proceedings "if authorized by the Court upon receiving a well-grounded request therefore, when the Inter-American public order of human rights is affected in a significant manner and the statement in question regards a topic included in the statement of an expert witness offered by the Commission."

34. Goldman, "History and Action," p. 877.

35. In 2011 Ecuador proposed the creation of a new human rights forum within UNASUR, the Union of South American Nations. Ministry of Foreign Affairs, Trade, and Integration of Ecuador, "Proposal for the Creation of a South American Human Rights Coordination Body." See Gabriela Kletzel and Camila Barretto Maia, "The Challenge of Complementarity in Latin America's New Institutional Architecture for Human Rights," in *The Inter-American Human Rights System: Changing Times, Ongoing Challenges*, edited by César Rodríguez-Garavito and Nelson Camilo Sánchez León (Due Process of Law Foundation, 2016), pp. 39–40, www.dejusticia.org/en/publication/challenges-to-the-inter-american-system-of-human-rights/.

36. IACHR, "Indigenous Communities of the Xingu River Basin, Pará, Brazil," PM-382/10, (April 1, 2011).

37. See Ana Maria Mondragón, "Corporate Impunity for Human Rights Violations in the Americas: The Inter-American System of Human Rights as an Opportunity for Victims to Achieve Justice," *Harvard International Law Journal* 57 (Spring 2016), https://harvardilj.org/wp-content/uploads/sites/15/Ana_0708.pdf; see also Raisa Cetra and Jefferson Nascimento, "Counting Coins: Funding the Inter-American Human Rights System," in *Changing Times, Ongoing Challenges*, pp. 84–5, and Victoria Amato, "Taking Stock of the Reflection on the Workings of the Inter-American Commission on Human Rights," Due Process of Law Foundation, *Aportes* Magazine 5, 16 (June 2012), p. 5, http://dplf.org/sites/default/files/aportes_16_english_webfinal_0.pdf.

38. Amato, "Taking Stock," p. 8.

39. IACHR, PM 406–11—Emilio Palacio, Carlos Nicolás Pérez Lapentti, Carlos Pérez Barriga, and César Pérez Barriga, Ecuador. See also "UN and IACHR Special Rapporteurs for Freedom of Expression State Deep Concern over Decision to Affirm Judgment against Journalists in Ecuador," IACHR Press Release R20/12, www.oas.org/en/iachr/expression/showarticle.asp?lID=1&artID=884.

40. IACHR, *Report on the Situation of Human Rights in Venezuela*, OEA/Ser.L/V/II.118 doc. 4 rev. 2, December 29, 2003, www.cidh.org/countryrep/venezuela2003eng/intro.htm.

41. Ibid.

42. "El secretario de CIDH incomoda a gobiernos de Ecuador y Venezuela," *El Universo*, April 2, 2012, www.eluniverso.com/2012/04/02/1/1355/secretario-cidh-incomoda-gobiernos-ecuador-venezuela.html/.

43. See "IACHR and Inter-American Court Appreciate General Assembly Decision on Budget Increase," IACHR Press Release 83/12, www.oas.org/en/iachr/media _center/PReleases/2017/083.asp.

44. William F. Schulz and Sushma Raman, *The Coming Good Society: Why New Realities Demand New Rights* (Harvard University Press, 2020), pp. 127–30.

45. IACHR, "Corruption and Human Rights: Inter-American Standards" (2019). OEA/Ser.L/V/II. Doc.236/19, www.oas.org/en/iachr/reports/pdfs/CorruptionHR .pdf.

46. "Pompeo Cuts OAS Funds over Advocacy of Legal Abortion," *Washington Post*, March 26, 2019, www.washingtonpost.com/world/national-security/pompeo-cuts-oas -funds-over-advocacy-of-legal-abortion/2019/03/26/4ea5314d-d7e0-48de-b636 -e552447430b0_story.html?noredirect=on.

47. "Inter-American Human Rights Court Backs Same-Sex Marriage," *BBC News*, January 10, 2018, https://www.bbc.co.uk/news/world-latin-america-42633891.

48. Ana Chacób Mora, "The Evangelical Wave Hits Democracy in Costa Rica," *Open Democracy*, March 20, 2018, https://www.opendemocracy.net/en/democraciaa bierta/is-democracy-in-danger-in-costa-rica-too/

49. See, for example, Daniel Cerqueira, *El Derecho a Un Medio Ambiente Sano en el marco normativo y jurisprudencia del Sistema Interamericano de Derechos Humanos* (Due Process of Law Foundation, 2020), p. 31, www.dplf.org/es/resources/el-derecho -un-medio-ambiente-sano-en-el-marco-normativo-y-jurisprudencia-del-sistema.

TWELVE

Caught between Geopolitics, Democratic Regression, and the "Sovereign Backlash"

The African Human Rights System

SOLOMON DERSSO

In this period of rising populism, nationalism, and various forms of bigotry as well as the assertion of statist policies of sovereignty and national interests, amid intensifying rivalry among global actors, numerous questions arise about the impact of these global developments on the human rights situation in Africa. Indeed, as a region that is often affected by major shifts in the international system, Africa may not be spared from the global tensions and trends affecting the protection of human rights. In examining whether and how these global developments threaten human rights in Africa, three variables merit consideration.

The first relates to how existing trends endogenous to the continent affect the human rights agenda and how the human rights institutions function in the context of these trends. Many of the challenges facing the African human rights system arise from the existence of conditions that cast doubt on its relevance to the lived experiences of most of the continent's population, given the perpetration of human rights violations and abuses by governments and other actors, often with impunity.[1] At a time when this system has become more essential than ever as a platform for the promotion and protection of human rights as a result of declining democratic governance, the reduction of civic space, and the persistence of conflict and terrorism, organizations charged with defining and defending human rights have come under enormous pressure from governments. In particular, states have exerted pressure on the region's premier human rights body, the African Commission on Human and Peoples' Rights (the African Commission or Commission), invoking, among others, African values and sovereignty.

The second variable is the kind of human rights issues that the adverse developments in the global arena give rise to on the African continent. During the forty years since the adoption of the African Charter on Human and Peoples' Rights (the African Charter, or Charter), the founding treaty establishing the African human rights system, changes in the international environment from the Cold War to the so-called global war on terror have had a direct impact on the conduct of states vis-à-vis human rights, in turn profoundly affecting the human rights landscape on the continent.

The third factor is how adverse global developments interact with and affect existing challenges to human rights in Africa. In a context of deepening contestations, perennial institutional challenges, and calls by states for the institutional reform of the African Union (AU), the combination of these adverse global trends and regional developments—some but not all related to global trends—could severely undermine human rights in the continent. The various threats to the African human rights system and consequently to political, civil, economic, and social rights risk becoming more acute in the maw of a changing global system.

The African Human Rights System: A Brief Overview

The African Charter is the founding human rights treaty on which the edifice of the regional system was built.[2] Right from the start, this system was more than a regional manifestation or articulation of international human rights.[3] It was a product of the historical, political, socioeconomic, and cultural experiences of the continent, and it has evolved. This can be gathered not only from the equal legal status that it has accorded to civil and political rights and to economic, social, and cultural rights, but also from the place of honor it has accorded to peoples' collective rights and its enunciation of the duties of individuals.[4]

One of the major achievements of the African Charter at the time of its adoption, and in later developments, was the establishment of a legal regime, as part of the Organization of African Unity (OAU) system (now the African Union), for the promotion and protection of human rights. This is significant in two major ways.

First, in making human rights a matter of continental concern and hence not merely subject to the exclusive jurisdiction of states, it established the first paradigmatic departure in the OAU's conception of the principles of state sovereignty and noninterference.[5] The African Charter not only enunciated the catalog of rights and freedoms by which states parties to the Charter consented to be legally bound, it also established a mechanism for the monitoring and implementation of these rights and freedoms and for holding states accountable.[6]

Second, in embracing human rights and extending their scope and articulation, the Charter ended the debate about whether human rights were "non-African." This is of particular importance as the African Charter opens further avenues for the recognition and articulation of human rights at both the continental and national levels. It inspired the adoption of various human rights and democracy and governance norms within the OAU and its successor, the AU. This also accounts for the huge space given to human rights in the AU's founding treaty, the Constitutive Act.[7] The African Charter and the various other human rights instruments that succeeded it also served as sources of inspiration in the elaboration of national bills of rights and various laws giving effect to specific human rights. The African human rights system also contributed to the recognition of the legitimacy of the work of civil society organizations, human rights defenders, political opposition, and the media, despite the increasing assault to which they have been subjected in recent years.

Apart from establishing the African Commission on Human and Peoples' Rights (ACHPR, the African Commission), the African Charter paved the way for the establishment of other human rights institutions. In 1990, under the African Charter on the Rights and Welfare of the African Child, the African Committee of Experts on the Rights and Welfare of the Child (The Child Rights Committee) was constituted, dedicated to securing the rights of children. The 1998 Protocol to the African Charter on Human and Peoples' Rights established the African Court on Human and Peoples' Rights (ACtHPR) to complement the African Commission. While the latter has a wide mandate covering the monitoring, investigation, promotion, and quasi-judicial adjudication of human rights, the African Court's mandate is exclusively limited to receiving and adjudicating complaints on violations of human rights. These three institutions, supported by national human rights institutions and civil society organizations, make up the human rights bodies of the African human rights system.[8] And together they have become an avenue to hear and respond to human rights violations affecting various sectors of African citizens.[9] Despite initial doubts about whether they could hold governments accountable, first the African Commission and later the other two human rights bodies have become important sites for exposing human rights violations in

African states and supporting the human rights work of civil society organizations and the media.

The Existing Bleak State of Human and Peoples' Rights

Despite the achievements of the African human rights system, particularly at a normative level and even in holding states accountable, there remains a major gulf between the richness of the legal instruments and the practice of states and the lived realities of people on the continent. There is no doubt that even on this score the African human rights system has registered some gains. During the past four decades of its development and implementation, direct colonial rule and apartheid have ended. One-party and military dictatorships have fallen. Despite recent regression (in the practice of states), democracy has gained traction as the only legitimate system of government, and human rights are widely accepted. Yet, the challenges of implementation and noncompliance, as well as institutional problems, continue to pose serious dilemmas. Against this background, the recent global trends toward assaults on human rights amid rising tensions make efforts to promote and protect human and peoples' rights highly fraught.[10]

To understand how these global trends weaken support and provide space for greater violation of those rights, it is necessary first to look at the current political and human rights environment within Africa, which is being shaped by four trends: democratic regression, a spike in the number and intensity of conflicts, an appalling increase in levels of poverty and socioeconomic deprivation, and the increased strain on the human rights system itself.

Democratic Regression

According to an Afrobarometer survey conducted across thirty-four African countries, 71 percent of people now support and demand a democratic system of government.[11] This is consistent with some key trends on the continent including popular support for the work of civil society groups, human rights defenders, and the media. Most importantly, it closely tracks demographic changes centered around the majority of an increasingly literate and politically engaged youth population.

Nevertheless, despite growing public support for democratic governance and human rights, the continent, like other parts of the world, has continued to witness the shrinking of civic space.[12] Governments have been using both legal and extralegal measures in a major assault on freedom of expression, freedom of association and assembly, and freedom of the press. The legal regimes they use include the adoption of laws with requirements that limit access to foreign funds and entail cumbersome registration processes. As the 2018 report by the German Institute for Global and Area Studies pointed out, since the turn of the century, the number of governments in Africa imposing restrictions on the operations of civil society organizations (CSOs) has been on the rise.[13] For example, Angola, Benin, Burundi, Eritrea, Rwanda, Sierra Leone, Somalia, Sudan, Uganda, and Zimbabwe have all adopted policies to restrict foreign funding for domestic civil society groups, while Ethiopia's 2009 law prohibiting CSOs and charities from receiving more than 10 percent of their funding from foreign sources resulted in the closure of the majority of these bodies. A paper by Afrobarometer in 2019 highlighted that, apart from laws, governments also resort to the use of "an ever-expanding array of tools and tactics, including suspension of Internet access, surveillance systems, licensing requirements, prohibitive fees, and even raids, arrests, and government violence."[14] As some of these tactics make clear, in the context of the public's mobilization online to exercise rights and hold officials accountable, the manipulation of digital technology has also become a frontier for authoritarian control.

Another manifestation of the continent's democratic governance deficit is the rise of authoritarianism and the decline of democracy and good governance.[15] As in other parts of the world, democratization in Africa has continued to deteriorate.[16] According to the 2021 Freedom House report, the number of countries in Africa that are "not free" increased from fourteen in 2006–2008 to twenty in 2021, and in that year only seven countries, mostly small island states, were ranked "free," the lowest figure since 1991. The 2020 Mo Ibrahim African Governance Index found that over the past decade, twenty countries, home to 41.9 percent of Africa's population, had experienced declines in indicators that measure security and the rule of law (-0.7) and participation, rights, and inclusion (-1.4), even while achieving progress in human development (+3.0), and foundations for economic opportunity (+4.1).[17]

The prevalence of what political scientists call "constitutional coups" has deepened the regression in the process of democratization.[18] The enthusiastic embrace by thirty-eight African states of constitutional clauses limiting presidential terms during the third wave of democratization in the 1990s has been reversed in recent years, creating a wave of executive consolidation and perpetuation of power through constitutional manipulation. Since the early 2000s, at least sixteen countries removed or weakened constitutional limits on terms of office of presidents in pursuit of prolonging their grip on power indefinitely.[19] Together with the recent spike in military seizure of power, as witnessed in

Chad (2021), Guinea (2021), Mali (2020 and 2021), and Sudan (2019 and 2021), these developments, compounded by the AU's wavering in its long-standing zero policy against coups,[20] have cast a shadow on its ban on unconstitutional changes of government.[21]

Another sign of the slide in democracy in Africa is the decline in popular confidence in elections. According to a poll by Afrobarometer in 2020, "while most Africans believe in elections as the best way to select their leaders, popular support for elections has weakened."[22] With leaders perfecting the art of "winning" elections that they convene for the sole purpose of legitimizing themselves—characteristic of what Fareed Zakaria has called "illiberal democracies" or of Kenneth Roth's "zombie democracies"—many countries are "stuck with ageing leaders or family dynasties" or electoral monarchies or authoritarians.[23] At the same time, elections are increasingly being held in an environment characterized by insecurity, fear, and violence, often deliberately created as a means of winning elections.[24]

The rise of political violence is also further testimony to the waning observance of democratic and human rights principles, a phenomenon to which state violence contributes significantly. According to the Armed Conflict Location and Event Data Project (ACLED), in over one-third of African countries in 2020, state forces were the most active agent engaging in political violence.[25] Just as the so-called global war on terror was instrumentalized and abused to stifle fundamental freedoms and imprison, assault, and torture political dissidents, opposition political leaders and supporters, human rights defenders, and journalists, so the COVID-19 pandemic has also been misused for attacking these sectors of society.[26]

Spike in the Number and Intensity of Conflicts

Mirroring the global spike in the number of conflicts has been an upsurge in African conflicts in recent years.[27] A report by the Peace Research Institute Oslo (PRIO) and Uppsala University showed an increase from twelve conflicts observed within ten countries in 2007, to thirteen countries affected by eighteen civil wars involving the state as one of the parties by 2017.[28] Both figures have risen since then, with twenty-one conflicts in 2018 and even more in 2020, when Africa was the only continent to witness an increase in the number of conflicts.[29] The most dramatic rise relates to nonstate conflicts, mostly reflecting the spread of terrorist actors on the continent.[30] Whereas in 2011 there were twenty-four nonstate conflicts, in 2017 the number had soared to fifty.[31]

It is indicative of the changes in the demographic structure of countries, and the increasing expression of discontent about the abysmal political and socio-economic conditions affecting the majority of Africans, that protests and riots (a total of 5,660 in 2017) have now become the leading conflict events on the continent.[32] While not all these incidents amount to conflicts that pose a threat to international peace and security, in certain instances they are the precursors to and manifestations of such conflicts, as witnessed in Burundi in 2015.[33]

What is of particular significance and concern in the context of human rights is that, as a recent study by the African Commission established, the vast majority of victims of these conflicts and violence are civilians, including children.[34] The tragedies underscore the pervasive lack of regard for human rights and guarantees of international humanitarian law.[35] The African Commission and the African Committee of Experts on the Rights and Welfare of the Child, in a joint statement issued in February 2020, lamented that "Violent conflicts, whose frequency, geographic scope and lethality increased in 2019, have led to the most serious of violations of human and peoples' rights in Africa including mass murder, mutilations, sexual violence particularly against women, and destruction of property and livelihoods, and displacement of millions of peoples in which children are most affected, with indelible marks left on their lives."[36]

Scandalous State of Poverty and Socioeconomic Deprivation

The vast majority of people on the continent lead an existence stripped of the essential conditions for a dignified life. In 2020, the number living in extreme poverty (which according to the World Bank is less than $1.90 per day) jumped to over half a billion. What this means is that some 520 million people lack the income and other resources necessary to meet basic needs.[37] Living in places susceptible to violence and crime and lacking social services and sanitary conditions, they suffer from ill health, lack of social capital, and severe material deprivation.[38]

The pervasiveness of such conditions of poverty and socioeconomic deprivation makes the normative and institutional progress of human rights in Africa hollow for a large percentage of the population. This crisis of legitimacy of the human rights system is not merely a result of the gulf between the promise of the human rights agenda and the lived experiences of the peoples of the continent, but also stems from the failure to make these structural conditions of deprivation priority areas of concern. The persistence of these appalling conditions is, of course, also a consequence of the trinity of burdens weighing on Africa, namely the burden of the democratic governance deficit and failure of governments, the burden of history, and the burden of the deeply skewed power structure of the international economic system.[39]

The COVID-19 pandemic exposed the scandalous magnitude of these conditions and their ramifications. First, and not surprisingly, despite commitments that African states made in 2001 under the Abuja Declaration to allocate 15 percent of their annual budgets to health, the health care systems of most, if not all, countries on the continent were poorly equipped to respond to any health crisis, let alone a pandemic of COVID-19's unprecedented scale. According to a survey undertaken by Reuters, despite some variations, most countries in Africa "have severe shortages of medical personnel, especially critical care nurses and anesthesia providers," and Africa "averages less than one intensive care bed and one ventilator per 100,000 people."[40] Second, many people lacking access to water, sanitation, health care, and decent shelter have been unable to comply with the elementary requirements of regular handwashing and social distancing.[41] Third, in the global structure of power in which 99 percent of Africa's vaccines are imported, the lack of access to ingredients for COVID-19 vaccines and the technology for their generic manufacture on the continent mean that populations are deprived of the most effective route to ending the pandemic and its disastrous consequences.[42]

Although not specific to the COVID-19 crisis, gender-based violence reached epidemic proportions during the pandemic, highlighting the pervasiveness of gender oppression on the continent. The sense of despair engulfing the unemployed and the young has also deepened. It is not surprising that, despite the death of nearly 20,000 migrants between 2014 and 2018,[43] "turning the Mediterranean Sea into a graveyard,"[44] increasing numbers of mostly young people, desperate to find a better life elsewhere, continue to embark on the perilous journey across the Sahara to reach Europe. Others hand themselves over to smugglers in the Horn of Africa and Sinai to be thrown onto dangerous boats crossing the Red Sea to the Gulf countries and Israel.

A Human Rights System under Increasing Strain

Beyond the dire human rights environment in which the African human rights system operates, as highlighted above, the institutions charged with implementing and enforcing the rights and freedoms recognized in this system face a number of institutional and structural challenges. The African Commission, as the premier human rights body, is legally dependent on the African Union Commission (AUC), the administrative and technical arm of the AU. According to Article 41 of the African Charter, the authority to appoint the secretary of the African Commission is vested in the (secretary-general) chairperson of the AUC. The effect of this is that the African Commission does not have control over the recruitment, administrative, and financial management of its Secretariat. Dependent on the AUC's notoriously slow and unpredictable recruitment process, the Commission operates with a chronically understaffed Secretariat.

Additionally, all the members of the Commission operate on a part-time basis. The Commission and other human rights bodies are underfunded by the AU's core budget. The result of this is that all the organizations charged with human rights in the AU have to rely on external support for the implementation of their mandates. This financial dependence, with its supply-heavy pressure, has had the unwanted consequence of eroding the autonomy of these institutions in executing their mandates and in setting their priorities.

At the same time, the staffing, actions, and decisions of the Commission, the Court, and other institutions charged with protecting human rights depend on the political organs of the AU. These include the Permanent Representatives Committee, the Executive Council, and the Assembly of Heads of State and Government, all bodies made up exclusively of member states. The AU's Executive Council, in which the foreign ministers of AU member states are represented, is charged with the election of the members of the human rights bodies and the consideration of their activity reports, thereby politicizing the work of the institution and others like it. Article 59 of the African Charter stipulates that the African Commission must submit its reports to the Assembly. And while the Constitutive Act of the AU stipulates under Article 23 that the Assembly may impose sanctions for noncompliance with AU decisions, the latter has never invoked this authority for the failure of states to implement the legal recommendations and decisions of the human rights bodies, including those of the African Court. This has created a huge gulf between the promise of the actions and decisions of the human rights organs to defend victims and deliver justice, and their translation to concrete outcomes on the ground.

It is not uncommon for states to oppose or even reject these recommendations and decisions. Unlike in the OAU era, during which the Assembly routinely "authorized" the publication of the African Commission's report without any significant discussion or debate, since the early 2000s state representatives on AU political bodies contest and even demand revisions of those recommendations, at times alleging that the human rights bodies have unsavory motives.

The Pressures of Global Trends

The most defining post–Cold War global trends have been the end of the United States' "'unipolar' moment," the rise of emerging powers (most notably China), and the advance of technology.[45] But another has been the resurgence of nationalism and populism accompanying "'the unravelling of the international order."[46] Of particular significance in this respect are the implications of these changes for human rights and the human rights system. There are concerns that in the context of the growing rivalry resulting from the so-called retreat of Western liberalism, as Edward Luce put it, and the rise of China and resurgence of Russia, the rules governing the operation of the international system (including human rights) since World War II have come under increasing pressure.[47]

In the face of the decline of the United States and its European allies, and the declining delivery of the liberal peace agenda, the international system's support for democracy and human rights has weakened as well.[48] In the context of the post–Cold War winds of change that led to the rise of democratization in Africa, the United States and the European Union (EU) have since the early 2000s, in particular, pursued strategies for promoting human rights and democracy.[49] They have employed various instruments oriented to the use of carrots (such as political dialogue, democracy aid, and increased development assistance) rather than sticks (sanctions and other forms of negative conditionality). Their relative decline in shaping global governance has compounded the challenge to the liberal agenda posed by existing questions about the efficacy of the instruments and the normative coherence of democracy and human rights promotion by these global powers. This created the opportunity for African governments such as Uganda that lack commitment to democratization and human rights to sustain forms of collaboration with the United States and the EU focusing mainly on those reform areas that do not affect the power of the incumbent.

China outpaced the United States to become Africa's largest trading partner in 2009. Its investment on the continent also more than doubled, to 40 billion dollars, in the five years from 2011. Beyond the economic sphere, the rivalry also involves competing models of political systems and development. In contrast to Africa's traditional partners, which advocate democracy and a private capitalist-based model of political governance and economic development, China, drawing on the successes of its own "authoritarian capitalism," presents autocratic and technocratic forms of political and economic development models with a heavy state role as a viable option for African countries.[50]

This has increased the tendency of African governments not to go beyond paying lip service to democracy and human rights; they may signal ostensible respect for them to the United States and the EU but only with limited, often cosmetic, policies.

While these trends have evolved over the years, a more challenging aspect of multipolarity for human rights and democracy in Africa is the deepening polarization and rivalry between Western powers and China and Russia. If this rivalry descends into a zero-sum game in which each seeks to achieve dominance of influence in Africa, it could have serious repercussions for human rights and democracy. First, the space for concerned African countries to maneuver shrinks as the rival geopolitical powers struggle to line up allies, increasingly forcing states to take sides. This potential binary choice eliminates the capacity for states and leaders to balance cooperation with the United States and the EU on democracy and human rights with support for infrastructural development cooperation with China.[51]

Second, the growing rivalry could have adverse impacts for human rights and democratization similar to those of the Cold War era. Most notably, it carries the risk of strengthening the existing democratic and human rights challenges by lending support to authoritarian tendencies. As Chester Crocker, a former US diplomat, pointed out and Africa's Cold War experiences attest, great-power competition and a reduced focus on development can lead to "western firms and governments more interested in commercial access and 'getting along' with existing governments than with durable political and economic development."[52]

Third, the most disturbing aspect of great-power contestation is its impact on peace and conflict on the continent. This was particularly evident when the "new Africa strategy" of the United States was launched in December 2018. When unveiling the strategy, John Bolton, then national security adviser to the Trump administration, pointed out, following the logic of the U.S. Defense Strategy, that the greatest threat to U.S. interests came not from poverty or Islamist extremism but from China and Russia.[53] This prompted the *New York Times* to publish an editorial with the caption "Bolton outlines a strategy for Africa that is really about countering China."[54] But under Joe Biden's presidency, there has been no change in the U.S. approach to China and Russia. If anything, the United States seems more determined to contain these two powers and recoup some of its losses on the continent. From a human rights perspective, the fundamental flaw of the condescending framing of this Africa strategy about "countering China" is that it treats Africa as a mere theater of great-power struggle, ignoring the agency of a continent of 1.3 billion people.

Making this picture even more complicated, great-power rivalry over Africa is aggravating a "new scramble,"[55] with countries of varying levels of economic and security power, including from Asia and the Middle East, actively seeking to expand their political and security influence across the continent.[56] This does not bode well for stability and human rights. As one example, the rivalry among the Gulf countries for influence in the Horn of Africa has given Eritrea a unique opportunity to break out of its isolation, providing a much-needed breathing space and external validation to President Isaias Afwerki's authoritarian rule.[57]

One of the implications of this deepening rivalry in Africa will be the risk of internationalizing conflicts, with various powers giving support to opposing parties. A scenario that exemplifies this point has emerged in Somalia. While the federal government has sided with Qatar and Turkey, various states of the country's federation have aligned themselves with the United Arab Emirates (UAE). This has exacerbated existing tensions between the federal government and regional governments, further undermining the precarious security situation in the country.[58] Moreover the current rivalry between Russia and France in the Central African Republic is stoking political instability and aggravating conflict and insecurity there.

If such rivalry were to involve the major powers as happened in Syria, it would not only paralyze the prospect of peaceful resolution, conflicts would also degenerate further into theaters of war crimes and crimes against humanity. This has been the case in the large-scale displacement and refugee flows in Syria and to a lesser extent Yemen. At the same time this renewed big-power competition has hamstrung the UN Security Council, preventing it from taking collective action against insecurity and the attendant violations of human rights and humanitarian law in conflict situations, including those in Africa.[59]

Apart from the shift in global power relations and the adverse ramifications of the rise of competition between the major powers, many parts of the world have seen a resurgence in nationalism and populism. This period has now become characterized as "the sovereign backlash."[60] From Brexit to Trump, "populist sovereignism" has challenged the role of the human rights system and international human rights enforcement mechanisms. Under the Trump administration, the United States withdrew from the UN Human Rights Council. It also denied U.S. entry to the Prosecutor of the International Criminal Court (ICC), targeting particularly African members of the Office of the Prosecutor. In the United Kingdom, it was in the name of "taking back control" or sovereignty that the "leave" camp won in the referendum on continued EU membership. Meanwhile, in Europe, major gains were made by right-wing populist parties in national politics.[61] These internal political developments have shifted the EU's priority in its partnership with Africa to the so-called migration crisis. Apart from the lack of mutuality and congruence between the EU and Africa on the nature of the migration problem, the policy approaches that the EU has sought to pursue have not only led to breaches of human rights, international humanitarian laws, and refugee laws, but also exposed the hypocrisy in the EU's advocacy for human rights in Africa.[62]

Not surprisingly, Africa did not escape the global spread of nationalism and populism. This contagion effect has led to the rise of populist authoritarianism in the continent, evidenced by the tactics of leaders in Burundi, Tanzania, Uganda, Zambia, Zimbabwe, and potentially Tunisia. A second, related consequence has been the enthusiastic reception by strong leaders in Africa, China, and Russia of President Donald Trump's dictum that "it is the right of all nations to put their own interest first."[63]

The defense of sovereignty has also been used in Ethiopia's pushback, supported by Russia and China, against the call of the EU, the United Kingdom, and the United States for an end to the conflict in Tigray. When the UN humanitarian chief announced that "there is famine now in Tigray," Western countries, the UN, and other humanitarian agencies called for a humanitarian ceasefire.[64] On the same day, China's foreign minister, in a telephone conversation with his Ethiopian counterpart, stated that "China opposes foreign interference in Ethiopia's internal affairs." He added, echoing Ethiopia's demand for Western countries to respect its sovereignty by insisting that the situation in Tigray was a domestic matter: "Ethiopia's domestic issues should be resolved primarily through the efforts of the Ethiopian government."[65] Similarly, the Russian ambassador to Ethiopia said that "Russia has repeatedly stated its position that this [situation in Tigray] is an exclusively internal affair of Ethiopia."[66]

In the elections in Côte d'Ivoire, Guinea, Tanzania, and Uganda, the incumbent leaders used various instruments to orchestrate their retention of power. In all four elections, state security forces unleashed violence on opposition leaders and their protesting supporters. Expressions of concern by the United States and the EU, for instance, with respect to the election-related violence in Uganda, did not induce any change of behavior. In Somalia, in a display of his authoritarianism, President Abdulahi Formajo ignored the political agreement on the convening of national elections that was reached among rival political forces on September 27, 2020. He used the lower house of Parliament to announce the extension of his term for two years, bringing the country to the brink of major violence.[67]

Technology has also allowed autocrats to consolidate their power and trample on various rights, leaving human rights norms and bodies struggling to keep up. The adverse impact of this can be seen in at least two ways. First, surveillance technology and internet disruptions or suspension of specific platforms, as happened in the Ugandan elections early in 2021, have been used to target dissidents and stifle civic space. Second, governments have also manipulated technology to influence public opinion, especially around elections. Illustrating this trend, on June 16, 2021, Facebook announced that it had removed sixty-five Facebook accounts, fifty-two pages, twenty-seven groups, and thirty-two accounts on Instagram for violating its policy against coordinated inauthentic behavior.[68] Facebook's investigation linked the coordinated operation to individuals associated with the Ethiopian government's Information Network Security Agency.

Another, broader impact of new technology on human rights relates to the theft of personal information and its sharing by big tech companies that harvest such data to shape the market and people's political preferences. As Kofi Yeboah pointed out, the data—conversations, thoughts, decisions, consumption patterns, fears, concerns, and emotions—thus collected "can be used to inundate citizens with targeted misinformation about political opponents. For example, one month prior to Kenya's election, Kenyans woke up to an online video titled Raila 2020 which communicated that Kenya would become extremely violent, food would be scarce, there would be water shortages and so on if Raila Odinga was allowed to be president."[69]

There is thus an increasingly urgent need to address the various human rights issues arising from big tech through measures such as robust data protection laws and effective regulation of the industry, in line with international human rights law.

The African Human Rights System Faces the "Sovereign Backlash"

Under the African Charter, the African Commission on Human and Peoples' Rights reports to the AU Assembly. While the power of the Assembly to "consider" African Commission reports was delegated to the Executive Council in 2003, in more recent years the Commission's reports are in practice considered by the Permanent Representatives Committee (PRC), a body made up of the permanent representatives of all AU member states.[70] The growing interest of AU member states, particularly since early 2000s, in closely "considering" the report by debating its contents has been a welcome development. Unfortunately, it has not been without its downsides. As Frans Viljoen pointed out, this increased engagement was accompanied by "increasing attempts at bedeviling and thwarting scrutiny."[71] The result has been encroachment on the power of the Commission.

When the Executive Council was considering the report of the African Commission in June 2004, Zimbabwe's foreign minister objected to its publication on the grounds that his country had not had an opportunity to respond to the Commission's fact-finding report on it. Anticipating future frictions, the Executive Council withheld authorization for the publication of the Commission's entire report. Considering that the African Charter only empowers the AU Assembly to "consider'" the report, the withholding of authorization to publish the report lacked firm legal basis and undermined the mandate of the Commission.

Over the years, the session to consider the African Commission's report has become a platform for member states to contest the legitimacy of unfavorable Commission pronouncements on countries' human rights situations. The report often triggers a reaction in the overwhelming majority of AU members. For example, representatives of over thirty member states reacted to the report submitted during the February 2021 AU Summit. On various occasions, contestation over the report has been punctuated by acrimony and heated pushback, with member states insisting that the Commission review its report to water down unfavorable references or even erase concerns completely.

In invoking sovereignty and in the resultant pushback against the AU's progressive norms and the African human rights system, member states have been employing the language of "African values." Such was the case when several member states sought a reversal of the Commission's decision to grant observer status to the Coalition of African Lesbians (CAL), a South African gay advocacy civil society organization. In June 2015 this culminated in a decision by the AU's Executive Council on the Activity Report of the Commission to withdraw the observer status it had granted to CAL.[72] In justifying its decision, the Executive Council, mirroring the reasoning of cultural conservativism often used by populists, urged "the ACHPR to take into account the fundamental African values, identity and good traditions," and expressed its opposition to the African Commission's granting of observer status to nongovernmental organizations (NGOs) "who attempt to impose values contrary to the African values." This also came at a time of increased campaigning in parts of Africa by conservative religious groups, notably U.S. evangelical movements (see also Melani McAlister's chapter 7).[73]

This has understandably given rise to legitimate concerns that, were this decision to be implemented, then the Executive Council might have other African Commission decisions withdrawn or reversed. CAL and the Centre for Human Rights of the University of Pretoria filed a joint request for an advisory opinion before the African Court in November 2015, requesting it to provide an interpretation of the scope of the supervisory powers of the political organs of the AU vis-à-vis the African Commission.

By the time the African Court declined the request on procedural grounds, the relationship between the African Commission and some member states was at a breaking point.[74] When the African Commission presented its forty-third Activity Report at the January 2018 Summit, the issue of CAL became the flashpoint for member states seeking to severely curtail the Commission's independence. The report noted that the decision to grant CAL observer status was "properly taken" and that it was the duty of the Commission to protect the rights in the African Charter "without any discrimination because of status or other circumstances." Accusing the Commission of refusing to implement a clear decision of the Executive Council, several member states floated a proposal to establish an open-ended committee of the PRC that would be charged with getting the issue of CAL conclusively finalized and defining criteria for granting observer status to NGOs, as well as addressing other issues including a revision of the Commission's working methods, the criteria for the appointment of its members, development of a code of conduct for the Commission and its members, and the need to adopt appropriate measures to avoid third-party interference in its work.

Initially, with the issue of CAL having been used to stir homophobic sentiments, the proposal received the support of a number of AU member states. It was accordingly captured as one of the proposals in the PRC's draft report on its consideration of the African Commission's report. However, by the time the PRC's report was considered at the AU Executive Council level, successful diplomatic work by the delegation of the African Commission meant that all but one of the states that had supported the proposal at the PRC level changed their position on the establishment of the ad hoc open-ended group. Instead, the Executive Council decided that the African Commission and the PRC should convene a joint retreat on the issues affecting the relationship between the Commission and AU member states. This was held from June 4 to 6, 2018, in Nairobi, Kenya.

The African Commission avoided the most intrusive measures for which some AU member states had initially advocated.[75] However, the Executive

Council persisted in demanding that the Commission implement its decision on the withdrawal of CAL's observer status. Against the background of worrying developments on the continent—notably the decision of the Southern Africa Development Community (SADC) to permanently disband the SADC Tribunal, following a number of unfavorable decisions the subregional court had adopted against Zimbabwe—the African Commission finally relented and caved in to this request.[76] At its twenty-fourth extraordinary session held from July 30 to August 8, 2018, the Commission adopted a decision withdrawing CAL's observer status.

Although this regrettable incident led to widespread legitimate condemnation of the African Commission by civil society organizations, it has not stopped the Commission from calling for the protection of the rights of Lesbian, Gay, Bisexual, Transgender, Intersex, Queer (LGBTIQ) persons, insisting that the rights in the African Charter belong to all human beings irrespective of their status, and that violating the rights of LGBTIQ persons on account of their status would be contrary to the Charter's standards.

This type of backlash is not unique to the African Commission. The African Court has faced a similar challenge. In response to various unfavorable decisions it took, four out of the ten states parties to the Court Protocol that made up the Article 34(6) declaration have withdrawn their declaration, thereby denying their citizens direct access to the Court. In its 2020 report on the state of the African human rights institutions, Amnesty International characterized this development as "threatening to push the [Court] towards the edge of an existential crisis."[77] Out of the thirty states that ratified the Court Protocol, only Benin, Burkina Faso, Côte d'Ivoire, Gambia, Ghana, Malawi, Mali, Rwanda, Tanzania, and Tunisia have made the declaration under Article 34(6) accepting the Court's competence to receive cases directly from individuals and NGOs. Direct access previously accounted for nearly all the cases that the Court had received from individuals and NGOs.[78]

The Court had started to face a backlash in 2016. Following its decision with respect to *Ingabire Victoire Umuhoza* v. *Republic of Rwanda*, Rwanda withdrew its Article 34(6) declaration, arguing that it "was being exploited and used contrary to the intention behind its making" by providing a platform for "convicted genocide fugitives." Rwanda also raised the issue of the human rights bodies attempting to operate like appellate courts, hence exceeding their authority. In 2019, Tanzania, the host of the Court, followed suit under the authoritarian drift of the administration of President John Magufuli. While the vast majority of cases with the African Court are from Tanzania, its withdrawal seems to have been inspired as much by the issue of the Court seemingly operating as an appellate court reviewing the decision of national courts as by the unfavorability of its decisions of the state.

In April 2020, two other countries, Benin and Côte d'Ivoire, announced the withdrawal of their Article 34(6) declarations. Both used the sovereignty justification for their decision. Benin accused the Court of "interfer[ence] in issues related to state sovereignty and issues that do not fall within its jurisdiction." Similarly, Côte d'Ivoire argued the Court's "serious and intolerable" actions not only undermine its sovereignty but are also "likely to cause a serious disturbance of the internal legal order of State" and to "undermine the foundations of the rule of law by establishing genuine legal uncertainty."

Conclusion

The African human rights system still plays a key role in supporting the efforts of national institutions and civil society organizations to create the conditions for the enjoyment of human and peoples' rights and to hold perpetrators of human rights violations accountable. By developing new and powerful bodies of precedence and jurisprudence, as well as through advocacy and promotion, and the documentation and condemnation of incidents of human rights violations, the system has proven wrong those who thought that it was too weak to hold states accountable. Despite serious challenges to the protection of human rights, it has contributed to the widespread and increasing acceptance of human and peoples' rights on the continent.

In recent years, this system has sought to address existing and emerging human rights challenges in the face of the deteriorating political and security situation across the continent and the added pressure of global trends. The regression of democratization has weakened the support of states and the political and institutional context for the effective promotion and protection of human rights. These conditions underscore the necessity for the African human rights institutions to expose and condemn violations, including attacks against civil society, opposition groups, and the media. They should also deepen their engagement and close working relationship with national human rights commissions and other constitutional bodies such as ombudspersons, electoral commissions, and police oversight bodies. As recent experiences of the role of the judiciary in Kenya, Malawi, South Africa, and Zimbabwe have shown, the African human rights system can also contribute to arresting democratic backsliding in Africa by supporting and leveraging the role of the judiciary.[79]

There is also a need to leverage and systematically support the role of civil society organizations and the Network of African National Human Rights Institutions. Apart from supporting one another and enhancing their coordination within the AU framework, including through the African Governance Architecture, the African human rights institutions could safeguard the space for their effective operation by working closely with states willing and able to lend diplomatic support for their work. Within the context of the AU, they should adopt a coordinated approach to engagement in the AU institutional reform process to ensure that their independence and autonomy are safeguarded and their capacity and working arrangements are strengthened. They should also use and expand existing mechanisms for dialogue with AU policy bodies and member states, which are critical channels for addressing the situation in which recent reversals have been witnessed.

Despite the challenge of exerting the level of influence required to change the conditions that result in increased conflict and insecurity, the African human rights institutions should use all available avenues to ensure that human rights violations in conflict situations are addressed. They can do this by supporting, participating in, and initiating the deployment of human rights monitors and fact-finding missions and commissions of inquiry to investigate human rights violations in conflict situations. The African Commission's experience in undertaking a human rights investigation in Burundi in 2015, and its recent establishment of a Commission of Inquiry on the Situation in Tigray, Ethiopia, serve as useful precedents to learn how best to initiate and deploy such mechanisms. At the institutional level, states and activists need to build on the consultative meeting between the African Commission and the AU Peace and Security Council (PSC) and that between the Child Rights Committee and the PSC. As highlighted in the African Commission's study, this should in particular lead to a more systematic consideration of the human rights dimension of conflicts in the PSC's deliberations and policy decisions on each conflict situation with which it engages.[80]

Generally, it is critical that the African human rights institutions elevate their game in the promotion and protection of human and peoples' rights by ensuring that their actions always have a solid technical and legal basis and resonate with the needs of the public; this will help to limit the impact of their exposure to attacks that could severely erode their role. Additionally, apart from enhancing complementarity among themselves and with international bodies, including through joint actions, African human rights institutions should work to raise their public profile and enhance their support base among the African public. Equally important are the quality and intensity of their outreach to state actors, and the close working relationships that they maintain with independent national human rights institutions. In terms of the contemporary global trends challenging human rights, as I have pointed out elsewhere, "There is no other time than today for the regional and global multilateral platforms to elevate their role and importantly forge ever stronger partnership in upholding the ideals of human and peoples' rights."[81]

The public legitimacy of the human rights system also depends on the extent to which it addresses the challenges of crippling poverty and inequality affecting the majority of the population suffering from increasingly systematic socioeconomic deprivation. There is a need to expand the approach to human rights work beyond court litigation and reactive expressions of outrage. Equally important is prioritizing the focus on the promotion and fulfillment of socioeconomic rights. As Mark Malloch-Brown aptly observes, governments, multilateral organizations, and civil society need "to address the challenges people actually face, looking beyond narrow political rights to address the deeper causes of economic and social exclusion."[82] This will be the key factor determining whether people's faith in human rights and the international and regional institutions built to defend them will deepen or suffer further erosion in the years to come.

Notes

1. The mainstream human rights discourse and practice reduce the threats to human rights largely to the level of the state, thereby ignoring or paying little attention to other serious conditions of unfreedom. See Solomon Dersso, Speech at the Dialogue between Regional Human Rights Protection Commissions in the Context of the Pandemic Hosted by the Inter-American Commission of Human Rights, August 12, 2020, www.achpr.org/public/Document/file/English/Statement%20at%20the%20dialogue%20between%20regional%20human%20rights%20systems%20.pdf; Mark Malloch-Brown, "The Fight for Open Societies Begins Again," Project Syndicate, July 7, 2021, www.project-syndicate.org/commentary/renewing-the-fight-for-democracy-human-rights-open-societies-by-mark-malloch-brown-2021-07.

2. The African Charter was adopted at the Eighteenth Assembly of Heads of State and Government of the Organization of African Unity (OAU) at Nairobi in July 1981, and entered into force on October 21, 1986, ILM 21 (1982) 58.

3. It is worth noting that the African Charter reiterates the OAU Charter's recognition of the UN Charter and the Universal Declaration of Human Rights. Importantly, it affirms in its Preamble "that fundamental human rights stem from the attributes of human beings, which justifies their international protection."

4. On social and cultural rights, see ACHPR Communication 155/96, "The Social Economic Rights Action Centre and the Centre for Social and Economic Rights

v. Nigeria." On collective rights, see ACHPR, "State Reporting Guidelines and Principles on Articles 21 and 24 of the African Charter" (2018); Solomon A. Dersso, "The Jurisprudence of the African Commission on Human and Peoples' Rights with Respect to Peoples' Rights," *African Human Rights Law Journal* 6, 2 (2006), https://hdl .handle.net/10520/EJC52059; Makau Mutua, "The Banjul Charter and the African Cultural Fingerprint: An Evaluation of the Concept of Duties," *Virginia Journal of International Law* 35 (1995), p. 339.

5. See African Commission on Human and Peoples' Rights and the Centre for Human Rights, *Celebrating the African Charter at 30: A Guide to the African Human Rights System* (Pretoria University Law Press, 2011), p. 7. Subsequently, with the adoption of the Constitutive Act of the African Union, this approach was encapsulated in Article 4(h) of the Constitutive Act mandating the AU's intervention in its member states in cases of "grave circumstances, namely genocide, war crimes and crimes against humanity." For more, see "The Role of the African Human Rights System in the Operationalization of Article 4(h) of the AU Constitutive Act," in *Africa and the Responsibility to Protect*, edited by Dan Kuwali and Frans Viljoen (Oxford, U.K., and New York: Routledge, 2014).

6. For a more recent review of the role of the African Commission, see Manisuli Ssenyonjo, "Responding to Human Rights Violations in Africa: Assessing the Role of the African Commission and the African Court on Human and Peoples' Rights (1987–2018)," *International Human Rights Law Review* 7, 1 (2018), https://doi .org/10.1163/22131035-00701003.

7. See Konstantinos D. Magliveras and Gino J. Naldi, "The African Union: A New Dawn for Africa?," *International and Comparative Law Quarterly* 51, 2 (2002), https:// www.jstor.org/stable/3663236; Abadir M. Ibrahim, "Evaluating a Decade of the African Union's Protection of Human Rights and Democracy: A Post-Tahrir Assessment," *African Human Rights Law Journal* 12, 1 (2012), www.scielo.org.za/scielo.php ?pid=S1996-20962012000100003&script=sci_abstract.

8. See Amnesty International, "The State of the African Regional Human Rights Bodies and Mechanisms 2019–2020," October 21, 2020, www.amnesty.org/en /documents/afr01/3089/2020/en/. On the role of national human rights commissions and NGOs, see Nobuntu Mbelle, "The Role of Non-Governmental Organizations and National Human Rights Institutions at the African Commission," in *The African Charter on Human and Peoples' Rights: The System in Practice, 1986–2006*, edited by Malcom Evans and Rachel Murray (Cambridge University Press, 2008), p. 289.

9. See, in general, Ssenyonjo, "Responding to Human Rights Violations in Africa."

10. "Basic Freedoms under Assault, Secretary-General Tells Human Rights Council, Launching Call to Revive Respect for Dignity, Equality amid Rising Tensions," UN Press Release SG/SM/19985, February 24, 2020, www.un.org/press/en/2020 /sgsm19985.doc.htm.

11. Robert Mattes, "Democracy in Africa: Demand, Supply and the Disaffected Democrat," *Afrobarometer Policy Paper* 54 (2019), https://afrobarometer.org/publica tions/pp54-democracy-africa-demand-supply-and-dissatisfied-democrat.

12. David Kode, "Conflict Trends 18/01: Civic Space Restrictions in Africa," AC-CORD, May 31, 2018, www.accord.org.za/conflict-trends/civic-space-restrictions-in-africa/; for an article on how this is happening in the rest of the world, see Jean Bossuyt and Martin Ronceray, "Claiming Back Civic Space: Towards Approaches Fit for the 2020s," European Centre for Development Policy Management, May 18, 2020, https://ecdpm.org/publications/claiming-back-civic-space-towards-approaches-fit-for-2020s/.

13. Hannah Smidt, "Shrinking the Civic in Africa: When Governments Crackdown on Civil Society," German Institute for Global and Area Studies, *GIGA Focus Afrika* 4 (November 2018), www.giga-hamburg.de/en/publications/11568057-shrinking-civic-space-africa-when-governments-crack-down-civil-society/.

14. Carolyn Logan and Peter Penar, "Are Africans' Freedoms Slipping Away?," *Afrobarometer Policy Paper* 55 (2019), p. 23, https://afrobarometer.org/publications/pp55-are-africans-freedoms-slipping-away.

15. Chester A. Crocker, "African Governance: Challenges and Their Implications," *Governance in an Emerging New World Order* 119 (January 2019), www.hoover.org/research/african-governance-challenges-and-their-implications.

16. Freedom House, "Freedom in the World, 2019: Democracy in Retreat," https://freedomhouse.org/report/freedom-world/2019/democracy-retreat.

17. Ibrahim Index of African Governance, Mo Ibrahim Foundation, November 25, 2020, https://mo.ibrahim.foundation/news/2020/2020-ibrahim-index-african-governance-key-findings.

18. See André Mbata B. Mangu, "South Africa's Contribution to Constitutionalism, Rule of Law and Democracy," in *Regional Integration in Africa: What Role for South Africa?*, edited by André Mbata B. Mangu (Koninklijke Brill NV, Leiden, the Netherlands, and CODESRIA, Dakar, Senegal 2020), pp. 15–52.

19. Joseph Siegle and Candace Cook, "Circumvention of Term Limits Weakens Governance in Africa," Africa Centre for Strategic Studies, September 14, 2020, https://africacenter.org/spotlight/circumvention-of-term-limits-weakens-governance-in-africa/.

20. The AU Peace and Security Council argued that Chad's security situation required special treatment when it did not sanction the unconstitutional seizure of power by the military. This position is clearly contrary to the terms of the AU norm banning unconstitutional military seizure of power. See Amani Africa, "Consideration of the Factfinding Mission on Chad," May 10, 2021, https://amaniafrica-et.org/consideration-of-the-fact-finding-mission-on-chad/.

21. See Solomon Ayele Dersso, "Defending Constitutional Rule as a Peacemaking Enterprise: The Case of the AU's Ban of Unconstitutional Changes of Government," *International Peacekeeping* 24, 4 (2017), https://doi.org/10.1080/13533312.2017.1345314.

22. Fredline M'Cormack-Hale and Mavis Zupork Dome, "Support for Elections Weakens among Africans, Many See Them as Ineffective in Holding Leaders Accountable," *Afrobarometer Dispatch* 425 (February 9, 2021), https://afrobarometer.org

/sites/default/files/publications/Dispatches/ad425-support_for_elections_weakens_in_africa-afrobarometer_dispatch-7feb21.pdf.

23. See Fareed Zakaria, "The Rise of Illiberal Democracy," *Foreign Affairs* 76, 6 (Nov.–Dec. 1997), pp. 22–43, https://www.jstor.org/stable/20048274; Kenneth Roth, "The Age of Zombie Democracies: Why Autocrats Are Abandoning Even the Pretense of Democratic Rituals," *Foreign Affairs*, July 28, 2021, https://www.foreignaffairs.com/articles/americas/2021-07-28/age-zombie-democracies; Tonny Onyulo, "How These African Leaders Subvert Democracy to Cling to Power for Life," *USA Today*, October 23, 2017, www.usatoday.com/story/news/world/2017/10/23/haging-african-leaders-cling-power-through-corruption-constitutional-changes-and-fraudulent-election/771984001/.

24. Sarah Jenkins, "The Politics of Fear and the Securitization of African Elections," *Democratization* 27, 5 (2020), www.tandfonline.com/doi/abs/10.1080/13510347.2020.1742112.

25. Clionadh Raleigh and Roudabeh Kishi, "Africa: The Only Continent Where Political Violence Increased in 2020," *Mail and Guardian*, February 1, 2021, https://mg.co.za/africa/2021-02-01-africa-the-only-continent-where-political-violence-increased-in-2020/.

26. Solomon Ayele Dersso, "We Need an Outpouring of Outrage about Africans Being Killed by Security Forces," *Mail and Guardian*, June 10, 2020, https://mg.co.za/africa/2020-06-10-we-need-an-outpouring-of-outrage-about-africans-killed-by-security-forces/.

27. The Armed Conflict Location and Event Data Project (ACLED), "Ten Conflicts to Worry about in 2020," January 2020, www.acleddata.com/wp-content/uploads/2020/01/ACLED_TenConflicts2020_Final.pdf.

28. Ingrid Vik Bakken and Siri Aas Rustad, "Conflict Trends in Africa, 1989–2017," *Conflict Trends* 6 (Oslo: PRIO, 2018).

29. Raleigh and Kishi, "Africa: The Only Continent."

30. Solomon Ayele Dersso, "African Peace and Conflict Diplomacy in Uncertain Times," in *Diplomacy and the Future of World Order*, edited by Chester A. Crocker, Fen Osler Hampson, and Pamela Aall (Georgetown University Press, 2021), p. 124.

31. Crocker, "African Governance."

32. Olawale Ismail, *Reforming for Peace: The State of Peace and Security in Africa 2018*, Tana Forum, April 17, 2018, p. 8.

33. It was disputes over the announcement on the third-term candidacy of the incumbent president of the country that triggered the political crisis in April 2015, which degenerated into a dangerous violent confrontation. For details, see ACHPR, *Report of the Delegation of the African Commission on Human and Peoples' Rights on its Fact-Finding Mission to Burundi, 7–13 December 2015* (2016), https://www.achpr.org/news/viewdetail?id=198.

34. ACHPR, *Addressing Human Rights Issues in Conflict Situations: Towards a More Systematic and Effective Role for the African Commission on Human and Peoples' Rights*, 2019, www.achpr.org/public/Document/file/English/ACHPR%20Conflict%20Study

_ENG.pdf, https://www.achpr.org/public/Document/file/English/ACHPR%20Con
flict%20Study_ENG.pdf.

35. The nature of the violence targeting civilians in Mozambique's Cabo Delgado
Province and in Ethiopia's Tigray Region manifested "gratuitous degradation [that]
was a marked feature in many of the incidents of brutality" in the South Sudan civil
war during 2013–2015, as documented in the AU Commission of Inquiry on South
Sudan. See AU, "A Separate Opinion" by Mahmood Mamdani, a member of the AU
Commission of Inquiry on South Sudan, October 20, 2014, p. 9, www.peaceau.org
/uploads/auciss.separate.opinion.pdf.

36. ACHPR and ACERWC, Press Statement on the Occasion of the Thirty-Third
Assembly of the Heads of State and Government of the African Union, www.acerwc
.africa/press-statement-on-the-occasion-of-the-33rd-assembly-of-the-african-union/.

37. On the multidimensionality of poverty going beyond income, see generally,
Blessing Gweshengwe and Noor Hasharina Hassan, "Defining the Characteristics of
Poverty and Their Implications for Poverty Analysis," *Cogent Social Sciences* 6, 1 (2020),
www.tandfonline.com/doi/full/10.1080/23311886.2020.1768669.

38. Ibid.

39. See Solomon Ayele Dersso, "Taking Stock of the African Charter on Human
and Peoples' Rights Forty Years On," *The Elephant*, July 23, 2021, www.theelephant
.info/long-reads/2021/07/23/taking-stock-of-the-african-charter-on-human-and
-peoples-rights-forty-years-on/.

40. Katharine Houreld, Davice Lewis, Ryan McNeill, and Samuel Granados,
"Virus Exposes Gaping Holes in Africa's Health Systems," Reuters, May 7, 2020,
https://graphics.reuters.com/HEALTH-CORONAVIRUS/AFRICA/yzdpxoqbdvx/.

41. In a remark that exposes the scandalous lack of access to essential services such
as water, communities in a province in South Africa expressed their "thanks to the
virus" when the government started to provide water as part of the effort to counter the
pandemic. See Mandla Khoza, "'We Thank Virus for the Water' Say Grateful Mpuma-
langa Community," *Sowetan Live*, April 7, 2020, www.sowetanlive.co.za/news/south
-africa/2020-04-07-we-thank-virus-for-the-water-say-grateful-mpumalanga-community/.

42. Solomon Ayele Dersso, "African Union Wants Vaccine Patent Waiver," *Mail
and Guardian*, February 10, 2021, https://mg.co.za/africa/2021-02-10-african-union-
wants-vaccine-patent-waiver/; Dersso, "Taking Stock of the African Charter on
Human and Peoples' Rights Forty Years On."

43. "Over 20,000 Migrant Deaths in Mediterranean since 2014—IOM," Info-
Migrants, March 9, 2020, www.infomigrants.net/en/post/23295/over-20-000-migrant
-deaths-in-mediterranean-since-2014-iom.

44. "Europe Has Turned Mediterranean into Migrant Graveyard, NGO President
Claims," InfoMigrants, February 21, 2020, www.infomigrants.net/en/post/22931
/europe-has-turned-mediterranean-into-migrant-graveyard-ngo-president-claims.

45. Jean-Marie Guéhenno, "International Organizations–Down but Not Out," in
Diplomacy and the Future of World Order, edited by Crocker, Hampson, and Aall,
pp. 31, 34.

46. Robert Malley, "Ten Crises to Watch in 2019," *Foreign Policy*, December 28, 2018, https://foreignpolicy.com/2018/12/28/10-conflicts-to-watch-in-2019-yemen-syria-afghanistan-south-sudan-venezuela-ukraine-nigeria-cameroon-iran-israel-saudi-arabia-united-states-china-kurds-ypg/.

47. See Edward Luce, *The Retreat of Western Liberalism* (New York: Atlantic Monthly Press, 2017); Dersso, "African Peace and Conflict Diplomacy," p. 124.

48. Joanne Wallis, "Is There Still a Place for Liberal Peacebuilding?," in *Hybridity on the Ground in Peacebuilding and Development: Critical Conversations*, edited by Joanne Wallis et al. (Australian National University Press, 2018), p. 83.

49. Christine Hackenesch, "Not as Bad as It Seems: EU and US Democracy Promotion Faces China in Africa," *Democratization* 22, 3 (March 2015), p. 421, https://doi.org/10.1080/13510347.2014.1002476.

50. Ibid.

51. Ethiopia and Rwanda have sought to do this since the mid-2000s. See Christine Hackenesch, *The EU and China in African Authoritarian Regimes: Domestic Politics and Governance Reforms* (London: Palgrave Macmillan, 2018), Intro. and ch. 3 and 4.

52. Crocker, "African Governance."

53. Mark Landler and Edward Wong, "Bolton Outlines a Strategy for Africa That's Really about Countering China," *New York Times,* December 13, 2018, www.nytimes.com/2018/12/13/us/politics/john-bolton-africa-china.html.

54. Ibid.

55. Solomon Ayele Dersso, "Africa: From Scramble to Theatre of Rivalry for Global Superpowers," *Addis Fortune*, February 9, 2019, https://addisfortune.news/africa-from-scramble-to-theatre-of-rivalry-for-global-superpowers/.

56. Alex Vines, "Continental Drifts towards Africa," *Mail and Guardian*, January 4, 2019, https://mg.co.za/article/2019-01-04-00-continental-drifts-towards-africa/.

57. Harry Verhoeven, "Amid Red Sea Rivalries, Eritrea Plays for Independence," United States Institute of Peace, March 11, 2020, www.usip.org/publications/2020/03/amid-red-sea-rivalries-eritrea-plays-independence.

58. In a report that he submitted to the Peace and Security Council of the AU, the AU Commission chairperson noted in March 2018 that federal member states had started security initiatives (supported by the UAE) that were at variance with the Somalia Transitional Plan. Amani Africa, "Briefing on the Horn of Africa," *Insights on the Peace and Security Council,* November 21, 2018, http://amaniafrica-et.org/images/Reports/BriefingonHoA.pdf.

59. Richard Gowan, "A Decade after Failing to Stop Massacres in Sri Lanka, What Has the UN Learned?," *World Politics Review,* March 19, 2019, www.worldpoliticsreview.com/articles/27664/a-decade-after-failing-to-stop-massacres-in-sri-lanka-what-has-the-u-n-learned.

60. Chester A. Crocker, Fen Osler Hampson, and Pamela Aall, "A Challenging Time for Peace and Conflict Diplomacy," in *Diplomacy and the Future of World Order*, edited by Crocker, Hampson, and Aall, pp. 3, 8.

61. See Stephan de Spiegeleire, Clarissa Skinner, and Tim Sweijs, *The Rise of Populist Sovereignism*, The Hague Centre for Strategic Studies, 2017, https://hcss.nl/wp-content/uploads/2017/09/The-rise-of-Popular-Sovereignism-what-it-is-where-it-comes-from-and-what-it-means-for-international-security-and-defense.pdf.

62. See Eric Reidy, "The Legal Battle to Hold the EU to Account for Libya Migrant Abuses," *The New Humanitarian*, August 10, 2020, www.thenewhumanitarian.org/analysis/2020/08/10/Libya-migrant-abuses-EU-legal-battle; Joe Penney, "Europe's Outrage over the African Migrant Slave Trade in Libya Is Hypocritical," *Quartz Africa*, November 29, 2017, https://qz.com/africa/1140661/libya-slave-trade-african-migrant-trade-outrage-by-eu-is-hypocritical/.

63. Robert Mugabe of Zimbabwe welcomed Trump's sovereignism when he told the state television that "America for America, America for Americans—on that we agree," and added "Zimbabwe for Zimbabweans." The authoritarian leaders of Burundi and Uganda were among the first to congratulate Donald Trump on his election. President Yoweri Museveni of Uganda expressed his "love for Trump." Egypt's President Abdel Fattah Al-Sisi praised Trump "on his unique personality." See Solomon Ayele Dersso, "African Peace and Conflict Diplomacy," in *Diplomacy and the Future of World Order*, edited by Crocker, Hampson, and Aall.

64. "Ethiopia's Tigray Crisis: UN Aid Chief Says There Is Famine," *BBC News*, June 10, 2021, www.bbc.com/news/world-africa-57432280.

65. "China Opposes Foreign Interference in Ethiopia's Internal Affairs: Chinese FM," *CGTN*, June 11, 2021, https://news.cgtn.com/news/2021-06-11/China-opposes-foreign-interference-in-Ethiopia-s-internal-affairs-10ZT2IcYfPa/index.html.

66. "Russia Will Continue to Be Reliable and Loyal Partner of Ethiopia: Amb Evgeny Terekhi," *Fana Broadcasting Corporate*, June 11, 2011, www.fanabc.com/english/russia-will-continue-to-be-reliable-and-loyal-partner-of-ethiopia-amb-evgeny-terekhin/.

67. "Somalia's Parliament Votes to Extend Embattled President's Term," *Al Jazeera*, April 12, 2021, www.aljazeera.com/news/2021/4/12/somalias-parliament-votes-to-extend-embattled-presidents-term.

68. Facebook, "Removing Coordinated Inauthentic Behavior from Ethiopia," June 16, 2021, https://about.fb.com/news/2021/06/removing-coordinated-inauthentic-behavior-from-ethiopia/.

69. Kofi Yeboah, "How AI Is Transforming Africa's Political Landscape," in *Decoding Digital Democracy in Africa*, edited by Nic Cheeseman and Lisa Garbe (Democracy in Africa/Digital Civil Society Lab, 2020), pp. 17–20, at p. 18, http://democracyinafrica.org/wp-content/uploads/2021/06/Decoding-Digital-Democracy-Booklet_Final_loRes-2_WITHEDIT.pdf.

70. AU Doc Assembly/AU/Dec.II(II).

71. Frans Viljeon, *International Human Rights Law in Africa*, 2nd ed. (Oxford University Press, 2012), p. 187.

72. AU Doc EX.CL/Dec.887(XXVII), decision on the 38th Activity Report of the African Commission on Human and Peoples' Rights adopted during the Twenty-

Seventh Ordinary Session of the AU Executive Council, June 7–12, 2015, Johannesburg, South Africa.

73. See Siri Gloppen and Lise Rakner, "The Perfect Enemy: From Migrants to Sexual Minorities," Chr. Michelsen Institute, CMI Brief 2019:05, www.democraticbacklash .com/the-perfect-enemy-from-migrants-to-sexual-minorities.

74. African Court on Human and Peoples' Rights (ACHPR), "Request for Advisory Opinion by the Centre for Human Rights of the University of Pretoria and the Coalition of African Lesbians, Application 002/2015," September 28, 2017, www .african-court.org/en/images/Cases/Judgment/002-2015-African%20Lesbians-%20 Advisory%20Opinion-28%20September%202017.pdf.

75. For a discussion on the decision of the Executive Council on the outcome of the joint retreat, see Japhet Biegon, "The Rise and Rise of Political Backlash: African Union Executive Council's Decision to Review the Mandate and Working Methods of the African Commission," *European Journal of International Law* (blog), August 2, 2018, www.ejiltalk.org/the-rise-and-rise-of-political-backlash-african-union-executive -councils-decision-to-review-the-mandate-and-working-methods-of-the-african -commission/.

76. Erika de Wet, "Reactions to the Backlash: Trying to Revive the SADC Tribunal through Litigation," *European Journal of International Law* (blog), August 5, 2016, www.ejiltalk.org/reactions-to-the-backlash-trying-to-revive-the-sadc-tribunal -through-litigation/.

77. Amnesty International, "The State of the African Regional Human Rights Bodies and Mechanisms," (2020), p. 6.

78. Based on the Court's statistics reported as of September 2019, of the 238 applications it had received, individuals made 223 applications and NGOs made 12 applications. See Nicole De Silva, "Individual and NGO Access to the African Court on Human and Peoples' Rights, The Latest Blow from Tanzania," *EJIL: Talk!*, December 16, 2019, https://www.ejiltalk.org/individual-and-ngo-access-to-the-african-court -on-human-and-peoples-rights-the-latest-blow-from-tanzania/.

79. Nic Cheeseman, "Can the Courts Protect Democracy in Africa?," *Africa Report*, May 21, 2021, www.theafricareport.com/90612/can-the-courts-protect-democracy-in -africa/.

80. ACHPR, *Addressing Human Rights Issues in Conflict Situations*.

81. Solomon Ayele Dersso, Remarks on the Occasion of the AU–UN High Level Dialogue on Human Rights, African Union Headquarters, Addis Ababa, Ethiopia, April 24, 2018, www.achpr.org/public/Document/file/English/comm_dersso_remarks _on_au_un_dialogue_.pdf.

82. Malloch-Brown, "The Fight for Open Societies Begins Again."

THIRTEEN

Human Rights and Geopolitics in the Middle East, North Africa, and Afghanistan

ASLI Ü. BÂLI

The twentieth anniversary of the September 11 attacks offered a searing reminder that they resulted in a "double tragedy"[1]—the loss of life caused directly by the attacks and the resulting U.S. wars and interventions that engulfed in violence so much of the Middle East and North Africa (MENA) region, broadly construed here to include territories from Afghanistan to Morocco. An avalanche of commentary on the anniversary and the "global war on terror" (or GWoT) converged around a narrative of despair. The wars in Afghanistan and Iraq were both effectively lost by the United States while the GWoT spread from South Asia into the MENA region to little effect in terms of addressing the long-term challenge of terrorism.[2] Instead, these wars laid waste to the human capital and physical infrastructure of country after country across a large swath of the Muslim world.[3] Groups like al Qaeda and the Islamic State proliferated in this same expanse, often as a direct consequence of the attempts to destroy them, as wars weakened the states in the region and errant drone strikes motivated new generations to coalesce around jihadi resistance.[4] Amid the chaos and violence of two decades of counterterrorism and war—and the calamitous withdrawal from Afghanistan—a human rights agenda that at the close of the twentieth century had gained ground globally was dramatically set back, nowhere more definitively than in the Muslim world and the MENA region.

While the lasting impact of the violence visited on—and spawned within—the region as a consequence of the "war on terror" cannot be overstated, it would also be wrong to overlook another critical anniversary. In the long term, the MENA region may come to be more profoundly transformed as a consequence of internal dynamics set in relief by the Arab uprisings a decade ago (and similar grassroots mobilizations in the Iranian Green Movement and the Turkish Gezi Park protests) than by the churning brutality of the GWoT.[5] The mass mobilizations in the streets of almost all major Arab capitals was an important turning point that marked the end of what had appeared to be a relatively stable postcolonial social and political status quo. Unable to sustain their end of an authoritarian social contract—one that traded socioeconomic development for public quiescence—autocratic republics and despotic monarchies suddenly faced the real possibility of overthrow by largely nonviolent, popular uprisings.[6] The old repertoire of painting opponents as terrorists and repression as counterterrorism faltered as the middle classes joined protests that grew large enough to overwhelm security forces.

Of course, some regimes doubled down on coercion, committing massacres in full public view.[7] In those cases, unarmed protests were gradually transformed into armed insurgencies and eventually civil conflicts that a decade later continue to rage in Syria, Yemen, and Libya. But elsewhere, the uprisings demonstrated for the first time just how fragile the sclerotic authoritarian regimes of the region had become. Where the military and security forces defected from the regime or at least became willing to dispense with the figureheads who were the focal points of protests—as in Tunisia and Egypt—barriers of fear and habits of acquiescence were broken seemingly overnight. The overthrow of long-ruling authoritarian presidents like Zinedine Ben Ali and Hosni Mubarak precipitated some immediate changes, but it will only be in the long run that the true measure of the events that unfolded in 2011 can be assessed.[8]

The Arab uprisings were significant in part because indigenous actors seized control of the narrative and defied the stultifying repression of the counterterrorism frame. These popular mobilizations occurred spontaneously, transcended borders and diffused a set of demands across the region that were formulated bottom-up rather than through borrowed Western framings and donor tutelage.[9] They were also significant because they exposed in a stark way the ebbing U.S. commitment to the region and the increasingly hollow rhetoric of human rights and democracy emanating from the West more generally. Rather than supporting prodemocratic popular uprisings, the United States and the European Union (EU) took a selective approach, supporting the overthrow of anti-Western regimes but looking to shore up authoritarian allies, especially in the

Gulf.[10] The French response to the Tunisian uprising, like the U.S. response to events in Egypt, was overtaken by the momentum of protesters, but the consternation at the ouster of reliable allies was unmistakable and bore little resemblance to the decades-long purported advocacy of democratization by Western actors.[11] None of this was lost on public opinion in the region, any more than the subsequent disavowal of human rights obligations when refugees fleeing conflicts in Libya and Syria threatened to arrive on European shores.

The Human Rights and Humanitarian Situation Ten Years after the Uprisings

The decade since 2011 has seen a decline in the human security landscape across the region.[12] Water scarcity and climate change have affected the region deeply, with Yemen's capital, Sana'a, projected to become the first major city to run dry.[13] The rise of authoritarian surveillance tools in an age of social media and the proliferation of drone technologies and cyber weaponry across the region have been other factors in closing political space and making civilian populations more vulnerable—as Thompson Chengeta describes in chapter 9.[14] Finally, the COVID-19 pandemic and the inadequacy of the region's health infrastructure—from shortages of basic personal protective equipment for medical workers to an inability to obtain vaccines—has underscored the fundamental failure of MENA states to provide for the well-being of their peoples.[15] Taken together, war, drought, deprivation, and inequality have produced a large-scale migration crisis, with millions displaced and seeking to flee the region. Moreover, regional stability has continued to deteriorate owing to the metastasizing GWoT violence in Iraq and Afghanistan and the civil conflicts in Syria, Libya, and Yemen. Following the North Atlantic Treaty Organization (NATO) intervention in Libya, not only North Africa but also the Sahel region came to be awash in weapons, besieged by warring factions and Islamist militias and fundamentally destabilized by the collapse of the Libyan state and economy.[16] In Syria, the civil conflict was exacerbated by spillover effects from Iraq and was quickly transformed into a proxy war with arms and funds pouring in from the Gulf and the West, the rise of the Islamic State group, and an aerial counterterrorism campaign that produced devastation from Mosul in Iraq to Raqqa in Syria.[17] Finally, in Yemen, Saudi-United Arab Emirates (UAE) intervention, with the support of the United States and the United Kingdom, has produced one of the most severe humanitarian crises of the twenty-first century.[18]

While humanitarian crises and violence in the region have been exacerbated by ongoing direct and indirect Western intervention, successive U.S. administrations and their allies have signaled waning interest in the region as geopolitical competition shifts to East Asia.[19] The low probability that any other global powers—whether the EU, Russia, or China—will seek to fully replace the United States in propping up a failing regional order means that on the geopolitical front far-reaching changes in the MENA region are inevitable.[20] Notwithstanding the wars, authoritarian retrenchment, and dystopian inequality now characterizing the region, a reduced Western presence, especially if it means declining American support for pro-Western autocrats, may provide a precarious window of opportunity for bottom-up transformation.

Acting on that opportunity will prove challenging, to say the least. The Tunisian case illustrates well the perilous circumstances of postauthoritarian transitions.[21] Even a successful democratic uprising cannot reverse overnight long-accumulated human rights deficits and inequalities. The risk of authoritarian reversion remains ever-present.[22] In particular, the failure to address socioeconomic grievances—that is, the immense shortfall in meeting the economic and social rights of the region's growing population—endangers any project that pursues political liberalization but does not tackle yawning inequalities. At the same time the decade of democratic developments in Tunisia is at least suggestive of the possibility of alternative, postauthoritarian trajectories as well, particularly if these developments could be paired with a social agenda that enjoys international support and economic assistance.[23] If the domestic movements that have emerged across the region in the last decade demanding rights, dignity, and freedom find a way to translate nascent opportunities into the energetic action that will create a tipping point, the conditions for new configurations of political authority and social rights may yet emerge.

Is human rights the right framework for attempts to turn the page on the MENA region's decades of repression, violence, climate-related crises, and impoverishment? The question remains open. On the one hand, developments at the multilateral level and among key actors may mean that a more capacious framework of economic and social rights—one that encompasses robust international obligations to address global rights to health, a clean environment, adequate water, and sustainable development more generally—is now emerging.[24] The growing consensus about the magnitude of global challenges, and a generation of progressive activism, have reshaped the debates in the United Nations' (UN's) corridors in Geneva. On the other hand, this change may come too late to resuscitate the damaged credibility of human rights as a normative framework in the MENA, especially given inconsistent international commitment to supporting human rights in the region.[25] Moreover, without a massive injection of humanitarian assistance—perhaps as a form of reparative justice for decades of plunder and sponsorship of regional autocrats—new commitments to economic and social rights at the international level will mean little to the drought-stricken, conflict-ridden de-development that has put at risk the subsistence of populations across the region. The magnitude of these crises can make human rights frameworks seem toothless.

Perceptions of international human rights frameworks in the region are also tainted by the double standards with which they have been applied: some of the worst abusers have long been shielded from scrutiny by their Western sponsors while crippling sanctions have been imposed on anti-Western actors even during the pandemic.[26] The resistance to holding Saudi Arabia's reckless Crown Prince to account for flagrant human rights violations while imposing sanctions on Iran—affecting access to medical supplies in the midst of the pandemic—neatly illustrates this dynamic. Still, human rights is also part of the vernacular of popular demands in the region. Whether protesting against impunity for domestic violence in Recep Tayyip Erdoğan's Turkey or the failure of accountability following the immense explosion in the port of Beirut, or police brutality in Abdel Fattah al-Sisi's Egypt, the region's protesters continue to frame their grievances in the language of human rights.[27] Events in Sudan and Algeria in 2019–2020, the collapse of the long-standing order in Lebanon, and continuing expressions of grassroots indignation in Iraq, all suggest the latent possibility of renewed uprisings.[28] Such mobilizations, in turn, harbor transformative potential for the better realization of human rights in the region.

The rest of this chapter offers a brief overview of the current human rights situation in the Middle East and North Africa and considers how the uprisings have affected understandings of human rights in the region. If the uprisings gave voice to popular demands for regime accountability, the absence of accountability a decade later attests to the failure of existing international human rights mechanisms to impose a meaningful framework of responsibility even in the most extreme cases, such as the atrocities in Syria, the plundering of Libya, or the proxy wars in Yemen. The chapter concludes with a consideration of the ways in which geopolitical factors have inhibited the realization of human rights progress in the region, using the example of the Afghanistan withdrawal to illustrate the perverse dynamics of Western intervention and advocacy for human rights. With the West now pivoting away from the MENA region, the question remains whether international actors will support the humanitarian assistance and multilateral conflict resolution that is a prerequisite for the pursuit of human rights in the region.

Internal Challenges to Human Rights
in the MENA Region

The Middle East and North Africa remain notoriously inhospitable to a binding regional human rights framework. Like Asia—and unlike Europe, the Americas, and Africa—the Middle East has no binding regional human rights law, though two regional human rights instruments have been drafted, one by the members of the Organization of the Islamic Conference (OIC) and another by the League of Arab States.[29] In addition, some of the North African countries—including Algeria, Egypt, Libya, and Tunisia, but not Morocco—are signatories of the African Charter on Human and Peoples' Rights, and thus technically subject to the jurisdiction of the African Commission on Human and Peoples' Rights (African Commission) and the African Court of Human and Peoples' Rights (African Court), though they have been less engaged with the African human rights system than sub-Saharan African countries.[30] Most countries in the region are also parties to the core multilateral human rights treaties, including the International Bill of Rights comprising the International Covenant on Civil and Political Rights (ICCPR) and the International Covenant on Economic, Social, and Cultural Rights (ICESCR).[31] Additional international human rights instruments addressing protections for the rights of women and children and the prevention and prohibition of torture have also been widely ratified by the states of the region, albeit with significant packages of reservations concerning specific provisions.[32] Thus the core binding framework for human rights in the region is the multilateral human rights system centered on the United Nations Human Rights Council and the various treaty bodies associated with the international human rights instruments ratified by the countries of the region. Though the UN system, as well as major transnational human rights organizations like Human Rights Watch and Amnesty International, do extensive reporting on human rights in the Middle East, there is no regional or international enforcement mechanism empowered to adjudicate human rights claims that emerge from the region.[33]

The challenges to human rights in the Middle East are as formidable as the available enforcement mechanisms are weak. For two decades, the war on terror has provided a framework that strengthens the hands of authoritarian governments in the region at the expense of human rights.[34] And in the last decade, every country where protests occurred during the Arab uprisings has experienced a significant deterioration in its human rights record.[35] Peaceful protests in Syria gave way to an armed revolt met by brutal repression by the regime of Bashar al-Assad, resulting in the deaths of hundreds of thousands and the displacement of millions.[36] The uprisings in Libya and Yemen, while very different in their initial trajectories, have degenerated into vicious civil wars that have devastated the population, brought on famine conditions, and eviscerated hopes for a democratic transition or the protection of human rights—all of which is further exacerbated by the global pandemic.[37] Elsewhere, for instance in Egypt and Bahrain, early achievements by protesters were followed by counterrevolutionary repression and the ratcheting up of the authoritarian police states ruling the countries.[38] The GWoT provided the pretext of counterterrorism as cover for escalating crackdowns on opposition groups.[39] The monarchies of the region—in the Gulf, Jordan, and Morocco—faced more muted protests that were met in each country by a mix of accommodation and repression.[40] Ultimately, protests have not resulted in political liberalization, nor have they reined in counterterrorism depredations or forced any of these governments to tackle the destabilizing levels of socioeconomic inequality in their countries. Today, alongside regime violence, the health and well-being of citizens across the region are threatened by high unemployment, lack of economic opportunity and growing immiseration, tied to climate change–driven water scarcity as well as state mismanagement of the agriculture sector, and wide-ranging corruption in public services.[41]

The crisis in economic and social rights is especially striking for a region that has considerable resources. Oil wealth continues to be a source of revenue for the Gulf Cooperation Council (GCC) countries and remittances for other parts of the region, though even the GCC states have struggled with the effects of climate change and the impact of a pandemic-related decline in oil demand.[42] Elsewhere in the region, a combination of population growth, privatization, and corruption has led to growing inequality and unsustainable levels of unemployment, as wealth is concentrated in fewer hands and a larger proportion of the society experiences declining standards of living from one generation to the next.[43] Thus, it is no surprise that citizens across the region describe economic deprivation as the leading human rights issue in their country and corruption as a major cause of political unrest and deteriorating rights.[44] Another long-standing problem that contributes to economic malaise is the failure to protect women's rights, with little progress on reforms in family, labor, criminal, and nationality laws that entrench de jure discrimination against women.[45]

Underlying the dire state of human rights in the MENA region is the abiding reality of authoritarian rule. Far from addressing demands for reform, authoritarianism is resurgent in much of the region, with citizens experiencing a marked decline in political freedoms including freedom of speech, assembly, and expression.[46] Violence is endemic even in the countries not experiencing armed conflict: abductions, torture, killings of journalists and political opponents, police brutality, extrajudicial killing, summary executions, and violent crackdowns on peaceful protest all remain depressingly common across the region.[47] There is a widespread perception that Western actors are contributing to this dire picture with tacit or even explicit support for authoritarian actors and a willingness to turn a blind eye to depredations committed in the name of counterterrorism.[48] The situation is even more drastic in countries engulfed by war—Libya, Syria, and Yemen—where violations of international humanitarian law involve the daily targeting of civilians in mass attacks, producing casualties numbering in the tens or even hundreds of thousands, and counterterrorism pretexts have transformed local conflicts into geopolitical proxy wars. Finally, the rare democracies of the region have also witnessed bouts of escalating state violence presented as counterterrorism— such as the Israeli strikes on Gaza in 2021 and Turkish military action against Kurdish groups in the country's southeast in 2015—as well as democratic erosion or backsliding.[49] In short, few regions can compete with the MENA in terms of an overall deterioration in protection of human rights in the twenty-first century.

The Afterlives of the Uprisings

Despite this bleak portrait, however, there is real ferment in the region around a human rights agenda. At least one analyst has argued that the Arab uprisings "can be viewed as the world's first human rights revolution."[50] The transnational wave of protest movements was galvanized by demands for human rights in a Middle Eastern vernacular. The specific demands that reverberated across the region—for dignity, bread, and justice—represent a grassroots articulation of a fundamental human rights framework, underscoring the indivisibility of civil, political, economic, and social rights.[51] Fed up with counterterrorism frameworks legitimizing state repression and the corruption and economic mismanagement that blight the prospects of ordinary people, the uprisings asserted popular demands in a rights-based register. Yet implicit in the uprisings was also a critique of Western human rights advocacy that cleaves civil and political rights—and the agenda of promoting good governance and democracy—from economic and social rights. The core, shared assessment of publics across the region from Tunis to Sana'a was that regimes that failed to deliver socioeconomic rights to their populations must fall. In the wake of the uprisings, the failure to meet popular demands for a decent standard of living remains a source of profound destabilization for the region's autocracies.[52]

That the protests were neither led (nor in many cases even joined) by Islamists is also telling.[53] Demands to overthrow authoritarians like Ben Ali and Mubarak were not grounded in political Islam but in basic demands for human dignity. The reflexive habit of presenting domestic dissent as Islamist menace was, accordingly, unavailable to the autocratic regimes confronting uprisings. Though many resorted to repression to foreclose political change, the tired scripts of counterterrorism no longer provide the same mantle of authoritarian legitimacy they did before 2011.

The uprisings focused attention on the real sources of popular dissatisfaction in the MENA region. The pro-Western regimes were destabilized not out of anti-imperialism or an embrace of political Islam, but because they governed through coercion and were unable to deliver the prerequisites for realizing basic human rights. The Taliban, which took power in Afghanistan in the midst of the American withdrawal, would do well to heed this basic reality. The region's corrupt, pro-Western regimes are brittle and unstable because of their brutal and incompetent record of governance. Opportunistic actors—from Sisi in Egypt and Kais Saied in Tunisia to the Taliban in Afghanistan—may be able to seize power in a context of destabilization and widespread public discontent with the status quo, but their own governments will be equally unstable, dependent on coercion, and unable to deliver socioeconomic growth unless they address the failings of the prior regime. Analysts across the spectrum caution that governing is more difficult than conquest in the case of Afghanistan, and the same is true across the MENA region.[54] Governing requires securing the basic human rights of the population, whatever the regime type and geopolitical orientation; the alternative is ongoing instability.

This basic insight was memorably given voice during the Arab uprisings by popular chants that spread across the region's borders. The language of human rights was explicitly deployed by citizen-led movements for a range of reasons. First, universality as a characteristic of human rights has a resonance that captures the imagination of publics and enables them to convey the transcendent character of their demands. The basic idea that we are *all* entitled to certain rights regardless of where we live and who governs is intuitively appealing and facilitates the broad diffusion of human rights frameworks. Second, the transnational character of human rights claims enabled local movements to make demands that were globally legible. The conscious invocation of human rights and creative public campaigns using humor, graphic arts, and social media to project demands internationally enabled protesters both to convey the legitimacy of their anti-authoritarian uprisings and to seek the protection offered by global media coverage of their regimes' responses. Finally, the embrace of human rights articulations by protesters enabled them to resist regime efforts to characterize their movements as terrorist or insurgent mobilizations, seizing the high ground in the battle over global public relations.

The result of the prodemocratic and prohuman rights character of the uprisings was that Western governments had a difficult time coming to the aid of their authoritarian clients as these sought to repress citizen revolts. From initial French efforts to support Ben Ali's authoritarian regime to American ambivalence in response to the Egyptian uprising against Mubarak, Western governments repeatedly found themselves on the "wrong side of history" as decades of purported democracy promotion suddenly faltered in the face of an anti-authoritarian mass mobilization.[55] In the end, half-hearted efforts to steady Ben Ali's regime gave way as the Tunisian military's decision to stand aside ensured its fall, while Mubarak's allies—led by the United States—secured a caretaker role for the Egyptian military once it became clear that the president had to go. Rather than invoking human rights, Western powers limited themselves to calls for an "orderly transition," widely seen in the region as code for a tightly orchestrated transfer of power that would maintain the existing geopolitical balance of power.[56] The key priority conveyed by this framing was that the uprisings should not alter the pro-Western character of Arab regimes in transition. By contrast, where regimes that were not solidly in the Western camp became destabilized—such as in Syria or Libya—full-throated support for protesters and regime change was the order of the day among Western capitals.

The legacy of these double standards has profoundly marked the MENA region. In particular, the decision by the UN Security Council, with U.S. leadership under the administration of President Barack Obama, to intervene in Libya, followed by the failure to authorize similar multilateral intervention in Syria, put paid to the doctrine of the "responsibility to protect," and bred cynicism across the region about the human rights pieties of the West.[57] Indeed, the intervention in Libya vividly illustrated the destabilizing quality of the prevailing geopolitical order that defined the MENA region, and the way it undermined human rights. Pax Americana after September 11 came with a belligerent swagger that did more to destabilize the region than maintain order. With Libya, the Security Council became an instrument for an intervention that tarnished the image of multilateralism with the brush of NATO-led regime change.[58] A decade on, neither UN initiatives nor U.S. priorities enjoy the influence they once did in the region, opening the door to a geopolitical reordering with potentially far-reaching implications for human rights. These trends have been further cemented by the withdrawal from Afghanistan, seen as a full American retreat from the region and even as a capitulation to actors once reviled for their records of human rights abuse.[59]

Europe's reputation has not fared much better over the decade since the uprisings. The European response to Syrian refugees, as one example, represented another nadir in Western human rights credibility. The massive flow of Syrian refugees into neighboring MENA countries from 2011 to 2015 was never recognized as a "crisis" by European actors, so long as migration could be limited to the eastern Mediterranean. After millions of displaced Syrians had been absorbed by countries such as Lebanon, Jordan, and Turkey with little international assistance or European attention, the summer of 2015 suddenly witnessed a global panic when refugees reached European shores.[60] The result was an object lesson in the limits of Western humanitarianism. Lebanon, with a population of under four million, found itself hosting over a million Syrian refugees by 2014, at a time when Western countries systematically failed to meet their financial pledges to humanitarian relief efforts coordinated through the UN.[61] Yet when a similar number of refugees arrived in Europe—where the population is over one hundred times greater than Lebanon's—the unraveling of refugee protocols and the stark refusal of wealthy capitals to absorb even small numbers of displaced people exposed the racial biases and shallow commitments of European countries accustomed to lecturing their neighbors on human rights.[62]

From the perspective of geopolitics and human rights, the Arab uprisings and their aftermath have left a dual legacy. The uprisings demonstrated that the human rights paradigm has substantial traction at the grassroots level among Middle Eastern publics. At the same time, faith in the formal international human rights machinery at the United Nations is at an all-time low, and human rights rhetoric from Western capitals retains little leverage. Whether considering the ransom paid by Europe to Turkey and the Libyan Coast Guard to deter migrants—by warehousing them at best and enslaving them at worst[63]—or the betrayal of Afghan allies literally cast off by Western evacuation efforts,[64] the region's publics view normative claims from the West with a skepticism that may become fatal to international human rights frameworks and the organizations that promote them.

Geopolitical Obstacles to Progress on Human Rights in the MENA Region

The above survey of the state of human rights in the MENA countries makes clear that the geopolitical significance of the region has had an adverse effect on the realization of rights for those who live there. A decade into the "war on terror," even those countries not subject to invasion and occupation had been disfigured by counterterrorist violence. The authoritarian police states of the region eagerly repurposed counterterrorism to their own ends, targeting dissidents and opponents with the same treatment that the United States meted out to its adversaries. Regime circles grew richer and better equipped— corruption was fueled by ever-growing counterterrorism budgets[65]—while those outside those cliques confronted impoverishment as economies faltered. Out of this decade-long escalation of violence and inequality emerged the uprisings that swept the region. If the geopolitics of the GWoT contributed to these uprisings, a decade later it is the selective U.S. disengagement from the MENA region that will scramble the internal distribution of power there and its relation to the broader regions to which it remains connected, from Europe to the Indian Ocean to the Horn of Africa.

Twenty years after the United States and NATO invaded Afghanistan, the sudden withdrawal and the collapse of the Afghan government has definitively undercut the perceived reliability of Western commitments to stability and the defense of human rights in the region. Allies and adversaries alike understand that U.S. foreign policy doctrine has shifted away from high-minded rhetorical support for human rights—including women's rights—to a focus on the narrower "national security interests of the American people."[66] The initial decision to withdraw from Afghanistan—and to negotiate with the Taliban to the exclusion of the government of then-Afghan president Ashraf Ghani—may have been taken by the Trump administration, but President Joe Biden chose to follow and engaged in little consultation with allies. In the Middle East, the message received is that the U.S. commitment to regional alliances has become more tenuous.[67] The Biden administration may not be using the "America First" label, but it has embraced a transactional approach to foreign policy.[68]

The Western pivot away from the MENA region creates a void that will be filled by new forms of geopolitical competition within and beyond it. On the one hand, Israel, Saudi Arabia, the United Arab Emirates, Iran, Qatar, and Turkey are immersed in intense intraregional competition that has exacerbated sectarian divisions and fueled the region's proxy wars.[69] On the other hand, external powers—particularly Russia and China, but perhaps increasingly also India and Pakistan—may become more active in the region.[70] If Afghanistan serves as a testing ground for a new geopolitical framing of the MENA, for now it seems that the non-Western external powers are content to hedge their bets. On the one hand, China, Turkey, and Iran may engage to a limited extent with the new Afghan regime both to avoid a destabilizing collapse and to assert a potential role in shaping new trade routes and access to natural resources.[71] At the same time, none of these powers seems keen to assume principal responsibility for maintaining order or countering terrorism or narcotics trafficking in the country. Understanding the implications of this new geopolitical context for human rights requires contextualizing the significance of the withdrawal from Afghanistan.

To the extent that this withdrawal marks a repudiation of the liberal internationalist model of intervention and nation-building, there has been much concern that it also sounds a death knell for human rights.[72] Yet it is worth remembering that from the neocon project of regime change to the neoliberal effort to rebuild so-called failed states, over a quarter century of interventions in the MENA countries have left most of their targets worse off as false promises have ended in bitter recriminations, from Somalia to Iraq to Afghanistan. Against this backdrop of failed intervention, the significance of the Afghan withdrawal for human rights in the region may not be as dire as feared. Put simply: if military interventions cost tens of thousands of civilian lives (based on conservative estimates) without producing stable or secure states, then abandoning such interventionism may have some counterintuitive benefits.

This leads directly to the second core implication of the Afghanistan withdrawal: while the United States long touted its commitments to human rights—and notably women's rights—in Afghanistan, the sidelining of this agenda in favor of other geopolitical imperatives has been a constant. The speed of the withdrawal and the prioritization of securing Western citizens without putting in place a plan to protect local Afghan allies was only the most recent reminder of underlying U.S. priorities.[73] The West's half-hearted commitment to human rights in Afghanistan raised and then dashed expectations in ways that may have left local communities worse off in the short run and deeply skeptical about the international human rights agenda in the long run. In the end, the withdrawal has left Afghans to their own resources to find ways to protect human rights on the ground without Western support.[74] While the scenes of chaos, desperation, and panic at the end of August bode ill for the immediate protection of human rights in the country, in the medium term the withdrawal of Western militaries and nongovernmental organizations (NGOs) may create the space for indigenous civil society to develop local priorities and resources with respect to protecting rights, however they may be framed. After all, human rights require, at a minimum, the very basics of security and stability that have been denied to most Afghans in over four decades of externally driven war on their territory. The rapid rise of a new government with local sources of support in the midst of the American withdrawal may paradoxically be a hopeful sign in the longer term for securing a prerequisite for realizing human rights: an end to war. While few expect the Taliban to establish a rights-respecting government, reducing armed conflict would constitute an improvement for the human rights of civilians in many parts of the country outside the capital, despite the painful backsliding on women's rights.[75] Moreover, it has been widely reported that the Taliban consolidated control over the territory through local political bargains, which may result in forms of accountability to the rural and provincial parts of Afghanistan that were long absent from the Kabul-centered governance of the past twenty years.[76]

On the other hand, whatever the course of events on the ground in Afghanistan, the country will remain trapped in a set of geopolitical framings that will have a significant impact on its human rights trajectory. Alongside the shallow Western commitment to human rights in the region, geopolitical obstacles to realizing those rights are also exemplified by the experience in Afghanistan. First, there is a real risk that the United States will respond to military defeat by inflicting economic punishment on its former adversary, the Taliban.[77] Going beyond an asset freeze by, for example, designating the Taliban, now the de facto government of Afghanistan, as a foreign terrorist organization would be a form of economic warfare, strangling the country, cutting aid delivery, blocking trade, and impeding the ability of ordinary Afghans to access essential imported goods. Steps along these lines would arguably be an even greater enduring betrayal of the Afghan people than the chaotic withdrawal itself, impairing economic recovery and accelerating a mass exodus of refugees. Afghanistan is a poor country; much of its GDP over the past twenty years has depended on donors,[78] half the population faces food shortages—including over three million children experiencing severe malnutrition—and millions have been internally displaced. As Adam Tooze has argued, what Afghanistan needs is an "amply funded multilateral humanitarian effort to ensure life can continue as far as possible and millions of people are preserved from disaster."[79]

Beyond the threat of punitive sanctions, all the factors that undermine human rights across the whole region are also in play in Afghanistan. These include the possibility of new nonstate actors challenging Taliban control, continued counterterrorism airstrikes by Western forces, geopolitical competition resulting in proxy wars, the ravages of climate change, the unequal global response to the pandemic, and the rush to stave off a migration crisis by placing physical obstacles in the way of desperate people seeking to flee. With the Taliban government cut off from Afghan sovereign assets and facing sanctions, the escalating humanitarian crisis in the country is just the most recent example of the risk of man-made famine in the region.[80] That these starvation conditions have been externally imposed in countries such as Yemen and Afghanistan in the midst of a global pandemic only underscores the degree to which the epidemic of human rights abuse in the Middle East is tied to geopolitical factors.[81]

Over the past decade, the return of great-power proxy wars—notably in Syria and Yemen—has disproportionately affected the MENA region. The withdrawal from Afghanistan may accelerate this trend, with the decrease of the U.S. appetite for extended deployments and the intensification of strategic competition. As China expresses interest in Afghan trade routes and rare earth minerals,[82] the Biden administration's avowed commitment to "over the horizon" defense strategies may mean a doubling down on drone strikes and cyber intervention, arming local proxies to counter Chinese influence without offering alternative sources of Western investment.[83] Indeed, even in the midst of the U.S. withdrawal, there remained the risk that leaving Afghanistan might mark the beginning of a new chapter of the "forever war."[84] The rise of private military security contractors, the impact of digital technologies, unmanned weaponry and cyber warfare, and competition with China are all aggravating factors that portend continued war-making through technological surrogates and proxy forces.

Against this stark reality, prospects for human rights remain more imperiled by geopolitics than by actions and decisions by local powers in the MENA region. From a human rights perspective, it is worth remembering what is actually owed to Afghanistan by international actors instead of a future of proxy wars, sanctions, and continued carnage. What human rights would require in that country—and across much of the MENA, for that matter—is, at a minimum, accountability for two decades of devastation under the guise of the war on terror, and related proxy wars, which have extinguished millions of lives and crippled the future of generations. Yet instead of massive humanitarian assistance and acknowledgment of these terrible costs, the region is increasingly walled off from its neighbors, seen as an incubator of threat or a transit site for migration. In this context, for the people of the MENA region, claims about Western—and especially American—commitments to democracy or the pursuit of human rights is understood simply as so much geopolitical propaganda and apologia for empire. Changing this basic reality and rehabilitating human rights frameworks requires fundamentally rethinking the geopolitical approach to the region in a way that centers on the human security of the region's people rather than prioritizing authoritarian clients, weapons sales, counterterrorism, and continued investment in a global economy fueled by the region's carbon resources, trade routes, and rare earth minerals.

Conclusions and Recommendations

In some ways the COVID-19 pandemic, as much as the Afghanistan withdrawal, has brought the September 11 era to an end. Global priorities have shifted away from the war on terror, and the pandemic has underscored a logic of rivalry with China. Two decades of misdirected resources, bookended by a forced reckoning with the official incompetence and mendacity of American war planners in Afghanistan,[85] have left behind a destabilized and immiserated MENA region.

The parting U.S. drone strike in Kabul, initially described as a successful attack on Islamic State affiliates but later shown to have massacred ten civilians from a single family, including seven children, serves as a synecdoche of the war on terror.[86] Like the tens of thousands of Afghan civilian deaths that preceded them, these children's deaths might never have been acknowledged but for enterprising reporting; and even now they will be little more than a footnote to the geopolitical imperatives that shaped both the war and the evacuation. Both literally and figuratively, Afghan civilian lives barely register in a geopolitical order that imposes at best limited accountability on Western war planners. For all the pious invocation of human rights during the decades-long military engagement in Afghanistan, the actual rights of Afghans—including those left to reckon with the devastating fallout of the U.S. withdrawal—remain little more than a rounding error in the avalanche of bitter retrospectives published since the last U.S. soldier was evacuated. Meanwhile, the EU began quietly funding a Turkish effort to build a 330-mile wall along its eastern border with Iran to prevent Afghan migrants from entering the country and transiting to Europe.[87]

Afghanistan is now seen primarily as a migration and terrorism risk to be mitigated, rather than as a country to which humanitarian protection and human rights support are owed.[88] The lightning speed with which the country was abandoned will remain a powerful indictment of the West for those in the MENA region and beyond. Western publics, too, should recognize that benevolent intentions delivered through aerial bombardment have neither improved human rights nor persuaded populations on the ground of the virtues of a global hegemon often indifferent to the death and dislocation it produces.

What then are the prospects for human rights in the region for the next decade, as the West pivots away? The post-9/11 war on terror facilitated a metastasizing global approach to counterterrorism that enabled, legitimized, and accepted massive human rights abuses. Perhaps now space may become available for the peoples of the MENA region to pursue indigenous solutions to endemic challenges as the GWoT winds to a close. If there is to be international support for human rights in the region going forward, it must heed the lessons of the harms wrought by external actors so far this century, as well as the voices of civil society actors on the ground.

This would mean, first, prioritizing economic and social rights in a region where the inequality and impoverishment that fueled uprisings a decade ago have only been exacerbated. International humanitarian assistance to address the ravages of war, pandemic, water scarcity, and climate change—all of which imperil the subsistence of millions from Libya to Afghanistan—would be the right starting point. A human rights–informed approach to migration management cannot depend on building higher walls around Europe or at the borders of countries such as Australia and the United States. Instead, it requires substantial transfers of resources to, and investments in, territories where populations are at risk of famine and epidemics of preventable diseases. The legacy of withdrawal from Afghanistan might yet include improvements in human rights in the region if accountability for the damage inflicted in the past two decades took the form of long-term and sustainable investment rather than sanctions that will further immiserate the civilian population.

Instead of embracing a new over-the-horizon strategy, the United States would do well to internalize the lesson that its military interventions have neither stabilized the MENA region nor achieved durable counterterrorism objectives. As the Afghanistan debacle illustrates, the most that can be achieved militarily is temporary threat management at a staggering cost to civilian populations. To improve the prospects of human rights in the coming decade, a reversal of priorities is required, beginning with reinvestment in multilateral efforts at conflict resolution and an end to proxy wars through incentives to the Gulf countries and Turkey to desist from their current strategies, and the inclusion of adversaries such as Russia and Iran in planned negotiations about theaters of conflict where these states are present. Should such efforts succeed, moreover, a postconflict context will require massive reconstruction. Rather than treating this as an opportunity to impose heavy-handed conditions on aid, the United States might lead international efforts to facilitate rebuilding while insisting on narrowly framed, specific, and achievable human rights priorities such as humanitarian access to all regions.

What is needed more broadly in the region has been well articulated by Fionnuala Ní Aoláin, the UN Special Rapporteur on the promotion and protection of human rights and fundamental freedoms while countering terrorism. She argued that the twentieth anniversary of September 11 required nothing less than a "genuine reckoning on the use and abuse of counterterrorism measures and institutions."[89] The future of human rights in the Middle East depends not only on a formal end to direct U.S. and Western intervention, but also a fundamental rethinking of the geopolitical logics and counterterrorism framings that have enabled lawless violence and repression. Yet neither Western actors nor their Chinese and Russian competitors have shown interest in such a reckoning.

International peace and stability, and improvements in human rights in the MENA countries, cannot be realized through the region's authoritarian status quo, nor can these goals be delivered through military intervention. Calls for "restraint" in the halls of power in Washington should be heeded not through increased reliance on air power and partnerships with regional autocrats, but by reimagining stability in the MENA region in terms of the welfare of its citizens.[90] In the meantime, achieving human rights goals requires a return to first principles—those that were articulated by broad publics across the region during the 2011 uprisings. Bread, dignity, and justice—that is, providing a minimum core of economic and social rights, ending authoritarian repression, and achieving a measure of accountability for past harms—were the shared aspirations articulated by mobilized citizens a decade ago. Counterterrorism and intervention have undermined these objectives. The possibility of pursuing a locally determined human rights trajectory depends on an end to the wasted human and financial capital of the war on terror, its many proxy conflicts, and the Western war profiteering it enabled.[91] Given the adverse consequences of direct and indirect interventions in the region over the last two decades, perhaps the best news for human rights in the MENA is that geopolitical interest in the region may be waning.

Geopolitics have long been at cross-purposes with human rights in the MENA region. An agenda to reverse this equation would entail humanitarian reparations, divestment from alliances with autocrats, and investment in grassroots partnerships with civil society actors articulating their own locally inflected agenda for human rights. For now, such a reversal may remain beyond reach. Instead, in the space left following an American pivot to other geopolitical priorities, a more attainable hope is that the MENA states might define a stable order among themselves.[92] If they do, perhaps such stability will enable the region's peoples to pursue tangible, local solutions that will incrementally address their own human rights demands with less direct geopolitical interference.

Notes

1. David Leonhardt, "A Missing Legacy," *New York Times*, September 10, 2021 (describing the "double tragedy" of September 11).

2. Jared Keller, "American Lost the Iraq War—These Cables Show How," *The New Republic*, November 25, 2019; Anthony Cordesman, "America's Failed Strategy in the Middle East: Losing Iraq and the Gulf," Center for Strategic and International Studies, January 2, 2020.

3. Murtaza Hussain, "Over Two Decades, U.S.' Global War on Terror Has Taken Nearly 1 Million Lives and Cost $8 Trillion," *The Intercept*, September 1, 2021.

4. Itamar Rabinovich, "Reflections on the Long-Term Repercussions of September 11 for US Policy in the Middle East," Brookings, September 7, 2021.

5. Mohamed Ali Adraoui, "How the Arab Spring Changed the Middle East and North Africa Forever," *The Conversation*, May 26, 2021.

6. Omar Dahi, "Understanding the Political Economy of the Arab Revolts," MERIP (Middle East Research and Information Project), Summer 2011.

7. See, for example, Heiko Wimmen, "Syria's Path from Civil Uprising to Civil War," Carnegie Endowment for International Peace, November 22, 2016.

8. Jillian Schwedler, "Taking Time Seriously: Temporality and the Arab Uprisings," Project on Middle East Political Science, May 2016.

9. Merouan Mekouar, "No Political Agents, No Diffusion: Evidence from North Africa," *International Studies Review* 16, 2 (2014), pp. 206–16.

10. Alexander Marquardt, "Obama Mideast Speech Faces Disappointed and Disillusioned Arab World," *ABC News*, May 19, 2011; Marina Ottaway, "Bahrain and the Conundrum of Democracy Promotion," *Georgetown Journal of International Affairs*, June 14, 2021.

11. Robert Marquand, "An Embarrassed France Backpedals from Its Support of Tunisia's Ben Ali," *Christian Science Monitor*, January 20, 2011; John Nichols, "The Nation: Biden Is on the Wrong Side of History," *NPR*, January 31, 2011 (noting then-vice president Biden's support for maintaining Mubarak in office despite a popular uprising).

12. Johan Schaar, "A Confluence of Crises: On Water, Climate and Security in the Middle East and North Africa," *SIPRI Insights on Peace and Security,* July 2019.

13. Hadil Al-Mowafak, "Yemen's Water Crisis: A New Urgency to an Old Problem," Peace Lab, April 6, 2021.

14. Marie Lamensch, "Authoritarianism Has Been Reinvented for the Digital Age," Center for International Governance Innovation, July 9, 2021; Federico Borsari, "The Middle East's Game of Drones: The Race to Lethal UAVs and Its Implications for the Region's Security Landscape," Italian Institute for Political Studies, January 15, 2021.

15. "MENA: COVID-19 Amplified Inequalities and Was Used to Further Ramp Up Repression," Amnesty International, April 7, 2021. The oil-rich Gulf states fared better because of their prior investment in health infrastructure, though the pandemic has had adverse long-term impacts on their economies. "COVID-19, Subdued Oil Price to Leave Much of the Gulf in the Red This Year—Fitch," Reuters, April 27, 2021.

16. "UN's Guterres Warns of 'Impact' on Sahel Region from Libya War," *Al Jazeera English*, January 23, 2020.

17. Azmat Khan, "The Uncounted," *New York Times*, November 16, 2017 (on civilian toll of U.S. air campaign in Iraq against Islamic State); and "All Feasible Precautions? Civilian Casualties in Anti-ISIS Coalition Airstrikes in Syria," Human Rights Watch, September 24, 2017.

18. "After Years of Conflict, Yemen Remains the World's Worst Humanitarian Crisis," United Nations Population Fund, December 7, 2020.

19. Tyler Page and Natasha Bertrand, "White House Shifts from Middle East Quagmires to a Showdown with China," *Politico*, January 29, 2021.

20. Jon Hoffman, "Neither Russia nor China Could Fill a U.S. Void in the Middle East—Nor Would They Desire to," *Foreign Policy*, September 15, 2021.

21. Bouazza Ben Bouazza, "Tunisia's Saied Strengthens Presidential Powers in Decrees," *Washington Post*, September 23, 2021.

22. "Stemming Tunisia's Authoritarian Drift," International Crisis Group, January 11, 2018.

23. Kersten Knipp and Khaled Salameh, "Tunisia: A Political Crisis Fueled by Economic Woes," *Deutsche Welle*, July 27, 2021.

24. Rajesh Mirchandani, "Five Global Issues to Watch in 2021," United Nations Foundation, December 23, 2020.

25. Michele Dunne, "Support for Human Rights in the Arab World: A Shifting and Inconsistent Picture," Carnegie Endowment for International Peace, December 28, 2018.

26. Even the defenders of current priorities acknowledge the apparent double standard. See, for example, Eric Mandel, "Why the Double Standard on Human Rights with Saudi Arabia and Iran?," *The Hill*, January 28, 2021.

27. See, for example, Esra Yalcinalp, "Women Rise Up over Withdrawal from Istanbul Convention," *BBC News*, March 26, 2021; Leela Jacinto, "Beirut Blast Propels Activist from Street Protests to Political Action," *France 24*, February 8, 2021; and Declan Walsh, "Rare Protests against Egypt's Leader Erupt in Cairo and Elsewhere," *New York Times*, September 20, 2019.

28. See, for example, Peter Bartu, "The New Arab Uprisings: How the 2019 Trajectory Differs from the 2011 Legacy," Al Jazeera Centre for Studies, January 13, 2020, https://studies.aljazeera.net/en/reports/2020/01/arab-uprisings-2019-trajectory -differs-2011-legacy-part-1-200105102004189.html.

29. Cairo Declaration on Human Rights in Islam (OIC, 1990); Arab Charter on Human Rights (Arab League, 2004). In addition, Turkey is the sole state in the region that is a member of the Council of Europe and therefore bound by the European Convention of Human Rights and the jurisdiction of the European Court of Human Rights. This situates Turkey somewhat differently from other countries in the region and for the purposes of this chapter, the focus will be on the countries of the region that are not party to the Council of Europe.

30. Libya under the Qaddafi regime was the North African country that was the most engaged with the African human rights system, but since 2011 its participation has waned dramatically. Of the other countries, Egypt is currently behind by two

reports in its reporting obligations to the African Commission, and Algeria and Tunisia are behind by three or more reports. Only Tunisia has ever had a contentious case brought against it before the African Court—that case was brought in 2021 and is currently pending. In 2011, the Court was asked to issue an advisory opinion on the situation in Libya, but the request was denied.

31. The following countries have ratified the ICCPR: Algeria, Bahrain, Egypt, Iran, Iraq, Israel, Jordan, Kuwait, Lebanon, Libya, Morocco, Palestine, Qatar, Syria, Tunisia, Turkey, and Yemen. All of these countries have also ratified the ICESCR, together with Oman, which has only joined the ICESCR. The governments of OmanSaudi Arabia, and the United Arab Emirates have neither signed nor ratified the ICCPR.

32. The Convention on the Elimination of Discrimination Against Women has been ratified by all the countries of the region save Iran. As of 2020, when Qatar and Oman both acceded, the Convention against Torture was also ratified by all of the countries in the region with the exception of Iran. The Convention on the Rights of the Child has been ratified by every country of the region.

33. Again, the North African countries subject to the jurisdiction of the African Court and Turkey's participation in the Council of Europe remain outliers in this respect. Moreover, of these countries, only Turkey has ever faced enforcement action under the contentious jurisdiction of a regional human rights court.

34. Shadi Hamid, "Sound and Fury in the Post-9/11 Middle East," *Foreign Affairs*, September 8, 2021; Chris Rogers and Jordan Street, "If the US Wants to Push Back on Authoritarian Agendas at the UN, Get Counterterrorism Rights," *Just Security*, February 1, 2021.

35. Michael Safi, "Life Has Got Worse since Arab Spring, Say People across Middle East," *The Guardian*, December 17, 2020.

36. "Factbox: The Cost of Ten Years of Devastating War in Syria," Reuters, May 26, 2021 (detailing documentation of the deaths of over 227,000 civilians and the displacement of over half of Syria's population of 23 million).

37. "In Libya and Yemen War Zones, COVID-19 Adds a Second Front," *PBS News*, May 6, 2020.

38. Jonathan Fenton-Harvey, "Regional Uprisings Confront Gulf-Backed Counterrevolution," MERIP, Fall/Winter 2019.

39. Mirjam Edel and Maria Josua, "How Authoritarian Rulers Seek to Legitimize Repression: Framing Mass Killings in Egypt and Ukbekistan," *Democratization* 25, 5 (2018), pp. 882–900.

40. Yasmina Abouzzohour, "Heavy Lies the Crown: The Survival of Arab Monarchies, 10 Years after the Arab Spring," Brookings, March 8, 2021.

41. Michael Robbins and Amaney Jamal, "The State of Social Justice in the Arab World: The Arab Uprisings of 2011 and Beyond," *Contemporary Readings in Law and Social Justice* 8, 1 (2016), pp. 127–57, at p. 130.

42. Gawdat Bahgat, "Socio-Economic and Political Impact of COVID-19 on GCC States," in *The Politics of Pandemics: Evolving Regime-Opposition Dynamics in the MENA*

Region, edited by Karim Mesran and Annalisa Perteghella (Washington: Atlantic Council, 2020).

43. Lydia Assouad, "Inequality and Its Discontents in the Middle East," Carnegie Middle East Center, March 12, 2020.

44. Robbins and Jamal, "The State of Social Justice in the Arab World," pp. 139–42.

45. See generally, United Nations Development Programme, *Human Development Reports—Gender Inequality Index* (2020).

46. "Human Rights in Middle East and North Africa—Review in 2020," Amnesty International, 2021.

47. A survey of documented human rights conditions reflected in Human Rights Watch's *2021 World Report* corroborates this description for the following countries: Algeria, Bahrain, Egypt, Iran, Iraq, Jordan, Kuwait, Lebanon, Libya, Morocco, Oman, Qatar, Saudi Arabia, Syria, Tunisia, the UAE, and Yemen. Similar patterns can be gleaned from Amnesty International's "Human Rights in the Middle East and North Africa—Review in 2020."

48. Rafiah Al Talei, "The Dilemma of US Democracy and Human Rights Promotion in the Middle East," Carnegie Endowment for International Peace, May 27, 2021.

49. Ceylan Yeginsu, "Turkey's Campaign against Kurdish Militants Takes Toll on Civilians," *New York Times*, December 30, 2015; "Gaza: Apparent War Crimes during May Fighting," Human Rights Watch, July 27. 2021.

50. Rosa Brooks, "Lessons for International Law from the Arab Spring," *American University International Law Review* 28, 3 (2013), pp. 713–32, at pp. 714–15.

51. Jordan Paust, "International Law, Dignity, Democracy and the Arab Spring," *Cornell International Law Journal* 46, 1 (2013), pp. 1–19, at p. 1.

52. Rami G. Khouri, "How Poverty and Inequality Are Devastating the Middle East," Carnegie New York, September 12, 2019.

53. Fait Muedini, "The Role of Religion in the 'Arab Spring': Comparing the Actions and Strategies of Islamist Parties," *Oxford Handbooks Online,* July 2014.

54. Carter Malkasian, "How Will the Taliban Rule? Governing Afghanistan Is More Difficult Than Conquering It," *Foreign Affairs*, August 23, 2021.

55. Shadi Hamid, "The Struggle for Middle East Democracy," Brookings, April 26, 2011.

56. Dan Robinson, "Obama: Egypt Needs Orderly Transition," *VOA News*, January 29, 2011.

57. For an early discussion of the likely long-term implications of the Libya intervention for the "responsibility to protect" doctrine, see David Rieff, "R2P, R.I.P.," *New York Times*, November 7, 2011.

58. Philippe Bolopion, "After Libya, the Question: To Protect or Depose?," *Los Angeles Times*, August 25, 2011.

59. David Zucchino, "Kabul's Sudden Fall to Taliban Ends U.S. Era in Afghanistan," *New York Times*, August 15, 2021.

60. Kenneth Roth, "The Refugee Crisis That Isn't," *Huffington Post*, September 3, 2015; and Kelly Greenhill, "Open Arms behind Barred Doors: Fear, Hypocrisy and Policy Schizophrenia in the European Migration Crisis," *European Law Journal* 22, 3 (2016), pp. 317–32.

61. "Syrian Refugees in Lebanon Surpass One Million," UNHCR/WFP, April 3, 2014 (quoting then-UN High Commissioner for Refugees António Guterres stating that international support for Lebanon "is totally out of proportion with what is needed.").

62. Shada Islam, "Europe's Migration 'Crisis' Isn't about Numbers. It's about Prejudice," *The Guardian*, October 8, 2020.

63. Kyilah Terry, "The EU–Turkey Deal, Five Years On: A Frayed and Controversial but Enduring Blueprint," Migration Policy Institute, April 8, 2021; and Joey Ayoub, "How the EU Is Responsible for Slavery in Libya," *Al Jazeera English*, November 29, 2017.

64. Phil McCausland, "U.S. Withdrawal Leaves Afghan Allies Grappling with Fear, Anger and Panic," *NBC News*, August 31, 2021.

65. Zoltan Barany, "Arms Procurement and Corruption in the Gulf Monarchies," Center for Strategic and International Studies, May 11, 2020.

66. Jake Sullivan, the Biden administration's national security adviser, stated that the president viewed the withdrawal decision as serving the "national security interests of the American people." Jake Sullivan, White House Press Briefing, August 17, 2021.

67. Broader worries about the credibility of U.S. deterrent capabilities after the Afghan withdrawal, by contrast, seem overblown. The United States has made clear for nearly a decade its intention to pivot to Asia, and while some Islamist nonstate groups may be emboldened by the American withdrawal, for many states the redeployment of resources to countering China may actually enhance U.S. credibility in East Asia. The agreement concluded in 2021 to provide Australia with nuclear-powered submarines is an early indicator of how aggressive U.S. foreign policy may now become in the Asia-Pacific region. Ishaan Tharoor, "A Landmark Submarine Deal May Be Aimed at China, but It Has Upset France," *Washington Post*, September 17, 2021.

68. In his first major address, Secretary of State Antony Blinken announced that the administration's foreign policy would prioritize "the needs and aspirations of the American people." Antony J. Blinken, "A Foreign Policy for the American People," March 3, 2021.

69. Joost Hiltermann, "Tackling Intersecting Conflicts in the MENA Region," International Crisis Group, February 13, 2018.

70. Ali Wyne and Colin P. Clarke, "Assessing China and Russia's Moves in the Middle East," *Lawfare*, September 17, 2021.

71. "Adapting to a New Reality in Afghanistan," International Institute for Strategic Studies, August 20, 2021.

72. Zack Beauchamp, "The War on Terror and the Long Death of Liberal Interventionism," *Vox*, September 8, 2021.

73. Nicole Narea, "Biden Had a Chance to Save US Allies in Afghanistan. He Wasted It," *Vox*, August 17, 2021.

74. Thomas Meaney, "Like Ordering Pizza," *London Review of Books* 43, 7 (September 9, 2021).

75. For example, the UN reported that more women and children were killed in the first half of 2021 than in the first six months of any year since the UN began systematically keeping count more than a decade ago. "As US Withdraws, Civilian Casualties in Afghanistan Reach Record High," *NPR*, July 26, 2021.

76. Malkasian, "How Will the Taliban Rule?"

77. Adam Smith, "The Humanitarian and Policy Challenges of U.S. Sanctions on the Taliban," *Just Security*, August 23, 2021.

78. "Biden Administration Freezes Billions of Dollars in Afghan Reserves, Depriving Taliban of Cash," *Washington Post*, August 17, 2021.

79. Adam Tooze, "Don't Abandon Afghanistan's Economy Too," *Foreign Policy*, August 27, 2021.

80. Marc Santora, Nick Cummings-Bruce, and Christina Goldbaum, "A Million Afghan Children Could Die in 'Most Perilous Hour,' U.N. Warns," *New York Times*, September 13, 2021.

81. "Deadly Consequences: Obstruction of Aid in Yemen During COVID-19," Human Rights Watch, September 14, 2020.

82. Iain Marlow and Enda Curran, "As US Exits Afghanistan, China Eyes $1 Trillion in Minerals," *Al Jazeera English*, August 24, 2021.

83. James Webb, "US Over-the-Horizon Capabilities Robust, but Use Requires 'Strategic Refinement,' Experts Say," *Military Times*, September 7, 2021.

84. Asma Khalid, "Biden Pledged to End the Forever Wars, but He Might Just Be Shrinking Them," *NPR*, September 8, 2021.

85. Craig Whitlock, "At War with the Truth: The Afghanistan Papers," *Washington Post*, December 9, 2019.

86. Matthieu Aikins, "Times Investigation: In U.S. Drone Strike, Evidence Suggests No ISIS Bomb," *New York Times*, September 10, 2021.

87. Ayla Jean Yackley, "The Turkish Wall Built to Keep Out Refugees from Afghanistan," *Financial Times*, September 15, 2021; Nektaria Stamouli, "Turkey Puts Its Migrant Security System on Display for Europe," *Politico*, January 3, 2022.

88. Lauren Cerulus, "Europe Needs Security 'Screening' of Afghan Refugees, Top Official Says," *Politico*, August 26, 2021.

89. Fionnuala Ní Aoláin, "Human Rights Advocacy and the Institutionalization of U.S. 'Counterterrorism' Policies Since 9/11," *Just Security*, September 9, 2021.

90. Emma Ashford, "Strategies of Restraint: Remaking America's Broken Foreign Policy," *Foreign Affairs*, September/October 2021.

91. "Human and Budgetary Costs to Date of the U.S. War in Afghanistan," Costs of War Project, Watson Institute at Brown University, August 2021.

92. Trita Parsi, "Middle East Cooperation Appears to Be Breaking Out—the Untold Story," *Responsible Statecraft*, September 20, 2021.

Conclusions

Reforming, Rebuilding, Modernizing the International Human Rights System

ANA LANKES AND CHRISTOPHER SABATINI

In June 1993, 171 states and representatives from eight hundred nongovernmental organizations (NGOs) met in Vienna at the second United Nations (UN)-hosted World Conference on Human Rights to take stock of the condition of the international human rights system and seek ways to strengthen it.[1] After nearly two weeks of discussions, governments agreed to a common declaration and plan of action that, among other things, created new instruments, such as the high commissioner for human rights and mechanisms to bolster the UN's capacity to monitor children's, women's, and Indigenous rights. The discussions leading up to the Vienna Declaration and Programme of Action were heated. Disagreements raged over whether human rights should be considered universal or culturally relative, whether economic, social, and

---

* To help sharpen the recommendations of the authors and editors of this book, in May 2021 Chatham House convened a meeting of human rights activists from around the world. Participants included activists in general human rights organizations as well as those representing the rights of migrants, women, ethnic minorities, and Lesbian, Gay, Bisexual, Transgender, Intersex (LGBTI) communities. The meeting was held under the Chatham House Rule. As noted in the Introduction, this concluding chapter contains many of the ideas and recommendations discussed during that exchange.

cultural rights should be given precedence over civil and political ones, whether development should be considered a right, and whether or not to call out states with particularly egregious records of rights violations, such as Cuba, China, Syria, and Iran.[2] In the end, the declaration affirmed the universality of human rights and stressed that democracy, development, and respect for rights are mutually reinforcing.

Three decades on, these discussions are still being had, but new currents are challenging even those delicate rhetorical pledges. The normative and institutional infrastructure that gave birth to the modern human rights system became central to the global order that emerged after World War II and spawned popular expectations of states and the international system. The foundation of human rights norms and commitments emerged alongside and was part of the broader momentum toward freer, integrated commerce and investment, multilateralism to reduce conflict and promote peace, and the processes of decolonization and racial integration in the United States. While parallel systems of trade and cooperation formed during the ideological confrontation between the West and the Soviet Union, broader notions of universal rights and multilateral systems to promote peace and human dignity and the protection of universal rights remained global, despite being politicized and instrumentalized at times. However, the division between political and civil rights and economic and social rights became a central point of challenge between the West and the Soviet Union and its allies.

After the collapse of communism, and the unravelling of the Soviet Union and the Eastern bloc, the Western liberal infrastructure stood triumphant. As such, it became—temporarily, at least—the sole means to integrate former Eastern-bloc countries and much of the Global South into world trade, international financial institutions such as the Bretton Woods system and private finance, and the international and regional norms set up to promote and defend human rights. Since their creation, those systems had consolidated primarily around the Western, liberal core of political and civil rights. This was a reflection of the predominant powers that had driven their development, the specific challenges of decolonization or dictatorship, and the relative ease of litigating and enforcing those rights relative to more complex social and economic rights (as I described in chapter 1). But this felicitous world convergence around the Western liberal order was not to last.

The world is now more plural. The liberal ideals that briefly reigned supreme at the end of the Cold War no longer have the same collective pull on popular aspirations, global discourse, states' foreign and domestic policies, or state alliances. The difficult discussions during the Vienna Summit hinted at divisions that would only grow and fundamentally shape a new global human rights landscape. The rise of China and the reassertion of Russian activism and power against the West are recasting the international balance of power. Parallel to this, the growing economic power of countries within the Global South—comprising states in Africa, Asia, and Latin America—combined with the declining influence of Western powers relative to China have given greater voice to long-standing demands of the global poor. In human rights terms this has meant greater emphasis on economic and social rights. This is not limited to individual, domestic demands on governments; there are also more calls to re-balance global discussions about rights and the obligations of international organizations in favor of those rights.

China's success in reducing poverty has amplified its global soft power as a model of economic and political development, while it has also used its bi-lateral assistance and investment as an alternative to more traditional develop-ment assistance and multilateral financial institutions. As Rosemary Foot detailed, Beijing has explicitly sought economic and political alliances with states that shared its rejection of liberal democratic norms or those that just needed economic investment to boost their development aspirations but indi-cated some ideological and diplomatic affinity and support. For those in the Global South that liked to believe they could be on the cusp of breaking out of the periphery, it was an understandably attractive offer, promising economic assistance—not always delivered—with implicit diplomatic solidarity. While the hard policy implications are yet to be evaluated, the long-term implica-tions of these financial, diplomatic alliances hang over the current global lib-eral order as China seeks increasingly to assert its geopolitical ambitions over Hong Kong and Taiwan, and over states that challenge its domestic human rights policies.

At the same time, economic globalization and automation have undermined worker security, while the fragmentation of party systems has created a fertile field for political movements tapping into and directing fear and discontent toward the perceived fallout of globalization. The resulting anger has erupted in the rise of nationalist movements, and in some cases public rejection of in-ternational norms and rules to defend human dignity and human rights do-mestically and internationally. In France, the Netherlands, the United States, and the United Kingdom, such nationalist movements rail not just against a perceived economic and cultural threat to native workers, but also against al-leged broader threats to local laws from international legal regimes. These sen-timents have influenced public debates and fueled the election of nationalist, populist governments in Brazil, Hungary, the Philippines, and, at least until

2020, the United States. Whether or not these individual leaders or movements will remain a political force, at least for the medium term they will retain their capacity to affect national politics in their ethnic chauvinism and promotion of popular rejection of perceived intrusions on national sovereignty.

As the balance of international, economic, and domestic political power has changed since the 1990s in ways that shape the future of human rights protections, so too has technology. While often overlooked among the broader challenges—Russia, China, populism, and the odd alliances that have been formed among them—technology is now an unexpected threat to the human rights order, sometimes in conjunction with the malign actors mentioned above, but often too, employed by autocracies and democracies alike. The capacity of the international human rights system to respond requires an upgrade not just of the international institutions to monitor and evaluate these threats, but also of human rights groups and their capacity to understand, track, and report their implications to international bodies and to the broader public.

The changes outlined above in the spheres of geopolitics, domestic politics, and technology are a challenge not only to international human rights norms and institutions but also to the broader post–World War II liberal order of free trade, financial integration, and a broader commercial and financial rules-based system. An often unremarked keystone of that broader order has been human rights. This book has attempted to understand developing trends both as they affect human rights and as part of a broader momentum in global politics.

In attempting to pick apart, understand, and address the novel pressures of geopolitics and technology on human rights and the international human rights regime, we focused in the last section of the book on the regional impact of these pressures. In some regions there have been greater advances in human rights defense and jurisprudence than have been achieved by global bodies. But our authors demonstrate that in all the regions we considered—with or without vigorous human rights norms and bodies—the protection and defense of political, civil, economic, and social rights have also become caught up in the global crosswinds of nationalism, national sovereignty, and great-power politics that threaten not only the immediate protection of individual rights but broader regional systems of rights as well.

In Part I, Rosemary Foot and Alexander Cooley show how China and Russia are actively reshaping global human rights institutions and norms. Both actors have used their vetoes in the UN Security Council to block international action against human rights abuses and put pressure on the UN Human Rights Council to reduce attention to country-specific resolutions. They have also set up regional counterordering initiatives that shore up authoritarian regimes, such as the Shanghai Cooperation Organization and the Commonwealth of Independent States. These actions are reshaping normative agendas by elevating the doctrine of sovereign equality over that of popular sovereignty and state responsibilities to protect human dignity. China, in particular, has used its economic clout to advance an alternative vision to liberal democracy, arguing that development is a foundational right from which other human rights flow, thus subordinating civil and political rights. Nandini Ramanujam and Vishakha Wijenayake look at Russia's historical role in pushing for socioeconomic rights and state sovereignty, and argue that while there remain challenges in Russia's domestic and international human rights agenda, socioeconomic rights may provide an avenue for meaningful engagement with Moscow and with it broader reform of the human rights debate. All three chapters argue that ideological confrontations with either of these states are unhelpful. Instead, existing human rights bodies should do more to focus on development, the absence of which has led many countries in the Global South to support China's approach. But governments and multilateral bodies should not do that to the exclusion of or even by minimizing civil and political rights. In the final chapter of Part I, Rana Moustafa argues that multilateral bodies must do more to protect human rights amid international crises like COVID-19. As she details, the pandemic gave greater scope and license for autocrats to consolidate power while much of the world was distracted by domestic concerns and political polarization over how to deal with its effects, and her conclusion is that the response of the existing multilateral organizations proved inadequate.

Part II focuses on how changes in domestic politics and the organizational capacity of new constituencies are a threat not only to human rights domestically but also to the international human rights framework and geopolitics more broadly. Gerald Neuman argues that the rise of exclusionary populism across the globe is threatening the operation and integrity of international human rights norms and bodies. Exclusionary populism denies the legitimacy of any opposition and undermines institutional checks and balances. This has led several populist regimes to withdraw from international human rights bodies or cut funding for them, and in some cases they vote together with autocratic governments on issues of sovereignty and accountability, while challenging the capacity of liberal democracies—often cast as elitist and distant from the interests of the people—to enforce human rights norms and standards. Some populist regimes have been helped by domestic religious groups who seek to protect "the rights of the family" and have at times been given undue influence in shaping foreign human rights policies, as Melani McAlister outlines.

Both authors argue for efforts to bridge divides among nationalist populists and diverse religious groups. For example, policymakers should learn from some populist critiques, cultivate the support of moderate religious actors, and selectively deploy local values frames to reduce the fear of rapid cultural change. Above all, they must address the root causes of populism, such as economic insecurity. At the same time, the funding and independence of international monitoring bodies must be bolstered to protect against populist and autocratic efforts to undermine them, while religious groups—or any single domestic constituency—must not be allowed to hold undue influence over human rights policy.

Part III analyzes the role of emerging technologies in undermining human rights. Emily Taylor, Kate Jones, and Carolina Caeiro look at how geopolitical competition has carried over to the internet, where China is seeking to reshape technical standards to permit increased surveillance. Thompson Chengeta considers the racial implications of developing autonomous weapons systems (AWS) and law-enforcement and surveillance technologies using artificial intelligence. He argues that these instruments disproportionately threaten the rights of people of color, but more broadly that they undermine the right to justice because they make it difficult to ascribe accountability in the event of their unlawful use (whether this is intentional or not). Both chapters call for human rights considerations to be taken into account throughout the process of developing new internet protocols or AWS, or drafting technical standards. This could be done by including more NGOs and civil society organizations in the bodies that determine internet protocols, and by granting human rights bodies greater access in the drafting of regulations and participation in monitoring human rights protections with regard to the application of AWS and the impact of regulations affecting the use of technology on human rights.

These challenges have been felt and have torn at one of the most notable successes of the past seventy-five years, regional human rights systems. The last four chapters, in Part IV, are dedicated to those often-overlooked systems and the effects of changing geopolitics on their operation and authority. Solomon Dersso shows how increasing great-power competition in Africa permits authoritarian governments such as Eritrea's, which receive military support from foreign patrons, to act with impunity. The complex machinations of Russia, China, the Gulf states, and Turkey in central, eastern, and northern Africa can contribute to greater instability, as in Libya, making it nearly impossible to guarantee human rights. Urfan Khaliq and Santiago Canton and Angelita Baeyens explain how rising illiberal populism and states' reassertion of sovereignty have seriously challenged regional human rights systems in Europe and Latin America, respectively, by reducing their funding and eroding cooperation. Aslı Ü. Bâli demonstrates how great-power politics have corrupted human rights in the Middle East and North Africa, whether through intervention or through neglect (most recently in the case of the U.S. withdrawal from Afghanistan). Those policies have not only affected individual rights in countries such as Egypt or Afghanistan but also undermined the political, economic, and social promise of the Arab Spring.

Taken together, the trends and factors analyzed in all four sections of the book are eroding the basic foundation of human rights. Our aim is to kickstart a wide-ranging dialogue among scholars, policymakers, and activists on how to confront these challenges and strengthen the fraying consensus. In some cases, responding will involve work within countries to address the economic insecurity and social and political illiberalism that have eroded human rights protections. In others, countering elected autocrats will require international leadership to identify, establish, and monitor effective mechanisms to react to violations. International norms and multilateral institutions need to be updated to focus on these emerging threats, find ways to generate sustainable funding, and elevate the discussion around economic and social rights amid rising global inequalities. This is not an exhaustive list of issues. Climate change and the rights of migrants and refugees are certainly others, as we discussed in the Introduction. But even successful integration and strengthening of these rights will depend on domestic political constituencies and effective international norms and bureaucracies to deal with them. The protection of human rights, more than ever, has become a domestic political messaging problem as well as an international challenge.

International Norms, Popular Discontent, and Populists

The main challenge to today's human rights systems comes not from the decay of the systems themselves, but from the rising global power of China, Russia, and a group of like-minded countries that have formed a cynical common cause against them domestically and internationally. As several chapters in this book demonstrated, regional and international human rights systems have come under increasing attack in the past twenty years from member states reasserting their sovereign prerogatives. The fundamental consensus around human rights and democracy based on imperfect international cooperation in the post–Cold War era is evaporating. This change has gone hand in hand with

growing authoritarianism, often by democratically elected leaders with a varying popular mandate, who have become a new breed of human rights abusers.
These regimes are not the medal-festooned juntas of military officers or outright dictators of the past, but elected governments that gradually undermine
checks and balances and the rule of law to clamp down on critical voices. This
has complicated a human rights system that until recently had focused largely
on coups, dictatorships, and egregious cases of human rights through death
squads, gulags, and censorship, rather than the subtle erosion of checks and
balances on power—often with popular acquiescence, if not support—that has
tended to precede those abuses.

These elected authoritarians pose new and specific challenges to human
rights. Their geographic and ideological range is broad, and include presidents
Nayib Bukele in El Salvador, Rodrigo Duterte in the Philippines, Vladimir
Putin in Russia, and Recep Tayyip Erdoğan in Turkey, as well as prime ministers Narendra Modi in India and Viktor Orbán in Hungary, and former president Hugo Chávez in Venezuela. But they all share an affinity with the ac-
cumulation of personal power behind the façade of elections and the trappings
of democracy.

How should the international community and local civil society groups respond when voters themselves back antidemocratic and rights-abusing leaders?
One starting point is to recognize the red flags that signal an elected government's potential slide into authoritarianism. Over the last two decades, easily
identifiable patterns of institutional manipulation and democratic backsliding
have become apparent. Governments across the world have engaged in what
Lucan Way and Steven Levitksy call "competitive authoritarian" tactics,[3] which
include using state resources to promote the reelection of incumbents, redirecting public funds to uncritical media outlets and getting allies to buy opposition
channels, introducing reforms that reduce the independence of electoral commissions, and weakening or abolishing term limits, while maintaining the ve-
neer of electoral democracy. These steps generally do not elicit immediate international outcry. But by the time more obviously autocratic measures are taken,
such as gaming electoral systems to perpetuate their retention of power and
politicizing the armed forces, it is usually too late to respond effectively.

These tactics must be recognized and challenged to discourage would-be
authoritarian governments from emulating one another. Autocratic demonstration effects have already led to cross-border learning that has eroded democratic institutions and standards, domestically and internationally.[4] For example, in 2020, Nicaragua's dictators (President Daniel Ortega and his wife and

president Rosario Murillo) almost directly copied a "foreign agents law" and a cybersecurity law passed in Russia in 2012 that curbed free speech and severely constrained the rights of civil society organizations to operate.[5] Poland followed Hungary's lead in undermining judicial independence by lowering the retirement age for judges in its constitutional court in order to get rid of critical voices.[6] In Bolivia, actors affiliated with the ruling party brought independent media outlets to heel and removed critical content, imitating tactics previously honed in Venezuela.

Individual cases of autocrats repressing their own populations and learning from one another to do so are, of course, nothing new.[7] The difference today is that many have at least a fig leaf of elected democratic legitimacy.

In the light of these challenges and the analyses in the preceding chapters, we present several ideas and suggestions that heads of state, multilateral institutions, and activists should pursue.

- **Update and expand international institutions to identify and react to modern threats to human rights stemming from elected autocrats.** Rights-respecting governments, including non-Western ones, should collaborate to create a platform that can define the early warning signs of rights violations and spell out clearly when and how they would react collectively. Ideally, this should be based within the UN framework and be as inclusive as possible in order not to be seen as a Western-led politicized project. This platform could be tasked with creating a checklist of red flags, such as skewing the electoral playing field, harassing the media, politicizing the judiciary, and throwing up obstacles to the independent operation of civil society organizations. It could also outline the types of voluntary bilateral and multilateral tools it stands ready to deploy. These could include diplomatic isolation, targeted Magnitsky-style sanctions,[8] enhanced monitoring by international and other UN bodies, and greater support for civil society groups to address democratic deficits. Such a platform could create the framework for a cogent, defensive, and proactive strategy against nascent authoritarianism. But a note of caution is necessary. U.S. and European Union (EU) sanctions and their threat have proven increasingly less effective in deterring antidemocratic acts and autocrats in, for example, Hong Kong, Nicaragua, and Russia—a further sign of the diminished power of Western governments to impose their will in the current global environment. In these cases greater efforts at coordinating sanctions policy and ensuring its effectiveness should be key.

- **Focus on renewing countries' democratic social fabric and popular understanding of human rights.** On a domestic level, dealing with populist or authoritarian elements will prove difficult. Ideally, respect for human rights and democracy should be instilled as early as possible. NGOs, multilateral organizations, community leaders, and national governments need to work to educate and connect their citizens to the world of human rights, to prevent the rise of parties hostile to minorities and democratic principles. Efforts to engage citizens politically and to educate populations in human rights can raise awareness about the work of local, regional, and international human rights mechanisms, and can shore up public support for them. As mentioned both by Santiago Canton and Angelita Baeyens with respect to the Inter-American System of Human Rights, and Solomon Dersso in regard to the African System of Human Rights, lack of public awareness about human rights courts leads to low public engagement with such bodies and a dwindling number of direct petitions from citizens. Expanding the budgets of these organizations will permit them to have a greater presence on the ground in ways that, as Canton and Baeyens detailed, will make human rights more personally relevant to the millions of citizens for whom regional and international systems have remained distant. As Alexander Cooley noted in his chapter, "viewing international policy or global governance as a separate sphere, detached from domestic politics, is no longer viable." This also applies to the next recommendation.

- **Understand and respond to economic insecurity stemming from globalization, the changing nature of work, and imperfect social safety nets.** In all countries, the threat of exclusionary populism must also be combated by addressing its root causes: economic insecurity and anxiety over cultural change. As Gerald Neuman made clear, populism, defined most simply as a strategy that dichotomizes politics as a struggle between "the people" and a perceived corrupt "elite," undermines democracy and human rights by narrowing the definition of what constitutes "the people," leading to a rejection of pluralism and checks on and dissent from what leaders define as the "popular will." Both right-wing and left-wing populism thrive in contexts of high economic insecurity and deep social cleavages. Yet liberal democratic leaders have sometimes focused on civil and political rights and ignored social and economic ones. As several chapters in this volume have noted, that has hurt the appeal of human rights discourse in parts of the Global South, where calls for social and economic rights can have greater resonance. It has also contributed to the rise of exclusionary populists in the West. One suggestion that emerged from the preceding chapters and the multiple workshops held in developing this book is that human rights groups should make greater efforts to collaborate with development economists to shape policies sensitive to such disruptions. The United States could also signal a new commitment to economic inclusion by ratifying the International Covenant on Economic, Social, and Cultural Rights.

- **Engage a broad segment of civil society, including a diversity of religious groups, in foreign policy and human rights policy.** The undue influence in politics of powerful religious groups that seek to undermine or split the human rights agenda needs to be countered. As Melani McAlister shows, the U.S. evangelical and conservative Catholic lobbies have significantly shaped the country's health and human rights policy abroad in ways that distance it from allies and the modern human rights agenda. The human rights community and human rights–supporting governments need to recognize the danger posed by the disproportionate and sectarian influence of religious fundamentalist groups and should create independent monitoring mechanisms to ensure that a plurality of religious views is included. As McAlister highlighted, evangelicals in the Trump administration convened a "Commission on Unalienable Rights" to offer an alternative to the modern, progressive consensus in international human rights law, and disseminated its report, translated into several languages, allowing other illiberal regimes to pursue self-serving reinterpretations of their human rights obligations. Today, the U.S. State Department will need to demonstrate its more inclusive view of human rights to counteract that widely disseminated report; and it should either resign from, disband, or reform the International Religious Freedom of Belief Alliance founded by the Trump administration to bring together right-wing populist governments claiming to defend Christianity against other religions and the influence of sexual minorities. Neither the commission nor the alliance should have been enabled to gain such weight or such broad dissemination of their publications. To prevent any single group, whether religious, business, or other, from gaining an overwhelming, narrow influence on U.S. human rights–related foreign policy, Congress and/or the State Department could consider the creation of an independent, diverse commission comprising legal experts and civil society participants to ensure that such policy reflects a consistent, nonpartisan approach.

In a similar vein, Western democracies should do more to engage and support civil society in individual countries. This includes a specific focus on groups in closed or closing societies such as Cuba, China, the Philippines, Russia, Turkey, and Venezuela. Such groups have come under mounting formal and informal pressure but remain key voices advocating for human rights and the universal vernacular of human rights internationally. As Nandini Ramanujam and Vishakha Wijenayake argue, this should involve legal assistance to those groups as they push back against state efforts to deny their legal and political space.

- **Recommit to a broad human rights agenda among liberal democracies, including in non-Western countries.** The most important way to strengthen respect for international human rights is for rights-respecting countries to speak out consistently against authoritarian backsliding and put their own houses in order. Calls to respect the universality of human rights will not be taken seriously if countries that purport to uphold such rights apply them only selectively. Public efforts by the United States and other countries to downplay systematic human rights violations in Israel, Pakistan, or Saudi Arabia, among others, cheapen the values and commitments of human rights supposedly embodied in the international system. At the same time, dehumanizing rhetoric and policies toward migrants in the United States; the United Kingdom; and in other countries in Europe, such as Denmark and the Netherlands, have eroded, in ways that are difficult to measure but powerful, the delicate respect for human dignity and the importance of laws and policies to protect it, nationally and internationally. Renewing, restoring, and sustaining the international human rights order requires the founders and one-time supporters of that order to show greater commitment to the objective discussion of the rights and dignity of human beings; and ultimately all governments, including those that once claimed to be champions of these rights, must pledge to safeguard them.

- **Improve the capacity to monitor and punish states and businesses promoting or selling technology that violates human rights conventions and practices.** The use of automated weapon systems, artificial intelligence (AI), and surveillance technology, and attempts to reform internet protocols—as detailed both by Thompson Chengeta and by Emily Taylor, Kate Jones, and Carolina Caeiro—demands greater scrutiny by multilateral organizations, democratic governments, and human rights NGOs. Such actions should also involve greater inspection of and restrictions on the role of certain nonstate actors, such as arms manufacturers and tech companies, that enable rights violations. For example, under international guidelines, defense contractors are obliged to respect international humanitarian law.[9] But this has not always been the case. The international community needs to be more vigilant and assertive in demanding accountability. The United States and United Kingdom manufactured weapons sold to Saudi Arabia that were responsible for the tragic killing of civilians—including children—in Yemen.[10] The sale of surveillance technology from Israel has also been abused by governments to covertly track journalists and civil society.[11]

- **Ensure greater technology awareness among human rights bodies, norms, and activists.** Privacy concerns and surveillance will become increasingly pressing problems in the field of human rights, as shown by Taylor, Jones, and Caeiro. Better global standards, which include human rights considerations, would protect privacy online and discourage governments from providing licenses to apps and software that could be used for unlawful surveillance. Creating better technology standards and global regulations on the development and deployment of online and digital surveillance and tracking technology may prevent governments from licensing their use, but it is only a first step. All standards development organizations, such as the International Telecommunications Union and the Internet Engineering Task Force (IETF), must ensure they lower the entry barriers for civil society and human rights organizations to participate as members. Where such groups already have a voice, as in the IETF's Human Rights Protocol Considerations Research Group, they should have a greater say on the development of controversial technologies. Finally, a UN body could be created and tasked with producing human rights guidelines for technology standards organizations as well as alerting the international human rights community to rights-threatening technological developments, including spyware, AWS, or AI. The UN Human Rights Council should commission standards on the state collation of data and surveillance, to identify technology and its use that are not compatible with international human rights law.

- **Ensure that international bodies, including multilateral organizations and human rights groups, reflect global diversity.** One of the easiest and most important ways in which human rights institutions can gain greater legitimacy internationally and in local settings is by becoming more diverse. The accusation that "human rights are a Western imposition," weaponized frequently by actors who have an interest in diluting or ignoring such rights, would have far less purchase if these bodies were not overwhelmingly staffed by people from Western countries. They could become more diverse, first by instituting stronger affirmative action policies; second, by making greater efforts to look for local actors in recruitment drives; and, third, by consulting more actively and in greater depth with local communities, such that every policy has the input of the people it will affect. This also applies to the recommendation to increase the budgets of international and regional human rights bodies to enable greater on-the-ground presence, which will ensure inclusion and diversity.

- **Explore existing and potentially new platforms to more effectively challenge and mobilize action on severe human rights abusers.** What can be done in the hardest cases, when states continue to violate human rights despite diplomatic and economic pressure? One response is to repurpose existing frameworks to tackle governments and elected leaders that have blocked traditional human rights channels and mechanisms. For example, a resolution presented by Liechtenstein at the UN General Assembly—rather than the Security Council, where it would have been blocked—created the International, Impartial and Independent Mechanism (IIIM), a body that has collected evidence of human rights violations in Syria since the start of the civil war. The Gambia spearheaded a resolution to create a similar mechanism for Myanmar through the General Assembly, and also got the backing of the Organisation of Islamic Cooperation to take Myanmar to the UN's International Court of Justice (ICJ) to face charges of ethnic cleansing against the Rohingya people. These platforms engage countries that otherwise do not participate actively in human rights forums. Another such framework is the UN's Universal Periodic Review, which examines the human rights record of member states every five years. The point is that activists can use existing tools in innovative ways to tackle the most recalcitrant regimes. Along these lines, there has also been a growing movement to use individual country courts to prosecute cases of crimes against humanity and genocide. Since World War II, fifteen countries have used the concept of universal jurisdiction to pursue such cases in country courts. This was done, for example, in Spain for the arrest of the former Chilean dictator Augusto Pinochet in 1998, and most recently in the 2019 case filed by the Burmese Rohingya Organisation UK (BROUK) in Argentina's federal courts for crimes committed by the government of Myanmar against Rohingya populations.[12] Regardless of the merits of those cases and their outcome, country judicial systems offer another platform for raising demands for justice over egregious human rights abuses and increasing popular awareness of these cases.

- **Upgrade, reform, and protect international and regional human rights bodies.** Some existing mechanisms require serious reform to become more effective. International monitoring bodies such as the UN Human Rights Council (UNHRC) have at times been captured by authoritarian states, which then act as a bloc, distorting and emasculating the body and its processes, as detailed by Rosemary Foot. The UNHRC needs to be reformed to impose stricter membership criteria and create a more competitive, transparent electoral process as well as subject members to routine inquiries about human rights practices. In the case of the worst offenders, the threshold for suspending members should be lowered; at a minimum, acceptance of UNHRC monitoring mechanisms should be a requirement for membership of the body prescribing them. Furthermore, budgets for international human rights–monitoring bodies should be protected or increased; anti–human rights regimes have consistently sought to reduce the impact of such bodies by cutting their funding and limiting their independence. The chairpersons of the ten UN Treaty bodies warned in 2020 that underfunding was putting their work at risk. Almost all chapters in this book mention underfunding for human rights bodies as a serious impediment to their operation: for example, the Inter-American System of Human Rights receives only 19 percent of the overall budget of the Organization of American States (OAS); this means that it has few full-time staff and no subregional offices. Similar dynamics affect the African Commission on Human and Peoples' Rights. The capacity of these important bodies to realize human rights in their regions hinges on more effective funding and the associated on-the-ground presence.

- **Strengthen international solidarity in defense of human rights.** The political, economic/financial, and legal costs of violating human rights must be increased. States are increasingly disregarding civil and political rights because the costs of doing so are low. Part of this stems from a declining attention and commitment to human rights. But in part it is also because Russia and China brazenly support rogue regimes, both economically and diplomatically, for their own ideological and diplomatic ends. This calculus must be changed. Strengthening sanctions regimes would be a start. Recent threats and implementation of sanctions regimes over human rights have had little effect. The reason is that they are too easy to bypass, and their implementation can be patchy. Greater efforts need to be made to coordinate sanctions multilaterally and ensure that the private sector is on board. Under both the Trump and Biden administrations, the United States has piled up sanctions on individuals, regimes, and organizations, at times with little regard for their effectiveness in meeting intended goals or for their costs.[13] In the case of the EU sanctions imposed against Russia after the latter's annexation of Crimea in 2014 (and before Russia's invasion of Ukraine in 2021), the German government's refusal to halt the building of the Nordstream 2 pipeline, and the fact that German businesses increased their investments in the country since 2014, diluted the original sanctions and later those in 2021. A global Magnitsky-style compact may help ensure greater international compliance and create clear criteria for imposing sanctions, which should also always be targeted to avoid or minimize the cost to civilian populations. Such a compact could also create a monitoring mechanism to minimize breaches and ensure private sector support, and to evaluate their efficacy objectively.

If a global compact on sanctions seems far off, then individual states can do more to enhance the symbolic weight of sanctions. As one example, the United States has sanctioned the architect behind the Uyghur genocide, Chen Quanguo, the Communist Party secretary for Xinjiang and a member of the Nineteenth Politburo. As the previous secretary for Tibet, he was also behind the massive repression, Sinicization, and increased surveillance of that region. Other states should join in those sanctions. Bodies that have strong sanctioning tools, such as the EU, should also not be afraid to use them against members when (as, for instance, in the case of Hungary and Poland) they defy its core values, even if the primary outcome is simply to send a strong signal to other members.

Refocusing and potentially ramping up the international sanctions regime today requires examination of three factors. The first is history and the conditions that affect successful sanctions policies. Many sanctions today have failed, including broad multilateral efforts. Part of that failure is that they are often too ambitious and lack clear goals and policy to leverage sanctions. A second consideration is that while the West applies sanctions frequently, today many other countries are willing to help repressive rights-violating regimes evade them. Some, such as China, have a large economic market and resources that can be used to assist such regimes; others—such as Russia and Iran—provide diplomatic or intelligence support because of their own sanctions. In these cases, sanctions-backing governments must figure out how to coordinate to close off these routes more effectively.[14] Third, governments that use sanctions against rights violators must publicly recognize that for the first time in recent history, a new, powerful geopolitical actor, China, is not only less vulnerable to sanctions but also willing to impose them itself on governments, and even on private institutions and individuals. The effect is not only to diminish the moral authority of sanctions but also to threaten governments and national businesses, making it potentially difficult in the future to invoke them.

- **Be honest about the challenges today and the need for an upgrade.** One of the central recommendations of this book is the need to be introspective. Human rights groups need to evaluate what has worked, where, and why. There needs to be a greater understanding about differentiating between human rights strategies in closed societies such as China's, or in failed states such as Somalia, as opposed to those in democracies such as Denmark or the United States. Trying to understand why the "golden era" of human rights, from the 1970s until the early 2000s, has ended is important to prepare for the future. The dynamics and reasons behind the withering of the basic consensus around human rights in the past two decades, alongside a reversal in the third wave of democratization, need to be understood. And that understanding should be built into any effort by the one-time defenders of the liberal international order to engage with and reform the global human rights regime.

- **Consider whether it is time for a new Vienna Convention on Human Rights.** Calling such a global discussion would not be without risk. There are too many states today that would seek to undermine consensus and dilute rather than uphold human rights. Before such a forum is called, there will need to be questions about whether to convene it only among a coalition of the willing, or to make it broad-based, and how to ensure that nonstate actors, particularly NGOs and civil society groups, have their voices heard. Private sector stakeholders, particularly in technology, and experts in economics, development, technology, and sanctions should also be included, alongside representatives from moderate religious groups. The challengers to the current human rights regimes are already building their own alternative human rights movement: China has created a South-South Forum on Human Rights, which has met twice, with an agenda of promoting development as a right over traditional political and civil rights. Western liberal governments need to step up to do the same. Unfortunately, U.S. president Joe Biden's December 2021 virtual Democracy Summit was too perfunctory and too focused on international challenges, and at the same time not sufficiently focused on the specific shortcomings and threats to international human rights, or on collective responses.

A global, broad-based forum led by liberal democracies could, if done correctly, be an important step in evaluating and restoring the international human rights regime in a complex and contentious world. It would open up a global discussion on the successes of the grand human rights experiment started seventy-five years ago and on ways to help it evolve and thrive in the future. Within that discussion, the principles of human rights and their universality should remain central. But that is not to say that the norms and institutions and even goals that sought to embody and advance these principles cannot be updated. Indeed, as this book has argued, they must be—as must our domestic discussion and commitment to human rights within our borders.

Notes

1. Kevin Boyle, "Stock Taking on Human Rights: The World Conference, Vienna, 1993," *Political Studies* 43 (1995), pp. 79–95, https://onlinelibrary.wiley.com/doi/pdf/10.1111/j.1467-9248.1995.tb01737.x.

2. "A Rights Meeting, but Don't Mention the Wronged," *New York Times*, June 14, 1993, https://www.nytimes.com/1993/06/14/world/a-rights-meeting-but-don-t-mention-the-wronged.html.

3. Lucan Way and Steven Levitsky, "Elections without Democracy: The Rise of Competitive Authoritarianism," *Journal of Democracy* 13, 2 (April 2002).

4. Christopher Sabatini and Ryan Berg, "Autocrats Have a Playbook, Now Democrats Need One Too," *Foreign Policy*, February 10, 2021, https://foreignpolicy.com/2021/02/10/autocrats-have-a-playbook-now-democrats-need-one-too/.

5. "Nicaragua: Law Threatens Free, Fair Elections," Human Rights Watch, December 12, 2020, https://www.hrw.org/news/2020/12/22/nicaragua-law-threatens-free-fair-elections.

6. "EU Court Rules Poland's Lowering of Judges' Retirement Age Is Unlawful," *The Guardian*, June 24, 2019, https://www.theguardian.com/world/2019/jun/24/eu-court-rules-polands-lowering-of-judges-retirement-age-unlawful.

7. As detailed in John Dinges, *The Condor Years: How Pinochet and His Allies Brought Terrorism to Three Continents* (New York: The New Press, 2005).

8. Magnitsky sanctions refer to U.S. and other countries' legal authority to target individuals' bank accounts and visas for crimes of corruption and human rights abuses. For more information, see https://home.treasury.gov/policy-issues/financial-sanctions /sanctions-programs-and-country-information/global-magnitsky-sanctions.

9. For defense contractors obligations to respect international humanitarian law, see https://www.ohchr.org/documents/publications/GuidingprinciplesBusinesshr_eN .pdf.

10. Bruce Riedel, "It's Time to Stop US Arms Sales to Saudi Arabia," Brookings, February 4, 2021, https://www.brookings.edu/blog/order-from-chaos/2021/02/04 /its-time-to-stop-us-arms-sales-to-saudi-arabia/.

11. Stephanie Kirchgaessner, Paul Lewis, David Pegg, Sam Cutler, Nina Lakhani, and Michael Safi, "Revealed: Leak Uncovers Global Abuse of Cyber-Surveillance Weapon," *The Guardian*, July 18, 2021, https://www.theguardian.com/world/2021 /jul/18/revealed-leak-uncovers-global-abuse-of-cyber-surveillance-weapon-nso -group-pegasus.

12. Tun Khin, "Universal Jurisdiction, the International Criminal Court, and the Rohingya Genocide," in *OpinioJuris*, October 23, 2020, http://opiniojuris.org/2020 /10/23/universal-jurisdiction-the-international-criminal-court-and-the-rohingya -genocide/.

13. Christopher Sabatini, "America's List of 'Undemocratic and Corrupt Actors' Just Keeps Growing," *New York Times*, October 5, 2021, https://www.nytimes .com/2021/10/05/opinion/us-sanctions-venezuela.html.

14. Daniel Drezner, "The United States of Sanctions," *Foreign Affairs*, September /October 2021, https://www.foreignaffairs.com/articles/united-states/2021-08-24 /united-states-sanctions.

Contributors

Editor: Christopher Sabatini
Senior Research Fellow, U.S. and the Americas Programme, Chatham House, United Kingdom

Angelita Baeyens
Vice President of International Advocacy and Litigation, Robert F. Kennedy Human Rights

Asli Ü. Bâli
Professor and Faculty Director, Promise Institute for Human Rights, UCLA School of Law, United States

Carolina Caeiro
Academy Associate, U.S. and the Americas Programme, Chatham House, United Kingdom

Santiago Canton
Director, Peter D. Bell Rule of Law Program, Inter-American Dialogue, United States

Thompson Chengeta
Reader in Law, Liverpool John Moores University, United Kingdom

Alexander Cooley
Claire Tow Professor of Political Science, Barnard College, New York, United States

Solomon Dersso
Commissioner, African Commission on Human and Peoples' Rights, The Gambia

Rosemary Foot
Professor, Emeritus Fellow, St Antony's College, University of Oxford, United Kingdom

Kate Jones
Associate Fellow, International Law Programme, Chatham House, United Kingdom

Urfan Khaliq
Professor, Public International and EU Laws, Cardiff School of Law and Politics, Cardiff University, United Kingdom

Ana Lankes
Argentina and Chile Correspondent, *The Economist,* United Kingdom

Melani McAlister
Professor of American Studies and International Affairs, The George Washington University, United States

Rana Moustafa
Assistant Professor, International Law, Alexandria University, Egypt

Gerald Neuman
J. Sinclair Armstrong Professor of International, Foreign and Comparative Law, Harvard Law School, United States

Nandini Ramanujam
Co-Director and Director of Programs, Center for Human Rights and Legal Pluralism, McGill University, Canada

Emily Taylor
Associate Fellow, International Security Programme, Chatham House;
Editor, *Journal of Cyber Policy*, Chatham House/Taylor & Francis, United
Kingdom

Vishakha Wijenayake
O'Brien Fellow, Center for Human Rights and Legal Pluralism, McGill
University, Canada

Index

Note: Figures are indicated with italicized page numbers. Note information is indicated with n and note number following the page number.